THE GOVERNMENT OF
MODERN BRITAIN

Oxford University Press, Ely House, London W.1

GLASGOW NEW YORK TORONTO MELBOURNE WELLINGTON
CAPE TOWN SALISBURY IBADAN NAIROBI LUSAKA ADDIS ABABA
BOMBAY CALCUTTA MADRAS KARACHI LAHORE DACCA
KUALA LUMPUR HONG KONG TOKYO

The Government
of Modern Britain

BY

FRANK STACEY

Senior Lecturer in Government
University College of Swansea

CLARENDON PRESS · OXFORD

1968

© *Oxford University Press 1968*

PRINTED IN GREAT BRITAIN BY
W. S. COWELL LTD, BUTTER MARKET, IPSWICH

TO
MARGARET

PREFACE

THIS is a study of British central government which I hope will be of use to students taking Politics as a degree course. It has been developed from lectures which I have given to university students of Politics in their first and second years.

Many people who come to the study of British government have only a general background knowledge. I have therefore begun most of the chapters in an introductory way and have led on to a more sophisticated consideration of the subject, as well as to discussion of some of the controversies which have arisen in recent years. In doing so, I have drawn upon many of the excellent monographs which have appeared since the Second World War on aspects of the work of Parliament, of elections, of parties and pressure groups, and of the administrative machine. I have endeavoured to bring the treatment of each subject up to date, including my own researches and assessments. My aim has been to map out the field for the student and to indicate some of the ways in which he can pursue his studies of British government to a further level. My frame of reference has been broadly the period from 1945 to 1967, although I have gone back before 1945 where it seemed desirable to fill in the essential background. Footnotes give full details of sources, but for the sake of convenience I have also listed at the end of each chapter the books, articles and other publications which will probably be of most value to the reader who wishes to take his studies further.

I owe a great deal to the many friends and colleagues who have given me advice and encouragement. I am especially grateful to those who have read and commented on parts of the manuscript. My thanks go to Sir Kenneth Wheare, Professors Samuel H. Beer, Peter Bromhead, J. M. Brown and Alun Davies, and to Donald Anderson, Richard Bryden, Kenneth O. Morgan, Peter Nicholson, John C. Rees, and John Sabine, and to Margaret Stacey, my wife.

I have benefited from discussion with many public servants and Members of Parliament. It would be invidious to mention any of them by name except for the Speaker of the House of

Commons, Dr. Horace King, who, when Chairman of Ways and Means, was most helpful in answering my questions and discussing numerous aspects of parliamentary procedure with me. The Secretary of the Council on Tribunals also helped me a great deal through his comments on the first draft of Chapter XVI. I wish to make clear that the responsibility for all statements of fact and opinion in this book is entirely my own.

Finally, I should like to thank Mrs. E. M. Morgan, Miss June Pratten, and Miss Sylvia Thomas, who typed the manuscript.

Department of Political Theory   FRANK STACEY
and Government,
University College of Swansea
September 1967

CONTENTS

TABLES

ABBREVIATIONS

The following abbreviations are used in the footnotes:

Cd., Cmd., Cmnd.   Command Paper (the official abbreviation has varied from time to time).

H.C.   House of Commons Paper.

H.C. Deb.   House of Commons Debates.

S.O.   Standing Orders of the House of Commons. Public Business.

CHAPTER I

Free Elections

WHAT is the essential test of whether a country has a democratic form of government? There are many possible answers to this question, but if there is to be one single answer perhaps the most satisfactory is that the members of the legislature must be elected by the people in free elections and must be required to seek re-election at fairly frequent intervals. The government must in turn be responsible to the legislature and be capable of being defeated by it. This is the principle of parliamentary democracy. If the head of the government is not responsible to the legislature, he must be elected by the people for a limited term, as in the presidential system, in the United States.

Who May Vote?

When, however, we say that the members of the legislature must be elected by the people, what do we mean by 'the people'? Must we say that in a democracy there must be universal adult suffrage, both male and female? If so, then Switzerland, in which women do not have the vote, is not a democracy, neither is Rhodesia in which the majority of Africans is not yet enfranchised. It is clear that there is room for difference of opinion here, but it seems reasonable to argue that democracy does imply universal adult suffrage. Britain has only enjoyed such a franchise since 1928. Until 1918, no woman had the vote, although nearly all men had been entitled to vote since 1884. The Representation of the People Act, 1918, gave the vote to all men and to women over thirty who owned, or whose husbands owned, lands or premises of an annual value of at least £5. The inequity of having a property qualification for women which did not apply to men, and a higher age qualification than for men, was soon realized. In 1928 these limitations on female suffrage were removed and women gained the vote on the same basis as men.

What is meant by the term adult suffrage? In Britain the law at present accords the vote to men and women who have attained the age of 21. It is sometimes argued that the vote should be given at an earlier age. During and after the Second World War, young men were conscripted for military service at 18. Again, both men and women are liable for income tax when they are wage earners. Should not those who pay tax also have the right to vote? Many young men and women of 18 are better informed about politics than many of their seniors are. On the other hand, it can be argued that a degree of maturity and experience in the voter is desirable.

The Communist Party was the first political party in Britain to come out clearly in favour of lowering the age qualification to 18, presumably because the 1936 Soviet Socialist Constitution gives the vote to all Soviet citizens at the age of 18, although, in practice, it does not give them the right to a choice of candidates. In 1959, a Committee of the Labour Party on Youth recommended voting at 18. The Liberal Party, in its manifesto for the 1964 General Election, proposed that a Royal Commission should consider the question of lowering the voting age to 18. On 12 May 1965 the Speaker announced in the Commons that an all-party Conference on Electoral Law, with himself as chairman, would consider the question of the minimum age for voting, among other topics. The Labour Party proposed to this Conference that the age qualification should be lowered to 18.

When we say that all adults are entitled to vote, this does not mean that all have the opportunity to vote. The effectiveness of the right to vote depends in the first place on the effectiveness of the machinery of registration. In Britain registration is the concern of the Electoral Registration Officers, who are Town Clerks in the County Boroughs, and County Clerks in the County areas. The registers are compiled annually, in the autumn. The Registration Officers send a canvasser to every house in the constituency. The canvasser checks the name on the old register and leaves a form which must be filled up and returned by the head of the household. The form requires him to state the names of everyone who will be present in the house on a named day in October, who is over 21 or approaching the age of 21, and is either a British subject or a citizen of the

Republic of Ireland. Failure to complete and return the form is an offence. A new register is then compiled from the returns and can be inspected at public offices and certain post offices. Until a named day in December, members of the public can inspect the register and can challenge the non-appearance or wrongful appearance of names.

The system is in general effective and is certainly more satisfactory than systems which require the citizen to go himself to a public office to get his name on the register. Under such systems, many citizens may not bother or may forget to register. More sinister, they may be intimidated or obstructed from registering. This is still the case in certain Southern States in the United States where coloured voters find it difficult to secure registration. In Britain there are relatively few complaints about the compilation of registers. In Swansea in 1951 someone complained to the Conservative agent that his dog had been put on the register. How it had got there was a mystery. Presumably the canvasser had helped the householder to fill up the form and so 'Toby Davies', who had made his presence felt in a canine way, found himself transformed into one of the adult human residents of the house. The interesting point was that the householder complained to the Conservative agent, who in turn drew the attention of the Electoral Registration Officer to the fault in the register. No one attempted to personate the dog and vote on his behalf.

The atmosphere on this sort of question in Northern Ireland is, generally speaking, very different. Tension there is often acute between Catholics and Protestants. There is less general confidence in the fairness of the registration officers. D. G. Neill found, in 1951, several cases in which it was alleged that the registration officers were negligent and politically biased in the work of compiling the registers. He also found widespread evidence of personation of electors.[1] In Britain there is little evidence of sharp practice because the political atmosphere is calmer and there is a general acceptance that the rules of the game will be observed.

The system is far from perfect, however. When general elections are held in October, as they often are, they are held

[1] See D. G. Neill, 'The Election in Northern Ireland' in D. E. Butler, *The British General Election of 1951* (Macmillan, 1952) pp. 220–35.

on a register which is nearly a year old. It would be better if registers were revised twice a year instead of annually, but this would be more costly. The system is also largely dependent on the intelligence and sense of responsibility of the householder. One simple reform could improve matters. Much more should be done by poster displays in shops and post offices etc. to inform people when the register is open for inspection. A more difficult, but still desirable, reform would be to provide for amendment of the register after December each year if errors are found after the normal challenge period has ended.[1]

Some people living in Britain are excluded from voting even if they are over 21. We have seen that voters must be British subjects or citizens of the Republic of Ireland. People who are certified as mentally deficient or mentally ill may not vote, neither may peers of the realm, if they are members of the English peerage. This is because English peers receive a writ of summons to the House of Lords and are excluded from the business of the Commons. Persons serving a term of imprisonment also cannot vote unless they have been sentenced to a term of less than 12 months in which case they may vote by post from prison. The Returning Officer in each constituency, who is normally the mayor in borough constituencies or the sheriff in county constituencies, is excluded from voting in the election over which he presides. This is to signalize his impartiality. Finally, anyone who has been convicted of corrupt or illegal practices in the course of an election is excluded from voting for a five year period. Convictions under this Act are nowadays very rare in Britain as bribery and intimidation are almost unknown.

With few exceptions, then, everyone over 21 has the vote and much public money is expended to ensure that those who are qualified to vote are able to do so. Seamen and members of the armed services are able to vote by proxy or by post, if they are away from home. The postal vote is available for people in other occupations which take them periodically away from

---

[1] On this point see D. E. Butler and A. King, *The British General Election of 1964* (Macmillan, 1965) p. 221.
The Speaker's Conference in February 1966 recommended that the Government should arrange for a feasibility study of the use of computer techniques in compiling and keeping up-to-date the electoral register. (Cmnd. 21917. Conference on Electoral Law: Letter from Speaker to Prime Minister, 8 February 1966.)

home, and for voters who have moved to another constituency since the compilation of the register.[1] It can also be secured, on a doctor's certificate, for people who are incapacitated by blindness or illness from voting in person.

The postal vote was introduced, on a permanent basis, by the Representation of the People Act, 1948. It is a reform which has had considerable advantages for the Conservative Party. The Nuffield election studies have estimated that the Conservatives have consistently won a larger share of the postal votes than Labour has done. For example, Butler and King estimated that, if there had been no postal vote, the Labour Party in 1964 would have had an overall majority of between 20 and 40, instead of only 4.[2] Small wonder then that the Conservative election manifesto in 1964 should contain the proposal that people absent from their constituencies on holiday should be permitted to vote by post. The question of absent voting generally was one of the matters referred to the Speaker's Conference on electoral reform in 1965.

The question of electoral advantage, however, must not be allowed to obscure the moral principle that everyone who wishes to vote should be given the opportunity to do so. Other changes in electoral administration since 1948 have had the same object in mind. For example there are many more polling booths than there used to be. Even a tiny rural hamlet now often has its own polling booth, where previously voters had to travel considerable distances to vote in the nearest large village or town. Polling booths are also now open for long periods: from 7.0 in the morning to 9.0 in the evening at parliamentary elections. In these various ways Parliament has chosen to maximize voting opportunities in Britain rather than to make voting compulsory. At the last five general elections in the United Kingdom the percentage poll has been as follows: 82·5 per cent. in 1951, 76·8 per cent. in 1955, 78·7 per cent. in 1959, 77·1 per cent. in 1964 and 75·8 per cent. in 1966. These percentages compare favourably with a country like Australia which has compulsory voting, where the percentage poll is normally around 90 per cent.

[1] Voters who have moved to a neighbouring constituency *within the same borough* are not, however, entitled to postal votes.
[2] Butler and King: op. cit., pp. 226–7.

The Representation of the People Act, 1948 which introduced certain new voting facilities, such as the postal vote, was also responsible for taking away certain voting rights. Before the passage of the Act, certain categories of people had been entitled to more than one vote. Occupiers of business premises could claim a vote in the constituency in which their business was situated, in addition to their vote as residents, provided that their residential qualification was in a different constituency. Not more than one business vote could be claimed by each individual: the proprietor of a chain store could not claim an additional vote for each one of his one hundred and one different branches. Graduates of British universities were also entitled to a vote additional to their votes as residents in a constituency. The university votes were cast in twelve university constituencies distributed, between 1918 and 1948, among the universities of England, Wales, Scotland, and Northern Ireland. The Act of 1948 abolished both the university and business votes and introduced the principle of 'one man, one vote'. During its passage through the House of Commons, the Conservative opposition strongly criticized these changes, and the Conservative Party in the 1950 election was pledged to restore university representation. However, Conservatives in office between 1951 and 1964 made no attempt to restore either the university or the business vote.

John Stuart Mill put forward the most developed argument in favour of plural voting in his book *Representative Government* first published in 1861. He advocated giving additional votes to people holding positions of responsibility in all walks of life—to foremen as well as to business proprietors—and to those holding university degrees or professional qualifications.[1] He also thought that people who did not hold a position of responsibility or have a high standard of education should be able to qualify for more than one vote by passing a special examination in which they could show knowledge of civic affairs. By these means he hoped to give greater weight in the electoral decision to the minority of electors who were well informed and had a responsible attitude.

Much more can be said in favour of such a system as this than of the practice of granting additional votes only to gradu-

---

[1] J. S. Mill, *Representative Government* (Blackwell, ed. 1946) pp. 217–18.

ates and business men. But the whole idea of plural voting has been steadily losing ground since Mill's day. For one thing, universal suffrage has not had the undesirable effects on British politics which Mill feared it might. His fear that it might result in a House of Commons consisting largely of the unintelligent and ill-informed has proved quite unfounded. For another, better schooling nowadays ensures that every voter has reached a reasonable minimum standard of education. A high standard of education is, anyway, no guarantee of political wisdom. Finally, the idea of educational qualifications for voting has been discredited by abuse. For example, some of the Southern States in the United States have used educational tests to deny the vote to large numbers of coloured people. Again, the present suffrage in Rhodesia ensures the dominance of the European voter by requiring a high educational standard for admission to the more influential 'A' Electoral Roll and a lower, but still for most Africans unattainable standard, for entry to the 'B' Roll.

Impartial Administration of Elections

When, therefore, we say that the members of the House of Commons are elected by the people, we mean that they are chosen by all men and women over 21, with very few exceptions, who choose to vote, and that no one has more than one vote. But are they freely elected? Just what is implied by the phrase 'free elections'?

The most important requirement is that elections should be fairly administered. In Britain we are so accustomed to fair administration of elections that we barely realize what an important pre-condition of free elections this is. To appreciate its importance it is well to look at an example of elections in which, although opposition candidates were tolerated, all the weight of the administration was thrown in favour of the candidates who supported the existing regime. The classic example is found in the Second Empire in France. It was then customary for the administration to give all kinds of advantages to the 'official candidates' who supported Napoleon III. They were provided with special posters to indicate their official status—the famous *affiches blanches*. Government servants, from the Prefects of Departments to the postmen, were instructed to influence opinion in favour of the official candidates.

In Britain, public servants must be entirely neutral and it is made clear that no propaganda in favour of any candidate must be displayed anywhere near the polling booth. In the 1950 parliamentary election in Oxfordshire an assistant agent was amazed to hear on polling day that in one of the remoter villages in the constituency, a poster in favour of the other party's candidate was being displayed at the entrance to the polling booth. His mind flew back to Napoleon III, but, taking a grip on the present, he telephoned the Chief Constable and made a complaint. The Chief Constable at once sent a police car to have the offending poster removed. He later telephoned to apologize and explained that this was the first time the particular school in question had been used as a polling booth, and that the poster had been left over from a political meeting on a previous day. The rarity of an incident such as this is significant.

The manning of polling booths and counting of votes is entrusted to the employees of the local authorities who work under the direction of the Returning Officer assisted by the Town or County Clerk as the case may be. All candidates are entitled to witness the count and to appoint tellers to assist. They have the right to demand a recount where they think they have observed any errors in the distribution or counting of ballot papers or when the result is very close. The Returning Officer also consults the candidates about doubtful ballot papers: papers in which words have been written in, or the cross marked on or very near the line instead of squarely in the box against the candidate's name.[1] The system therefore ensures that the counting of votes is as accurate and impartial as possible.

Another pre-requisite of free elections is that bribery and intimidation should be excluded. In the 1860s in Britain, corruption of voters was still widespread. W. B. Gwyn, for example, comments that 'Two-thirds of the Bridgwater voters newly enfranchised by the Reform Act of 1867 were considered by well qualified opinion to be corrupt'.[2] Corruption and

[1] British case law is rich in decisions of the election court upon what does or does not constitute a valid ballot paper. They are well summarized by A. N. Schofield, *Parliamentary Elections*, 2nd ed. (Shaw, 1955) pp. 373–87.

[2] W. B. Gwyn: *Democracy and the Cost of Politics in Britain* (Athlone Press, 1962) p. 65.

intimidation were in time virtually eliminated by the secret ballot, introduced in 1872, and the Corrupt and Illegal Practices Act of 1883 followed by a series of court decisions which have defined these practices very fully. For example, intimidation has been held even to extend to undue spiritual influence. A priest who threatens one of his flock with excommunication, or withholding of the sacraments, if he does not vote in a certain way, is guilty of undue influence.[1]

It is important that disputes about the validity of elections should be heard in impartial courts. Since 1868 a disputed return in a constituency has been decided by judges of the Queen's Bench who can void the election if they find evidence of any irregularity. The judges are independent of the executive and their decision is likely to be much more fair than the majority vote of the legislature, which is an alternative method of deciding disputed returns. This was the method used by the House of Commons before 1868 and by the French National Assembly in the Fourth Republic.

The process in the National Assembly gave rise to bitter controversy, and the decisions reached were often neither consistent among themselves nor free from party prejudice.[2] A better method was adopted when the Constitution of the Fifth Republic gave the function of deciding disputed returns to the Constitutional Council. This body is not a court but is independent of the legislature. It consists of three members nominated by the President of the Republic, three by the President of the National Assembly and three by the President of the Senate. They hold office for nine years. Former Presidents of the Republic are ex-officio members of the Constitutional Council.

Freedom of Speech and Freedom to Organize Political Parties
The most obvious requirement for free elections is freedom of speech. No matter how fairly the election itself is conducted, it is not a free election if candidates can be made to suffer fines or imprisonment on account of their political views. British law imposes some limits upon what is said and written during an election campaign. A person uttering a libel or slander may be

[1] Schofield, op. cit., p. 413.
[2] See Peter Campbell, 'Verification des Pouvoirs in the French National Assembly', *Political Studies* Vol. I. No. 1. (Feb. 1953).

proceeded against in the courts for what is said in an election campaign or at any other time. The law is in a real sense a protector of freedom of speech. It permits fair comment but discourages the 'smearing' of one candidate by another. Where the law of libel is more lax, political parties have been able to get away with the most unscrupulous smearing of their political opponents. For example, in the Third Republic in France, right-wing groups, from time to time, used the most unscrupulous smear tactics against the centre and left, knowing that if they threw enough mud some of it would stick, however unjustified the accusations they made.

There is also, in Britain, the law of seditious libel. But the modern interpretation of a seditious libel is a narrow one. In effect, the law allows the most fundamental and hostile criticism of the existing system of government and organization of society. It categorizes as a seditious libel only language calculated 'to incite others to public disorders, to wit, rebellions, insurrections, assassinations, outrages, or any physical force or violence of any kind'.[1] Thus, Fascist, Communist, or Anarchist speakers have freedom to express their political views in Britain provided they do not specifically incite their audiences to acts of violence.

This degree of freedom of expression is not found in all countries which lay claim to be democracies. In the United States, for example, the Smith Act of 1940 made it a crime to be a member of a group in the knowledge that it advocates the violent overthrow of the Government. Several Communists have been fined or imprisoned under this Act, and in some (but not all) cases the Supreme Court has upheld their conviction.[2] There is keen debate on the question of whether or not such a limitation of freedom of expression is necessary. It is sometimes argued that it is vital for the democracies to defend themselves against the advocates of political systems that seek to replace

---

[1] Mr. Justice Coleridge in the case of *The King* v. *Aldred* (1909), quoted more fully by E. C. S. Wade in his appendix to A. V. Dicey, *Introduction to the Law of the Constitution*, 9th ed. (Macmillan, 1939) p. 579.

[2] For example on 5 June 1961, the Supreme Court upheld the conviction under the Smith Act of Junius Scales. But the conviction of another Communist, John Noto, was reversed on the grounds that 'the mere abstract teaching of the moral propriety or even moral necessity for a resort to force and violence, is not the same as preparing a group for violent action and steering it to such action'.

democracy by dictatorship. Yet, where limitations are placed
on the expression of political views, there cannot be said to be
free elections in the fullest sense.

Again, elections are not fully free where there is not freedom
of political organization. The Federal Republic of Germany
which has proscribed the Communist and the Nazi parties
cannot therefore be said to permit completely free elections.
But whether these departures from the principle of free elections
should be condemned is another matter. Certainly there is a
strong argument for preventing the revival of Nazi organizations in West Germany by making any form of Nazi party
illegal. One should judge each such departure by the circumstance of the case. The ideal is complete freedom of political
organization, just as complete freedom of expression is the ideal.
Where there is any falling away from these ideals it is regrettable, although sometimes it may be shown to be necessary.

Freedom to Stand for Election
There should also be freedom to stand for election. In Britain
there are certain categories of people who may not sit in the
House of Commons. In general, people who are disqualified
from voting are also disqualified from sitting in the Commons.
In addition, members of the Clergy of the Church of England,
the Church of Scotland, the Church of Ireland, and of the
Roman Catholic Church may not sit in the Commons. Also
excluded are undischarged bankrupts and the holders of
certain offices under the Crown. Until 1957, the law on this
question was determined by the Succession to the Crown Act of
1707 and was full of anomalies. Any office of profit under the
Crown then constituted disqualification and some, but not all,
contractors to the Crown were also disqualified.

The House of Commons Disqualification Act of 1957 clarified
and reformed the law. No contractors to the Crown are now
disqualified, and only certain stated offices under the Crown
involve disqualification. The principal categories are Civil
Servants, members of the regular armed forces, full-time police-
men (except for members of the British Transport Commission
Police), full-time judges and members of the boards of nationalized industries. Some people in these categories can sit in the
House of Lords. For example, some of the judges are Law Lords

and the chairman of the National Coal Board, Lord Robens, is a Life Peer. The ancient sinecures of the Stewardship of Her Majesty's Chiltern Hundreds, or of the Manor of Northstead, still disqualify from membership of the Commons. Acceptance of one of these offices is the only way by which a Member of Parliament may resign his seat.

In general, the law on disqualification is now sound enough apart from the question of the excluded clergy. It seems ludicrous that members of the Clergy of the Churches of England and Scotland, and Roman Catholic priests, should be excluded from the Commons, while non-conformist ministers are not. Even clergymen of the dis-established Anglican Church in Wales may sit in the Commons under the provisions of the Welsh Church Act of 1914.

Although, theoretically, any British citizen who does not fall within the excluded categories may sit in the House of Commons if elected, the need to meet the cost of an election campaign in fact restricts the right to stand. Independent candidates and candidates nominated by the small parties also have to reckon, as part of the cost of the campaign, the probable loss of the £150 deposit. This deposit is exacted by existing legislation from every candidate, who forfeits his £150 if he secures less than one-eighth of the votes cast in the constituency.

Candidates nominated by the two giant parties, the Conservative and Labour parties, have only rarely forfeited their deposits in recent elections. On the other hand, a high proportion of the candidates of the smaller parties—the Liberals, Communists, Welsh Nationalists, and Scottish Nationalists—regularly lose their deposits. For example, in the 1964 general election, all thirty-six Communist candidates, and twenty-one out of twenty-three Welsh Nationalist candidates, lost their deposits. Out of 365 Liberal candidates, 53 lost their deposits. Only five Conservative and eight Labour candidates did. The system is therefore very hard on the smaller parties who are also far less wealthy.

The idea of the deposit is to reduce the likelihood of frivolous candidatures. This object could be achieved much more fairly by requiring, instead of a deposit, that every candidate must submit to the returning officer a nomination paper bearing the signatures of 200 registered electors in the constituency where he wishes to stand. Such a requirement would ensure that each candidate had secured a sizeable degree of support in the constituency, while it would not penalize the smaller parties and independents as the present deposit does. An alternative reform would be to reduce the qualification for retention of the deposit from one-eighth to one-sixteenth of the votes cast. At present, a candidate who obtains more than six thousand votes may often forfeit his deposit although he clearly has the support of a substantial body of electors in the constituency.

J. F. S. Ross, who has been one of the most eloquent advocates of the abolition of election deposits, also proposed that the State should make grants to candidates which would meet the whole or part of the cost of their election campaigns—the size of the grant increasing, up to a specified maximum, in relation to the number of votes received.[1] This is one of the most radical projects yet devised for reducing the influence of wealth in politics. There is little doubt that much of the power of the Conservative and Labour parties flows from their ability to attract funds from the business and professional classes in the one case and from the trade unions in the other. But objections can be made to Mr. Ross's scheme on the grounds not only of its cost to the taxpayer, but also that it would weaken the voluntary principle in party organization. At present the need to secure funds for fighting elections is one of the chief stimulants to parties, impelling them to try to increase their membership and to organize social functions which, in addition to raising money, in some degree broaden public interest and contact with party workers.

Reducing the Influence of Wealth in Elections

Existing legislation sets severe limits to the influence of wealth during the period of the election campaign. The Representation of the People Act, 1948, requires that candidates shall not exceed limits of expenditure which vary according to the number of electors in each constituency. In county constituencies, the permitted expenditure per candidate is £450 plus 2d. per elector. In borough constituencies, the formula is £450 plus 1½d. per elector. The maxima are higher in the county constituencies, as they are often scattered rural areas which

---

[1] J. F. S. Ross, *Parliamentary Representation* 2nd ed. (Eyre & Spottiswoode, 1948) pp. 204-7.

involve greater expense in organization. Thus, in a county constituency with an electorate of 60,000 the maximum expenditure permitted to each candidate is £950. In a borough constituency with 60,000 electors, the maximum is £825. These maxima are severe when it is considered that expenditure will include the fee for an agent's services, the cost of producing election addresses (postage of the addresses is provided free by the State), the cost of posters, of hiring halls for meetings and committee rooms, of expenses for visiting speakers, of secretarial services, and of many other incidental expenses.

Before 1948, permitted expenditure was considerably higher —at the 1945 election, £1,300 could be spent in a borough constituency with 60,000 electors. The effect of lowering the limit has been to curtail certain party activities. For example, nowadays much less is normally spent on posters than before the war, and election addresses are usually printed on smaller sheets of paper. With the cost of printing constantly rising since 1948, the restriction on expenditure has become more and more stringent and in 1965 was due for revision. It was one of the subjects which was referred to the Speaker's Conference on electoral reform in that year. A restriction on expenditure is clearly desirable but not to the point where it is difficult for the parties to make effective appeals to the electors or to get their candidates known.

It is, on the face of it, very anomalous that while expenditure is strictly controlled during the election campaign, there is no control on expenditure by the parties at other times. In the period between May 1963 and October 1964, which was the period of intensive build-up for the 1964 general election, the Labour Party spent £314,000 on press advertising, posters, and other public relations activities. In the same period the Conservative Party spent £992,000, over three times as much, on advertising and publicity. In addition, the Steel Federation, individual steel firms and other organizations, like Aims of Industry, spent no less than £1,896,000 in anti-nationalization campaigns. The total spent on publicity which was anti-Labour in tone was £2,888,000, more than nine times Labour expenditure.[1]

---

[1] Richard Rose, 'Pre-Election Public Relations and Advertising', in Butler and King, op. cit., pp. 368–78.

This lack of balance must cause concern. Expenditure by the parties could at all times be limited by law. This would result, no doubt, in some of the funds which are at present expended by the parties being diverted to campaigns like that organized by Aims of Industry. It would be possible to restrict such campaigns by making illegal any forms of advertising which are not trying to sell a distinct product or service. This would exclude prestige advertising and all forms of propaganda advertising, including advertisements such as those sponsored by Christian Action. This is, in effect, the situation on independent television where the Independent Television Authority prohibits all advertising which is in any way political in content. To extend this practice to advertising in the press would however seem a severe restriction on 'freedom to advertise'.[1]

Another provision of the Representation of the People Act, 1948 which was intended to restrict the influence of wealth in elections was the section which forbade candidates from using more than a stated number of cars for taking voters to the polls. The limits imposed were determined, as with the control of expenditure, by the number of electors in the constituency. One car could be used for every 1,500 electors in county constituencies and one for every 2,500 in boroughs. Each agent had to register the cars used by him with the Returning Officer, and registered cars displayed an official windscreen label. Drivers of all other cars were forbidden from giving 'lifts' to the polling stations to anyone other than to members of their own household. The provision was difficult to enforce and there was some evasion of the law. The police could not check upon the occupants of every unregistered car stopping outside a polling booth, for example. But the law did make it difficult for agents to use unregistered cars for several journeys to the poll. Its object was therefore attained, in part if not in whole.

This section of the Act was repealed by a Conservative majority in Parliament in 1958. The ending of the restriction gave no great advantage to the Conservatives, because increasing affluence has meant that it is almost as easy for local

---

[1] A provision in the Companies Act, 1967, requires all companies to give to shareholders information about contributions to political funds. This provision may help to reduce the disparity in expenditure between the two main parties; it should improve public knowledge about the sources of party funds.

Labour parties as it is for Conservative parties to get enough people to volunteer their cars on polling day.

It is interesting to notice that J. S. Mill in 1861 not only advocated a severe restriction of election expenditure by candidates, but also wanted to forbid them from conveying voters to the poll. He argued that the State should meet the cost of providing carriages to take sick people to the poll.

Freedom of the Press

Just as freedom of speech is essential if there are to be free elections, so it is vitally important that there should be a free Press. The Press in Britain is free in the sense that it is, in peace time, in no way controlled by the Government. Newspapers may print whatever news and comment they choose with the qualification, as with the principle of freedom of speech, that they are subject to the laws of libel. They are also limited by the law of contempt, which forbids the publication of anything affecting a case before the courts which might tend to influence the result of a trial. These limitations do not, in general, infringe the principle of freedom of the Press as they are necessary to ensure that accuracy is respected and that proceedings in court are fair. The extent of the limitation imposed by Parliamentary privilege is more open to question and is discussed later, in Chapter VII.[1] The Press is also limited in what it can publish by the Official Secrets Acts.

Just as the Government should not control the Press, neither should any one business interest or any small group of interests. The essence of a free Press is a competing Press. It was the fear that competition was fast disappearing from the newspaper world which has led to the setting up, since 1945, of two Royal Commissions on the Press. The first, which reported in 1949, concluded that: 'There is nothing approaching monopoly in the Press as a whole or, with the single exception of the London financial daily, in any class of newspaper'.[2] In 1960, however, the *News Chronicle* went out of circulation, even though it had 1,206,000 readers, mainly owing to the difficulty of securing sufficient advertising revenue in the face of the competition of commercial television. The *News Chronicle*, which had been a

---

[1] See below p. 174.
[2] Report of the Royal Commission on The Press 1947–1949, p. 175 para. 664.

Liberal paper, was merged with the Conservative *Daily Mail*. This large scale merger was one of the reasons for the setting up of a second Royal Commission on the Press, in 1961. This Royal Commission, which reported in September 1962, concluded that the increasing concentration of ownership contained potential dangers for the freedom of the Press, and that some method should be adopted for regulating amalgamations in the public interest. The Labour Government in 1964 introduced its Monopolies and Mergers Bill which sought to give effect to this recommendation. The Bill, which became law in 1965, provides that no major merger of newspapers can take place without the approval of the Board of Trade following on a report by the Monopolies Commission. The Royal Commission in 1962 also recommended that the Press Council should be reconstituted with a lay chairman and given the function of reporting to the public on developments which may tend towards greater concentration or monopoly in the Press. The Press Council revised its constitution accordingly in 1963 and appointed Lord Devlin as its first lay chairman.

The extent to which concentration of ownership of the national daily papers has already taken place is shown by Table I. It will be seen that the national press is now dominated by four

TABLE I

Circulations in 1966 of the national dailies

		Circulation	% of total	Political leaning
	Daily Express	3,953,612	25·6	Conservative
Jointly	Daily Mail	2,381,223	15·5	Conservative
owned	Daily Sketch	849,396	5·5	Conservative
	Daily Telegraph	1,354,146	8·8	Conservative
	The Times	273,148	1·8	Non-committed/ Conservative
Interlocking	Daily Mirror	5,077,548	32·9	Labour
ownership	The Sun	1,247,818	8·1	Labour
	The Guardian	282,709	1·8	Labour/Liberal
		15,419,600	100·0	

The figures are average circulations in the period January to June 1966. The *Morning Star* has not been included since its circulation is relatively very small.

groups: the *Daily Express*; the *Daily Mail* and the *Daily Sketch* which are jointly owned; the *Daily Telegraph*; and the *Daily Mirror* and the *Sun* which have interlocking ownership. In terms of political leaning, the first four of these papers are Conservative and between them account for 55·4 per cent of the circulation of morning dailies. The *Daily Mirror* and the *Sun* are Labour and have 41·0 per cent of the total circulation. The situation does not therefore give cause for alarm but certainly wants watching.

A limiting factor on the influence of the Press has been the development of radio and television. The Press in Britain was probably at its highest peak of influence just before the introduction of broadcasting in the 1920s. A large literate public had permitted the popular dailies to develop mass circulations and there was no rival to the Press as a means of disseminating information. Nowadays the existence of television and radio acts as a very effective check on the accuracy of news appearing in the Press.

Although both the British Broadcasting Corporation and the Independent Television Authority are State owned, they are independent corporations. The Postmaster-General has overall responsibility for both corporations, but he is not empowered by statute to interfere with the content of programmes except by express and public directive. In practice this power is very rarely used, and both corporations provide objective news and feature programmes which are fair-minded and are not biased towards any one party.

Time for party political broadcasting is provided free on both networks, and the time allotted is divided between the principal parties in a ratio agreed between the parties on the one hand and B.B.C. and I.T.A. on the other. At the 1964 general election the agreed ratio was Conservative 5, Labour 5, Liberal 3. It had been agreed that a party had to nominate fifty candidates to qualify for a party political broadcast.[1] The excluded parties criticized this arrangement, and for the 1966 general election the Scottish and Welsh Nationalist parties were each allotted a five-minute broadcast on B.B.C. and Independent Television and a five-minute sound broadcast.

In general the system is a fair one, especially when compared

[1] Martin Harrison, 'Television and Radio', in Butler and King, op. cit., p. 157.

with Radiodiffusion Television Française which, until 1965, continually favoured President de Gaulle, particularly in the presentation of news and features. In 1965 arrangements for the Presidential election were fairer than they had been at previous elections. Equal time was allowed on television to each of the five candidates, including President de Gaulle. Also, a Control Commission kept watch on the fairness of news bulletins. The added scope for opposition candidates probably helped to make the election a surprisingly close-run affair for de Gaulle.

The Problem of Constituency Boundaries

Most of the pre-requisites of a free election have now been examined, but there is one further condition which needs to be fulfilled. Constituency boundaries should be impartially and fairly drawn. It is possible for a governing party so to manipulate constituency boundaries that it obtains much more than its fair share of seats. This can be done, broadly speaking, in two ways. You can maximize your own voting strength by drawing together into one constituency scattered groups of supporters who are in a minority in each of several existing constituencies. Alternatively, you can minimize the opposing party's voting strength by lumping its voters together in one constituency, drawing them away from marginal constituencies where they threaten your control.

The use of either technique can be easily discerned from the electoral map as it produces totally artificial constituencies which are often of extraordinary shape and size. The technique is thought to have been first consciously employed in Massachusetts in 1812 during the administration of Governor Gerry. It is said that one of the constituencies in the state had the shape of a lizard. 'Why, this district looks like a salamander!' remarked an observer. 'Say rather a Gerrymander!' replied an opposition editor. Gerrymandering is still carried on in some American states. In 1959 the 12th congressional district in New York state was shaped like an elongated sea horse, for example, while the 26th district in California resembled the head and horns of a moose. Both were recent creations and had been devised in the interests of the majority party.[1]

[1] See an article (with maps) by George B. Merry in the *Christian Science Monitor* 11 June 1959, p. 4.

Gerrymandering, in the full sense of the word, has been virtually unknown in Britain. In the nineteenth century there were vast disparities in the size of the electorate between one constituency and another. This led the Chartists to campaign in 1838 for equal electoral districts as well as universal male suffrage, annual parliaments, secret ballot and the payment of M.P.s. Equal electoral districts have not yet been achieved, although since 1944 their attainment has been recognized by law as desirable. The worst disparities in the size of constituencies were removed by re-distribution in 1867, 1885, and 1918.

After the passage of the Representation of the People Act of 1928, a new problem was created. Previously re-distribution had always been closely accompanied by extension of the franchise. This sugared the pill for the party which stood to lose by re-distribution. Although it would lose seats by re-distribution, it might gain some by extension of the franchise. After 1928, no extension of the franchise was possible without lowering the qualification age—a reform which then found little favour. Consequently nothing was done about re-distribution, and by 1939 extensive population changes had produced wide variations in the sizes of constituencies. There were then 20 constituencies with more than 100,000 electors and 13 constituencies with under 30,000 electors.

It was obvious that some new system for re-distribution needed to be devised. The Speaker's Conference in 1944 approved the proposal that four permanent boundary commissions should be set up, one each for England, Wales, Scotland, and Northern Ireland. The commissions would have the task of reviewing constituency boundaries and suggesting revisions to Parliament at frequent intervals. In this way, re-distribution could take place regularly and would only need to be relatively minor in character, the electoral map being constantly adjusted to the population map. The task of recommending revisions would also be placed in the hands of an impartial authority.

These proposals were embodied in legislation in Acts of 1944, 1946, and 1948 which were consolidated in the House of Commons (Redistribution of Seats) Act 1949. The Speaker of the House of Commons was made ex-officio chairman of each commission. There were four other members of each commission, chosen for their knowledge of population and allied questions and their independence of party politics. For example, the members of the English Commission comprised, in addition to the Speaker, the Registrar-General, the Director-General of the Ordnance Survey, a nominee of the Home Secretary (who is concerned with the administration of elections), and a nominee of the Minister of Health (who at that time was concerned with the oversight of local government). The commissions were instructed to review constituency boundaries at intervals of not less than three, nor more than seven years.

The new system, although basically well devised, has not worked as well as had been hoped. One must distinguish, however, between the work of the English Commission and that of the other three commissions. In respect of the work of the commissions for Wales, Scotland, and Northern Ireland there has been little controversy. This is mainly because these commissions have relatively few constituencies to look at and have had sufficient time to consult with and take account of the views of local authorities and local party organizations. The English Commission, on the other hand, has run into two major controversies, in 1948 and 1954.

Before discussing these controversies it is important to note the terms of reference of the commissions. They were each to establish an electoral quota by dividing the total eligible electorate by the number of seats available. Scotland was to have not less than 71 seats, Wales not less than 35, and Northern Ireland not less than 12. The total number of constituencies in the United Kingdom was to be not substantially greater than 625. The electorate in each constituency was to be made 'as near to the electoral quota as is practicable'. On the other hand, the commissioners were instructed that constituencies should not cut across local government areas except when it was necessary to disregard local boundaries so as to avoid excessive departures from the quota.

The problem for the English Commission was difficult enough in balancing these often contradictory requirements when faced with re-drawing the boundaries of over 500 seats. Its problem was made the more difficult by a further rule which was, and is, distinctly ambiguous. The commissions were instructed that they might depart from the two main principles (of equal electoral districts and respect for local government

B

boundaries) 'if special geographical conditions, including in particular the size, shape and accessibility of a constituency, appear to them to render a departure desirable'. What does this rule mean? Does it apply only in exceptional circumstances and mean that, for example, in the mountainous parts of Wales and Scotland, where population is very scattered, it is desirable to have constituencies whose electorate is far below the electoral quota? Or has it a more general application? Does it mean that rural constituencies in general should have a lower electoral quota than urban constituencies?

It was, in effect, on the ambiguity of this rule that controversy centred in 1948. When the English Commission's proposals reached the Commons, Labour backbenchers complained that it had interpreted its function so as to favour, in general, the rural areas against the urban areas. They pointed out that under the Commission's proposals the average electorate in the county constituencies was 6,000 fewer than the average in borough constituencies. The Labour Government yielded to this protest and asked the English Boundary Commission to allot 17 extra seats to boroughs which had constituencies with large electorates. The Conservative opposition attacked the changes as 'shameless gerrymandering' but, even after the changes, the average electorate for English rural constituencies was more than 2,000 fewer than the average in borough constituencies. In fact, it is probable that re-distribution as a whole cost Labour between 20 and 30 seats at the 1950 general election.[1]

With a major re-distribution carried through in 1948, it seemed possible that revision of constituency boundaries would not again create great problems. In fact, controversy over the proposals of the English Commission was even fiercer when the next review took place, in 1954, than it had been in 1948. The reasons are a little hard to find, particularly as in theory the Commission should have had only minor changes to recommend after the lapse of such a short space of time. One reason seems to have been that the Commission went back to its original interpretation of the geographical conditions rule, giving substantially greater representation to the county

[1] This is the estimate of H. G. Nicholas in *The British General Election of 1950* (Macmillan, 1951) p. 4.

constituencies than to the boroughs. In the second place, the commissioners began their work rather late in the day, starting in August 1953 a review which had to be completed by August 1955. Consequently the process was hurried, and although local authorities and local parties were asked to comment on the Commission's proposals in the first instance, they were not given a chance to comment on the revised proposals. Finally, in the opinion of many, the Commission gave too much emphasis to securing equal electoral districts and too little attention to respecting local boundaries. When the Orders in Council embodying their proposals reached the Commons in 1954 they evoked a storm of protest from both sides of the House. Many local authorities were aggrieved at the proposed changes and three of them, Hammersmith, Fulham, and Manchester, attempted, although unsuccessfully, to challenge the validity of the Orders in the Courts. In the Commons, Sir Winston Churchill, the Prime Minister, recommended that the House should approve the Orders. But he pronounced himself very dissatisfied with the process of revision. He suggested that there should be a longer interval between revisions, possibly 10 to 15 years instead of 5 to 7 years.[1]

This proposal was followed by the House of Commons (Redistribution of Seats) Act of 1958. The Act extended the period between general reviews to 10–15 years. It also gave the commissioners greater latitude to depart from the quota in order to respect local government boundaries. It did not, however, attempt to define and clear up the ambiguity in the 'special geographical conditions rule'. It made a useful change in the composition of the commissions. A judge was to be appointed deputy chairman of each commission, while the Registrar General and the Director of the Ordnance Survey were to become assessors instead of members of the commission.

In some ways the lengthening of the period between reviews was a desirable change. Constituency party workers do not like frequent changes in boundaries because they break up

---

[1] By far the best discussion of the handling of redistribution, between 1944 and 1954, is to be found in an article by David Butler, 'The Redistribution of Seats', *Public Administration*, Vol. XXXIII, Summer 1955, pp. 125–47.
See also his book *The Electoral System in Britain Since 1918*, 2nd ed. (Clarendon Press, 1963) pp. 213–20.
See too R. L. Leonard, *Guide to the General Election* (Pan, 1964) pp. 31–7.

established patterns of co-operation to which they have grown accustomed. On the other hand the longer period means that constituencies are bound to vary considerably in size, and the commissions are only likely to make interim revisions in exceptional cases, for example on the creation of new towns. By 1964 considerable disparities had already appeared. There were then 15 constituencies with between 80,000 and 90,000 electors, including Billericay with 96,762.[1] At the other extreme, and excluding the small, deeply rural constituencies, there were some urban constituencies with very small electorates, for example Paddington South with 35,226 and Kelvingrove with 28,407.

There is clearly scope for improvement in the system of boundary revision. We have seen that virtually all the controversy has centred on the work of the English Commission. This gives a clue to the chief anomaly in the system. It does not make sense to have one commission for England with an electorate of over twenty-nine million, and one commission for Wales with an electorate of little over 1,800,000 and one for Scotland with an electorate of just under 3,400,000. Instead of having one commission for England, there should be one for each of the eight English regions which, in 1964 and 1965, were given responsibility in economic planning: the North, North West, Yorkshire-Humberside, West Midlands, East Midlands, East Anglia, South West and South East. Each one of these regions has a larger electorate than Wales and two of them, the North West and the South East, have a larger electorate than Scotland. A commission for each English region would have a much less mammoth task than that which faces the English Commission at present. It would then be possible to have adequate consultation with local authorities and local parties in each region, and to give due weight to their views. It would also be possible to shorten the period between general reviews, since 10–15 years is certainly too long.

The other change which should be made is to define the 'special geographical conditions rule' in an unambiguous way. Such a definition should surely make clear that only constituencies where the population is exceptionally sparse may have a

---

[1] For the general election in March 1966 Billericay had topped the 100,000 mark with 101,904 electors.

much lower electoral quota than the average. The electoral map should not, in general, favour the countryside against the town.

However, though one can point to the need for changes of detail in the new method of boundary division developed since the Second World War, it is basically sound. The other recent changes in the electoral law have also, as we have seen, enhanced the fairness of the system. In general we may say that parliamentary elections in Britain are free elections in a very full sense. But there is one aspect in which British elections are often held to be most unfair. The relationship between votes cast and seats won can be severely criticized, and the next chapter will examine such criticism.

FOR REFERENCE

D. E. BUTLER, *The British General Election of 1955* (Macmillan, 1955).

D. E. BUTLER, *The Electoral System in Britain Since* 1918, 2nd ed. (Clarendon Press, 1963).

D. E. BUTLER, 'The Redistribution of Seats' in *Public Administration*, 1955, pp. 125–47.

D. E. BUTLER and A. KING, *The British General Election of 1964* (Macmillan, 1965).

D. E. BUTLER and A. KING, *The British General Election of 1966* (Macmillan, 1966).

D. E. BUTLER and R. ROSE, *The British General Election of 1959* (Macmillan, 1960).

R. L. LEONARD, *Guide to the General Election* (Pan, 1964).

R. B. McCALLUM and A. READMAN, *The British General Election of 1945* (Cass, 1947).

W. J. M. MACKENZIE, *Free Elections*, 2nd ed. (Allen & Unwin, 1964).

J. S. MILL, *Representative Government* (1861).

H. G. NICHOLAS, *The British General Election of 1950* (Macmillan, 1951).

C. O'LEARY, *The Elimination of Corrupt Practices in British Elections 1868–1911* (Clarendon Press, 1962).

R. ROSE, *Influencing Voters* (Faber, 1967).

J. F. S. ROSS, *Parliamentary Representation*, 2nd ed. (Eyre and Spottiswoode, 1948).

A. N. SCHOFIELD, *Parliamentary Elections*, 3rd ed. (Shaw, 1959).

H. STREET, *Freedom, the Individual and the Law* (Pelican, 1963).

Cmd. 7700, Report of the Royal Commission on the Press 1947–1949.

Cmnd. 1811, Report of the Royal Commission on the Press 1961–1962.

CHAPTER II

The Method of Election

The Relative Majority System

ELECTION to the House of Commons is by relative majority in single-member constituencies. This method of election is to be found also in most countries of the British Commonwealth (in, for example, Canada, New Zealand, and India) and in the U.S.A. It is unknown, however, in Western Europe outside Britain: most of the countries on the Continent which have a democratic system use one of the various types of proportional representation, as does the Republic of Ireland.

Under the relative majority system, as applied in Britain, the candidate who receives the largest number of votes is declared elected even if he has not secured more than half the votes cast. Thus if, in a single member constituency, the Conservative candidate secures 21,000 votes, the Labour candidate 20,000 and the Liberal candidate 10,000, the Conservative is declared elected even though well over half the votes (in this case 30,000 out of 51,000) have been given to the other candidates. As a result, a party will often win a clear majority of seats in the House of Commons when it has received less than half the votes cast in the country as a whole.

Table II shows how ten out of the thirteen General Elections between 1922 and 1966 produced an absolute majority for one party; but on only two occasions (in 1931 and 1935) did the party winning the election secure 50 per cent or more of the votes cast in the United Kingdom as a whole. In only two cases were the majorities small. These were in 1950 when the Labour Party had a majority of only five, and in 1964 when it had a majority of only four, over all other parties. The other majorities have all been comfortable ones: ranging from a majority of 17 for the Conservatives in 1951 to the sweeping majority of 331 which that party obtained in 1931.

So the system can be severely criticized on the grounds that it

TABLE II

British General Elections 1922–66

	Party winning an overall majority in the Commons	No. of seats gained	Majority over all other parties	% of votes gained by majority party
1922	Conservative	345	75	38·2
1923	(None—Minority Labour Government)			
1924	Conservative	419	223	48·3
1929	(None—Minority Labour Government)			
1931	Conservative	473	331	55·2
1935	Conservative	432*	249	53·7
1945	Labour	393	146	47·8
1950	Labour	315	5	46·1
1951	Conservative	321*	17	48·0
1955	Conservative	344*	58	49·7
1959	Conservative	365*	100	49·4
1964	Labour	317	4	44·1
1966	Labour	363	97	47·9

* Includes National Liberals (and National Labour in 1935).

frequently gives the whole governing power, normally for a period of four to five years, to a party which did not win the support of a majority of voters.[1] Yet the governing party can secure the passage of legislation which the other parties fundamentally oppose and which is possibly disliked by the majority of electors. For example, many of the nationalization measures, passed by Parliament during the lifetime of the Labour Government between 1945 and 1950, were vigorously opposed by the Conservative and Liberal parties. Those two parties had between them gained 48·8 per cent of the votes cast at the 1945 General Election to Labour's 47·8 per cent (see Table III). Yet Labour had an unassailable majority of seats in the House of Commons, of 146 over all other parties, and the nationalization programme was passed in its entirety. Similarly, in 1954 the Conservative majority in the Commons secured the passage

[1] Under the Parliament Act of 1911, General Elections must be held at least every five years. The Lords must approve legislation to extend the life of Parliament.

TABLE III

Seats and Votes in Britain 1945–66

(*Party winning the General Election is italicized*)

		Seats	% of Votes Cast
1945	Conservative	213	39·8
	Labour	*393*	47·8
	Liberal	12	9·0
	(Others 22)		
1950	Conservative	298	43·5
	Labour	*315*	46·1
	Liberal	9	9·1
	(Others 3)		
1951	*Conservative*	*321*	48·0
	Labour	295	48·8
	Liberal	6	2·5
	(Others 3)		
1955	*Conservative*	*345*	49·7
	Labour	277	46·4
	Liberal	6	2·7
	(Others 2)		
1959	*Conservative*	*365*	49·4
	Labour	258	43·8
	Liberal	6	5·9
	(Others 1)		
1964	Conservative	304	43·4
	Labour	*317*	44·1
	Liberal	9	11·2
1966	Conservative	253	41·9
	Labour	*363*	47·9
	Liberal	12	8·6
	(Others 2)		

of the Television Act which inaugurated commercial television. This measure was vigorously opposed by the Labour and Liberal parties in the House but it became law despite the fact that at the General Election of 1951 the Conservatives had won only 48·0 per cent of the votes while the Labour and Liberal parties had achieved a combined total of 51·3 per cent.[1] Far-reaching changes such as these cannot easily be undone by subsequent governments. Yet under the British system they can be initiated

[1] There had been no mention of an Independent Television Bill in the Conservative Manifesto at the 1951 general election.

by governments which enjoy comfortable majorities at West-minster but have gained the support of only a minority of the electors. Is not such a situation, it may be argued, fundament-ally undemocratic?

Another, and related, consequence of the electoral system is that normally the smaller parties are greatly under-represented. The Liberal Party has suffered most severely from the working of the system in recent years. For example in 1964 the Liberals received 11·2 per cent. of the votes cast in the general election, yet they won only nine seats. Under a fully proportional system they would have secured seventy seats. One should not over-look the fact, either, that in 1964 the Liberals only contested 365 seats out of the whole 630. Had they contested every seat their proportion of the national poll would have been much larger.[1]

These then are the two main criticisms which can be made of the British electoral system. First, it frequently gives a parlia-mentary majority to a party which has only won a minority of votes at the General Election. Second, it heavily under-represents the smaller parties. Certain commentators have made wider criticisms. For example, in his book, *Parliamentary Representation*, J. F. S. Ross says of British elections: 'a general election is a gamble of which no one can predict the result with any certainty, and that result seldom accords with the wishes of the electorate as expressed by their votes'.[2] The first part of this statement has no basis in fact. Recent analyses of general election results have shown that the electoral system has a logic of its own and that it is predictable in operation.[3]

Since the Second World War, the party which has secured the largest number of votes has usually won more than its fair share of seats. The party with the second largest aggregate of votes has normally received fewer seats in relation to votes, while the other parties have been always heavily under-represented. When the margin of votes between the two main parties is small, as it was in 1950 and 1951, the majority for one party in the House of Commons is a small one. But, as the

[1] Butler and King (op. cit., p. 295) estimated that if the Liberals had fought everywhere in 1964 they would have won 16½ per cent of the total vote.

[2] Ross: op. cit., p. 169.

[3] See especially Butler, op. cit., Part II. The Working of the System. See also the appendixes to all the Nuffield General Election studies.

margin of votes widens, the majority in seats increases more rapidly. In fact this process has been expressed in terms of a mathematical formula known as the 'Cube Law'.[1] This formula states that if the popular vote is divided between the two main parties in the proportion A:B, the seats in Parliament will be divided $A^3:B^3$.

The formula can be used nowadays to predict the results of elections with remarkable accuracy, provided that a bias, normally present in the system since the redistribution of seats in 1948, is taken into account. This bias is occasioned by the fact that Labour votes tend to be concentrated into industrial constituencies while Conservative votes are more evenly spread throughout the country. There are more 'safe' Labour seats such as Llanelly, Neath, and Barnsley, where Labour majorities are regularly 20,000 or more, than there are comparable safe Conservative seats. As a result, the Labour Party normally gains fewer seats in relation to votes than the Conservative Party does. Table IV illustrates how this comes about.

TABLE IV

Labour votes are 'wasted' by being concentrated in industrial constituencies

1951 General Election

| | Votes | | Seats | |
	Labour	Conservative	Labour	Conservative
Neath	24,129	10,367	1	
Battersea, South	17,237	17,731		1
Chislehurst	30,699	31,679		1
Totals	72,065	59,777	1	2

Taking the results in the Neath, South Battersea, and Chislehurst constituencies together we see that Labour polled 72,065 votes but won only one seat, whereas the Conservatives, who polled only 59,777 votes, won two seats. In the country as a whole of course, the disparity between seats and votes is not so great, but the fact remains that there are more Neaths and

[1] See M. G. Kendall and A. Stuart, 'The Law of Cubic Proportion in Election Results', *British Journal of Sociology*, Vol. I. No. 3.

Barnsleys than there are safe Conservative seats like South Kensington or Worthing.

It was the operation of this factor which resulted in the Conservatives winning a majority of seats in 1951 although they received 0·8 per cent less of the popular vote than Labour did (see Table III). At the two following general elections, in 1955 and 1959, this bias continued to operate against the Labour Party. But in 1964 it virtually disappeared. As Butler and King have pointed out, in 1951 Labour was 230,000 ahead of the Conservatives in votes but 26 behind them in seats. In 1964, Labour was 200,000 ahead in votes but 13 ahead in seats. Butler and King attributed the disappearance of the bias to the relatively low percentage poll, on average, in safe Labour seats. Labour was not piling up votes where they were not needed to the extent it had done in previous elections.[1]

Allowing for the fact, however, that this bias against Labour may operate, it can be said that the British electoral system is predictable and not capricious in the way it works. A British general election is not a gamble. Neither is it true to say, as J. F. S. Ross does, that the result of an election 'seldom accords with the wishes of the electorate as expressed by their votes'. A general election result may not clearly reflect the state of opinion in the country but it does register a swing in opinion from one main party to another. It overemphasizes, on most occasions, the degree of swing in opinion but it does not misinterpret the direction of swing.

It is fair to point out, however, that the argument put forward by Ross in *Parliamentary Representation* was based largely upon an analysis of the working of the system in the 1920s and 1930s. During this period, and especially in the 1920s, there were three and not two main parties and, as a result, the working of the system seemed much more haphazard than it has seemed since the Second World War. With three main parties in the field, it is much more difficult to predict the effect of a given

---

[1] Butler and King, op. cit., pp. 295–6.
See, however, H. Berrington, 'The General Election of 1964' in *Journal of the Royal Statistical Society* (1965), pp. 17–66. Berrington argued that the disappearance of the bias against Labour in 1964 was not wholly to be attributed to the fall in turnout in safe Labour seats. It may have resulted in part from other causes, e.g. from the fact that as there had been no major redistribution of seats since 1954 many safe Labour seats had relatively small electorates.

percentage swing in opinion in terms of the party gains and losses which will result. In the 1920s the situation was made more confusing by the fact that the parties varied widely in the number of seats which they contested in the general elections of 1922, 1923, 1924 and 1929. But it is an unusual situation in Britain for there to be three main parties in the field. The very working of the system tends to drive out one of the parties and to restore a duality. The situation arose in the 1920s because Labour was replacing the Liberals as the main opposition to the Conservatives. When once the Labour Party had proved itself to be electorally stronger than the Liberal Party, the Liberals began to suffer from that acute under-representation which, as we have seen, tends to be inflicted upon the third party in Britain.

As the present electoral system in Britain undeniably tends to over-represent one of the two main parties and under-represent the other parties, would it be desirable to replace it by some form of proportional representation? This question can only be answered if we examine the way in which systems of proportional representation work and compare them with the British system. Many contradictory statements are made about proportional representation. For example, it is said that it promotes a multi-party system whenever it is adopted. On the other hand, it is sometimes claimed that proportional representation has resulted in a reduction in the number of parties. Again it is said, mainly by opponents of proportional representation, that it enhances the power of the party machine; while advocates of proportional representation often claim that it enlarges freedom of choice for the elector and emancipates him from party control. In fact all of these contradictory statements have an element of truth in them because they relate to different systems of proportional representation, or to different circumstances in which they are operating. It is clearly necessary to examine the different systems and to try to determine their effects.

Proportional Representation: The Party List System

There are two main systems of proportional representation (P.R. for short) in use in the world today. First, there is the party list system which is to be found in one form or another in Belgium, Holland, Italy, Switzerland, and the Scandinavian countries. Second, there is the system of the single transferable vote which is in use in the Republic of Ireland and in Tasmania. It is also used for election of the Senate in Australia.

The party list system was used in the Fourth Republic in France. In the later years of the Fourth Republic, the system was modified, but in November 1946 it existed in reasonably pure form and the general election in that month will be taken as an example of the system. The country was divided into 104 multi-member constituencies. In the main, each department, which is comparable to an English county, formed one constituency but a few of the more populous departments were subdivided into two or more constituencies. The average number of seats allotted to a constituency was five, although some constituencies returned as few as two, and some as many as eleven deputies. In each constituency, each political party drew up a list of its candidates, limited in number to the number of seats to be filled. On polling day, the elector voted by choosing one of the party lists and placing it, in an envelope, in the ballot box. He was not allowed to erase any names and add other names from the list of a different party. This type of list is known as a 'blocked list'. When cross-voting between lists is allowed it is normally known as *panachage*.

Seats were allotted as follows. We will suppose that, in a typical five-member constituency, 200,000 valid votes were cast. The electoral quota was determined by dividing the number of valid votes by the number of seats. In this case the quota would be 40,000. The votes recorded for each list would then be counted. A list securing 40,000 votes would be entitled to one seat, a list winning 80,000 votes to two seats, and so on.

When, for example, a list was accorded two seats, the first two names on the list were declared elected. The order in which the names appeared on the list had been decided by the political parties. The system therefore placed great power in the hands of the party machine and greatly limited the elector's freedom of choice. It is true that in November 1946, the electoral law provided that voters could alter the order of preference on a party's list. But alterations of the order were taken into account only if 50 per cent or more of the voters for a list altered the order. In fact this condition was extremely rarely fulfilled and therefore the provision for preferential voting, within the list, was in effect a dead letter. In Norway, voters may alter the order on the party list but may not cross vote. In practice there, too, the order fixed by the party always stands.[1] It is indeed the general experience with the party list system that the party choice prevails even where cross-voting is allowed, although blocked lists clearly intensify party control.

In the example of the list system we have just examined, round figures have been given for the sake of simplicity. In practice, party lists will not secure exact multiples of the quota, and not all seats will be allocated by virtue of the quota. The votes over and above the quota can be weighed in various ways, but the two commonest are the systems known as the 'largest remainder' and the 'highest average'.

The system of the largest remainder is very simple. Suppose, for example, that in a five-member constituency, where 200,000 votes are polled, they are divided among the party lists as follows: M.R.P. 90,000, Socialist 58,000, Radical 52,000. The M.R.P. gain two seats and the Socialists and Radicals gain one seat each by virtue of the multiples of the quota (40,000) which they achieve. The Socialists have a remainder of 18,000 votes, against the 12,000 and 10,000 remainders of the Radicals and M.R.P. respectively. The Socialists are therefore accorded the fifth seat.

However, under the highest average system, the fifth seat in this case would go to the M.R.P. This is how the system would work. After seats have been allotted by the quota, the total of each party's vote is divided by the number of seats gained plus one. Thus the M.R.P.s total of 90,000 would be divisible by three and the Socialist 58,000 and the Radical 52,000 would be divisible by two. The resulting averages would be: M.R.P. 30,000, Socialist 29,000, and Radical 26,000. The M.R.P. would therefore secure the fifth seat.

This example illustrates the varying effects which different methods of allocating the votes in a list system may have. The 'largest remainder' method favours the smaller parties at the expense of the larger, while the 'highest average' method favours the larger parties at the expense of the smaller. François Muselier has calculated what would have been the effect of either system on the electoral fortunes of the Communist Party

[1] H. Valen and D. Katz, *Political Parties in Norway* (Tavistock, 1964) p. 64.

if employed at the 1951 election in France. Under the system of the largest remainder, the Communists would have won 160 seats; with the highest average they would have won 181 seats.[1]

In France in 1946, the highest average method was used and this, together with the operation of the 'blocked list' system, had a marked effect on the party structure of the Assembly. The electoral system helped to strengthen the larger parties and to improve party discipline, since the party organizations played such a large part in deciding who was elected. Whereas in 1940 there had been fourteen parliamentary groups in the Chamber of Deputies, and only two parties (Socialist and Communist) with effective national organizations, in 1946 there were only six parliamentary parties or groups, and three of these (the M.R.P., Socialists, and Communists), who dominated the Assembly, were well organized parties. Of course, the electoral system was not the only factor in bringing about this change. Another major factor had been the fall of France, which brought with it the discredit of the parties of the right who were the least well organized and disciplined. A further influence was the Resistance, in which the M.R.P., Socialists and Communists were the leading elements. Nevertheless the change in the electoral system was important, particularly in view of the electoral system which had preceded it.

In the Third Republic, for the great bulk of the period from 1871 to 1940, the system in use had been a relative majority system in single-member constituencies with two ballots. Under this system, if a candidate secured an absolute majority of votes at the first ballot he was at once declared elected. But if no candidate secured an absolute majority, a second ballot was held a fortnight later at which only a relative majority was required for election. This system gave rise to vigorous bargaining between local party groups in the interval between the two ballots. It encouraged small parties to remain in the field. It enhanced the power of the local committee and, by contrast, weakened such national party organizations as existed. The introduction of any of the types of party list system of P.R. was therefore likely to reduce the number of parties in France, and the methods used in 1945 and 1946 were especially calculated to do so.

[1] F. Muselier, *Regards Neufs sur Le Parlement* (Editions du Seuil, 1956) p. 125.

French experience illustrates the way in which we must consider not only the type of P.R. used, but also the electoral system which was used before it was introduced. Both factors will condition the effect of the introduction of P.R. in any country. The same applies of course to any non-proportional system. In the Fifth Republic, when the second ballot in single-member constituencies was re-introduced, it had quite different effects from the effect it had had in the Third Republic. For one thing, the interval with P.R. in the list system, followed in 1951 and 1956 by a system permitting alliance of party lists, had helped to reduce the number of parties and strengthen party discipline. For another, the predominance of General de Gaulle and the party which supported him, the U.N.R., produced a new situation. Elections in 1958 and 1962 under the second ballot system greatly favoured the U.N.R. and enabled it to gain a share of seats well in excess of what it could have gained by a system of P.R., or by the relative majority system with one ballot as in Britain. In 1958, for example, the U.N.R. gained 212 seats out of 552, having received only 20·4 per cent of the votes cast at the first ballot. Under the British system it would probably have won less than 150 seats. This curious effect is explained largely by the fact that the Communists were heavily disfavoured by the second ballot, the non-Communist parties frequently combining against them between the ballots in favour of the U.N.R. candidate.

Can we generalize about the working of the party list system in Western Europe as a whole? We cannot, since conditions before it was introduced have varied so much from country to country. But we can make certain observations. First, in all the countries which have the party list system of P.R., there are several important parties in the legislature. Consequently, it is rare to find one party forming the government with an absolute majority of seats over the other parties. In September 1967, only the Social Democratic Party in Sweden was in this situation. All the other countries—Holland, Belgium, Italy, Switzerland, Norway, Denmark, and Finland—had coalition or minority governments. A multi-party situation was found everywhere and coalition governments were normal. But although each one of these countries had a multi-party system, it was not possible to say that this was a result of the introduction of P.R. In all seven countries there were three or more sizable parties before the introduction of P.R. But it is clear that the adoption of P.R. in one of the party list systems has everywhere helped to maintain a multi-party system.[1]

The Single Transferable Vote
The single transferable vote (or S.T.V.) is the system of proportional representation which has been most often advocated in Britain. Indeed it was in operation between 1918 and 1948 for those university constituencies which had two or three M.P.s. In 1917, the House of Commons approved in principle a proposal that 100 urban seats should be filled by this method of P.R. But when detailed plans for implementing the idea were submitted by the Boundary Commission, the majority in the House rejected them and so this limited experiment with P.R. was never made. In 1965 'methods of election with particular reference to preferential voting' was one of the topics referred to the Speaker's conference on electoral law. This heading would presumably cover the examination of the working of the single transferable vote. The system has been in use in the Republic of Ireland since 1922, and it is used in Tasmania, Malta, and Gibraltar. It is also used for elections to the Upper House, the Senate, in Australia.

If it were to be adopted in Britain, it has been suggested that the country should be divided into constituencies electing between three and seven Members. The densely populated urban areas would be divided into five-, six- or seven-member constituencies. The more sparsely populated rural areas would have three- or four-member constituencies. In some of the less populous parts, such as the Highlands of Scotland, it might be advisable to preserve the existing single-member constituencies, but this would be exceptional. Thus Bristol, which at present has six single-member constituencies, could become one six-member constituency. In such a six-member constituency the voter would be confronted with a ballot paper on which would

[1] For the fullest discussion of the relationship between the number of parties and different electoral systems see:
Maurice Duverger, *Political Parties* (Methuen, 1954) especially Book II Chap. I, and Maurice Duverger, *L'Influence des systèmes électoraux sur la vie politique.* (Librairie Armand Colin, 1950).
See also Peter Campbell, *French Electoral Systems,* 2nd ed. (Faber, 1965).

appear the names of all the candidates listed in alphabetical order. He would not choose amongst party lists as in the party list system. He would be invited to place a figure 1 in the blank space next to the name of the candidate whom he most favoured, a figure 2 against the candidate whom he thought next most suitable, and so on. This form of ballot paper would obviously give much more freedom of choice to the voter than the party list system does. He could readily cross vote between the parties and could exercise his preference among the candidates put forward by a party.

An example is given below of a ballot paper in the constituency of Wilmot, Tasmania in February 1955. (In this election

A Ballot Paper under the Single Transferable Vote in the Constituency of Wilmot, Tasmania, February 1955

Six Seats

	BEST C. R.	Liberal
	BEST MILLIE	Liberal
	BETHUNE	Liberal
	BOUCHER	Liberal
	CASHION	Labour
	FAGAN	Labour
	FISHER	Liberal
	HAAS	Labour
	HOMFRAY	Liberal
	McNEIL	Labour
	SPURR	Labour
	THOMPSON	Liberal

Voters were required to insert the figures 1 to 12 against the candidates' names in order of preference.

voters were required to use all their preferences in order to cast a valid vote; by contrast, in Ireland the voter may use as few or as many preferences as he chooses.) The first stage in counting the votes is to establish the quota. This is done by dividing the number of valid votes cast by the number of seats plus one. To the resulting figure one is added. Thus in Wilmot, 32,553 valid votes were cast. The quota therefore was:

$$\frac{32,553}{6+1} = 4,650 + 1 = 4,651$$

The first preference votes were cast as follows:

Fagan	(Lab.)	5,983
Cashion	(Lab.)	4,224
Best, C. R.	(Lib.)	4,037
Bethune	(Lib.)	2,760
Best, Millie	(Lib.)	2,727
Fisher	(Lab.)	2,722
Spurr	(Lab.)	2,652
Thompson	(Lib.)	1,831
Homfray	(Lib.)	1,739
McNeil	(Lab.)	1,664
Boucher	(Lib.)	1,336
Haas	(Lab.)	878

Fagan (Labour) was the only candidate to attain the quota with his first preference votes, so he was the first to be declared elected. His surplus was then distributed and this enabled Cashion (Labour) to attain and exceed the quota. Cashion's resulting surplus was then distributed but did not permit any other candidate to attain the quota. The following candidates at the bottom of the poll, Haas (Labour), Boucher (Liberal), McNeil (Labour), Homfray (Liberal), and Thompson (Liberal) were in turn excluded and their next available preferences distributed. This helped to secure a quota for Best, C. R. (Liberal), Bethune (Liberal), and Best, Millie (Liberal). No one else obtained a quota but Spurr (Labour) was elected to the sixth seat as his total was now, at 4,494, nearest to the quota. The successful candidates therefore were:

Fagan	(Labour)
Cashion	(Labour)
Best, C. R.	(Liberal)
Bethune	(Liberal)
Best, Millie	(Liberal)
Spurr	(Labour)

It is clearer to give this actual example of the distribution of votes under S.T.V. than to describe the rules for the distribution of votes, which are complex.[1]

Although S.T.V. gives far more freedom of choice to the elector than the party list system does, it should not be thought that it produces, in practice, much effective cross-voting between the parties. For example, the results in Wilmot, and in other Tasmanian constituencies, show that Liberal voters tend to give their first six preferences to Liberal candidates, and the party 'how to vote' cards ask them to do this. Very few Labour members are therefore elected by distributed votes from 'Liberal' ballot papers and vice-versa.[2] The habit of mind of voting for the party, in order to maximize your party's chances in the legislature, is common under the single transferable vote as it is under the relative majority system. But S.T.V. does enable the voter to express a preference among the different candidates of his party. This is something which, we have seen, the party list system does only very exceptionally and which the relative majority system does not at all.

The single transferable vote also undeniably produces a result which is much fairer than the result produced by the relative majority system. If adopted in Britain, it would give greater representation to the Liberals. But it would not give a fully proportional result, even though it is described as a proportional system. When constituencies average only five members, it is difficult for candidates of the smaller parties to get anywhere near the quota and so stand a chance of election. The Communists, Welsh Nationalists, and Scottish Nationalists

[1] The regulations for distribution of votes are given in full in: E. Lakeman and J. D. Lambert, *Voting in Democracies*, 2nd ed. (Faber, 1959) pp. 247–75. The working of S.T.V. is described by W. J. M. Mackenzie, *Free Elections*, 2nd ed. (Allen & Unwin, 1964) pp. 60–9.

[2] Irish experience is similar. See B. Chubb, 'Ireland in 1957', in D. E. Butler (ed.) *Elections Abroad* (Macmillan, 1959) p. 218.

would probably still be excluded from Westminster or would be heavily under-represented. The Liberals would probably continue to be under-represented although less heavily than at present.

The only system which would give a fully proportional result is the system originally advocated by Thomas Hare and supported by J. S. Mill in his book, *Representative Government*. Under this system a form of the single transferable vote would be used, but the whole country would be one constituency. As J. S. Mill saw, this would allow every minority, which chose to organize, to secure a quota and be sure of sending at least one Member to Parliament. Thomas Hare's scheme has never secured much support. It would not have ended territorial representation, since he proposed that a national constituency should be superimposed on local constituencies. The votes for a candidate in his own locality would be counted first, and votes from outside would only be taken into account if needed to make up the quota. The system would be administratively very complex and not easily intelligible to the voter.

The proposal for multi-member constituencies averaging five members is then a compromise between the purest form of P.R., the national constituency, and the traditional single-member constituency. Can the five-member average be criticized in itself, on the grounds that it would make constituencies too large and lessen contact between the elector and the Member of Parliament? Undeniably, many constituencies would be large by present standards. Bristol, which we have referred to earlier, provides perhaps the ideal conditions for a multi-member constituency as it is reasonably homogeneous and compact. Other constituencies would be much more scattered and would be harder for the M.P. to keep contact with. But against the lessening of contact can be balanced the argument that under the present system, a Labour-minded elector may sometimes be disinclined to seek the help of his local Conservative Member. Whereas, under the single transferable vote, most constituencies would contain at least one Labour Member to whom he could take his case. The same would apply for Conservatives in largely Labour constituencies. Whether this advantage would compensate for the lessening of contact with M.P.s is a matter of opinion. It may, of course, be argued that

many constituents see little of their Members as it is. On the
other hand, many Members are very assiduous in visiting their
constituencies and in conducting 'political surgeries', at which
they take up the problems of individual constituents. Members
make no distinction between supporters or opponents of their
party in carrying out this service.

It is sometimes claimed that one of the defects of P.R. is that
it makes by-elections impossible. This is not strictly so, but in
practice they might not be provided for, since they would sometimes be inequitable in effect. By-elections are technically
possible by treating a multi-member constituency as one single-
member constituency and using the alternative vote instead
of the single transferable vote.[1] But the result would sometimes
falsify the actual swing of opinion. Let us take as an example a
constituency in which there are four Labour M.P.s and one
Conservative. The Conservative dies, making a by-election
necessary. If one were held in the constituency as a whole, it
would certainly be won by Labour. Even if the current trend
of opinion were towards the Conservatives, it would represent
a gain for Labour. Such a gain would seem particularly unreasonable and arbitrary if it threatened to dislodge a narrow
Conservative majority in the Commons.

There are other detailed questions of interest. Would P.R.
make the labours of the Boundary Commissions less difficult?
Probably it would, although it would not make the Commissions unnecessary. There would still need to be changes from
time to time in the boundaries of multi-member constituencies
if a broadly equal representation was to be maintained. Again,
would P.R. remove the bias against the Labour party which we
have found to be normally present in the existing system?[2]
It would lessen this bias but probably not altogether remove it.
For example, some of the multi-member constituencies in the
mining areas of South Wales would be Labour strongholds in
which very few Conservative or Liberal votes would be recorded.
The Labour party would still be 'wasting votes' in these constituencies, votes which ideally it would like to see transferred
to closely contested multi-member constituencies in some of
London's suburbs, for instance.

[1] See below pp. 48–9 for a description of the alternative vote.
[2] See above pp. 30–1.

The Systems Compared

It is now possible to sum up the effects of the different systems of P.R. and to contrast them with the relative majority system. Party list systems help to increase the power of the party organizations, although some variants of the system do so more than others. It is probable that the single transferable vote would not have a similar effect, but neither would it reduce the influence of the parties in Britain. One factor here, which we have already noticed, is that the habit of mind of voting for the party would be carried over into the new electoral system and would continue to be exploited by the parties, as it is in Tasmania. Another factor is that in the five-member constituency it would be as difficult for an Independent to secure election as it would be for a member of one of the smaller parties. Finally, in a multi-member constituency the cost of fighting an election would be even greater than it is at present. Under the single transferable vote, therefore, one would expect to find party organizations at least as influential as they are now. As regards the number of parties, we have seen that some types of the party list system are unfavourable to the smaller parties, some are more favourable. The most favourable is the system used in Israel which has a national constituency. This is the party list equivalent of the Thomas Hare system. But in all its forms, the party list system enables several large parties to contest for political power.

P.R. with the single transferable vote, and with constituencies averaging five members, would also under-represent the smaller parties. But it would reduce the effect of swings in opinion between the two largest parties, securing a fairer representation to each. It would also increase Liberal representation. If we refer again to Table III and consider that the Liberals have not been polling their real strength under the existing system, we can see that if Britain had had the single transferable vote since 1945, coalition or minority governments would have been the rule. Government by one party with an overall majority would have been the exception. Irish experience does not contradict this estimate. Since 1922 there have been sixteen elections in the Irish Free State, now re-named the Republic of Ireland. Only four of these elections have resulted in an overall majority for one party. Ireland too has a very imperfect form of P.R. Since 1947, out of 40 constituencies, 22 have only three Members. Nine have five Members and nine have four Members. The representation is even less proportional than it would be in Britain with an average of five Members.[1]

In choosing between the relative majority and proportional systems of representation, then, one question is of paramount importance. The other considerations, such as the effects on party organization, are important but subsidiary. The crucial question is whether minority or coalition governments are preferable to government by a party holding an overall majority of seats in the legislature. The evidence shows that in all countries that have proportional representation, whether of the party list or S.T.V. type, minority or coalition governments are normally to be found. Examination shows too that they would be frequently experienced in Britain if the single transferable vote were to be introduced. Whereas, under the existing relative majority system in Britain, coalitions or minority governments are rare. There were two short intervals of minority government between the wars: in 1923 and from 1929 to 1931. They occurred because one of the two main parties which normally contest for power in Britain was being replaced by a third. With the eclipse of the Liberal Party, the familiar British duality of parties has re-appeared.

There have also been coalition governments in this country since 1918. But on only one occasion was a coalition formed because no one party had a majority in the House of Commons. This was in 1931 when the Labour minority government was replaced by a coalition under the former Labour Prime Minister, Ramsay Macdonald, which included Conservatives, Liberals, and a few Labour Ministers. This government only lasted two months (from August to October 1931). In October 1931, a General Election gave an overwhelming majority of seats to the Conservatives. From then on the government was 'a coalition of convenience' rather than of necessity. From 1932 to 1940, the parties which made up the National Government (Conservative, National Liberal, and National Labour) had virtually identical programmes. Similarly, the coalitions under

[1] See Chubb, op. cit., p. 184.
See also J. L. McCracken, *Representative Government in Ireland* (Oxford University Press, 1958), and J. F. S. Ross, *The Irish Election System* (Pall Mall, 1959).

Lloyd George (1918 to 1922) and Winston Churchill (1940 to 1945) were not coalitions dictated by the state of parties in the Commons. During both periods the Conservatives had a large majority of seats and could have maintained a government on their own, but preferred to take part in a coalition. This in both cases was owing to special circumstances. The Churchill coalition was formed to demonstrate national unity in the desire to win the war. A coalition government was formed in the first world war for a similar reason, and the Lloyd George government from 1918 to 1922 was largely a continuation of the war-time coalition.

It is undeniable that the prevalence of minority and coalition governments in a country has a marked effect on its political system. A different effect is produced by normally having governments formed by a party with a clear majority of seats in the legislature. Differences can be seen both in the character of elections and in the relationship of governments to their legislatures.

An election in Britain is normally a contest between two large parties either of which will almost certainly attain a majority of seats in the House of Commons. The winning party will then be in a position to put into effect the programme which it has put before the electorate in its election manifesto. A British election therefore provides a choice of policies and a choice of which party is to govern. It is also, to some extent, a verdict on the success and the good faith of the party which has been in power. The system increases the element of responsibility in politics. At election time, the parties must not promise what they will not try to perform because they may be given full power and responsibility to put their policies into effect. Similarly, a party which has been in office can be held fully responsible for the administration of the country since it gained power.

The situation is very different in a country where there are several large parties and where coalition or minority governments are normal. Then the elector knows that the party he votes for is very unlikely to be able to put its programme into effect. If it becomes part of the governing coalition, it will only be able to carry out that part of its programme which the other parties in the coalition agree to. The resulting government policy may be different from anything which the coalition parties proposed at election time. At times, it may be difficult for a coalition government to arrive at any clear cut policy on major questions. With the Socialist, Radical, M.R.P., and Independents pulling different ways on economic, foreign, and colonial issues, there were periods in the Fourth Republic when French politics approached stalemate. French critics called it 'immobilisme'—government in neutral gear. The element of responsibility is diminished too. Normally, no party can be held fully responsible for what has been done by the government. One party in the coalition can often rightly blame the other parties for frustrating its programme. A party which has formed a minority government can blame the majority in the legislature for failing to pass the bills which the government introduced, or to approve all the appropriations and taxes which it proposed.

In some countries, a multi-party system gives rise to chronic ministerial instability. In France, between December 1946, when the Constitution of the Fourth Republic came into operation, and May 1958, there were twenty-two governments. The average life of a government was less than seven months. But not all countries with P.R. experience such instability. There may be some difficulty in forming a coalition after a general election has taken place. After the election in Holland in 1963, for example, more than two months went by before the parties could agree on the shape of the new government. But once a coalition has been formed in Holland, or in one of the Scandinavian countries, it usually remains remarkably stable and may survive for several years. Indeed, there are certain advantages in coalition government under these conditions. Changes made by the government will be agreed changes—agreed by a group of parties who together have more electoral support than a British government normally has. Whereas in Britain, as we have seen, policies can be forced through and legislative changes made by governments which do not have the support of a majority of the electorate. In this situation, there may be violent changes of policy from government to government. Much of the Iron and Steel Industry was nationalized by a Labour majority, de-nationalized by their Conservative successors, and re-nationalized by Labour in 1967.

Yet such a violent change in policy is in fact unusual. What is more significant about British experience since 1945 is that so many of the changes made by the Labour majority between 1945 and 1951 were not reversed by subsequent Conservative governments. Coal, gas, electricity supply, the railways, docks, inland waterways, and civil aviation were all industries which were nationalized in whole or in part between 1945 and 1950 and which were not returned to private ownership by the Conservatives after 1951. Indeed, a Conservative majority created a new nationalized industry. For, in 1954, Parliament passed an Act which gave to the United Kingdom Atomic Energy Authority responsibility for establishing nuclear reactors and providing electrical power on an increasingly large scale. It is significant too that when industries were nationalized between 1945 and 1950, fair compensation was always paid to the former shareholders. The public corporations set up to run these industries were also largely modelled on bodies such as the Central Electricity Board and the British Broadcasting Corporation which had been established by Conservative governments in the inter-war period.

Examination shows that although sweeping changes do occur under the British system, they are usually made in a way which is not entirely repugnant to the opposition party. The two main parties also draw upon each other's experience—rarely wholly rejecting what has been done by the outgoing party and often building upon it. In this way, the parties, while maintaining distinctive policies and attitudes, have always a large element of common ground between them. This comes about because they alternate in power and opposition and because they must both appeal to a wide section of the electorate. In popular stereotype, the Conservative Party is the party of the well-to-do and Labour the party of the working man. But, in fact, the Conservatives regularly gain the support of about one third of the manual workers and their wives, while Labour wins the votes of about one fifth of all salaried and professional men and women. As quite a small turnover of votes is magnified by the electoral system and can cause one party to be replaced in power by the other, neither party can afford to neglect the views of any sizeable section of the community. This makes for moderation in government and opposition.

The situation may be very different under P.R. Parties then often have a relatively narrow basis of support deriving from religious interest (e.g. the Catholic parties of France, Italy, Holland, and Belgium) or occupation (e.g. the farmer's parties in France, Sweden, and Norway). Such parties are concerned rather to strengthen their appeal to the interest upon which they are based than to win the support of a large cross-section of the community. They are often more sectarian and less moderate in attitude than the two main British parties.

One may say that the British system gives great power to the party winning an election, but it also helps to create a climate of opinion in which both Government and Opposition act with moderation and responsibility. Is this state of affairs so desirable that it is worth overlooking the inequities of representation which accompany it? This is a question which everyone must answer according to their opinion of where the balance of advantage lies. My concern has been to try to show that some of the statements made about P.R. are not well founded, but that it would have far-reaching effects if adopted in Britain. One must consider seriously whether much that is best in British politics is not in fact a product of the two-party system. That is not to say, however, that countries which at present have P.R. would benefit from changing to the electoral system used in Britain. Where a multi-party system has developed, the abandonment of P.R. would create very great resentment and, with four or more large parties in the field, would for some time give a very inaccurate picture of the state of opinion in the country concerned. This is perhaps a further argument for not adopting P.R. in Britain. Once the change to P.R. has been made, there is no going back, for it creates powerful vested interests against a return to the relative majority system.

Compromise Systems

(a) THE ALTERNATIVE VOTE   Are there systems of voting which embody a compromise between the relative majority and proportional systems? One such is the alternative vote which is used for elections to the Australian House of Representatives, where it is known as preferential voting. The Labour Government in Britain in 1930 introduced a bill which would have substituted the alternative vote for the relative majority system.

But the bill was drastically amended by the House of Lords and then abandoned by the Government.

The alternative vote in Australia takes place in single-member constituencies, but the voter, instead of placing a cross against the name of the candidate he favours, votes by inserting a 1 against his first choice and a 2 against his second, as with the single transferable vote. The first preference votes are counted and if a candidate secures an absolute majority of these, he is declared elected. But if no candidate secures an absolute majority, the candidate at the bottom of the poll is eliminated and his second preference votes are distributed to the remaining candidates. The process continues until one candidate secures an absolute majority and is declared elected. The system preserves the single-member constituency and the high degree of local contact between Member and voters which it permits. It is, in general, more favourable to the third party than the relative majority system (in Britain it would certainly mean that the Liberal Party would win more seats), but it produces a result that is far from proportional.

David Butler estimates that if the alternative vote had been in force 'in 1923 and 1929 the Liberals would have held a much more influential position in the deadlock of parties'.[1] It is likely that it would have lessened the decline of the Liberal Party which followed the 1929 election, although as he points out, the alternative vote would not prevent a party with less than 50 per cent of the votes from sometimes securing a large majority of seats in the Commons. In Australia it seems probable that the alternative vote has helped to maintain a three-party system. J. D. B. Miller comments that the smaller of the three parties in Australia, the Country Party, seems to benefit from preferential voting. The Liberal and Country Parties arrange to 'exchange preferences' in many constituencies and these arrangements seem to be especially helpful to the Country Party which habitually gets a bigger percentage of seats than of votes. In the three-party situation, governments in Australia are either Labour governments or coalitions of the Liberal and Country parties.[2]

[1] D. E. Butler, *The Electoral System in Britain since 1918*, p. 191.
[2] See J. D. B. Miller, *Australian Government and Politics* (Duckworth, 1954), particularly p. 86.

(b) THE WEST GERMAN SYSTEM   Another compromise system has been employed in Western Germany since the Second World War for elections to the Bundestag. The whole country was divided at the 1961 election into 247 single-member constituencies. In each of these constituencies, election was by relative majority as in Britain. But another 247 seats were filled by a list system of proportional representation. Each voter had two votes: one for an individual candidate in his single-member constituency and one for a party list. The effect of this ingenious system has been to produce a result midway between what would have been achieved by a fully proportional system on the one hand or by the relative majority system on the other. In both the 1953 and 1957 elections the Christian Democrats would, under the relative majority system, have secured a large majority of seats in the Bundestag. In fact, in 1953 they secured a majority of four, and in 1957 a majority of twenty-four over all other parties. In 1961 the Christian Democrats failed to secure an overall majority and formed a coalition government with the Free Democrats.[1] In 1965 they again failed to win an absolute majority. The coalition with the Free Democrats continued until late in 1966 when it fell apart and was replaced by a 'grand coalition' of the Christian Democrat and Social Democrat parties.

It should be noted also that under the electoral law of the Federal Republic, the smallest parties are placed at a special disadvantage. No party is allowed a list seat if it does not win at least three constituency seats or poll at least 5 per cent. of the valid votes cast in the whole of Western Germany. This discrimination against the smallest parties further decreases the proportionality of the result. Nevertheless, if anything like the West German system were to be adopted in Britain it would clearly tend to reduce the size of government majorities and would sometimes result in no one party securing an overall majority. This would have been the case for example in 1950, 1951 and 1964. The effect of adopting the alternative vote would be broadly similar, in that it would strengthen the position of a third party. If, then, there is a strong case against the

---

[1] See U. W. Kitzinger, *German Electoral Politics* (Clarendon Press, 1960), esp. pp. 19–20 and p. 279. See also J. K. Pollock *et al*: *German Democracy at Work* (Ann Arbor, 1955).

adoption of a proportional system in Britain, there is also a strong case against the adoption of one of the compromise systems. For they also would make coalition and minority governments less of a rarity.

FOR REFERENCE

D. E. BUTLER (ed.), *Elections Abroad* (Macmillan, 1959).

D. E. BUTLER, *The Electoral System in Britain Since 1918*, 2nd ed. (Clarendon Press, 1963).

D. E. BUTLER and A. KING, *The British General Election of 1964* (Macmillan, 1965).

D. E. BUTLER and A. KING, *The British General Election of 1966* (Macmillan, 1966).

P. CAMPBELL, *French Electoral Systems*, 2nd ed. (Faber, 1965).

R. A. DAHL (ed.), *Political Oppositions in Western Democracies* (Yale University Press, 1966).

M. DUVERGER, *L'Influence des systèmes électoraux sur la vie politique* (Librairie Armand Colin, 1950).

M. DUVERGER, *Political Parties* (Methuen, 1954).

U. W. KITZINGER, *German Electoral Politics* (Clarendon Press, 1960).

E. LAKEMAN and J. D. LAMBERT, *Voting in Democracies*, 2nd ed. (Faber, 1959).

J. D. B. MILLER, *Australian Government and Politics* (Duckworth, 1954).

J. F. S. ROSS, *Elections and Electors* (Eyre and Spottiswoode, 1955).

J. F. S. ROSS, *Parliamentary Representation*, 2nd ed. (Eyre and Spottiswoode, 1948).

CHAPTER III

Choosing the Candidates

I N the British electoral system, the voter normally has to choose between a Conservative, Labour, or Liberal candidate. He cannot, as under the single transferable vote, express his preference for one candidate of his chosen party rather than another. Great importance, therefore, attaches to the way in which candidates are chosen. In safe seats this is especially important, since nomination there is, to all intents and purposes, equivalent to election.

British and American Systems of Selection Compared

In Britain, the candidates are chosen by relatively small party committees in each constituency. In the United States, nearly all the states allow the ordinary voter to take part in choosing the candidate through one form or another of direct primary election. There are two main types of primary election, both conducted by the State authorities—the successful candidate in the primary election winning the right to run in the main election.

In the 'closed' primary, a voter must register as a Democrat, for example, if he wishes to help choose the Democratic candidate for the main election. Registering as a Democrat will exclude him from voting in the Republican primary. One disadvantage of the closed primary is that balloting is no longer fully secret. Taking part in a primary is a semi-public declaration of support for a party, if not for an individual. This may not be a grave disadvantage under modern conditions when unfair pressure on voters is uncommon. Some Americans are glad to proclaim their allegiance by wearing badges announcing 'I'm madly for Adlai' or 'L.B.J. for the U.S.A.'.

The ballot is kept secret where the 'open' primary is used. In this type of primary, the voter can choose candidates for both the Democratic and Republican nominations. The objection to this procedure is that it can permit irresponsible or 'wrecking' nominations, with Democrats combining to help choose the poorest Republican candidate, for example, so as to ensure the success of the Democrat in the main election. For this reason, perhaps, most states have the closed primary.

A more serious objection to primary elections, from the British point of view, is that they greatly increase the cost of elections. Candidates who are successful in the primary have to fight two campaigns. Therefore, the adoption of primaries would increase the influence of wealth in elections. Another objection is that primary elections are likely to give greater emphasis to the personal qualities of candidates and less emphasis to the policies which they support. Personal factors are important in the British selection process, but choice takes place within the framework of the established party policies and programmes. Finally, there seems to be little or no demand for primary elections in Britain. Pressure for the introduction of primaries in the United States arose from the knowledge that nomination by party caucus was often bedevilled by corruption or was in the hands of narrow oligarchies. British constituency parties seem to be largely free from these influences, but a closer look is necessary if we are to judge the nominating process in Britain.

Selection of Candidates in the Labour Party
The selection of candidates in the Labour Party is the task of the General Management Committee of each constituency party. This body is made up of delegates from all sections of the party in the division: from the ward parties, from affiliated trade unions, from women's sections, from Young Socialist branches, and from other affiliated organizations such as a Co-operative Guild. The size of the General Management Committee will vary widely according to the strength of the Labour Party in the constituency. In a seat where Labour is particularly active, there may be as many as 200 delegates. The average membership is probably around 120. Each year the General Management Committee (G.M.C.) elect an Executive Committee which is the body which initiates the process of selecting the prospective parliamentary candidate, when there is a vacancy.

c

The Executive Committee first invites affiliated organizations to make nominations. In practice, what frequently happens is that the Regional Organizer of the Labour Party circulates all affiliated organizations in the constituency (ward parties, trade unions, etc.). He sends them two lists of names approved by the National Executive Committee (N.E.C.). List A consists of persons nominated by trade unions whom those unions are willing to sponsor. List B consists of people who are not sponsored but who are considered by the N.E.C. to be suitable prospective candidates. It is quite common for the Regional Organizer to indicate that such and such candidates 'have expressed an interest in the constituency'. This may well be sufficient to secure nomination by one or more of the affiliated organizations. When the seat is winnable, people eager for nomination sometimes think it worthwhile to engineer themselves invitations to speak to affiliated organizations before the short list is drawn up.

The next stage is for the Executive Committee of the constituency party to draw up the short list. This will usually consist of from four to six names. The list must be approved by the General Management Committee (G.M.C.) and by the N.E.C. The N.E.C. rarely exercises its power to disallow any name on the list. When it does so, it is usually on the grounds that a person nominated is not eligible for membership of the Labour Party. This is designed to protect the party from infiltration by members of other parties, in particular the Communist Party.

The short list having been approved by the N.E.C., those lucky enough to appear on it are invited to attend a special meeting of the G.M.C. Each aspirant is invited to speak to the meeting for fifteen minutes and then answer questions. The delegates then vote by secret ballot. If one name wins more than half the votes cast, he is chosen as candidate. If no one secures an absolute majority at first, then a series of ballots follows, those at the bottom of the poll being eliminated on each occasion until an absolute majority is secured for one candidate. The G.M.C.'s choice must then be endorsed by the N.E.C. This usually follows automatically, but the N.E.C. must be satisfied that the candidate accepts the policy and programme of the Labour Party and that he undertakes, if elected, to abide by the standing orders of the Parliamentary Labour Party.

Although the N.E.C. plays a part in the selection of candidates, it is far from being a dominant part. Its role is really to vet the candidates rather than in any way to impose its choice. It will rarely press a name upon a constituency. Constituency parties are very independent and some prefer to have a local candidate. Well-known national figures have sometimes had difficulty in getting adopted even though they had the backing of the N.E.C. For example, in 1958, St. Helens constituency Labour Party chose a local man as their candidate instead of Tom Driberg who was at that time Chairman of the Labour Party. Similarly, Morgan Phillips was not selected in 1959 in North-East Derbyshire although he was Secretary of the Labour Party and a man of great ability. While some constituency parties, however, tend to prefer a local candidate, others seem glad to choose someone from outside the constituency. As a result, the Parliamentary Labour Party is a blend of those with a national and those with a local reputation.

Selection of Candidates in the Conservative Party

The process of selection in Conservative constituency associations is basically similar, but there are some differences. In the first place, the structure of the typical Conservative association is different. At the Annual General Meeting, which all local members of the Conservative Party may attend, the officers of the association are elected. These officers, together with representatives of the ward, or polling district branches, of Young Conservative groups and of Conservative Clubs, form the Executive Council. This Executive Council is, therefore, broadly comparable with the Labour General Management Committee. When a vacancy arises, the Executive Council appoints a small selection committee. The Chairman of the association normally heads this committee which usually includes the other principal officers of the association. The committee varies in size from six to twenty members.

This committee sifts the applications for nomination which have been received. In the Conservative Party, individuals are not prevented from nominating themselves, and for a safe or winnable seat it is not unusual for well over a hundred applications to be sent in.[1] The Chairman of the association

---

[1] A. Ranney, *Pathways to Parliament* (Macmillan, 1965) p. 58.

will also have conferred with the Vice-Chairman of the Conservative Party at Central Office, who has a special responsibility for the selection of candidates. The candidates department at Central Office maintains a list of candidates who have been interviewed by the Vice-Chairman and approved. From this list some names will be chosen by the Chairman of the constituency association for consideration with the names locally received.

From all the names put forward, the selection committee in the constituency prepares a short list of perhaps fifteen to twenty names. Those on the short list are invited to appear before the selection committee for interview, and the married men are often asked to bring their wives. After the interviews, the selection committee draws up a shorter short list which will normally include only two or three names. These two or three individuals are invited to attend a special meeting of the Executive Council at which each of them makes a speech for twenty minutes and then answers questions. The Executive Council then votes by secret ballot to choose the candidate. An absolute majority is usually required and the meeting usually goes on voting, with the weakest candidate each time dropping out, until an absolute majority is secured.

This is not the end of the process, however, as the Executive Council's choice must then be ratified by a general meeting of the Association. Usually such ratification is automatic, but not invariably so. In 1952 in Southport the general meeting of the Association refused to accept the Executive Council's choice and chose one of the other candidates who had appeared before the Executive.[1]

Such complete rejection of the Executive's choice is very unusual, but more than one case can be quoted of the choice being seriously challenged in the general meeting. This happened in October 1965, before a by-election in the Cities of London and Westminster constituency. *The Times* reported on 12 October that the Conservative candidate had been adopted after a stormy meeting of the Conservative association. The treasurer of the association, in fact, resigned in protest. Again, in 1954, in Swansea West, the Executive Council's choice was only approved in the general meeting by a narrow

[1] Ranney, op. cit., pp. 61–2.

majority. The dispute continued for some time afterwards in the correspondence columns of the local newspaper and some leading Conservatives conspicuously withheld support from the candidate in the general election in May 1955.

Such examples are exceptional. They do show that the general meeting can assert its right to challenge the Executive Council's choice. But, in practice, general meetings are very rarely assertive. As in the Labour Party, the central organization can exercise a veto over the choice of candidate. The Standing Advisory Committee on Candidates can withhold support from any candidate adopted by a local association, but it very rarely does this. It also, as we have seen, does suggest names for consideration, but it does not have the power, any more than the Labour N.E.C. does, to insist on the nomination of the candidate it favours. As in the Labour Party, a proportion of candidates nominated are local men. In the general elections of 1951, 1955, 1959, and 1964 not quite one-third of non-incumbent Conservative candidates were local men.[1]

Central Office has had relatively little success in inducing Conservative associations to adopt trade union candidates. Until 1964 there was only one Conservative trade unionist M.P. in the Commons. This was Ray Mawby of the Electrical Trades Union who was elected for Totnes in 1955. In 1964 he was joined by Sir Edward Brown as Conservative Member for Bath. Sir Edward, a member of the Association of Supervisory Staffs, Executives and Technicians, was Chairman of the National Union of Conservative and Unionist Associations in 1958–9. Yet it is reported that he went before twenty-nine constituency selection committees between 1954 and 1963, without being able to get a winnable seat, until he was selected at Bath.[2] Central Office has found it almost as difficult to get constituency associations to adopt women candidates. At the 1964 general election, only 4 per cent. of Conservative candidates were women: this, strangely, in a party in which most of the hard work in the constituencies is done by women. Finally, Conservative associations continue to prefer candidates who have been to public schools. At the 1964 general election 417

[1] Ranney, op. cit., p. 116.
[2] Ranney, op. cit., p. 34.

out of 630 Conservative candidates had been educated at public schools. So the efforts of Central Office to persuade associations to adopt more socially representative candidates have not been conspicuously successful. The majority of associations continue to have a bias against trade unionist and women candidates and in favour of the products of the public schools.

Labour and Conservative Methods Compared

We can now compare the process of selection in the Labour and Conservative Parties. As far as the influence of the central organization is concerned, we can say that there is little to choose between the parties. In both parties, the constituency associations have a great deal of autonomy. The central party organization can suggest names, but its views often go unheeded. Yet, in both parties, the choice takes place within the framework of party doctrine and programme. Both central party machines can veto the choice of candidate. The emphasis on acceptance of the party programme is more overt in the Labour Party. This still permits a great range of views within the Parliamentary Labour Party, and, on the other hand, the Conservative 'habit of loyalty', in a sense, takes the place of declaration of support for the party programme.

As far as the mechanism of choice is concerned, the Conservative method is oligarchic in that the small selection committee presents a narrow choice of candidates (usually only two or three) to the wider body, the Executive Council. The Labour General Management Committee, as we have seen, normally has a choice of from four to six candidates. On the other hand, the Conservative process is more democratic in that the final choice has to be approved by a general meeting of members of the Conservative Association. Even though ratification of the Executive Council's choice normally follows as a matter of course, this reference to the whole body of Conservatives is, potentially at least, more democratic. In both parties the choice of candidate is in effect made by a quite small body of party activists often consisting of less than 150 people. Yet this small body is representative of active members of the Conservative and Labour Parties in the constituencies. These, in turn, are a relatively small proportion of the electorate. Richard Rose has estimated that only about one in every 200 members of the electorate is an active party member.[1] But the possibility to be active is there and the parties welcome new members.

One factor which can influence the selection process is finance. Until 1948 it was permissible, in the Conservative Party, for a wealthy individual to influence selection in his favour by offering to pay the costs of fighting the election, and to meet a large part of the running costs of the Conservative association. This practice was severely criticized in 1948 by a Committee of the Conservative Party under the Chairmanship of Sir David Maxwell Fyfe.[2] The report was accepted, and since the beginning of 1949 severe restrictions have been placed by Central Office on the sums which may be contributed by candidates and Members of Parliament. No Conservative candidate may nowadays contribute to the cost of his, or her, election campaign, apart from personal expenses which under electoral law must not exceed £100. No candidate may contribute more than £25 a year to the funds of his, or her, Conservative association; no Member of Parliament may contribute more than £50 a year. These restrictions seem to be strictly adhered to. A candidate is no longer, then, selected in the Conservative Party with an eye to the length of his purse and his willingness to subsidize the activities of his local association.

The Labour Party also imposes restrictions, but they are not as severe as in the Conservative Party. As regards election costs, a sponsoring trade union may pay up to 80 per cent. of the maximum expenditure permitted by electoral law. The sponsoring union may also contribute up to £350 towards the running cost of a constituency party in a borough constituency or £420 in a county constituency.[3] Since 1957, candidates who are not sponsored may only pay their personal expenses at the election and may not donate more than £50 a year to the constituency party.

This situation obviously favours the sponsored candidate. Although Labour Party rules provide that questions of finance must not be discussed at the selection conference, it is an open

[1] Richard Rose, *Politics in England* (Faber, 1965) p. 93.
[2] The Interim and Final Reports of the Committee on Party Organization 1948 and 1949.
[3] Or 50 per cent. of a full-time agent's salary in a borough constituency, or 60 per cent. of his salary in a county constituency.

secret who is and who is not a sponsored candidate. As we have seen, candidates in the Labour Party are either on List A (sponsored) or List B (non-sponsored). Delegates know that if they choose an unsponsored candidate, the association will have to meet all the costs of the election and virtually all the running costs of the constituency organization between elections. The attraction of choosing a sponsored candidate is, therefore, considerable.

To place sponsored and unsponsored candidates on an equal footing, by making the same restrictions on contributions apply to each, might seem a desirable reform. This, however, would be to ignore the central role of the trade unions in the Labour Party. The unions were not only the major partner in the foundation of the Labour Party, but they continue to be the major source of funds for the party. It is, therefore, appropriate that trade union candidates should have some advantage in the selection process. Sponsoring by trade unions also widens the social base of the Parliamentary Labour Party since a high proportion of sponsored candidates are, or have been, manual workers. There is an argument, however, for lessening the differential between sponsored and unsponsored candidates. If, for example, the sponsoring union were allowed to contribute £100 a year to the constituency association, as against the £50 a year which the unsponsored candidate may contribute, this would still give the sponsored candidate an advantage, but the cards would not be stacked so heavily against the unsponsored man.

In practice, despite the advantages which sponsored candidates enjoy, sponsored M.P.s are a minority in the Parliamentary Labour Party. After the 1966 general election there were 132 trade union sponsored M.P.s, and eighteen who were sponsored by the Co-operative Party; the remaining 213 Labour M.P.s were unsponsored. The unions seem to be finding it increasingly difficult to find good sponsored candidates from amongst their members. Since before the 1964 general election, the Amalgamated Engineering Union has required all its potential sponsored candidates to pass a series of tests in public speaking and knowledge of politics, in an attempt to raise the standard of its candidates. The Transport and General Workers Union at the 1964 general election decided to sponsor some professional men—Dr. Jeremy Bray, for example, and Peter Shore, formerly head of the Labour Party's Research Department.[1] It is apparent that sponsored candidates do not have an automatic advantage at the selection conference. Delegates, in many places, are looking first and foremost for an able candidate whose attitudes and approach they like. The question as to whether he is a sponsored candidate may be a secondary consideration. It is particularly likely to be so where the seat is marginal.

The Social Composition of the House of Commons
One way of judging the process of selecting candidates is to look at the end product: the membership of the House of Commons. Table V gives the first or formative occupations of M.P.s of all three parties in the Commons elected in March 1966. It will be seen that three occupational groups predominated. Barristers and solicitors together accounted for 20·3 per cent of all M.P.s. Business accounted for 17·5 per cent, and 17·7 per cent of M.P.s had been workers. But although these three groups predominated, they by no means monopolized representation. Several other occupations were well represented: notably teachers (including both school and university teachers) with 12·3 per cent, journalists and publicists with 7·3 per cent, and farmers with 4·9 per cent. There was a fair sprinkling of other occupations, including former officers in the regular armed services, former civil servants or local government officers, and former party agents, etc. There were also twelve doctors or dentists, 1·9 per cent of all M.P.s.

If Conservative and Labour Members are compared, two chief differences emerge. First, more than half Conservative M.P.s (57·3 per cent) were associated with law or business. Just under a quarter of Labour M.P.s (23·7 per cent) came from these circles. Second, the largest single element on the Labour side were the former workers (30·0 per cent). Workers on the Conservative side were, as we have seen, very rare: only 0·8 per cent of all Conservative M.P.s. For the other occupations, Labour had many more teachers than the Conservatives had: 19·8 per cent to 1·6 per cent. Journalists and publicists were fairly evenly spread on both sides of the House.

[1] Butler and King, op. cit., p. 236.

TABLE V

HOUSE OF COMMONS, APRIL, 1966

The first or formative occupation of M.P.s

Occupation	Conservative	Per cent of Conservative M.P.s	Labour	Per cent of Labour M.P.s	Liberal[1]	Total[2]	Per cent of all M.P.s
Barristers, Solicitors	70	27·7	54	14·9	3	127	20·3
Business, Management	75	29·6	32	8·8	3	110	17·5
Workers	2	0·8	109	30·0	—	111	17·7
Teachers	4	1·6	72	19·8	1	77	12·3
Journalists, Publicists	17	6·7	29	8·0	—	46	7·3
Farmers	27	10·7	2	0·6	2	31	4·9
Armed Services	19	7·5	3	0·8	—	22	3·5
Civil Service, Local Government	13	5·1	9	2·5	—	22	3·5
Politicians	2	0·8	9	2·5	1	12	1·9
Doctors, Dentists	2	0·8	9	2·5	1	12	1·9
Other	22	8·7	35	9·6	1	58	9·2
Total	253	100·0	363	100·0	12	628	100·0

[1] The proportions of Liberals have not been calculated on a percentage basis because of the small total number.

[2] Not including the Speaker and the Republican Labour M.P.

Based on a table in D. E. Butler and A. King: *The British General Election of 1966* (Macmillan, 1966) p. 208, by permission of the publishers.

But the Conservatives had nearly all the farmers and most of the former regular officers. The Labour Party had more than four times as many doctors or dentists than the Conservatives, but the total number from this group was not very large (only twelve in all).

The total number of Liberal M.P.s was also too small for any meaningful contrast to be drawn between them and the other parties.

If we compare the membership of the House of Commons elected in 1966 with the membership of both Houses of the 89th Congress, elected in 1964, the Commons comes out favourably. In Congress there was a much greater predominance of lawyers. Out of the 535 members of the Senate and the House of Representatives no less than 305, or 57 per cent, had a legal background. There were also very few former workers or trade union officials in Congress: only three, or 0·6 per cent of the total membership.[1] The Commons, therefore, presented a much more even representation of some of the main occupational groups than Congress did. However, the Commons is very far from being, in terms of social composition, a 'mirror of the nation'. J. F. S. Ross has deplored this fact. He said of the Commons: 'the make-up of the House shows a lack of balance, an extreme disparity with the make-up of the community as a whole, that cannot be considered at all healthy or desirable. However personally estimable they may be, these hordes of lawyers, company directors, and trade union officials exclude from the House people of many other occupations that are at least as deserving of representation.'[2]

This attitude seems quite unrealistic. It is inevitable, and indeed desirable, that certain occupations should be greatly over-represented in the House of Commons. In the ranks of lawyers, company directors, and trade union officials there is a good proportion of able men who are brought into contact with and are well informed about public affairs. Many of them, too, have more opportunity to devote time to political campaigning and the duties of a Member of Parliament than people in other occupations have. Neither, as we have seen, do these three occupations monopolize representation in the Commons.

[1] Figures derived from the Congressional Quarterly, 29 December 1964, p. 2.
[2] J. F. S. Ross, *Elections and Electors* (Eyre and Spottiswoode, 1955) p. 445.

There are also sizeable groups of teachers, journalists, farmers, etc.

What is to be regretted is the small number of women in the House of Commons. After the general election in 1966 there were twenty-six women M.P.s or 4·1 per cent of the total. This compared more than favourably with both Houses of Congress which in 1964 had only twelve women members or 2·4 per cent of the whole membership. Nevertheless, the situation in the Commons is far from satisfactory. The woman's point of view is not adequately heard. The prejudice against selecting women candidates is, as we have seen, most marked in the Conservative Party. Of the twenty-six women M.P.s, only seven were Conservatives and nineteen Labour. But on the Labour side too the proportion of women M.P.s is low.

If we consider the educational background of M.P.s (Table VI) the clearest fact to emerge is that a high proportion (58·2

TABLE VI

Education of M.P.s, April 1966

Education	Conservative	Labour	Liberal	Total[1]	Per cent of all M.P.s
Elementary only	1	34	–	35	5·6
Elementary and adult education	1	46	–	47	7·5
Secondary only	17	53	2	72	11·5
Secondary and adult education	1	40	–	41	6·5
Secondary and University	29	124	3	156	24·8
Public School only	63	4	–	67	10·7
Public School and University	141	62	7	210	33·4
Totals	253	363	12	628	100·0

[1] Not including the Speaker and the Republican Labour M.P.
Based on a table in D. E. Butler and A. King: *The British General Election of 1966* (Macmillan, 1966) p. 208, by permission of the publishers.

per cent) had been educated at universities. On the other hand, a sizeable group (13·1 per cent) received only an elementary education or elementary education followed by adult classes. Here again the House of Commons was far from being a mirror of the nation. In the population as a whole the proportion who have been to universities is very small (less than 5·0 per cent) while the proportion who have received only an elementary education is very large. But what are we looking for in our M.P.s: more than average ability or representatives in the social sense? It seems, on the whole, desirable that the Commons should consist of a majority who are highly educated, while the views of those who have not had the same educational advantages should also be well represented.

The Commons, then, includes men and women drawn from a variety of occupations and with varying educational backgrounds. Every M.P. is, in a sense, a spokesman for the occupational group from which he has come, but he is also the spokesman for all the other occupations and callings to be found in his constituency. He is still the main channel of communication between the citizen and the Government. It is to the relationship between the Commons and the Government that we now turn.

For Reference

R. R. ALFORD, *Party and Society* (Murray, 1963).

J. BLONDEL, *Voters, Parties and Leaders* (Penguin, 1963).

I. BULMER-THOMAS, *The Party System in Great Britain* (Phoenix, 1953).

D. E. BUTLER and A. KING, *The British General Election of 1964* (Macmillan, 1965).

D. E. BUTLER and A. KING, *The British General Election of 1966* (Macmillan, 1966).

R. L. LEONARD, *Guide to the General Election* (Pan, 1964).

R. T. MCKENZIE, *British Political Parties*, 2nd ed. (Mercury Books, 1964).

The Political Quarterly, July–September, 1959, Special Number on the Selection of Parliamentary Candidates.

A. RANNEY, *Pathways to Parliament* (Macmillan, 1965).

P. G. RICHARDS, *Honourable Members*, 2nd ed. (Faber, 1964).

R. ROSE, *Politics in England* (Faber, 1965).

J. F. S. ROSS, *Parliamentary Representation*, 2nd ed. (Eyre and Spottiswoode, 1948).

CHAPTER IV

The House of Commons and the Government

THE British Constitution is continually changing. The relationship between the House of Commons and the Government is not the same today as it was in the 1930s and it has changed even more from what it was in 1867. Is there any value then in making Walter Bagehot's *The English Constitution* the starting point of our discussion? There is, because his little book, first published in 1867, was not only a brilliant analysis of the British political system of his time, but it has proved easily the most influential statement of the way in which British parliamentary democracy should work. Generations of British parliamentarians and students of politics have been stimulated, in particular, by his first chapter in which he discusses Cabinet government. Our political thinking, even today, draws heavily upon his ideas and the standard works on British Government have been deeply suffused with Bagehotian reasoning.[1] It is therefore particularly worthwhile to begin by looking closely at Bagehot's analysis.

The principal theme of Bagehot's first chapter was that it was an error to suppose that in Britain 'the legislative, the executive and the judicial powers are quite divided'—that there was a separation of powers.[2] In fact, he said, 'The efficient secret of the English Constitution may be described as the close union, the nearly complete fusion of the executive and legislative powers''.[3] The device which permitted this 'nearly complete fusion' was the Cabinet which was 'a combining committee— a hyphen which joins, a buckle which fastens, the legislative

---

[1] See for example the works of W. I. Jennings, particularly those listed below, p. 75.
A more left-wing authority whose works were as deeply influenced by Bagehot was H. J. Laski. See again p. 75.

[2] Walter Bagehot: *The English Constitution* (World's Classics, Oxford University Press, 1933) p. 2.

[3] ibid., p. 9.

part of the state to the executive part of the state'.[1] The members of the Cabinet were members of the House of Commons, or of the House of Lords, and the Cabinet was collectively responsible to the Commons. But, Bagehot claimed, although the Cabinet 'is a committee of the legislative assembly . . . it is a committee which can dissolve the assembly which appointed it'.[2] For the Prime Minister can request the Monarch to grant a dissolution—a request which the Monarch is almost bound to accept.[3] 'Either the cabinet legislates and acts, or else it can dissolve. It is a creature, but it has the power of destroying its creators. It is an executive which can annihilate the legislature, as well as an executive which is the nominee of the legislature.'[4]

The importance of this aspect of our Constitution, he said, could be best understood if we looked at a system in which there was a real separation of powers: the Presidential system in the United States. For 'the independence of the legislative and executive powers is the specific quality of the Presidential Government, just as their fusion and combination is the precise principle of Cabinet Government'.[5] Under the American Constitution, the President and the two Houses of Congress were elected by different processes and remained distinct. Neither the President nor any other Executive Officer could be at the same time a member of either House of Congress. The President could not dissolve Congress, neither could Congress by voting a motion of no confidence dismiss the President. This system, Bagehot claimed, resulted in weak and irresponsible government. The executive often could not command support in the legislature and was therefore 'crippled by not getting the laws it needs'. So, 'the executive becomes unfit for its name since it cannot execute what it decides on; the legislature is demoralized by liberty, by taking decisions of which others (and not itself) will suffer the effects'.[6]

A further drawback of presidential government, according to Bagehot, was that it could not educate a nation as cabinet government did. This education, he said, was provided by the great debates which went on in the House of Commons and

---

[1] Bagehot, op. cit., p. 12.   [2] ibid., p. 13.
[3] See below, Chapter X, pp. 248–9, for discussion of the question whether or not the Monarch could nowadays refuse a dissolution.
[4] Bagehot, op cit., p. 14.   [5] ibid., p. 14.   [6] ibid., p. 15.

which were closely followed by politically minded people in
the country. These debates attracted such interest because they
were preludes to the 'deciding catastrophes of cabinet government'.[1] The division at the end of an important debate might
produce a majority against the Government which would either
result in its resignation or in a request for a dissolution by the
Prime Minister. So English people found out about the great
issues of the day because they followed what was said in important debates in the Commons. But in the United States there
was not the same interest in debates in Congress because no
debate there could result in the fall of the government—
debates in Congress 'are prologues without a play'. Similarly,
the American Press, so Bagehot claimed, was inferior in quality
to the British Press because an American newspaper could not
turn out the government. 'Nobody cares for a debate in Congress which comes to nothing, and no one reads long articles
which have no influence on events'.[2]

Another line of criticism which he advanced was that the
Presidential system recruited less able men to the Executive and
to the Legislature than the Cabinet system did. 'The presidential government, by its nature, divides political life into two
halves, an executive half and a legislative half; and, by so
dividing it, makes neither half worth a man's having—worth
his making a continuous career—worthy to absorb, as cabinet
government absorbs, his whole soul'.[3] As being elected to
Congress was not a step on the road to membership of the
Executive, first-rate men did not aspire to become legislators.
Further, the method used to choose the President was far less
discriminating than the process by which Prime Ministers
were chosen. Few statesmen of real ability were chosen for the
presidential office and once a President had been chosen he
was virtually irremovable during his four-year term. Whereas a
British Prime Minister could be voted out of office, if circumstances changed and the nation needed a leader of different
capabilities. When Britain ran into difficulties during the Cri-
mean War, the Commons, he said, was able to vote out of office
the distinguished but pacific Aberdeen and 'put in the pugilist'
(Palmerston).[4] The final virtue, in other words, which he

[1] Bagehot, op. cit., p. 18.
[2] ibid., p. 20.   [3] ibid., p. 25.   [4] ibid., p. 26.

claimed for cabinet government was flexibility—ease in changing the Prime Minister when circumstances made change desirable.

The most obvious criticism of Bagehot's argument is that experience has shown that his consistently disparaging references to the American system of government were not justified. His notion that the American system attracts less able men to high office than the British system does has been shown to be spectacularly wrong. If a roll of honour of successful British Prime Ministers and American Presidents in the first half of the twentieth century were to be compiled, the record of the Presidents would be at least as good as that of the Prime Ministers. Judgements on this sort of question must inevitably be coloured by party feeling, but it would be difficult to deny the claims of Salisbury, Campbell-Bannerman, Asquith, Lloyd George, Churchill, and Attlee to be rated as men of outstanding ability and as on the whole successful Premiers. In the United States, Theodore Roosevelt, Woodrow Wilson, Franklin Roosevelt, and Truman must all rank as Presidents of outstanding ability and influence. This gives six Premiers to four Presidents, but the four Presidents held office for 33 years out of 50, while the six able Premiers were in office for only 29 years between them. What of the remaining years? The other Presidents and Prime Ministers included some able men, it is true, but none of such outstanding merit as those who have been named. If these less able Presidents and Premiers are compared, there cannot be much to choose between them. Certainly, Britain has never had to endure the equivalent of Warren Harding as Prime Minister, but if Harding is excluded then Taft, Coolidge, and Hoover stand comparison with Bonar Law, Baldwin, Ramsay Macdonald, and Neville Chamberlain.

Harold Laski, however, maintained essentially the same view as Bagehot. Writing in 1938, he said: 'The fact that our system has, on the whole, produced a succession of extraordinary men as Prime Ministers is, I suggest, a tribute of a quite special kind to the selective function of the House of Commons. . . . The contrast in this regard with Presidents of the United States is startling, for since the Civil War there have been fourteen Presidents of whom, I think, it is fair to say that only four would have reached the White House had they been subjected to the conditions through which a British Prime Minister arrives in Downing Street'.[1]

To be fair to Bagehot and Laski, Bagehot was writing at a time when the American Presidency was passing through an undistinguished period. Indeed from 1865 to 1901 there were no outstandingly able Presidents. The American system has since shown a capacity for development which Bagehot could hardly have imagined. American Presidents can today assert a leadership, both in the administrative and legislative spheres, which in 1867 would have seemed barely credible even to an American observer. The picture Bagehot gave of an executive unworthy of the name 'because it cannot execute what it decides on' is entirely inappropriate to the Presidency under Franklin Roosevelt, for example, either in the later stages of the New Deal or during the Second World War.[2]

Nevertheless, there is a continuing element of truth in Bagehot's contrast between the American and British systems. Congress can, at times, frustrate a President's programme, as the 80th Congress defeated President Truman's Civil Rights programme and withheld the power to control prices which he asked for. A President who has been confronted by a hostile Congress may, as Truman did in 1948, devote his election campaign to attacking the outgoing Congress for failing to support his policies. Such a situation is barely conceivable in Britain where a Prime Minister normally either has the support of the majority in the House of Commons or, if he loses that support, resigns or seeks a dissolution. It is accurate therefore to say that at a general election a British Prime Minister can usually be held responsible in the fullest sense for what has been done during his term of office. He is responsible not only for the administrative acts of his Government but also for the legislation which Parliament has passed under his guidance. That responsibility is only diminished on the rare occasions when a minority government has been in office.

It is indeed the emphasis in Bagehot's first chapter on the concentration of power in the British system, and the responsi-

---

[1] H. J. Laski, *Parliamentary Government in England* (Allen and Unwin, 1938) p. 243.

[2] See especially R. E. Neustadt, *Presidential Power* (Wiley, 1960) for a discussion of the role of the modern President.

bility that goes with it, which gives his analysis its continuing relevance. The main change which has occurred in the relationship between the House and the Government since 1867 has been the change brought about by the tightening of party discipline. In the 1850s and 1860s party discipline in the Commons was far weaker than it is today. Party groups in the Commons were much less cohesive than the well organized Conservative and Labour parties to which we are now accustomed. Government defeats in the House of Commons were relatively common and the Prime Minister never enjoyed the secure control of the Commons which he can now normally exert. For example, in 1866 a section of Liberals combined to vote against the Liberal Government's Reform Bill and procured the resignation of the Liberal Premier, Earl Russell. Russell's defeat led to two years of minority Conservative government under Lord Derby.

The strengthening of party discipline since 1867 has increased the power of the Prime Minister and the Cabinet but it has also increased their responsibility. What is different is the way in which governments are now held responsible. Whereas in Bagehot's day they were held responsible by the fear of defeat in the Commons, nowadays governments are chastened not by fear of defeat in the Commons but by fear of losing the next general election. As A. H. Birch has put it, we now have 'not so much a form of Parliamentary control of the executive as a form of voters' control, exercised through Parliamentary elections'.[1] The function of the Commons therefore is now to inform the government of the probable consequences of its policies. Debates have accordingly changed in character since Bagehot's day. They are now only very rarely the preludes to 'the deciding catastrophes in Cabinet Government'. They are part of a continuing process by which the Commons interrogates the government and scrutinizes its policies. It is the sanction which has changed.

In 1867 the sanction which discouraged a government from following unpopular policies was that of defeat in the Commons. In the 1960s the sanction is normally the fear of defeat at the next general election. This sanction may seem at times

---

[1] A. H. Birch, *Representative and Responsible Government*, (Allen and Unwin, 1964) p. 137.

somewhat ineffective. A government, as we shall see (below chapter XIII), may sometimes ride out a period of unpopularity and by timing a dissolution with an eye to the opinion polls win a further term of office. What, however, has been lost in responsiveness of government to short term parliamentary opinion has been gained in increased stability in government. Just how much has been lost in responsiveness to parliament is also a matter of dispute and this will be one of the principal lines of investigation in the next three chapters.

Before going on to discuss this question, we should note other aspects in which Bagehot's analysis has been held to be outdated or inappropriate. R. H. S. Crossman in an introduction to *The English Constitution* written in 1963, claimed that the system Bagehot described in his first chapter had been fundamentally transformed, not only by the strengthening of party discipline but by the disappearance of Cabinet Government and its replacement by Prime Ministerial Government.[1] This is a point of view which we shall examine in Chapter XI.

An earlier criticism of Bagehot's thesis in his first chapter was made by L. S. Amery.[2] He argued that the Cabinet is not appointed by the House of Commons and therefore cannot logically be described, as Bagehot described it, as a committee of the Commons. Instead, the Monarch selects a Prime Minister who then invites members of the House of Commons and of the House of Lords to join the Government as Ministers, either with or without a seat in the Cabinet. (Sometimes a Minister is appointed from outside Parliament, in which case he is either made a peer or found a seat in the Commons.) The House of Commons then either accepts or rejects the new Prime Minister and his Cabinet.

But although the House does not appoint the Cabinet, it has an important role in the process of selection. The Monarch will only appoint as Prime Minister an individual who has won the support of a large section of opinion in the Commons, and the Prime Minister is normally the leader of the majority party in the Commons[3]. Similarly most of the men and women whom

[1] Fontana ed. (1963), esp. pp. 51–6.
[2] L. S. Amery, *Thoughts on the Constitution*, 2nd ed. (Oxford University Press, 1953) pp. 21–8.
[3] For fuller discussion of the role of the Monarch in appointing a Prime Minister, see below Chapter X.

the Prime Minister will select as Ministers will have acquired their reputations as members of the House of Commons. So the Commons may be said to have an indirect role in the selection of the Prime Minister and his Cabinet and a direct role in supporting and maintaining the Government. The Cabinet is not a committee of Parliament in the ordinary sense. But it can be argued that it is a committee of a very special kind. To be fair to Bagehot, this was exactly what he was saying when he pointed out that the Cabinet is a creature of the legislature, but that it could destroy its creator through a dissolution.

There is another criticism which can be made of Bagehot's theoretical analysis which is really more telling. He speaks, as we have seen, 'of the close union, the nearly complete fusion of the executive and legislative powers' in the British Constitution. This is a considerable over-statement which becomes clear if one considers what a complete fusion of the executive and legislative powers would involve. A local authority in Britain is an example of an elected body which enjoys both legislative and executive powers. The Councillors who sit on a County Borough Council not only decide by-laws relating to local health questions, for example, but they also make administrative decisions about the functioning of the local health services which they control. An example of an executive body which has taken over all or nearly all of the legislative functions is the Council of Ministers in the Soviet Union. This primarily executive body, broadly equivalent to the British Cabinet, issues decrees which have the force of law and which are automatically ratified in the brief sessions of the Supreme Soviet.

It is obvious that the British system in central government is quite unlike either of these examples. The House of Commons is a legislative body, a minority of whose members are also members of the Government. Nowadays it is a large minority. In the Wilson Government in 1967 there were 85 Ministers who sat in the Commons. But this is still a minority in relation to the total membership of the House, which is 630. It is true that there is no separation, but neither is there anything approaching fusion. Rather we may say that in Britain there is 'Association of the Powers'—the legislative and executive branches of government are closely associated but are not fused.

Just as Bagehot's statement that there is a nearly complete

fusion of the executive and legislative branches in Britain is inaccurate, so is his statement that there is no separation between the judicial power and the other branches of government. There was in Bagehot's time, and there is today, a marked degree of separation between the judicial branch, on the one hand, and the legislative and executive branches on the other. The judges are independent of the executive in the sense that they hold office during good behaviour, and cannot be dismissed 'at the pleasure' of the Government. A judge can only be removed by a joint petition of both Houses of Parliament and by a judicial process in which the judge concerned must be heard. In fact, no judge has been removed since 1830.[1]

One of the functions of the judiciary is indeed to place a check upon the executive by ruling whether or not a Minister or one of his servants is acting within the powers granted to him by Statute. (See below Chapters VIII and XVI.) It is true that at the summit of the judicial profession all the powers are associated. The Lord Chancellor is not only head of the judiciary, but he is a member of the Cabinet and Chairman of the House of Lords. In his person, therefore, all the powers are confused, if not fused. But this does not affect the degree to which the judiciary is independent of the executive, since the powers which the Lord Chancellor enjoys over the judiciary are small. Again, the House of Lords, as well as being a legislative body, is also the highest court of appeal in the country. But when the House of Lords sits as a court it consists, by custom, of only the Law Lords. Here then also, in practice, separation between the judicial and the legislative branches is maintained.

While, however, one can point to these defects of detail in Bagehot's argument, the emphasis he placed on responsibility in the British system has proved a lasting one. Indeed, just as the British system emphasizes the responsibility of Government, so it promotes responsible attitudes in the Opposition. Today's Opposition may, following a general election, become tomorrow's Government. Therefore, the Opposition must always consider that, when it proposes alternatives to Government policies, it may before long become the Government and be morally bound to put its alternative policies into effect.

---

[1] See E. C. S. Wade and G. G. Phillips, *Constitutional Law*, 6th ed. (Longmans, 1960) p. 308.

The responsible position of the Leader of the Opposition has been recognized since 1937 by the payment to him of a salary out of public funds. This in no way obligates him to the Government, but signalizes his value as the official leader of the party which criticizes, challenges, and may sometime replace the existing Government.

The British people expect responsible government: this is commonly accepted. But do they also get responsive government? In that constant dialogue between the House of Commons and the Government, to which we have referred, how much attention does the Government pay to the criticisms voiced in the Commons? Does the House still, as Bagehot said, pour out 'in characteristic words, the characteristic heart of the nation?' Now that it is so difficult to defeat a Government in the House, does what is said there really count for much? These are some of the questions which will be examined in the next three chapters.

FOR REFERENCE

L. S. AMERY, *Thoughts on the Constitution*, 2nd ed. (Oxford University Press, 1953).

W. BAGEHOT, *The English Constitution*, with an Introduction by R. H. S. Crossman (Fontana, 1963).

A. H. BIRCH, *Representative and Responsible Government* (Allen and Unwin, 1964).

W. I. JENNINGS, *The British Constitution*, 3rd ed. (Cambridge University Press, 1950).

W. I. JENNINGS, *Cabinet Government*, 3rd ed. (Cambridge University Press, 1959).

W. I. JENNINGS, *Parliament*, 2nd ed. (Cambridge University Press, 1957).

H. J. LASKI, *Parliamentary Government in England* (Allen and Unwin, 1938).

H. J. LASKI, *Reflections on the Constitution* (Manchester University Press, 1951).

R. E. NEUSTADT, *Presidential Power* (Wiley, 1960).

H. V. WISEMAN, *Parliament and the Executive* (Routledge and Kegan Paul, 1960).

CHAPTER V

The House of Commons and Legislation

How effective is the House of Commons as a legislative Chamber? Is sufficient time now given to legislation, and are there adequate opportunities for proposing amendments? These are some of the questions which we will try to answer in this chapter.

Legislative Procedure

The legislative procedure of the House of Commons is calculated, if properly used, to provide opportunities for debating a bill both in broad outline and in minute detail. All debates are public and can be openly reported, except on the rare occasions when a bill is sent to a select committee. Furthermore, in general the passage of a bill covers a long enough period of time for interested sections of the public to be able to find out about the bill and to press for amendments. The first stage in the House of Commons is known as the first reading. No debate takes place at this stage, which is very brief. The Member who is introducing the bill, on being called by the Speaker, hands to the Clerk at the Table a 'dummy bill'. This is merely a sheet of paper on which is written the title of the bill and the names of the Members presenting and supporting it. The Clerk reads out the short title of the bill which is then ordered to be read a second time on a day named by the Member. The bill is then printed by order of the House. Copies are available to all members of the House and can be purchased from the Stationery Office by members of the public.

A considerable interval is usually provided between first and second readings so that those interested, both inside and outside the House, can study the text of the bill and examine its implications. Many of those interested will know, before it is printed, much of what the bill will contain. The draft of a Government bill will often have been discussed over a long

period between representatives of the Ministry introducing
the bill and interested bodies. The Minister in charge will try
to secure as much support as he can from them, and their
agreement to the bill, before ever it reaches the House of Commons. But these negotiations have gone on in private. Once the
bill has had its first reading, and is printed, the debate becomes
public.

Individuals and organizations who have not been consulted
by the Ministry can now press their views, and those who have
been consulted can appeal to the public to reinforce their
arguments. Criticisms and queries may begin to flow into the
office of the Minister in charge of an important bill very soon
after it has been published. The Minister of National Insurance
in 1946, James Griffiths, said when he opened the second
reading debate on the National Insurance Bill that in the first
six days after the bill was published, he had received 325 letters
from Members of Parliament alone, all on detailed aspects of
the bill.[1] So when the day allotted for the opening of the second
reading debate arrives, many Members will be already primed
with arguments for changes in the bill, arguments derived from
their own experience or researches, from contact with interested
bodies, or possibly stimulated by newspaper articles and edi-
torials.

The debate which takes place on second reading is a general
debate on the bill. The House is asked to approve the bill as a
whole before it goes on to be considered in detail in Committee.
Only two types of amendment can be discussed to the motion:
'That the bill be now read a second time'. A Member may move:
'That the bill be read a second time upon this day six months'.
If such a motion is carried the bill is in effect rejected and
proceeds no further. But an alternative method of rejection
is by carrying a reasoned amendment which states why the
House does not agree to the bill being read a second time. Some,
but not all, of the speeches in a normal second reading debate
deal with the general principles of the Bill. Many, probably the
majority, will be concerned with details; Members advocating
changes and hoping to prepare the way for amendments to be
moved at committee stage.

A second reading debate on an important bill normally is

[1] H.C. Deb. Vol. 418, Col. 1733.

allocated one parliamentary day. But a very important and controversial bill may be given two days. When a bill has been read a second time, there is normally an interval of several days before the committee stage begins. For example, debate on the second reading of the National Insurance Bill was completed on 11 February 1946 and the committee stage began on 26 February, just over a fortnight later. Similarly, the Commonwealth Immigrants Bill in 1961 was given its second reading on 16 November and committee stage began on 5 December.

When a bill involves expenditure of public money, a special financial resolution must be agreed to in committee of the whole House. A bill which involves spending public funds therefore has to undergo a stage additional to those which other bills must pass. But it is not normally a protracted stage. The Financial Resolution on the National Insurance Bill was in fact taken and agreed to on 11 February 1946, on the same day that the second reading debate on that bill was concluded.

Committee stage is, by contrast, the most time-consuming stage of all. It is now that the bill is considered in detail: clause by clause, schedule by schedule. Each clause (and schedule) is voted upon, the amendments to each clause being voted upon first before the clause is put in its amended, or unamended form. Debate at this stage may therefore go on for several weeks, especially when the bill is lengthy and controversial.

When the committee stage has been completed, the bill is reported as amended. Committee stage can take place in the whole House or in standing committee. Report stage is always in the whole House. Procedure at report stage is similar to procedure at committee stage in that amendments to individual clauses may be moved, but it is dissimilar in that only those clauses to which new amendments have been put down are discussed and voted upon. It does not therefore take so long as committee stage, but it provides a useful second opportunity for moving detailed amendments, and is particularly useful when a bill has been sent to a standing committee instead of to a committee of the whole House.

It is at committee and report stage that the ordinary Member of the House has his chance to get a government bill amended. Taking the National Insurance Bill of 1946 again as an example, one of the chief lines of criticism at second reading was that the

bill was unfair to self-employed persons who were to be required
to contribute more than employed people yet were entitled to
fewer benefits. At committee stage the position of many types of
self-employed persons was considered. Members representing
rural constituencies were concerned to know how the bill would
affect mole catchers, rabbit catchers, and hedgers and ditchers
—self-employed men but with low average earnings and therefore hardly able to afford a high contribution. Members from
constituencies including fishing villages raised the similar
problem of share-fishermen. These are groups of fishermen
who own a small boat collectively. Technically they are self-
employed men but, again, their average earnings tend to be low.
Other types of self-employed men and women, such as small
shopkeepers and private nurses, all had their champions. One
major concession was made by the Minister in standing committee. He accepted an amendment which placed self-employed
people on the same basis as the employed in relation to sick-
ness benefit.

The Minister in charge of the bill has several courses of
action open to him when faced with an amendment. He can
accept it as it stands, if he and his advisers think the amendment is desirable and suitably phrased. Or he can say that he
is, in general, in sympathy with the amendment but envisages
some difficulties if the amendment is approved as it stands. In
this case he may undertake to look into the question and if
possible introduce an amendment himself at a later stage.

Another alternative open to him is to say that this is a question which cannot be suitably dealt with in the bill but that he
promises to settle the matter by regulation after consultation
with all the interests affected. Such recourse to delegated legislation is nowadays frequently made by Ministers.[1] In such a case,
Members may ask the Minister what the effect of the regulations he intends to issue will be, and the Minister will often comply by describing his general attitude to the problem involved.

Finally, he may oppose the amendment altogether and ask
the committee to reject it.

Whatever course the Minister decides to take, he can, with
rare exception, be certain of getting the support of the majority

---

[1] The use made of delegated legislation and its constitutional implications are
discussed below in Chapter VIII.

of the committee. If his party has a majority in the full House of Commons, that majority is mirrored in the committee and party discipline is maintained there. Of course, if pressure is strong from within his party in favour of changes, he may decide to make concessions. But if he is resolved not to accept an amendment he will usually get his way even if this makes him unpopular with elements in his own party. Viscount Templewood (Sir Samuel Hoare) has described how, as Home Secretary in 1939, he was able to ignore Conservative opposition to some aspects of the Criminal Justice Bill of that year. The Conservative chief whip told him that nine-tenths of the Conservative Members in the House were opposed to the clause which abolished flogging as a judicial punishment. The Conservative Party had a large majority in the House and in the standing committee to which the bill was referred. Nevertheless the Minister stood firm, Conservative Members obeyed their Whip and the abolition clause was carried by a substantial majority. This bill did not become law at the time as its passage was interrupted by the outbreak of war in 1939. A bill with many of the same provisions (including the abolition of flogging) was introduced after the war and became the Criminal Justice Act, 1948.[1]

The statement that 'The Minister is in charge of the bill' can be taken in a literal sense. He is responsible for the bill not only in the form in which it is introduced into the House, but also in the form which it has taken on when it goes for the Royal Assent. The changes which he agrees to during the passage of the bill are normally changes in favour of which there is, in his view, a substantial weight of argument and opinion. They are not, except very rarely, changes forced upon him by the House against his will.

Supporting the Minister, of course, at every stage are his permanent advisers. They are always present but never obtrusive. In the whole House, the chief officials who have drafted the bill, or are expert in the subject under discussion, sit in a narrow pew under the Press Gallery on the Government side of the House. In standing committee, they sit in a comparable position at one side of the chairman's table. When a Minister needs advice he will normally scribble a note and send it via

---

[1] See Viscount Templewood, *Nine Troubled Years* (Collins, 1954) p. 234.

his Parliamentary Private Secretary who is sitting behind him. More rarely he will go over himself to confer with the Civil Servants in their box. In the final stages of the third reading debate on the Rent Bill on 5 July 1965, the Minister, R. H. S. Crossman, went over to the box, leant his elbows on top and was seen to be conferring deeply with his advisers. Such a frank admission of the need to consult an official is rare from a Minister, but it caused no surprise on this occasion.

When the report stage has been completed the bill goes to third reading. This stage is similar to second reading in that debate culminates in a division on the question of whether or not the bill shall be 'read a third time' and proceed further. No amendment may be moved to any clause in the bill. The House is again considering the bill as a whole but now in its amended form, as it has issued from committee and report. So debate is similar in character to debate on second reading, but, as with second reading, some speeches may be concerned with the general arguments for or against the bill, others may refer to points of detail. For when a bill has originated in the Commons it must go on to be discussed in the Lords, and there will be opportunities for detailed amendment there.

Legislative procedure in the House of Lords is basically similar to procedure in the Commons. There too a bill must receive its first and second reading, consideration in committee and on report, and third reading. There too a Minister is in charge of the bill if it is a Government bill. He may not be a Minister from the department concerned, as he invariably is in the Commons, for not all departments can be represented in the Lords. In such a case a Minister from another department or a Government Whip in the Lords may be briefed by the department concerned to take charge of the bill.[1] When a Labour Government is in office the position of the Minister in charge of a bill in the Lords differs considerably from the position in the Commons. A Labour Minister in the Lords cannot command a majority in support of the bill as Labour peers are in a minority there. Nevertheless the Conservative majority in the Lords normally uses its powers with restraint. Consequently, the committee stage on a Government bill in the Lords

---

[1] See P. Bromhead, *The House of Lords and Contemporary Politics* (Routledge and Kegan Paul, 1958) pp. 102–6.

is not unlike committee stage in the Commons, whether a Conservative or a Labour government is in office. It provides another opportunity for detailed changes to be urged upon the Minister, but amendments are not often carried against the Minister's advice even when Conservative peers have the power to outvote a Labour Minister and his supporters if they so choose. Governments, both Conservative and Labour, therefore, find committee stage in the Lords a useful opportunity for introducing amendments which debate in the Commons has shown to be desirable.

When a bill has been amended in the Lords, it returns to the Commons and the Commons have to decide whether they agree with the Lords amendments or not. If they disagree, then the bill goes back to the Lords for re-consideration. If disagreement persists, the bill fails, unless it is re-passed by the Commons in the same form in two successive sessions, one year having elapsed between the second reading on the first occasion and the third reading on the second occasion. If these conditions are complied with, the bill is passed without the approval of the Lords under the provisions of the Parliament Act, 1949.[1] When a bill has passed all its stages in both Houses or has complied with the provisions of the Parliament Act, it receives the Royal Assent and becomes law. In theory, the Monarch can withhold assent from any bill, but in fact the Royal Assent to a bill has not been withheld since 1707.

The way in which an important bill should be dealt with in Parliament can therefore be summed up as follows. The content of the bill is made known to the public first by being printed, then through cross-examination of the Minister at second reading and subsequent stages. Once interested sections of the public are fully aware of what the bill involves, they have more than one chance to express their views about it and to induce M.P.s or peers to move amendments. So the 'expressive' function of Parliament is performed, with the House of Commons acting as the main channel for probing a Minister about his intentions in a Bill, and for urging him to accept amendments which are often asked for by members of the public or by organized interests. The Government is kept in touch

[1] See below, Chapter IX, for a full discussion of this Act and the powers of the House of Lords.

with public opinion through the Commons and is influenced to adapt its legislation to accord more closely with public feeling.

But the process here described may on occasion be greatly modified. For example, when war threatened in the summer of 1939, the Emergency Powers (Defence) Bill, 1939, which gave very wide powers to the Government to make regulations, was passed by both Houses, within a few hours, on 24 August. Similarly, in November 1965 Parliament passed the Southern Rhodesia Bill through all its stages in a single sitting. This Bill gave the Government extraordinary powers to make Orders in Council to meet the situation created by the Unilateral Declaration of Independence in Rhodesia. So the normally long-drawn-out process can be compressed into one day if a crisis situation makes the rapid enactment of legislation desirable.

Even when there is not a crisis situation, some important bills are dealt with very quickly. For example, the Trinidad and Tobago Bill was given its first reading on 27 June 1962. Debate on second reading took place on 4 July and lasted less than two hours. The committee stage, report stage, and third reading were all taken on 6 July and, after passing all stages in the Lords, the bill received the Royal Assent on 1 August. This was an important bill providing for the independence of Trinidad and Tobago. It was not passed in an atmosphere of crisis, but it was recognized as an urgent matter on all sides and it was also non-controversial, all parties supporting the grant of independence.

Private Members' Bills

There are two principal ways in which the expressive function of the House of Commons in relation to legislation has been restricted since the mid-nineteenth century. First, the opportunities available to private members to get legislation on to the statute book have been greatly reduced. Second, various methods have been devised for curtailing debate and preventing long drawn out discussion of bills.

Until 1852, Government business had precedence on only two days a week. There were ample opportunities for private Members to introduce bills and some of the great social reforms of the nineteenth century resulted from their bills. One may instance the many reforms initiated in Private Members' bills by Lord Ashley (later Lord Shaftesbury). After 1852, Government business had precedence on three days a week and by the end of the century Government legislation predominated. Nowadays, only twenty Fridays in a Parliamentary session are normally reserved for private Members, ten for motions and ten for bills introduced by private Members. Private Members' time was revived in the session 1948-9. The Government had taken all the time of the House during the Second World War and for the three sessions following the war.

One of the most important Private Members' bills to become law since 1949 has been the Defamation Bill which received the Royal Assent in 1952. This measure made some major changes in the law of libel and slander. Many other bills introduced by private Members have produced useful if small-scale reforms. For example, the Heating Appliances (Fireguards) Bill which became law in the same session prohibited the sale of gas and electric fires without effective fireguards. It has undoubtedly made a valuable contribution to safety in the home. Another private Member's bill which was not of the first importance, but which did away with a great inconvenience, was Mrs. Barbara Castle's Public Lavatories (Turnstiles) Bill which received the Royal Assent in 1963 and required local authorities to abolish turnstiles in public lavatories.

In general it may be said that private Members are most likely to get a measure on to the statute book if it is largely uncontroversial. But controversial measures sponsored by private Members still, on occasion, pass into law if their sponsors can generate enough parliamentary interest in them and if the question at issue is not a matter of party politics. Examples of such bills in recent years are the Obscene Publications Bill and the Legitimacy Bill of 1958-9. These bills both dealt with the kind of topics which governments tend to shy away from. They offer no electoral advantage and they are awkward to handle, as feeling runs across party lines and the strongly held personal convictions of many Members are involved. The passage of each of these bills was a considerable achievement for their sponsors, Messrs Roy Jenkins and John Parker respectively.

An even more remarkable achievement was the **passage of**

Leo Abse's Sexual Offences (No. 2) Bill in 1967. This Bill, which legalized homosexual acts in private between consenting adults, faced determined opposition. Although it was not a Government bill, the Wilson Government allowed an all-night sitting for the completion of its report stage and third reading.

But the outstanding legislative reform which has been initiated by a private Member since 1949 has been the abolition of the death penalty. In the session 1955–6, Sidney Silverman introduced his Death Penalty (Abolition) Bill. The bill passed all stages in the Commons. The Conservative Government did not support the bill but found time for it to be discussed and allowed a free vote at every stage. The House of Lords, however, rejected the bill. The Conservative Government was not prepared to find time in the subsequent session for the bill and so enable it to become law without the Lords' assent, under the Parliament Act. Instead, the Government introduced their own Homicide Bill which limited the number of offences for which the death penalty could be imposed to murder by shooting or explosion, murder in the course of a robbery, murder of a policeman or warder, and murder on a second occasion.

As a result, many fewer murderers were hanged in the period between the passage of the Act in 1957 and 1964. It represented a partial victory for Silverman and the National Campaign for the Abolition of Capital Punishment. Their objective was achieved with the passage in 1965 of the Murder (Abolition of Death Penalty) Bill. The Wilson Government found time for the bill and allowed a free vote on it. Despite determined opposition from the opponents of abolition, it passed through the Commons with only one modification. Abolition was limited to a five-year period only, after which the position would have to be reviewed. The Lords inserted only three minor amendments including one empowering judges to recommend the term of years which should be served by every murderer sentenced to imprisonment for 'life'.

Procedure on a private Member's bill is identical to procedure on a Government bill, but there are several difficulties which beset the private Member. Private Members are competing with each other for the right to use the limited time which is reserved for them. Who shall have priority on private Members'

D

Fridays is determined by a ballot. A Member whose name is drawn out among the first six names is almost sure of getting a second reading debate for his bill. The first six Fridays out of the ten alloted to private Members' bills are normally given over to second reading debates. The Members who win the first six places in the ballot have the right to take the first place on each of the six days. Members who win an immediately lower place in the ballot—anything from seventh to twelfth—stand some chance of getting a second reading debate on their bills. They choose a second place on any of the six days and their bill will be discussed if time permits. Those with lower places in the ballot stand little chance of getting their bills considered, and every session there are many disappointed Members. The final four days, out of the ten allotted, are normally used for the report stage and third reading of those bills which have been given a second reading and have completed their committee stage in standing committee.

If a private Member does not win a place in the ballot he can still get a first reading for his bill, but he is not very likely to secure time for a second reading. There is also the procedure under the Ten Minute Rule whereby a Member may move that leave be given him to bring in a bill. He may make a short speech, lasting only ten minutes, in favour of his bill. One other Member may make a speech of similar length, after which a vote is taken.[1] A bill introduced in this way is unlikely to get a second reading, but the procedure does secure publicity for the bill. Silverman's Death Penalty (Abolition) Bill was in fact introduced in this way in 1955.

It is difficult enough then for a private Member to get his bill debated, but even if he wins a place in the ballot he is likely to encounter difficulties which rarely trouble Ministers. The private Member has no Whip, to ensure a majority for his bill or even to prevent the House being 'counted out'. The quorum

[1] Until October 1965 a motion to introduce a bill under the Ten Minute Rule procedure was taken immediately after Question Time on a Tuesday or Wednesday. On 27 October 1965 the House decided that for the session 1965–6, as an experiment, proceedings under this Rule should be held over until the end of the public business on those days. The object was to prevent time being taken from general debates in the earlier part of the day. This change had been recommended by the Select Committee on Procedure in March 1965.

(H.C. 149 of 1964–5 First Report from the Select Committee on Procedure, p. vii.)

of the House of Commons is forty Members. If any Member draws the attention of the Speaker to the fact that less than forty Members are present, he at once orders a count to be taken. The division bells ring once throughout the building and Members who are in the library or committee rooms hurry to reach the Chamber. If after four minutes from the ringing of the bell forty Members or more are present in the Chamber, debate continues.[1] But if fewer than forty are present the Speaker adjourns the House until the next sitting day.

It is rare, but not unknown, for the House to be counted out when Government business is under consideration. If a count is called for during Government business there will usually be sufficient Government supporters present in the building to make a quorum provided they can get to the chamber within four minutes. A private Member's bill is much more vulnerable if a count is called, as a Member depends entirely on there being enough Members sufficiently interested in his bill to be present in the Chamber or close at hand. To be counted out is also more disastrous for a private Member. For a Minister it means loss of face and losing a day. For a private Member it means that his bill is almost certainly lost for that session.

Another hazard which the private Member's bill may encounter is the danger of being 'talked out'. The ordinary business of the day is terminated on Fridays at 4 p.m. If 4 p.m. is reached and no division has taken place on the motion that the bill under discussion be read a second time, the bill in question fails to get its second reading and is lost. A small group of Members may therefore prolong discussion and 'talk out the bill'. Or they may prolong discussion on the first bill to prevent the second bill being reached. In either case, it is a rather ungentlemanly way of defeating a bill without having to vote against it. The stratagem can only be countered by moving the closure. This is a motion 'that the question be now put' and, if carried, it results in an immediate division on the question under discussion. But the Speaker will only accept the motion if he considers that sufficient time has been taken on the debate to permit every minority to make its views known. Even if he accepts the motion, standing orders require that at least 100

---

[1] In 1960 the time limit was extended from two to four minutes following a recommendation of the Select Committee on Procedure of 1958.

Members must vote for the closure if it is to be carried. It is, therefore, very difficult for a private Member to carry the closure and prevent his bill being talked out.

Government bills and private Members' bills are both 'public' bills. Public bills are quite distinct from 'private' bills, which are considered under an altogether different procedure. A public bill may be described as a bill which relates to the whole community, while a private bill relates to a specific locality or to an individual firm or other corporate body. A local authority which wishes, for example, to purchase land and establish an aerodrome will require to promote a private bill to secure the necessary powers for this purpose. The procedure on a private bill at committee stage is reminiscent of proceedings in a court of law. Counsel may appear for the promoters and opponents of the bill and witnesses may be cross-examined. The whole procedure on private business is quite distinct, and although it is an important subsidiary aspect of the work of Parliament it has little direct bearing on its role in the Constitution.[1]

Curtailment of Debate

The chief reason for the declining importance of private Members' bills in the last 100 years is to be found in the increasing activity of the State in social and economic questions. The demand for governments to intervene—to protect conditions of labour, to protect the health of the community, to establish national insurance and national health schemes, to combat unemployment—has become steadily stronger since the middle of the nineteenth century. The causes of this major trend are complex. Some factors can be singled out: the widening of the electorate in 1867 and 1884 which made the votes, and therefore the interests, of the working man more important to party leaders; the successive social enquiries which gave publicity to the seamier sides of life in an industrialized community. So governments came to have more ambitious legislative programmes, and there was less time for the private Member in the timetable of the average session.

---

[1] For a detailed historical survey see O. C. Williams, *History of Private Bill Procedure.* Vol. I (H.M.S.O., 1949).

The same trend has strengthened a second development which has served to curtail the expressive function of the House. In the middle of the nineteenth century no limits were set to debate on any question which was before the House. Debate continued until every Member who wanted to speak had had his say. The only restrictions were provided by the rules which enjoined Members against irrelevance and repetition. A Member who introduced irrelevant material into his speech or who unduly repeated himself during a speech could be called to order by the Speaker.[1]

Those halcyon days of almost unrestricted debate were brought to an end by the actions of a group of Irish nationalist Members in 1881. These Members, under the leadership of Parnell, developed the art of obstruction to a hitherto unknown pitch. Their objects were twofold: to prevent the passage of an Irish Coercion Bill which was then before the House, and in general to hold up business in the House until the Government was prepared to introduce Home Rule for Ireland. Endowed with the well-known eloquence of their nation, these Irishmen were able to speak at enormous length without repeating themselves or becoming irrelevant. They paralysed the work of the House of Commons so completely that the Prime Minister, Gladstone, was forced to consult with the Speaker to find some new device to curb this obstruction. On Gladstone's initiative, the Speaker was given power to make emergency rules to restrict debate, and the rules which he made that year provided the models upon which the modern closure and guillotine have been shaped.

Standing orders now provide that any Member may move that 'The question be now put'. The Speaker must then decide whether to accept the motion. He will accept the closure if he considers that it is not an abuse of the rules of the House, or an infringement of the rights of the minority. This last phrase is interpreted to mean that every section of opinion must have had a chance to speak on the matter before the House. If he accepts a closure motion, the Speaker puts it to the House at once without allowing any amendment or debate. But standing orders provide that even if a majority of the Members voting

---

[1] This power is still exercised by the Speaker and by the chairmen of committees of the Commons. *Standing Orders of the House of Commons*. Public Business. S.O. 22.

support it, the closure is not carried unless at least 100 Members vote for it.[1]

The closure is therefore an effective method of ending debate provided that discussion has been reasonably general and prolonged and that there are sufficient Members on hand to support the motion. The safeguards in the standing orders themselves prevent drastic imposition of the closure. It is furthermore provided that the closure may only be moved in full House when the Speaker is in the chair, or in committee of the whole House when the Chairman of Ways and Means, or the Deputy Chairman, is in the chair.[2] This ensures that the most experienced chairmen decide whether a closure motion may be accepted, for the Speaker and the two other chairmen mentioned are the senior presiding officers in the House. The closure may also be moved in standing committee, where the motion is not carried unless the number of Members supporting it is equivalent to the quorum of the committee.

The restrictions on the use of the closure which protect the rights of minorities may make it a clumsy instrument from the point of view of governments. If, for example, the Opposition, at committee stage, prolong debate on every clause of a long and important Government bill, the Minister may be forced to move the closure on every clause and even, conceivably, on every amendment discussed. As the chairman may not accept the closure until the clause or amendment in question has been fully discussed, the Opposition can, if it chooses, spin out debate to an inordinate length despite frequent use of the closure.

Some more drastic device is necessary in order to cope with such determined obstruction, and this is to be found in the guillotine. The technical name for what is popularly known as a guillotine is an 'allocation of time order'. It is in fact a timetable for the passage of a bill which lays down precisely how much time is to be allotted for each stage. The order may, for example, provide that twelve days are to be allotted on a certain bill for committee stage, two days for report stage and one day for third reading. It may go into greater detail and lay down that clauses 1 to 4 of the bill are to be discussed on the first day in Committee, clauses 5 to 11 on the second day and

[1] S.O. 31 and 32.   [2] S.O. 31.

so on. The order is debated by the House and, if approved, it goes into force automatically. So that even if, in the example given, only clause 2 has been reached at the end of the first day in committee, the Chairman puts clauses 1 to 4 to the vote. The 'guillotine' falls, chopping off debate on clauses 3 and 4 and consigning to limbo (or possibly to a later stage) any amendments which have been put down to those clauses.

The system is advantageous to governments as the Minister in charge of the bill knows exactly when his bill will complete all its stages in the House and he is freed from the problems entailed in repeatedly moving the closure. It can be inimical to the expressive function of the House, for usually whenever a guillotine is applied some clauses are voted without having been debated. Governments are therefore loath to ask for a guillotine and often only do so when debate on a bill has already been unduly prolonged.

There is a third method of restricting debate—a method which nowadays causes very little controversy. It is known colloquially as the 'kangaroo', but in standing orders as the power to select amendments.[1] This power is given to the chairman in committee of the whole House, or in standing committee, or to the Speaker at report stage. The chairman can, like a kangaroo, hop over some amendments and land on others. He can decide to omit certain amendments which are down on the order paper on the grounds that they cover substantially the same ground as the amendment which he selects. This is an effective counter to the obstruction caused by putting down to each clause a host of amendments, all substantially similar, but all otherwise requiring to be debated unless the closure is moved or a guillotine is in operation.

The kangaroo was first introduced in 1909 to curtail very determined obstruction by the Conservative Opposition to the Liberal Government's Finance Bill of that year. It was vigorously criticized at the time, but has since become quite uncontroversial as chairmen have on the whole used the power given to them fairly and wisely. Members usually recognize that it is in their interests to prevent unnecessary duplication and repetition in debate. Sometimes a Member will challenge the chairman's decision to omit the amendment which he has

[1] S.O. 33 and S.O. 59 5).

put down. If he can persuade the chairman that there are strong grounds for discussing his amendment, the chairman may change his mind, but usually the chairman's decision is recognized to be fair and reasonable.

It will be seen that the three main methods of curtailing debate—closure, guillotine, and kangaroo—have all emerged in response to obstruction by members of the Opposition. But they have not since been reserved for occasions when obstruction was at its most determined. The closure is nowadays used frequently, the kangaroo is used on almost every important bill at committee or report stage. So what were at first thought of as exceptional procedures have become normal devices to speed up the work of legislation and to permit a large number of Government bills to pass into law in any one session. Only the guillotine has remained an exceptional device. It has been in the past a government's heavy artillery for curtailing debate, called upon when real obstruction is encountered or threatened. It remains, therefore, a controversial method.

One point that should be recognized is that not all guillotines are of the most drastic kind. A guillotine which allows reasonable time for debate at the various stages, in relation to the length and complexity of the bill, is much less open to criticism than a really severe guillotine. Again, the Opposition may make a guillotine appear more drastic than it really is by spinning out debate on the early clauses in committee, to ensure that some clauses will have to be put to the vote without debate. They can then pillory the Government for applying the gag. This is a more or less respectable technique of opposition, justified on the grounds that a guillotine is always undesirable and that it is the duty of the Opposition to draw attention to its use. But there are some grounds for arguing that the guillotine could become a more normal procedure if both governments and oppositions were reasonable in their attitudes towards it—governments in allocating sufficient time, oppositions in seeing that time is effectively used.[1]

Standing Committees

There is another way in which the legislative work of the House can be speeded up—by making extensive use of standing

[1] See below pp. 105–6.

committees. It is open to question whether sending a bill to standing committee involves a curtailment of debate. In a sense it does, in that fewer Members have the opportunity of moving amendments, but from another point of view it does not, in that a longer time may be spent in discussing a bill in standing committee than would have been given to it in committee of the whole House. But it is significant that standing committees were first used by the House of Commons as a counter to obstruction.

Two standing committees were set up, at Gladstone's suggestion, in 1883 as a further move to deal with the Irish obstruction which had given rise to the introduction of the closure in 1881. They were little used until 1907 when the Liberal Government under Sir Henry Campbell-Bannerman had an ambitious programme of legislation which was being vigorously opposed by the Conservatives under Balfour's leadership. The Liberal Government in that year introduced a series of Standing Orders which established the modern system of standing committees. That the Conservative Opposition thought they involved curtailment of debate is shown by the fact that the Standing Orders of 1907 were discussed at great length, and discussion had finally to be cut short by the government imposing a guillotine. The Orders, as finally passed, set up four standing committees and provided that all bills would be automatically sent to them unless the House otherwise ordered.

Such a system can speed up the legislative output of the House considerably. The most time-consuming stage in legislation is committee stage, so that if many bills are taken in committee of the whole House there can be a serious bottleneck. If, on the other hand, nearly all bills are sent to standing committee and there are four such committees, the House can be considering up to four major bills at committee stage at the same time. The Liberal Government between 1907 and 1914 did not in fact use standing committees as extensively as this. In general, the most important measures of a session were sent to committee of the whole House, while many bills of lesser importance went to standing committee. This continued to be the practice between 1918 and 1939. In these inter-war years the pressure of legislation was not unduly severe in most sessions and obstruction was relatively rare.

During the Second World War it was foreseen that a new situation would have to be faced in the years following the war. Both the main parties, Conservative and Labour, were committed to extensive programmes of social reform and in particular to the establishment of a national insurance scheme, to some sort of national health service, and to an overhaul of the system of public assistance. In addition there were a number of reforms which had been in preparation just before the war but which had been put into cold storage for the duration of the war; for example, the Home Secretary, Sir Samuel Hoare, had to abandon the Criminal Justice Bill of 1939 when his senior Civil Servants told him that their wartime duties would make it most difficult for them to assist in the final stages of the bill and in putting it into operation.[1]

It was clear that, whichever party was in office at the end of the war, an unprecedentedly heavy burden would be placed upon the House of Commons. A committee of Ministers in the Churchill Coalition Government met to consider what could be done to tackle the problem. They produced a memorandum which recommended that more use should be made of standing committees, that in fact substantially all bills should be sent to standing committee. They also proposed that the number of standing committees should be increased, while the membership of each committee should be reduced in size. When the election of 1945 resulted in the formation of a Labour Government, with a clear majority, the question took on greater urgency. For the Labour Party was committed to an extensive programme of nationalization in addition to the programme of social reform which had been agreed to by the Coalition Government. One of the first actions of the new Leader of the House, Herbert Morrison, was to propose in the House of Commons that a Select Committee on Procedure be appointed to consider suggestions for speeding up the legislative work of the House. This motion was made and agreed to on 24 August 1945. The Labour Government submitted the memorandum, previously prepared by the Coalition Ministers, to this Committee which in its report endorsed their proposals.[2]

Changes were therefore made, at first by Sessional Order,

[1] Templewood, *op. cit.*, p. 234.
[2] H.C. 9-1 of 1945-6. 1st Report from the Select Committee on Procedure.

and in 1947 by revising the Standing Orders of the House. The main effect of these changes was to remove any limit on the number of standing committees which the House could appoint and to reduce the maximum permitted size of these committees from 85 to 50 members. It was left to the Government to decide how much use should be made of standing committees.

The Labour Government between 1945 and 1950 had no doubt of the use to which they could be put. In those years virtually all important bills were sent to standing committee at committee stage. The bills nationalizing large sectors of industry—the Coal Mines Bill, the Air Transport Bill, the Gas Bill, the Electricity Bill, the Transport Bill, the Iron and Steel Bill—were all taken in standing committee. The bills making important social reforms were dealt with in the same way— for example the National Insurance Bill, the National Health Service Bill, and the National Assistance Bill. There were in fact only two important bills which were sent to committee of the whole House. They were the Representation of the People Bill 1948, and the Parliament Bill which reduced the delaying power of the House of Lords and eventually became law in 1949. These were both bills of constitutional importance. Some minor bills were also taken in committee of the whole House.

It was this large-scale use of standing committees which, more than any other change in procedure, enabled the House of Commons to deal with an unparalleled volume of legislation in the years 1945–50. One has only to compare in any law library the size of the volumes of Public General Acts which became law in those years with the volumes published in any previous period to appreciate the extent to which legislative output was increased. Furthermore, the legislation of those years bulked large not only in the number of pages covered but also in its complexity and in the importance of the issues determined. It is therefore important to consider the consequences of forcing the pace in this way, and in the first place to assess the effects of such an increased use of standing committees.

Before doing so, it is necessary to examine the structure of standing committees. Standing orders from 1946 to 1960 provided that each standing committee should consist of a nucleus of twenty members to which could be added not more than thirty members in respect of each bill which the committee considered.[1] So the members of the nucleus were thought of as non-specialists; the added members were specialists chosen for their qualifications or known interest in the subject matter of a bill. Thus six standing committees were appointed in the years 1945–50. They were lettered A, B, C, D, E, and F. Standing Committee C, for example, was sent the Coal Industry Nationalization Bill in the session 1945–6. To its nucleus were added thirty members with experience of the coal industry or with some knowledge of the problems involved in the bill. When the Coal Industry Bill had been disposed of by that Committee, the thirty added members were dismissed and a different thirty were appointed to consider the next bill, which was the National Health Service Bill.

The members of the nucleus of a standing committee and the added members were nominated by the committee of selection. This committee consisted of eleven private members who were chosen for their long experience in the House and fair-minded attitude. They were nominated by the House at the beginning of every session and included members of all parties. In their work of nominating the twenty members who formed the nucleus of each standing committee, the selection committee were instructed by standing orders to 'have regard to the composition of the House'. They interpreted this instruction to mean that the party composition of the twenty members should mirror as exactly as possible the party composition of the whole House. They applied the same principle in selecting the added thirty members, although standing orders did not require them to do so. So each standing committee in its composition reflected the party composition of the whole House.

There was and is an additional standing committee which is distinct from the other committees and is different in composition. This is the Scottish Standing Committee. It consists of 30 members representing Scottish constituencies and up to 20 other members who are nominated for each bill which the committee considers. These additional members are chosen by the committee of selection so as to make the composition of the Scottish standing committee as a whole reflect the party

[1] S.O. 58 (1957).

composition of the full House. All Scottish bills are sent to this committee at committee stage.[1]

An important change in the composition of standing committees was made in 1960 after the report of the Select Committee on Procedure in 1959. The Procedure Committee recommended that the permanent nucleus of each standing committee should be done away with and that, as far as possible, the whole membership of a standing committee should consist of M.P.s specially interested in or expert upon the subject matter of a bill. This recommendation was accepted by the House, and since 1960 the membership of each standing committee has been chosen according to the subject matter of the bill under consideration, the expert members being chosen first and other members added, where necessary, in order to balance the party composition. This change has made it easier to man the standing committees, as has a further change made at the same time and also recommended by the Procedure Committee. This was a reduction in the average size of standing committees. Since 1960, standing orders have provided that the maximum size of a standing committee should be 50 and the minimum size 20.[2] The practice now therefore is for a standing committee on a major bill to number around 45 and on a minor bill around 25.

It is still none too easy, however, to find sufficient Members to man the standing committees. The committees hold many of their sessions in the morning when the House is not sitting (although they sometimes have afternoon sessions as well, during sittings of the House). Therefore it is difficult for those who combine other professions with their work as M.P.s to sit on standing committees. Work on a standing committee is also more rigorous than in the House, because those attending must actually be present in, or near, the committee room. It is not possible for Members to be on hand in the Library and merely turn up for divisions or part of the debate as they do for debates in the House, for there are no division bells when a vote is taken in standing committee. Members are summoned by the shouting of 'Division' down the corridor.

What is resented by many Members is that this work has to be shouldered by the minority of Members who devote all or most of their time to the work of the House. As a Conservative

[1] S.O. 61 and 62.   [2] S.O. 60.

M.P., Arthur Tiley, said in debate on the Television Bill in
1963: 'There are scores in this building who never seem to
appear on committees. This is "B" committee, and it is a "b"
committee. I am "b" well fed up!'[1] This outburst was occasioned by the request from the Minister in charge of the Bill,
Reginald Bevins, that the committee should arrange extra
sessions in order to expedite the Bill. The members of the committee were therefore particularly under strain at the time.
But this incident does illustrate the general conclusion that
by and large the committee of selection finds it difficult to
secure enough Members to man committees. K. C. Wheare
commented in 1955 that few Members who really deserve to
be on a standing committee for an important bill failed to obtain a place on it.[2] This of course was under the pre-1960
system, but a similar comment would probably be fair since
1960. One may say therefore that sending important bills to
standing committees has not resulted in any real diminution
of the rights of Members. Although it means that only around
45 instead of 630 Members have the opportunity to move
amendments at committee stage, those 45 are the most interested and best-informed Members on the subject of the bill.
It should also be remembered that the Members who are not on
the standing committee have the right to move detailed amendments at report stage. It has, too, been the practice since 1945
to give more time to a bill at report stage when it has been taken
in standing committee and not in committee of the whole
House.

The practice of sending all important bills, except bills of
constitutional importance, to standing committee between
1945 and 1950, did not then result in any real restriction on
debate. It did not at once, however, become the accepted practice of the House. It was not indeed until after 1955 that standing committees came to be used extensively again, and not
until 1960 that sending a bill to standing committee at committee stage came to be regarded as normal practice. This hiatus
occurred largely because governments between 1950 and 1955
had small majorities. After the General Election in 1950 the
Labour Party had an overall majority in the Commons of only

[1] *The Times* report of 3 April 1963.
[2] K. C. Wheare, *Government by Committee* (Clarendon Press, 1955), p. 146.

six. This entitled the Labour Party to a majority in standing committees of a fraction of one Member. The selection committee therefore at first composed the standing committees with an equal number of Labour and Opposition Members. This drew a protest from the Leader of the House, Herbert Morrison, that the Government's majority in the House should be reflected in the committees. Accordingly it was decided to give the Labour Party a majority of one in each of the standing committees. This did not look a very safe majority, however, and the Government decided to make relatively little use of standing committees during the session 1950–51. Only 13 Government bills were sent to standing committee during that session. Indeed the whole legislative programme was pitched in a minor key, with legislation on topics like the provision of cattle grids taking the place of the controversial and rousing measures of the previous five years.

After the 1951 general election, the Conservatives had an overall majority of 17. This too entitled them to only a small majority in the standing committees. It was not until after the general election of 1955, when they gained an overall majority of 60 in the House, that they received useful majorities in the standing committees. Even so, the Eden Government did not make such extensive use of standing committees as the Attlee Government had done between 1945 and 1950. Some important measures, which did not raise constitutional issues, such as the Housing Subsidies Bill of 1955–6, were taken in committee of the whole House. In the later 1950s, however, it came to be more and more accepted that important bills should be sent to standing committee. The most important bill in the session 1956–7 was the Rent Bill which was taken in standing committee, and the most important bill of the following session, the Local Government Bill, was also taken in standing committee.

Eventually, in 1959, the Procedure Committee recommended that all bills, except bills of major constitutional importance and those where the committee stage is only a formality, should be taken in standing committee.[1] This recommendation has been followed, and since 1960 it is easier to single out major bills which were *not* sent to standing committee. One such was

[1] H.C. 92-I of 1958 pp. iv—v at para. 5.

the Commonwealth Immigrants Bill of 1961–2. The Conservative Government originally intended to send this bill to
standing committee, but was strongly urged by the Leader of
the Opposition, Hugh Gaitskell, and by other Opposition
Members that it should be taken in committee of the whole
House. In deference to their view that the bill was of far-
reaching significance to the Commonwealth and that therefore
it was, in a sense, of constitutional importance, the Leader of
the Commons, Iain Macleod, agreed that the bill should be
taken in committee of the whole House.[1] Other bills of constitutional importance which were taken in committee of the whole
House in the session 1961–2 were the West Indies Act, which
ended the West Indies Federation, the Jamaica Independence
Act, the Trinidad and Tobago Act, and the Uganda Act.
Apart from measures of this character, all important bills
between 1960 and 1964 were taken in standing committee at
committee stage.

The use now made of standing committees represents a
major advance in the procedure of the House. It has raised the
legislative output of the House very considerably. The volume
and content of legislation passed in the period from 1945 to
1950 under the Labour Government was indeed quite un-
precedented. One of the criticisms of the House of Commons
made most frequently in the 1930s was that its procedure was
too slow and cumbersome. Critics, particularly on the Labour
side, argued that the parliamentary machine would break down
if faced with an ambitious programme of legislation. Sir Stafford Cripps, for example, claimed that a Labour government
would need to discard the traditional framework of parliamentary procedure if it was to stand any chance of getting a
socialist programme of legislation enacted. A Labour government, he said, would have to seek extraordinary powers through
the passage of a Planning and Finance Act at the beginning of
each session of Parliament.[2] But in the event, no such drastic
changes were necessary. The Labour Government of 1945–50
was able to get its heavy programme enacted by dint, largely,
of sending virtually all important bills to standing committee.

[1] See H.C. Deb. Vol. 648, cols 1170–5.
[2] Sir Stafford Cripps *et al.*, *Problems of a Socialist Government* (Gollancz, 1933),
pp. 55–6.

Another important factor was the increased use of delegated legislation made possible by the carry-over into peace-time of war-time emergency powers legislation. This will be discussed later in Chapter VIII. Between 1955 and 1964 the volume of legislation did not attain the peak reached in the period between 1945 and 1950. But it was nevertheless considerable and could hardly have been achieved without extensive use of standing committees.

Taking important bills in standing committee at committee stage is desirable because, besides increasing the output of legislation, it gives more time on the floor of the House for non-legislative business. This is obvious enough. A less obvious advantage is that, on balance, the quality of debate is better in standing committee than in committee of the whole House. The standing committees meet in committee rooms which open out of a long corridor on an upper floor of the House. Each room is rectangular in shape and provides space for the Government and Opposition members to sit facing each other with only a short distance separating the front-bench members on either side. In the no-man's-land in between, the shorthand clerks sit at a table taking down every word for the Standing Committee Hansard. At one end, on a slightly raised platform, sits the chairman of the committee flanked by the committee clerk and the Ministers' advisers, and at the other end there are a few seats for the press and public. The atmosphere is informal and the political temperature is, generally speaking, low. It all conduces to a reasonable and moderate attitude on both sides of the committee. The Opposition, on most occasions, are genuinely looking for ways in which the bill can be improved, from their point of view, while the Minister in charge of the bill gives as careful consideration to their amendments as to the amendments suggested on his side of the committee. It is a workshop of legislation in which, normally, the shaping and probing of the bill is the main task and making points of party advantage comes second.

When Labour was returned at the general election in 1964 with a majority of only four over all other parties, it was at first thought that the Wilson Government would have only a very modest legislative programme. The experience of 1950–51 was held to indicate that little could be done on such a small majority, at least in terms of legislation. In fact, the Wilson Government surprised the pundits by introducing, and getting on to the statute book, a greater volume of legislation than had been passed in an average session between 1951 and 1964. Nor was it all non-controversial or minor legislation. Although the most controversial item in the Labour programme, steel nationalization, was shelved, numerous far-reaching and controversial measures were passed. These included the Rent Bill which repealed the Conservative Rent Bill of 1957 and re-imposed rent control on a new and wider basis. This measure was not opposed as a whole by the Conservative Opposition, but it was opposed in detail at many points. Other important and controversial bills, passed in the session 1964–5, were the Control of Office and Industrial Development Bill, the Law Commissions Bill, the Trades Disputes Bill, and the Race Relations Bill. All important Government bills were sent to standing committee during this session. In fact, the Government found that its majority of one in each standing committee was safer than its majority of four and then, after a by-election defeat, of three in the whole House. Not that the Government was any less ambitious in the whole House, for while major measures were under consideration in standing committee, the Government was pressing through the whole House a Finance Bill which proposed the most far-reaching reforms of taxation since 1909.

The chief lesson of the parliamentary year 1964–5 was that a determined government could get through an ambitious legislative programme even with a tiny majority. But whether it could do this for session after session was more in doubt. There were frequent late-night sessions on the Finance Bill in 1965 and the wear and tear on Members was considerable. What was confirmed was the value of standing committees in periods of large or small majority.

The Guillotine in Standing Committee

While it is now generally accepted that most bills should be sent to standing committee, there is still controversy over the use of the guillotine in standing committee. Before 1947 it had been almost unknown for the guillotine to be used in standing committee. The Labour Government's memorandum to the

Select Committee on Procedure in 1945 had proposed a method by which the guillotine could be imposed in standing committee and the Committee had suggested certain modifications. Nevertheless, there remained a desire to avoid using the guillotine in standing committee, as it might seem a double restriction on debate. However, in the course of the session 1946–7, the Leader of the House, Herbert Morrison, came to feel that his programme of legislation was getting badly behind the clock. There had been, appropriately enough, some very long-winded debates on the Gas Bill in standing committee. The Minister in charge of the bill, Hugh Gaitskell (Minister of Fuel and Power), had ultimately to insist on all-night sittings in order to get the bill through standing committee. The Leader of the House concluded that if he was faced with similar obstructive tactics by the Conservative Opposition, on other important bills, they would have to be subject to a guillotine in standing committee. Slow progress was being made by the standing committees considering the Transport Bill and the Town and Country Planning Bill. So on 3 March 1947, the Government proposed, and the House of Commons approved, a guillotine resolution requiring that both bills should be reported to the House by Easter. Later on, in the session 1948–9, the Iron and Steel Bill was subjected to a guillotine in standing committee, the guillotine resolution in this case being proposed and approved immediately after second reading in the House and before the bill reached standing committee.

The imposition of the guillotine on these three bills was hotly criticized by the Conservative Opposition at the time. All three were bills of great complexity. The Transport Bill proposed to nationalize all railway networks in this country, the docks and hotels previously owned by the railways, most canals, long-distance road haulage and the whole of London's passenger transport system. The bill had 127 clauses and 13 schedules. As a result of the imposition of the guillotine, 37 clauses and 7 schedules were not discussed at all in standing committee.

This would seem a very drastic use of the guillotine. But K. C. Wheare pointed out that the time spent on the Bill was considerable.[1] Thirty-one sittings were given to the Bill in

[1] Wheare, op. cit. See his Chapter VI for discussion of this question and especially pp. 150–1.

standing committee. He considered that no important provision escaped discussion and remarked that of 37 clauses not discussed, 17 had no amendments tabled to them by the Opposition. He made similar observations on the use of the guillotine in standing committee on the Town and Country Planning Bill and the Iron and Steel Bill. Of the Planning Bill 50 clauses, and of the Iron and Steel Bill 58 clauses, were not discussed because of the operation of the guillotine. Yet the first of these bills was allowed twenty-five, and the second thirty-six, sittings in standing committee.

Support for Wheare's conclusion here was given by Peter Bromhead. He examined the time spent by the House of Lords on these bills. It is often said that when a bill has been extensively guillotined in the Commons, the inadequacy of debate there can be remedied by fuller consideration in the Lords. Where a bill has been drastically guillotined in the Commons, one would assume that the clauses not debated in the Commons would be debated at some length in the Lords. But Bromhead's analysis showed that, in these three bills, the clauses wholly or partly undebated in the Commons did not receive especially full discussion in the Lords. On the Transport Bill, only 14·7 per cent of the time in the Lords was given to the wholly or partly undiscussed clauses, on the Planning Bill only 9 per cent, and on the Iron and Steel Bill only 10 per cent. He concluded that, as the Lords is available for filling gaps caused by the guillotine and as the Lords had so little to say about guillotined clauses, 'it seems fair to assume that the device of the guillotine as used in the past 12 years, has not really stifled debate as grievously as has sometimes been suggested'.[1]

As often happens, the party which in opposition had been fiercely critical of the guillotine, found itself forced to resort to the guillotine when it came to power. Conservative governments from 1951 onwards were faced by determined Labour obstruction on some of their major measures. The Churchill Government accordingly imposed a guillotine in the session 1952–3 on the Transport Bill which denationalized part of

---

[1] See Peter Bromhead in *Parliamentary Affairs*, Autumn 1958, pp. 443–54. Contrast his view on the passage of the Transport Act of 1947, with that of B. Crick, *The Reform of Parliament* (Weidenfeld and Nicolson, 1964), pp. 108–9.

the long-distance road haulage system. This was in committee of the whole House, but Conservative Ministers also called for the guillotine in standing committee. It was imposed in standing committee on the Licensed Premises in New Towns Bill in 1951–2 and on numerous other major bills, for example on the Rent Bill in 1956–7 and the Pipelines Bill in 1961–2.

By 1959 there was evidence of a change of opinion in the House of Commons in relation to the guillotine. The Select Committee on Procedure, in that year, recommended that a form of guillotine should be applied to every bill in standing committee. They made this recommendation because, they said: 'It has been represented to us in evidence that protracted discussion on the early clauses of a bill in committee often results in inadequate treatment of the later clauses, and in drawing out the proceedings of the committee longer than is necessary. This is almost always avoided where a voluntary timetable has been adopted. There was general agreement in evidence as to the value of such timetables and their use wherever possible; and this, we consider, would also be the view of the House.'[1] But the voluntary timetable is difficult to achieve. One of the rare occasions when such a timetable was agreed upon on a major bill was in 1935 on the Government of India Bill.[2] A timetable for this bill was decided upon and successfully maintained by an informal committee representing all parties and groups interested in the bill.

The Procedure Committee in effect suggested that such machinery should become standard for every bill sent to standing committee, but that it should be backed by an element of compulsion. They proposed that a timetable should be prepared for every bill by a business committee representative of the House and to which there would be co-opted, in the case of every Government bill, two members appointed by the Government and two by the Opposition. The timetable they drew up would be enforced if the House voted to approve it. This proposal combines something of the idea of a voluntary timetable with the ordinary guillotine. It would be, in essence,

---

[1] H.C. 92-I of Session 1958–9. Report from the Select Committee on Procedure. Para. 7 at p. 5.

[2] See particularly Lord Hemingford, *Backbencher and Chairman* (Murray, 1946), pp. 170–1.

a guillotine, but a guillotine which had been prepared in consultation with the Opposition. The assumption was that on most Government bills the Opposition would be prepared to agree to a reasonable timetable and, even when the timetable had been imposed, the Opposition would have been consulted about the way in which time was to be allocated.

The Macmillan Government did not accept the Procedure Committee's suggestion. Some Members, however, continued to advocate this kind of reform. A group of Labour M.P.s and peers, under the chairmanship of Reg Prentice, in 1964 gave strong support to the idea of having an agreed timetable for the committee stage of every bill.[1] They considered that this would be the most important single innovation for saving time in legislative procedure.

The Select Committee on Procedure recommended reform on these lines in 1967. They suggested that a steering committee could be appointed for the committee and report stage of bills. The steering committee would consist of Members from both sides of the House and would sit under the chairmanship of the chairman, at committee stage, or the Speaker, at report stage. It would try to reach agreement on the time to be spent on the bill. Its recommendations would be reported but would not be binding on the House, or the standing committee, unless the Government secured the passage in the House of a motion giving effect to the steering committee's proposals.[2]

A proposal for saving the time of the House which was not approved by the Procedure Committee in 1959 was the suggestion made by Sir Edward Fellowes, Clerk of the House of Commons, that the report stage of many bills should be taken in standing committee. The Committee rejected this idea on the grounds that 'it would involve a departure from the principle that the whole House assumed responsibility for the detail of legislation'.[3] The Government concurred with their recommendation. There seems much to be said for keeping the report stage on the floor of the House, as it gives members not on the standing committee a chance to move amendments. It means

[1] See 'Three Dozen Parliamentary Reforms by one dozen parliamentary socialists', *Socialist Commentary*, July 1964, Para. 19 at p. V.
[2] H.C. 539 of 1966–7. 6th Report from the Select Committee on Procedure. Para. 17 at p. X.
[3] H.C. 92-I of 1958–9. Para. 10 at p. X.

that the whole House will still sometimes be considering minor details of legislation, but it has to be remembered that what seems a minor detail to many Members may be of vital concern to the individuals or groups affected by legislation.

In 1965, however, the Procedure Committee recommended that the second reading of some Government bills could be taken in standing committee. In October 1965, the House approved an Order giving effect to this proposal for the session 1965–6. The order provided that a Government bill could be sent to standing committee for second reading, on the proposition of a Minister, if twenty Members did not object to this being done. The standing committee for this purpose was to consist of not less than thirty nor more than eighty Members.[1] Clearly only the less controversial Government bills would be treated in this way.

Another useful proposal would be to allow bills to be carried over from one session to another. At present a bill which does not complete all its stages in one session is 'lost'. It must be re-introduced and given a first reading in the next session instead of being taken up at the point reached at the end of the previous session. This practice is very wasteful of the time of the House and there seems to be no good reason why it should be continued. The Socialist Commentary group recommended in July 1964 that 'at the end of each session the government should move a resolution to carry over such uncompleted legislation as it felt should not be lost'.[2]

Amendment of Government Bills

How can we sum up the changes made in the legislative procedure of the Commons since 1945? In general we may say that they have been well calculated to speed up the process of legislation without interfering with the expressive function of the House. We have seen that the time remaining for private Members can be effectively used for the introduction of bills on subjects with which the government of the day does not want to concern itself. More important, Government bills are still thoroughly debated and Members have effective opportunities to press amendments.

[1] H.C. Deb. Vol. 718, col. 292.
[2] Op. cit., Para. 24 at p. vi.

How far does this result in the withdrawal or significant amendment of Government bills? A number of examples can be found in recent years of bills withdrawn in response to criticism in Parliament. One may instance the Judges' Remuneration Bill in 1953, the Teachers (Superannuation) Bill and the Industrial Organization and Development Bill in 1954, and the Shops Bill in 1957. In the case of the Teachers (Superannuation) Bill, it was really a matter of suspension rather than withdrawal. The bill, which proposed to increase the proportion of teachers' contributions to superannuation from 5 per cent. to 6 per cent. of their salaries, was withdrawn in 1954 in the face of strong opposition from the teaching profession. But the bill was re-introduced and passed in the session 1955–6, and on this occasion the pill was sugared by the promise of a pay increase for teachers. The other bills were withdrawn in response to criticism from Conservative back-benchers.

It is when a government is faced with strong criticism from within the ranks of its own supporters that it is most likely to withdraw a bill. But amendment of a bill to meet criticism is much more common than withdrawal. For example, on the Rent Bill of 1956–7 a number of important amendments were accepted by the Minister or proposed by him in response to criticism. This Bill freed from rent control houses with rateable values above £40 in London or Scotland and £30 elsewhere. One amendment made during the passage of the bill through the Commons extended the security of tenure of tenants from six months, according to the bill as introduced, to fifteen months from enactment of the act. Other amendments accepted were designed in various ways to protect tenants from exploitation by landlords during the period of de-control. The amendments were stimulated by a group of Conservative back-benchers whose criticism was re-inforced by the attitude of the Labour Opposition, which was strongly critical of the bill as a whole.

A Conservative bill which was modified a great deal by amendments from the Labour side was the Offices Bill in 1962–3. Members of the Opposition in standing committee successfully moved amendments which strengthened the provisions of the bill by providing for a central as well as a Local Authority inspectorate, extended the bill's scope to coal depots and laid down more stringent safety and fire precautions. Again, a major concession was made to the critics of the Labour Government's Race Relations Bill in 1965. At second reading the bill was criticized on the grounds that it was more effective to tackle racial discrimination through a conciliation commission than by simply making it an offence at common law, as the bill proposed. This criticism was made both by Labour and Conservative back-benchers and by outside bodies such as the Campaign Against Racial Discrimination, the Institute of Race Relations and the British Caribbean Association. The Home Secretary, Sir Frank Soskice, deferred to this view and introduced amendments at committee stage which established a conciliation commission as the critics had proposed.

Many more examples could be given of amendments made in Government bills. Even where a bill is not amended in a major way, what is important is that possibilities for attempting to influence the Government, through debate, do exist and are effectively used.

For Reference

P. A. Bromhead, *Private Members' Bills in the British Parliament* (Routledge and Kegan Paul, 1956).

A. H. Hanson and H. V. Wiseman, *Parliament at Work* (Stevens, 1962).

W. I. Jennings, *Parliament*, 2nd ed. (Cambridge University Press, 1957).

Erskine May, *The Law, Privileges, Proceedings and Usages of Parliament*, 17th ed. (Butterworth, 1964).

H. Morrison, *Government and Parliament*, 3rd ed. (Oxford University Press, 1964), Chaps. X and XI.

P. G. Richards, *Honourable Members*, 2nd ed. (Faber, 1964).

K. C. Wheare, *Government by Committee* (Clarendon Press, 1955), Chap. VI.

H.C. 9-I of 1945–6. 1st Report from the Select Committee on Procedure.
H.C. 92-I of 1958–9. Report from the Select Committee on Procedure.
H.C. 149 of 1964–5. 1st Report from the Select Committee on Procedure.
H.C. 539 of 1966–7. 6th Report from the Select Committee on Procedure.
Standing Orders of The House of Commons. Public Business.

CHAPTER VI

The House of Commons and Administration

BAGEHOT could write in 1867 that 'generally the laws of a
nation suit its life; special adaptations of them are but subordinate; the administration and conduct of that life is
the matter which presses most'. Legislation nowadays bulks
much larger in the life of Parliament, but it is still true that the
debates which arouse most public interest are those which concern matters of administration and high policy. There are many
opportunities in an ordinary session of the House of Commons
for interrogating, criticizing, and attacking Ministers. Perhaps
the best known occasion, and one of the most valuable, is
Question Time.

Question Time
On every day of the Parliamentary week, except Friday, the
business of the House begins with a period of just over forty-five
minutes devoted to questions to Ministers. On Mondays,
Tuesdays, Wednesdays, and Thursdays the House meets at
2.30 p.m. After prayers and some brief and largely formal
business, Question Time begins and goes on to 3.30 p.m. Any
M.P. may put down a question to a Minister. If a Member
wants an oral answer, he must put an asterisk or 'star' against
his question and he must hand in his question to a clerk at the
Table, or in the Table Office, of the House at least 48 hours
before the time of reply.[1] This provision ensures that Ministers
have a reasonable opportunity to get replies prepared to
questions. If a Member does not star a question, he receives a
written reply which is printed in *Hansard*.

The advantage of an oral reply is that this may be followed
by supplementary questions. It is the supplementary questions
which give the chief interest to Question Time. A Minister's
answer may have been carefully prepared in his department in

[1] S.O. 8-(4).

order to avoid giving too much information or committing the Minister too clearly. The Minister reads out this answer when the number of the question is called. But the Member who has asked the question, or any other Member, may then ask supplementary questions. In these supplementaries, Members will try to probe the Minister further and sometimes to catch him off his guard.

Question hour is a testing time for a Minister. He must really know something of the background to the question he is answering. He is often the target for witticisms and raillery, and if he is a lively debater he will be prepared to give as good as he gets. A Minister wins the respect of the House if he makes a good showing at Question Time; conversely a Minister who evades the issue and is frequently ruffled by supplementaries loses its respect. A Minister can refuse to answer a question on a matter which is his responsibility by saying that it is not in the public interest for him to give an answer. But this is rarely done, because for a Minister to shelter behind the public interest is often felt to indicate a weakness in ability to handle supplementaries.

It is the cut and thrust of supplementary questions and answers which gives Question Time its dramatic quality and a high news value. Often, more space will be given in the popular newspapers to a few minutes from Question Time than to the whole of the rest of a parliamentary day. This does not indicate a distorted sense of values in relation to Question Time. The fact that a Minister is put into the limelight and made to stand up to a barrage of questioning helps to prevent highhanded action or maladministration in the departments. Question Time, of course, has its limitations. The chief one is the shortage of time allotted. Members are limited to two oral questions a day. Even so, there are usually many starred questions on the order paper which have not been answered when Question Time ends.[1] A Member whose question has not been answered orally is given a written answer unless he indicates that he wants the question postponed to another day. If a Member is persistent he can usually manage to get an oral

[1] In order to help relieve the congestion at Question Time, the Select Committee on Procedure proposed in 1959 that the number of oral questions allowed per Member per day should be reduced from 3 to 2. This proposal was accepted by the Government and Standing Orders were revised accordingly in 1960.

answer to his question in due course as a notice of the order in which Ministers will be answering questions on future days is posted in the division lobby.

Many Ministers are very effective in answering questions quickly and accurately. Their Civil Servants provide them with a well prepared file in which often a double page is set aside for each question. On the left-hand side is the answer to the question, which the Minister reads out quickly from the despatch box. On the right-hand side is material which may be useful in answering supplementaries. Ministers soon become practised in making use of this material or in turning away a supplementary with a courtesy or witticism as seems appropriate. In most cases both the first answer and the answers to supplementaries are very quickly given. But in some cases supplementaries come thick and fast at the Minister, when feelings run high and there is widespread dissatisfaction with his answer.

There is a difficulty here. Time spent on supplementaries cuts down the number of questions which can be answered in the question period. The Select Committee on Procedure in 1959 expressed the view that 'supplementary questions are more frequent and far longer, and the answers longer, than they used to be'.[1] They considered that this was the principal reason for many starred questions going unanswered every day. But supplementaries, as we have seen, are a most valuable device for cross-examining a Minister. Any restriction on supplementaries would, therefore, be undesirable. On the other hand, a Member who asks a long supplementary, which borders on a speech, is abusing the procedure of the House, and successive Speakers have tried to dissuade Members from this practice.

In 1965 the Select Committee on Procedure again considered the problem of congestion at Question Time. In their report they suggested that the maximum forward notice of questions should be twenty-one days. This was to prevent clogging of the Order Book in advance. So many Members were putting down questions well in advance that in March 1965 there were 1,149 questions down for oral answer.[2] As a result, when a

---

[1] H.C. 92-I of 1958–9, para. 38 at p. xxi.
[2] Figure quoted by the Leader of the House in the Debate on Procedure, 27 October 1965 (H.C. Deb. Vol. 718, col. 177).

question was reached it had often lost its topicality and topical questions were held back in the queue. The Leader of the House, Herbert Bowden, recommended in October 1965 that a limit of twenty-one days' forward notice should be accepted, and the House concurred in his view.[1] He did not, however, favour the other main suggestion of the Procedure Committee, which was that Members should be rationed in the number of questions, for oral answers, to eight a month.[2] He hoped that this restriction might be proved unnecessary if Members were more expeditious in asking supplementary questions.

The election of Dr. Horace King as Speaker in October 1965, coupled with a new determination on the part of Members not to abuse their rights in asking supplementaries, produced a remarkable improvement in Question Time. On 17 December 1965, the new Speaker told the House: 'In the first month of this Session, 756 Oral Questions received Oral Answers in the House. This compares with an average of about 550 in the first month of the previous 10 sessions or so and represents an increase of approximately one-third more Questions being answered in the hour.' This marked increase had been achieved through supplementary questions being on average much shorter, and not fewer.[3]

If this rate of dealing with questions can be maintained there seems little need for further rationing the number of questions which Members may ask, or for extending the time given to the question period. There are two arguments against lengthening Question Time in any considerable way. The first is that the general pressure on parliamentary time would increase. The second is that a major extension of the question period would probably detract from the interest which it at present arouses. Much of its attraction derives from the speed and liveliness with which questions are answered. If the period were to be much longer, the pace would slacken and interest would wane. One wonders, however, whether the question period should not be extended from just over forty-five minutes at present to a full hour. This suggestion was made by Tom Driberg

---

[1] H.C. Deb. Vol. 718, col. 292.

[2] H.C. 188 of 1964–5. Second Report from the Select Committee on Procedure. Question Time, p. vi at para. 8.

[3] H.C. Deb. Vol. 722, cols. 1613–15.

in the House on 8 February 1960.[1] A similar proposal was made to the Select Committee on Procedure in 1964–5 by the Study of Parliament Group.[2]

Questions to the Prime Minister can be put down on the Tuesday and Thursday of each week and are taken at 3.15 p.m. The Procedure Committee in 1959 recommended that this should be the practice. Until then, questions to the Prime Minister were not taken until Question 45. The greater time, on average, being taken on each question had resulted in this question being reached later and later in the question period. Very little time tended to be left, therefore, for questions to the Prime Minister, and many of the starred questions asked of him went unanswered. Since 1959 he has had a guaranteed fifteen minutes and thus usually has time to answer all his questions.

Question Time comes to an end at 3.30 p.m., but one type of question can be asked after 3.30 p.m. This is the private notice question. This type of question must deal with a topic that is clearly urgent in character. Instead of 48 hours' notice being required, it is only necessary for the Member to give notice of the terms of his question to the Minister, and the Speaker, not later than 12 o'clock on the day on which he is going to ask it.

In the matter of the admissibility of all types of question, the rules are carefully drawn. The governing principle is that the Minister to whom the question is addressed must be clearly responsible for the subject raised. Obviously, then, no Minister can be asked to account for the behaviour of, say, the American Secretary of State. Less obviously, Ministers in charge of departments which have a general oversight of nationalized industries cannot be asked about the day-to-day administration of those industries. This is because their control is limited by statute to general policy questions. Other rules exclude questions concerning the Sovereign and the Royal Family, foreign ambassadors, the decision of a court of law or anything

[1] H.C. Deb. Vol. 617, cols. 175–7.
[2] The Study of Parliament Group, 'Reforming the Commons' (*P.E.P. Planning*, October 1965) p. 301.

See also D. N. Chester and N. Bowring, *Questions in Parliament* (Clarendon Press, 1962), especially Chapter 12, for a discussion of the effectiveness of question time.

which is *sub judice*.[1] Despite these many restrictions, Members find little difficulty in keeping within the rules and asking questions of Ministers on a wide variety of topics for which they are responsible. The only field in which Members have felt real difficulty and resentment in recent years has been in asking questions on the nationalized industries.

Not all questions are asked by Members who are critical of a Minister's policy. Sometimes a Minister will himself arrange to be asked questions on a topic which will advertise the achievements of his department or influence opinion in a desired direction. Hugh Dalton described how he once did this. In August 1940, he was Minister of Economic Warfare. France, the Low Countries, Norway, Greece, and Yugoslavia had recently been occupied by Nazi Germany. There were voices raised in favour of applying a relaxed form of blockade to these countries which had so recently been our allies. Dalton was convinced that in the interest of weakening Nazi Germany and winning the war a strict blockade must be enforced. On 20 August Winston Churchill was to make a speech in the House arguing this point of view. Dalton described how at Question Time on that day he was asked, as Minister for Economic Warfare, a whole series of questions. He had drafted nearly all of them himself and his parliamentary private secretary had handed them out among friendly back-benchers. The questions were all designed to help emphasize the Government's case for maintaining a strict blockade.[2]

Adjournment Debates

Cases of 'planted' questions like this are not common. The great majority of questions are asked by Members who genuinely seek information or who are critical of a Minister's policy and are bringing pressure upon him to change it. A Member who is not satisfied by the answers given to his original question and to supplementaries will quite often say that he is not satisfied and that he intends 'to raise the matter on the adjournment'. Depending on the nature of the topic, he may be able to

---

[1] For further instances and discussion of inadmissible types of question see: P. G. Richards, *Honourable Members*, 2nd ed. (Faber, 1964); L. A. Abraham and S. C. Hawtrey, *A Parliamentary Dictionary*, 2nd ed. (Butterworth, 1964), pp. 169–70.

[2] Hugh Dalton, *The Fateful Years. Memoirs 1931–45* (Muller, 1957), pp. 357–8.

do this either under a special procedure under Standing Order
No. 9, or on the daily adjournment debate. An adjournment
debate takes place on a motion 'That this House do now
adjourn'. A debate opened in this way, as compared with a
debate on a reasoned motion (e.g. a motion which approves
or disapproves action by the Government, giving reasons for so
doing), has certain advantages. With a reasoned motion, nothing can be said which is not relevant to the motion, whereas
in an adjournment debate discussion is not so limited. The
Government, therefore, sometimes arranges to have a debate on
the adjournment on a major topic so as to permit a wide ranging
discussion. The debate which led to Neville Chamberlain's
resignation in May 1940 was a debate on his Government's
conduct of the war and took place on an adjournment motion.

A debate under Standing Order No. 9 is a very special kind
of adjournment debate. The Order provides that immediately
after questions a Member may move the adjournment 'for
the purpose of discussing a definite matter of urgent public
importance'. If the Speaker accepts the motion, and if forty
Members indicate their support for the motion by rising in their
places, a debate is fixed for 7 p.m. that day. At 7 p.m. the
scheduled business of the House is interrupted and the debate
takes place. The advantage of this procedure is that a full debate takes place on the same day that the motion is made and
at a time when a good attendance of Members is probable.
Debates under this Standing Order always arouse a great deal
of interest and are usually well reported in the Press. The disadvantage of this type of adjournment debate is that it dis-
rupts the timetable for the day. The Standing Order provides
that the business which has been interrupted by the debate
may be resumed when the debate is over and can go on, without any special motion, for a period long enough to make up
the lost time. Thus if the debate lasts for three hours, from
7 p.m. to 10 p.m., the resumed business can go on to 1.0 a.m.
This, besides being inconvenient for Members, poses a special
problem for the Government Whips. They must see that there
are sufficient Government supporters present to assure the
Government a majority at the end of the adjournment debate
and at any subsequent important divisions during the resumed
business. The pre-arranged timetable is all thrown out of gear,

Government supporters must be alerted and may have to be standing by for a division at a time when they thought they could be out of the House.

Partly because of its disruptive effects on the timetable, successive Speakers have tended to interpret the Standing Order in a more and more restrictive way. Before he accepts the motion the Speaker must be satisfied that the matter proposed for debate is definite, that it is urgent, and that it is important. This is laid down, as we have seen, by the Standing Order. Speakers in interpreting the Order have ruled that to be definite a motion must not be framed in general terms, but must deal with a particular case, that it must not deal with a hypothetical case or be based on uncorroborated report, and that official information must be available. To be counted urgent, the matter upon which the motion is based must have happened recently and be raised at the first opportunity, it must require the immediate attention of the House, and there must be no other opportunity in the near future to discuss it in the House. The matter must be of public importance and it must be something for which the Government is clearly responsible. It must not concern something which is *sub judice*, it must not deal with grievances which can only be remedied by legislation, it must not be a question of Parliamentary privilege, and it must not anticipate a motion which has already been scheduled for discussion by the House.[1]

The effect of these interpretations can be seen by considering some examples of motions rejected or accepted. On 2 March 1959, the Speaker refused to accept a motion for an emergency debate on the decision of the Government of the Federation of Rhodesia and Nyasaland to expel from that country a visiting British M.P., John Stonehouse. This question was urgent and important, but it was held by the Speaker not to be the responsibility of a Minister, as control of immigration had been specifically granted to the Government of the Federation by Order in Council in 1953.[2] The next day, 3 March 1959, the Speaker allowed an emergency debate on the declaration of a state of emergency in Nyasaland. This matter, besides fulfilling

[1] See Erskine May, *Parliamentary Practice*, 17th edn. (Butterworth, 1964), pp. 367-9.
[2] H.C. Deb. Vol. 601, col. 39-59.

E

all the other requirements, was clearly the responsibility of a Minister, the Colonial Secretary.[1]

On 7 December 1965 the Speaker refused to allow an emergency debate on the decision of the Wilson Government not to prevent the delivery of a cargo of oil, in a British tanker, to Beira in Mozambique. This oil was known to be destined for Southern Rhodesia, but at that time oil sanctions had not yet been applied. The Speaker refused to allow the motion for a debate, under Standing Order No. 9, since the matter had not been raised at the earliest opportunity. A question on the subject had been put on the Order Paper on the previous day. It could not, therefore, technically be classified as urgent.[2] On 8 December 1965, the Speaker refused to accept a motion for an emergency debate on the reported offer to the United States Government, by the Vietcong, of a Christmas truce in the war in Vietnam. The Speaker refused to accept this motion because it related to a matter which did not 'involve the administrative responsibilities of Her Majesty's Government'.[3]

As precedent has piled upon precedent in the interpretation of Standing Order No. 9, it has become increasingly difficult to achieve an emergency debate. The Select Committee on Procedure reported, in 1966, that in the first 20 years of this century there were 102 such debates, whereas in the 20 years between 1946 and 1966 there had only been 15. The Committee recommended that the rules should be changed 'to relieve Mr. Speaker of the need to be bound by previous interpretations of the standing order'.[4] In particular, they recommended that an emergency debate should be permissible on a matter which, although not currently a matter of ministerial responsibility, was potentially so, for example where there was a possibility of Government intervention in overseas affairs.

At present Members find great difficulty in initiating an adjournment debate under the emergency procedure. They have many more opportunities of introducing discussion on the daily adjournment debates. These debates take place after the allotted business for the day has been closed. The normal procedure

[1] H.C. Deb. Vol. 601, col. 223.
[2] H.C. Deb. Vol. 722, cols. 251–4.
[3] H.C. Deb. Vol. 722, cols. 426–7.
[4] H.C. 282 of 1966–7. Second Report from the Select Committee on Procedure, p. viii.

is for the business of the day to be interrupted at 10 p.m. A private Member then introduces a topic on the adjournment, the debate continuing until 10.30 p.m., when the Speaker rises and the House is adjourned without any vote being taken. This procedure is laid down in Standing Orders, which also provide that a Minister may move that the business of the day be excluded from the operation of the Order. In such a case Government business may go on after 10 p.m., sometimes well into the night. When, at last, that business has been completed, the adjournment debate follows for half an hour—say from 2.30 to 3 a.m. Another possibility is that Government business may end before 10 p.m. In this case, the adjournment debate may continue for longer than half an hour. The timing is different on Fridays, when normally other business ends at 4 p.m. and the adjournment debate lasts from 4 p.m. to 4.30 p.m.

There is competition among Members for the right to introduce daily adjournment debates. The time available is allotted in two ways. The subject for debate on one day in each week is selected by the Speaker from the topics put forward by Members. The right to initiate adjournment debates on the other days is decided by ballot, the ballot taking place once a fortnight to allocate the occasions for the next eight balloted days.

There is a wide variety of topics raised in these debates. Some Members raise the grievance of an individual constituent, some Members speak of the problems of their own town or region, some of a sectional interest, while some may prefer to make suggestions on a national or international question. As at Question Time, the topic raised must be the responsibility of a Minister, who is given notice so that a reply can be prepared in his Department. The spokesman is usually a Junior Minister, the Under-Secretary or Parliamentary Secretary for the Department. All that there is time for within the half-hour which is normally available is for the Member initiating the debate to introduce his topic, for one or two very brief interventions from other Members, and for the Junior Minister's reply.[1] Many daily adjournment debates can be thought of as

---

[1] On 13 July 1959, Dame Irene Ward introduced a debate at 10 p.m. on Arts Council Grants. She went on speaking until 10.30 p.m. when the Speaker rose. She thereby secured the first and last word in the argument and implied that she thought this more worthwhile than receiving a Ministerial reply. H.C. Deb. Vol. 609 cols. 169–78.

a sort of extended question. They often follow from questions that have been asked at Question Time and they enable Members to press a Minister further and to make a case and receive a reply in greater detail than is possible at Question Time.

There is no doubt that the opportunity to initiate debates on these occasions is popular with Members. But attending a daily adjournment debate introduced by another back-bencher is not so popular. Mr. Speaker Morrison, in giving evidence to the Select Committee on Procedure in 1958, said of the daily adjournment debates: 'I sit there night after night listening to them and three or four is quite a good attendance.'[1] It is understandable that at the late hour when these debates take place very few Members should be present. The thin attendances should not be held to indicate that these debates are of negligible importance. What is said in the debate appears in that day's *Hansard* and may, therefore, be read by Members who were not present. But, most important of all, it is a further opportunity to influence a Minister, part of the ceaseless effort by back-benchers to secure some modification or other of the official view or policy.

Debates in Government Time and in Opposition Time
Back-benchers initiating topics for debate come more into the limelight on the days on which the House adjourns for the Christmas, Easter, Whitsun, or summer recess. These days are wholly given over to debates initiated by back-benchers. Each day's business is rather like a string of daily adjournment debates. The Speaker allocates the time available from the list of Members who have indicated to him that they wish to introduce a topic for discussion. Debates on the ten Fridays allotted to Private Members' motions are similar in character.[2] These are the principal occasions when debates on aspects of policy and administration can be introduced by back-benchers.

Other debates can be classified as debates in Government time or debates in Opposition time. The first category are

[1] H.C. 92-I of 1958-9, p. 141 at Question 891.
[2] In response to the feeling that more time should be found for Private Members' motions, in addition to the ten reserved Fridays, the Macmillan Government allotted four half-days for this purpose in the session 1959–60. In subsequent sessions Governments have continued to give similar extra opportunities to Private Members.

debates which the Government finds time for because it wants the House to consider and approve some action by the Government, for example, an international settlement or negotiation. Or the Government may find time for a debate which the Opposition asks for to challenge some action or alleged inaction of the Government. The Leader of the House need not find time for such a debate but he normally will do so, particularly if the Leader of the Opposition can make out a reasonable case for the debate, on the grounds that there is public anxiety on the subject.

Negotiations go on between the Leader of the House and the Government Chief Whip on the one side, and the Leader of the Opposition and the Opposition Chief Whip on the other.[1] These are the 'usual channels' which are often referred to in the House. If agreement cannot be reached 'through the usual channels', the Leader of the Opposition may protest in the House either when the Leader of the House announces on a Thursday afternoon what is the business for the coming week, or at some other time. Normally, there is much give and take between the Leaders on the two sides. The duty of the Leader of the House is to get his Government's programme through; the duty of the Leader of the Opposition is to criticize that programme and sometimes to prevent its passage. Their interests would seem to be diametrically opposed, but both recognize the overriding duty to preserve the fabric of parliamentary government. So the Leader of the House will find time for debates the Opposition wants, while the Leader of the Opposition will only press opposition into obstruction at times of exceptionally strong feeling and difference of view. This tolerant attitude is, in the main, reinforced if the parties alternate in office fairly frequently.

[1] The Leader of the House was formerly the Prime Minister, if the Prime Minister was a Member of the House of Commons. Nowadays, the Leader of the House is always one of the Prime Minister's senior colleagues in the Cabinet. For example, Herbert Morrison was Lord President of the Council and Leader of the House from 1945 to 1951 in the Attlee Government. Harry Crookshank was Lord Privy Seal and Leader of the House under Churchill from 1951 to 1955, and R. A. Butler was Leader of the House in the Eden and Macmillan administrations from 1955 to 1961 while holding the offices first of Lord Privy Seal alone and then that of Lord Privy Seal and Home Secretary concurrently. Iain Macleod was Leader of the House from 1961 to 1963 and was succeeded by Selwyn Lloyd. In the Wilson Government, Herbert Bowden was Leader of the House from October 1964 to August 1966 when he was succeeded by Richard Crossman.

When the Opposition puts down a motion of censure on the Government, the convention is that the Government always finds time for it to be debated. To put down such a motion, therefore, is to ensure a debate. But the wise Leader of the Opposition will not put down censure motions too frequently or he runs the risk of making himself look ridiculous. For the censure motion is the heaviest artillery of criticism, it implies that the Government has lost the confidence of the country as a result of the action complained of in the motion.

Sometimes the Leader of the House will suggest that if the Opposition want a debate on a subject they should 'use one of their Supply days'. The Supply days have come to be regarded as Opposition time. Nominally, Supply days are concerned with financial business. The business before the House is to consider the Estimates of expenditure submitted by Ministers for their departments. But these Estimates are nowadays regarded as pegs upon which to hang debates on aspects of administration in the departments. There is normally only occasional and incidental reference to financial questions. The chief difference between debate on a Supply day and a debate in Government time is that the Leader of the Opposition chooses which Estimates shall be debated on which Supply day and, therefore, chooses the topic for debate. There are twenty-nine days in every session allotted by Standing Order to the business of Supply.[1]

The quality of debate on major policy questions, both in Government time and on Supply days, is often very high. There are two main lines of criticism which are made against these, the most important of all Parliamentary debates. The first is that so much time is taken up by the leading figures in the House. The Minister introducing the debate will often speak for nearly an hour, there may follow a long speech from the Opposition Shadow Minister. The debate may be wound up with a speech from the Leader of the Opposition followed by a reply from the Prime Minister. The order of speaking and the rank of Ministers taking part will vary greatly, but the general pattern is for a Minister and an Opposition front-bencher to

---

[1] On 14 December 1966 the House voted to amend S.O. 18 to increase the number of days allotted to Supply from 26 to 29. The Committee procedure for Supply was also abolished.

open and close the debate. In between, there is not a great deal of time left for other Members to contribute to the debate, and in this remaining period Privy Councillors often take a prominent part. All former Ministers are Privy Councillors and by custom they are given priority over other Members in the debate by the Speaker or Chairman. Consequently, Members who are not Privy Councillors find it difficult 'to catch the Speaker's eye' and contribute to the debate. Many a time a back-bencher, who thinks he has something important to say, will come with a speech prepared and not be called upon to make it.

This sort of experience has given rise to much frustration among back-benchers in recent years. Criticism on these lines was frequently voiced in the debate on 31 January 1958, which led to the setting up of a Select Committee on Procedure and in the letters to *The Times* which preceded this debate.[1] But it is easier to criticize than to make sound suggestions for improvement. The House and the interested public often want a full statement from the Minister. Equally, the Opposition speakers need time in which to develop their challenge to the Government and to make clear what their alternative policy would be. It would not seem desirable, therefore, to impose a time limit on front-bench speakers. The Select Committee on Procedure took this view in 1959, but asked the front-benchers on both sides to give a lead in keeping speeches as short as possible. They also recommended that Privy Councillors should no longer be given automatic priority over other Members in debate. The Macmillan Government did not accept this suggestion in 1960. R. A. Butler, as Leader of the House, said in the debate on the Procedure Report, that he thought that Privy Councillors' rights in debate should be retained but that the Speaker should use his discretion sometimes to call a private Member, 'when, for example, there is a string of Privy Councillors waiting to intervene and it is impossible for a private member to get in'.[2]

The Macmillan Government also rejected the Committee's

---

[1] See H.C. Deb. Vol. 581 Cols. 669 to 771.

Letters by Members to *The Times* among the following issues: 28 and 31 December 1957, 3, 6, 8, 10, and 23 January 1958.

[2] H.C. Deb. Vol. 617, Col. 40.

proposal for a time limit on speeches. The Committee had recommended the adoption of a suggestion made by a Labour M.P., Reginald Paget, that an hour should be set aside in major debates for brief speeches. These speeches should be limited to five minutes, and by convention they should not be interrupted by questions or interventions from other Members. This proposal had a mixed reception in the Commons. It was ridiculed by Sidney Silverman, for example, as 'Parliamentary Children's Hour'.[1] But many Members who thought five minutes too short a period, have favoured the principle of a time limit. In the debate of 8 February 1960, two Conservatives, Thomas Iremonger and Sir W. Robson Brown, spoke in favour of a ten-minute limit for back-benchers; another Conservative, John Hall, favoured fifteen minutes.[2]

In December 1963, more than 100 Members signed a Motion in favour of acceptance of the 1959 Procedure Committee's proposals for an hour of brief speeches during major debates. In the debate on Procedure on 27 October 1965, a Conservative Member, Edward Gardner, recalled this fact and reiterated the need for a time limit on speeches. A Labour Member, Trevor Park, expressed similar views. The Leader of the House, Herbert Bowden, in replying to the debate, said that he would be willing to experiment with an hour of five-minute speeches during major debates.[3] Nothing came of this suggestion, however, and in the following year the Procedure Committee changed their approach and proposed that, as an experiment, back-benchers should be limited to fifteen-minute speeches and front-benchers to thirty-minutes, extra time being allowed to make up for interruptions.[4] On 19 April 1967 the Leader of the House, Richard Crossman, announced that the Speaker was going to experiment with a fifteen-minute time limit for back-bench speeches during some major debates.[5]

The second line of criticism nowadays often heard about major debates is that too much has been pre-arranged in the

---

[1] H.C. Deb. Vol. 617, Col. 41.

[2] H.C. Deb. Vol. 617, Cols. 100–1, Col. 104, Col. 112.

[3] H.C. Deb. Vol. 718, Cols. 277, 258, and 282.

[4] H.C. 153 of 1966–7. First Report from the Select Committee on Procedure, para. 8 at p. vii.

[5] H.C. Deb. Vol. 744, Cols. 600–1.

Party committee meetings which precede these debates. The really keen debates, it is claimed, take place behind closed doors in meetings of Conservative and Labour Members. These meetings decide the line which the Party will take in the House, and individual Party members who disapprove of that line are under pressure not to speak against it and, even more, not to vote against it. The accuracy of this picture will be examined more fully in the next chapter.[1] Here what can be said is that many debates on major issues still excite great interest; they help to influence the Government and to educate public opinion. Debates in two international crises since 1945 can be taken as examples.

During the Suez crisis in November 1956, there was a series of debates in which the Labour Opposition, led by Hugh Gaitskell, set out in the clearest terms their disapproval of the Anglo-French landing at Port Said and the attempt to occupy the Suez Canal zone. After only eight days of operations, the British and French Governments announced a cease-fire and the withdrawal of their troops.

How far was this *volte-face* produced by the outcry raised in the British Parliament? Certainly there were other major influences on the Government. The United Nations Assembly voted a resolution calling on Britain and France to cease fire. The President of the United States, President Eisenhower, opposed the British intervention as did the Governments of all the British Dominions, except Australia and New Zealand. The American Administration also refused to give financial assistance to Britain in stemming a run on the pound which began after the Anglo-French landing. Finally, the Russian Premier, Marshal Bulganin, sent a message in which he warned Britain and France that Russia would intervene militarily against them if British and French troops were not withdrawn from Egypt. Opposition in the House of Commons was not then the main reason for the British withdrawal. But it played an important part, particularly since to the criticism of the Labour Opposition was added that of a group of Conservative Members, including two junior Ministers, Anthony Nutting and Sir Edward Boyle, who resigned from the Government when the ultimatum that preceded the landings was sent

[1] See below pp. 175–83.

to Egypt.[1] The world knew and the Government knew that Britain was deeply divided over the Suez intervention. The House of Commons played its part in acting as a major forum of debate and influence on the Government.

A Middle Eastern crisis in 1958 also proved to be of great interest in assessing the modern role of the House. On 17 July, British parachute troops were flown into Amman, the capital of Jordan, in response to an appeal from the King of Jordan for British protection against moves from Iraq, where a revolutionary regime had just taken control and assassinated both the King and the Prime Minister, Nuri-es-Said. A debate took place the same day in the House of Commons. In the debate, Hugh Gaitskell, as Leader of the Opposition, challenged the wisdom of this intervention and urged the Government to suggest a Summit Conference on the Middle Eastern crisis.[2] The situation was made more dangerous by the fact that a few days earlier the United States had landed troops in the Lebanon in response to an appeal from the Lebanese President for support against armed insurrection in his country. The Soviet Government had shown its hostility to both the American and British interventions. Three days after Gaitskell's speech in the House of Commons, the British Prime Minister, Harold Macmillan, received a telegram from Krushchev proposing a Summit Conference on the Middle East. The British Government accepted the proposal with, of course, the full support of the Labour Opposition. In fact, the Summit Conference on the Middle East never took place, but the proposal, and its acceptance by Britain and the United States, relaxed international tension over the Middle East. The turn of events was quite different from the crisis over Suez in 1956. But again it is clear that a debate in the House of Commons had an important influence on the Government and on British policy in the crisis.

Some of the most important debates in the session 1958–9 were on the Central African Federation. In March 1959 the Labour Opposition strongly criticized the declaration of a state of emergency in Nyasaland and the detention, without trial,

---

[1] Anthony Nutting resigned as Minister of State for Foreign Affairs and Sir Edward Boyle from his post as Economic Secretary to the Treasury.

[2] H.C. Deb. Vol. 591, Cols. 1512–18.

of many hundred members of the African Congress there.[1]
Leading Labour and Liberal spokesmen suggested that a Commission should be sent out to try to determine if the repressive
measures taken by the Government had been justified. The
Government agreed to appoint an independent commission
under the Chairmanship of Mr. Justice Devlin. When the
Commission's report was published in July 1959, it gave only
qualified approval to the Government's policy and strongly
criticized the repressive character of measures taken against
Congress members. The Government did not accept the criticisms in the Report and another lively debate took place in the
Commons in which the Labour Opposition and the Liberals
urged the Government to accept the report as a whole.[2]

In this example, again, we can see the Government being, to
some extent, influenced by the Opposition. But in the main, it is
an illustration of the Government and the Opposition being
unable to reconcile their differences. Nevertheless, both the
debates in March and July 1959 were very valuable in making
clear to the British people what was being done in Nyasaland
and the contrasting attitudes which the Government and the
Opposition took to the situation there. After the general election in October 1959, African questions soon ceased to be a
subject of major contention in the Commons. The Conservative Government decided to give independence to Nyasaland
and Northern Rhodesia and to agree to the dissolution of the
Central African Federation. This fully accorded with Labour
policy. Some grumblings of dissent were heard from the Conservative back-benchers, but, in general, a bi-partisan attitude
on these questions emerged.

The major debates in the period 1959–64 were on economic
questions, on Macmillan's attempt to take Britain into the
European Economic Community, and on defence. On none of
these issues were passions aroused to quite the intensity previously seen in the debates on Suez, or on African affairs before
October 1959. Frequently there were cross-currents in the
major parties, especially on the question of entry into the
Common Market, with neither party standing solidly for or
against entry into the E.E.C. Debates on these issues were, on

[1] H.C. Deb. Vol. 601, Cols. 279–342.
[2] H.C. Deb. Vol. 610, Cols. 317–444.

the whole, at a high standard, but an exception must be made here in the case of debates on defence. On defence matters, the Commons is often at a great disadvantage because not enough of the facts of the situation are known to M.P.s who are not in the Government. In this period, debates on defence seemed to become more and more unrealistic and often frustrating to leading members of the Opposition and to the interested public.

It is not possible for the period from October 1964 to July 1967 to say that certain topics tended to dominate debates in the House. There were important debates on economic policy, foreign affairs, defence and the social services. With the Wilson Government's decision in May 1967 to apply for membership of the Common Market, this question became the main focus of interest, as it had been in 1962. The Commons had a three-day debate from 8th to 10th May 1967 on the Government's decision. All the main trends of opinion were heard in this debate and the general quality of discussion was high.

Defence questions apart, major debates in the Commons since the Second World War have reached a generally high standard. They have educated the public. They have not excited quite the interest they did in Bagehot's day because they have not been preludes to 'the deciding catastrophes of cabinet government'. Yet one debate in 1963 did have something of this character. This was the debate on 17 June 1963, on Macmillan's handling, as Prime Minister, of Security in the Profumo case.[1]

The complications of this affair were considerable. The essential points, however, were as follows. On 22 March 1963, the Secretary of State for War, John Profumo, made a statement to the House of Commons in which he denied rumours about him that had been raised in the Commons. In particular, he denied that there was any impropriety in his association with Christine Keeler. Less than three months later, after more of the facts of the case had come to light, he admitted that this statement of his to the Commons had been untrue. He submitted his resignation to the Prime Minister on 4 June 1963, and it was accepted.

The Prime Minister, in the Commons debate, was criticized by the Labour Opposition and the Liberal Leader, Jo Grimond,

[1] H.C. Deb. Vol. 169, Cols. 34–170.

for not having asked for Profumo's resignation at an earlier stage. The Security Services, which are responsible to the Prime Minister, had known for some months that Profumo had been friendly with Christine Keeler, and her friend Dr. Stephen Ward, both of whom had also been seeing a great deal of a Russian naval attaché, Captain Ivanov. In fact, Christine Keeler was concurrently Ivanov's mistress. The Opposition's case was that the Prime Minister had handled the question incompetently. The debate excited very great public interest. It was clear that what was at issue was not the future of the Government but of the Prime Minister. Four Conservative back-benchers in the debate added their criticism to that of the Opposition. In the division at the end of the debate it was seen that the Government's majority had fallen from its nominal 97 to 69. It was estimated that 27 Conservative M.P.s had deliberately abstained in the division. In the course of the debate, one of the Conservative critics, Nigel Birch, a former Minister, had said that the Prime Minister should make way for a much younger colleague. Although Macmillan did not, in fact, resign until October 1963, and then on grounds of ill health, the debate, and the falling off of support which it revealed, had been a major setback to him.

Sources of Information for M.P.s

If the quality of debates is to be kept high, M.P.s must be well informed. Members get information at Question Time and from written answers to questions. Something also can be gleaned from the debates themselves. In addition, there are three main sources of information for Members. First, the Government itself provides information in the form of White Papers which may contain statements, with explanation, of intended policy, or may be largely factual. Some of these White Papers are periodic, some *ad hoc*. An example of the first type is the annual White Paper on Defence. This White Paper gives Members some insight into the defence position, as the Government sees it, and is regularly followed by a debate on defence policy. Until 1963 the Government produced, in a similar way, an Economic Survey which appeared before the Budget and helped to make more fully informed the subsequent discussion of the Budget in the Commons. It was discontinued by

Reginald Maudling, as Chancellor, because the forecasts in some previous years' surveys had proved to be very inaccurate. This was an unfortunate step, as the Economic Survey was a valuable contribution to debate.

Valuable although such White Papers are, it would not be enough if information were confined to what the Government is prepared to volunteer. There are two important independent sources of information. One of these is the reports of Royal Commissions and other independent committees set up to carry out inquiries and make recommendations. Recent examples are the Royal Commissions on Population and on Local Government in Greater London, and the Robbins Committee on Higher Education. Such committees are, of course, only set up if the Government agrees. They are indeed commissioned by the Crown, in the case of Royal Commissions, or by Ministers. But they always contain some independent and eminent people and their reports may not accord with the views of Government. In many cases they are commissioned because the Government itself is undecided and is willing that a problem should be carefully investigated and the various solutions publicly canvassed. Royal Commissions and their like, therefore, fit a special need. There remains a need for more continuous information about the activities of the Government, a need which is in part met by the reports of two Committees of the Commons. These are the Public Accounts Committee and the Estimates Committee.

These two committees form an important part, perhaps the most important part nowadays, of the apparatus by which the House controls expenditure in the departments. Put simply, the finance of Government has two sides—taxation and expenditure. The expenditure side can be divided again into the voting of sums of money by the House to the departments, and the actual spending of the money voted.

Over taxation the House still retains considerable control. The Government's proposals for taxation for the financial year are embodied in the Finance Bill. This Bill is preceded by the Budget resolutions which give immediate effect to the changes in taxation proposed by the Chancellor of the Exchequer in his Budget speech. Both the Budget resolutions and the Finance Bill are debated at great length by the whole House, sitting as Committee of Ways and Means. The Budget is normally introduced in April, and between then and the early part of July the bulk of the time of the House is taken up in discussing the Budget and Finance Bill. Members may move amendments to the smallest detail of proposed taxation. For example, back-benchers have moved that the purchase tax on saucepans be reduced and that the allowance of duty-free tobacco for old-age pensioners be increased. The Chancellor sometimes makes concessions to Members moving such amendments if he feels they have made a good case and if he has some scope for reductions in his tax programme.

The control exercised by the whole House over taxation is, therefore, detailed and effective. Its control over the allocation of money to the departments is much less close. The estimates of expenditure by each department are considered by the whole House when debating Supply. These Supply days are largely given over nowadays to discussion of administration in the departments. This is inevitable in view of the complexity of modern estimates. It would be impossible for the whole House to discuss coherently the complex pattern of expenditure of a modern department. This would be regrettable if there were no detailed control of expenditure by the House. In fact, detailed control is exerted through smaller bodies of M.P.s organized in the Committee of Public Accounts and the Estimates Committee.

The Public Accounts Committee

The Public Accounts Committee is the older of the two committees. It was first set up in 1861, and has had a continuous history ever since. It consists of fifteen Members of the House of Commons nominated in proportion to the party strengths in the full House. The Chairman is always a member of the Opposition and is usually a specialist in economic or financial questions. Its last three chairmen have been: Harold Wilson (1959–63), Douglas Houghton (1963–4) and John Boyd-Carpenter (1964–   ).

The Committee is assisted by the Comptroller and Auditor-General, who is an official of very great importance and unique position. He is an independent officer of the Crown. Independent in the sense that whereas Civil Servants hold office during pleasure (that is, theoretically they can be dismissed by the Government at any time), he holds office during good behaviour and, like a judge, can only be removed by the Crown on an address from both Houses of Parliament. As his title implies, he has two functions—that of Comptroller and that of Auditor. As Comptroller he controls the issue of public money from the Consolidated Fund to the departments. This control consists in keeping a watch on the money drawn from the Consolidated Fund and seeing to it that no more is drawn for any department than has been authorized by Parliament. His second function, that of Auditor, is even more valuable. He has a staff of more than 500 who are continuously at work auditing the accounts of the departments. As a result of this audit, he makes a report to the House of Commons, and this report forms the starting-point of the inquiries made by the Committee of Public Accounts.

In his audit, the Comptroller and Auditor-General is concerned above all with two things: first, whether the money has been spent as Parliament intended and, second, whether the departments have practised due economy. If there were no check on the way in which the money was spent by the departments, Parliamentary control of expenditure could become a mockery. Money voted for education could be spent on missiles, and that for hospitals on submarines. Such a crude transfer of funds is prevented by the Comptroller and Auditor-General in his function as Comptroller. It would still be possible for a department within its Vote, authorized by Parliament, to switch money from one sub-head to another. But elaborate regulations limit a department's freedom to do this. If, for example, the Ministry of Education finds during the financial year that it is going to have a surplus in the amount voted for school meals, it may not simply use the surplus to increase expenditure on educational research. It must first secure the consent of the Treasury to such a transfer, or virement, as it is called. Sometimes the Treasury will not give consent but will insist on the department concerned submitting a Supplementary Estimate to Parliament. It will so insist, for example, when the proposed new expenditure seems to be quite unforeseen in the estimates originally voted.

The Comptroller and Auditor-General looks in his audit for

cases of unauthorized virement or for virement which has been authorized by the Treasury but is not in his opinion justified. He mentions all such cases in his report. The Public Accounts Committee then summons the accounting officers of the departments concerned to appear before it and to explain their actions. The accounting officers are, in most cases, the Permanent Secretaries of the departments (in the case of departments whose Minister has the title of Secretary of State, the permanent head of the department is called the Permanent Under-Secretary). They, of course, do not like to incur a rebuke from the Committee. The system, therefore, gives a powerful inducement to the permanent heads of departments to try and avoid frequent virement. Similarly, it is a powerful incentive to them to prevent extravagance in their departments. For the Comptroller and Auditor-General is as active in exposing cases of extravagance as in pointing to irregular procedures, and it is probably even more damaging for a Permanent Secretary to be censured by the Committee for extravagance in his department.

Inevitably, the Committee is concerned chiefly with past expenditure. It does not begin its work until the audit has been completed and the Auditor-General's report compiled. It is in the main, therefore, looking at expenditure which has been voted by Parliament two years ago. But it does not look only at past expenditure and, nowadays, it frequently makes recommendations for future economies. For example, the Committee reported in the Session 1957–8 that, in its opinion, dispensing chemists had been making a concealed profit of around 14 per cent in making up prescriptions under the National Health Service. These unintended profits were being secured as a result of discounts made to the chemists by the manufacturers, discounts which had not been envisaged when the Drug Tariff had been drawn up by the Ministry of Health. The Committee recommended that there should be some immediate general reduction in the Drug Tariff and that further inquiries should be made to establish the extent of profits being made through discounts.[1]

The Committee has since returned to the question of the high cost of prescriptions in the National Health Service on several

---

[1] H.C. 256-I of 1957–8. 3rd Report from the Committee on Public Accounts, pp. xxviii and xxix.

occasions. In its 3rd Report for 1961–2 the Committee pointed out that in 1961 British pharmaceutical firms had spent £6,500,000 on sales promotion. The Committee suggested that the Ministry of Health should make strenuous efforts to induce the drug firms to eliminate excessive sales promotion activities and thereby bring about a lowering of the level of drug prices.

In its 3rd Report for 1962–3, the Committee pointed to the very high price of certain branded preparations. For example, one drug with a brand name, widely used in the National Health Service, was three times the price of the exact unbranded equivalent preparation.[1] Not surprisingly, the Committee found that some of the pharmaceutical firms were making extraordinarily high profits. In 1961, in a debate on the reports of the Public Accounts Committee, Harold Wilson pointed to the fact that eight subsidiaries of American firms had on average made nearly 73 per cent profit on capital employed, while British-owned companies had made profits averaging 20 per cent.[2] The Committee has performed a most valuable service in this field, keeping up a constant pressure on the Ministry of Health and urging it in a variety of ways to bring down the cost of drugs.

In a quite different field, the Committee pointed in the session 1958–9 to the very large profits being earned by the television programme companies under contract to the Independent Television Authority. The rentals paid by these companies to the Authority were very low in relation to the profits made, and the Committee recommended that, in future, rentals should be arrived at by competitive tender. In this way, a higher proportion of the profits of commercial television would be channelled to the Exchequer.[3] Although this specific proposal was not followed up, the Government was stimulated to examine other ways of increasing public revenue from the television companies. From 1961 to 1963 a Television Advertisement Duty was levied on the companies as a temporary provision. In 1963 the Television Act provided that rental payments were to be related to the net advertising receipts of the

---

[1] H.C. 275 of 1962–3. 3rd Report from the Committee on Public Accounts.
[2] H.C. Deb. Vol. 650, Cols. 645–6.
[3] H.C. 248 of 1958–9. 3rd Report from the Committee on Public Accounts.

companies. This brought a large increase of revenue to the Exchequer, while the companies still retained comfortable profits.

The Public Accounts Committee also did a valuable service in pointing to the constantly escalating costs of the development of guided missiles. In 1960, the Chairman of the Committee commented that Sea Slug, which had been estimated to cost between £1,000,000 and £1,500,000 to develop, was in fact going to cost over £40,000,000. Thunderbird, which was estimated to cost £2,500,000, was going to cost £40,000,000; and Firestreak, estimated to cost £4,000,000, was to cost £33,000,000.[1] The Committee called for new methods of estimating and control. It found an even costlier failure to estimate realistically in the case of the Bluestreak rocket project. The original estimate of the cost of this project was £50,000,000. By 1960, when it was largely abandoned, the estimated cost had grown to between £280,000,000 and £310,000,000.[2]

The Committee was also on the lookout for excessive profits being made by companies engaged in developing missiles. It found an outstanding case in 1964 when examination of the accounts revealed that Ferranti, the electronics firm, had made a profit of £4,500,000 in developing the Bloodhound Mk. I guided weapon. The Committee reckoned that this represented a profit of 63 per cent. on cost, and found this to be excessive.[3] In this case, the company concerned, after publication of the Committee's report and a debate on it in the Commons, agreed to return £2,250,000 of the profit it had made to the Treasury. It is apparent how important the Public Accounts Committee now is in the parliamentary scrutiny of expenditure.

The Estimates Committee
Alongside the Public Accounts Committee, and performing different but related functions, is the Estimates Committee. This Committee starts its work with the current estimates from the departments. It is, therefore, concerned to a greater extent with current expenditure and administration. The Committee came into being in 1912 and functioned until the outbreak of the First World War in 1914. It was revived

---

[1] H.C. Deb. Vol. 632, Col. 904.
[2] H.C. Deb. Vol. 650, Col. 651.
[3] H.C. 183 of 1963-4. 2nd Report from the Committee of Public Accounts.

after the War in 1921 and was continued until 1939 when the Second World War brought an end to its activities. In 1946 it was again revived and has continued to be appointed each session. But whereas the Public Accounts Committee was, early in its history, recognized to be doing valuable work, the Estimates Committee has had a more chequered career. In fact, it is only since 1946 that it has been considered a real success.

The reason for its increase in prestige lies in a change of approach which was made in 1946, although there had been glimmerings of a change before the Second World War. Until 1931 the Committee confined itself to the volumes of estimates. It would compare the current estimate for a particular service with the estimate for the previous year. If an increase in expenditure was proposed it would inquire into the reasons for an increase. This was a generally unprofitable approach because exactly the same sort of inquiry is undertaken by the Treasury every year before the estimates reach the House of Commons. However, in 1931 the Committee began to undertake general reviews of administrative activities. For example, in the session 1931-2 it produced a good report on borrowing by local authorities. The Committee was beginning to find its feet and acquire greater prestige.[1]

It was war-time experience which showed the way even more clearly. During the war, detailed estimates were not published for security reasons. An Estimates Committee was not, therefore, appointed, but in order to secure some general oversight of current expenditure a National Expenditure Committee was set up in 1939 and functioned until 1945. There had been a similar committee between 1917 and 1920, but the committee in the Second World War proved especially vigorous and successful. It undertook a whole series of inquiries into the general problems of war-time administration. It issued some excellent reports on such subjects as the training and supply of labour, and on other factors affecting output in industry. These reports were not only very informative to Members of the House of Commons but were often valuable to the Government. They dealt with topics which were at the root of many of the most

[1] See Basil Chubb, *The Control of Public Expenditure*, (Clarendon Press, 1952), pp. 131-3.

crucial difficulties which faced the Government on the home front. In order to speed up its inquiries, the Committee made extensive use of sub-committees and these sub-committees frequently visited factories, training schools, military establishments—anywhere where they felt they must see for themselves before sizing up a problem. They also took evidence from many people outside the Government service—from industrialists, trade unionists, managers, scientists—and took expert opinion of all kinds.

The Estimates Committee, revived in 1946, was aware of the achievements of the National Expenditure Committee and has, to a large extent, modelled itself upon it. It, too, has made extensive use of sub-committees, and the sub-committees have often been to see for themselves, and interview people on the spot. They have also taken evidence from many witnesses outside the Civil Service. The inquiries the Committee has made, although not so far ranging as many of those undertaken by the National Expenditure Committee, have dealt with large and important questions. The Committee now has forty-three members.[1] It is nominated in proportion to the party strengths in the full House of Commons. Its chairman is not, as is the chairman of the Public Accounts Committee, a member of the Opposition. He is a back-bencher on the Government side of the House. Since 1964 the chairman has been William Hamilton.

The Committee divides into seven sub-committees. In considering the sub-committee organization, we must distinguish between the periods before and after December 1965. In the earlier period the sub-committees were not specialized. They were lettered A to G. Sub-Committee A was a steering committee, and sub-committee G looked at the supplementary estimates. The other sub-committees investigated fields of expenditure according to the interest of each sub-committee chairman (subject to the approval of the steering committee). Since December 1965, the steering and supplementary estimate sub-committees have continued, but the other five sub-committees have been allotted specified fields of expenditure. The grouping is as follows: Defence and Overseas Affairs, Economic Affairs, Social Affairs, Technological and Scientific

[1] In 1960 the Estimates Committee was increased in size from 36 to 43 members.

Affairs, and Building and Natural Resources.[1] The chairmen of sub-committees are in some cases supporters of the Government and in some cases Opposition Members. In December 1965, three of the specialized sub-committees were chaired by Labour Members and two by Conservatives. The supplementary estimates sub-committee was chaired by a Conservative, and the chairman of the steering sub-committee was the chairman of the Estimates Committee itself, William Hamilton.

We have seen that the topics for inquiry are suggested by the chairmen of each sub-committee. The chairmen seem, in general, to have wanted to look at sectors in which there might be room for greater economy or more efficient administration. Thus, in the sessions 1946–7 and 1947–8, the Committee made a series of inquiries into aspects of civil aviation. They inquired first into the general question of Government oversight of the nationalized airways corporations, and then turned to examine in detail the construction of the Brabazon I, and similar types of aircraft, and of London Airport.[2] These were fields in which current and proposed expenditure was very heavy and the prospects of the nation getting value for money seemed very uncertain. Here the Committee was able to give some useful guidance to Parliamentary and public opinion. It concluded that the gigantic Brabazon air-liner would not be an economic development, but that the money spent on it was not entirely wasted as the project had yielded much information about the handling of large aircraft which would be of value in developing large, but not monster, types such as the Britannia.

On the construction of London Airport, the Committee's verdict was more favourable The expenditure involved seemed lavish and the scale on which the Airport was being planned appeared immense by pre-war standards. But the Committee accepted, rightly, as subsequent events showed, the argument of witnesses who claimed that the Airport needed to be as large

[1] See H.C. 21 of 1965–6. First Special Report from the Estimates Committee. Appointment of Sub-Committees and Allocation of Estimates to Sub-Committees.

[2] H.C. 144 of 1946–7. 6th Report from the Select Committee on Estimates. Civil Aviation.

H.C. 98 of 1947–8. 2nd Report. Cost of Construction of Brabazon I and Other Similar Types of Civil Aircraft.

H.C. 202 of 1947–8. 8th Report. Construction of London Airport.

as planned in order to cope with the expected increase of international traffic in the next decade. In the session 1960–1, the Committee returned to this subject and inquired into the working of London's airports. It suggested that an independent statutory authority should be set up to run the airports instead of their being under the direct control of the Ministry of Aviation.[1] The Government accepted this recommendation.

In the sessions 1956–7, the Committee made an inquiry into the supply of military aircraft. The Committee examined the Government's practice, at that time, of subsidizing the simultaneous development of two or more different aircraft with the same or similar specifications. It concluded that the simultaneous development of the Victor and Vulcan bombers had not been a mistake, but it condemned the continuation of orders for the Supermarine Swift when another fighter, the Hawker Hunter, had proved itself undoubtedly superior. It also condemned the placing of orders for many different types of helicopter. It recommended that fewer projected aircraft should be subsidized in future and it encouraged the Government's efforts to promote amalgamation of the aircraft firms into larger units.[2]

An equally far-ranging inquiry into the development of transport aircraft was made by the Committee in the session 1963–4. Some of the most interesting sections of its report dealt with the Anglo-French Concord project. The Committee criticized the Treasury for failing to take part in the initial negotiations with the French Government in preparing the agreement for the joint construction of this supersonic transport aircraft, whose cost of development, for the two countries, was thought likely to be around £170,000,000.[3] On the British side, the agreement had been prepared only by representatives of the Ministry of Aviation; the Treasury being kept informed.

The Committee considered that the Treasury should have taken a direct part in the negotiations. It was also critical of the terms of the agreement and particularly of the absence of

[1] H.C. 223 of 1960–1. 5th Report from the Estimates Committee. London's Airports.
[2] H.C. 34 of 1956–7. Second Report from Select Committee on Estimates. The Supply of Military Aircraft.
[3] On 19 October 1966 the Minister of Aviation announced that the latest estimate for the cost of development of the Concord was £500 million.

any break-clause providing for the contingency of a withdrawal of either country from the scheme.[1] The Treasury, in its reply to the Committee's criticism, rejected the suggestion that it should have taken a direct part in the negotiations, but, significantly, announced that in future the Treasury would be represented on the Anglo-French committee of officials supervising the Concord project.[2]

One of the most influential reports produced by the Estimates Committee was its report in 1958 on Treasury control of expenditure. The Committee voiced grave doubts whether the methods used by the Treasury, many of which had been introduced at a time when Government expenditure played a relatively small part in the national economy, were appropriate to the middle of the twentieth century. It recommended that a small independent committee should be set up to report 'on the theory and practice of Treasury control of expenditure'.[3] The Government did not set up an independent committee but instead commissioned an internal inquiry under the chairmanship of Lord Plowden. This group, partly of senior officials from the Treasury and other Departments, partly of outside authorities, reported to the Chancellor of the Exchequer in June 1961.[4] A year later the Treasury was re-organized to a large extent along the lines which the Plowden Committee recommended.[5]

The extent to which Governments accept recommendations made by the Committee varies very widely. On the one hand one can instance the Committee's report in the session 1956–7 on Her Majesty's Stationery Office.[6] The Committee made seven recommendations for changes in Stationery Office administration. The Treasury and the Controller of the Stationery Office accepted four of these and promised that a fifth should

[1] H.C. 42 of 1963–4. 2nd Report from the Estimates Committee. Transport Aircraft.

[2] H.C. 241 of 1963–4. 7th Special Report from the Estimates Committee. Transport Aircraft.

[3] H.C. 254 of 1957–8. 6th Report from the Select Committee on Estimates. Treasury control of expenditure.

[4] Cmnd. 1432. Control of Public Expenditure.

[5] See below Chapter XV.

[6] H.C. 33 of 1956–7. First Report from the Select Committee on Estimates. Her Majesty's Stationery Office.

receive careful consideration.[1] At the other extreme the Minister of Transport, Harold Watkinson, in July 1959 received the Committee's report on Trunk Roads with indignation. 'I will not accept the criticisms and intend to press on,' he was reported as saying. 'I can see no cause to make any change and don't propose to do so.' He claimed that the Committee's report was 'extremely misleading and inaccurate' and entirely rejected its contention that there had been no adequate national plan for developing trunk roads and that as a result there had been, in the Committee's words, 'an over-emphasis on motorways through fields to the neglect of the problem of urban bottlenecks'.[2] Such a major brush between the Committee and a Minister is very rare and, of course, gets much publicity in the Press. As a general rule, in fact, the Committee's reports get a wide coverage. They are felt to be newsworthy. This of itself indicates the value of the information which the Committee is able to impart.

It is apparent that party advantage is a secondary consideration for Members when they are sitting on these committees, The Estimates Committee had a majority of Conservative members in 1959, but it made, in its report on Trunk Roads fundamental criticisms of the road modernization scheme being undertaken by a Conservative Minister. When the Committee draws up its report there is sometimes cross-voting amongst Conservative and Labour Members. For example, in the session 1947–8, the Committee examined the work of the Civil Service Selection Board. This body had been set up after the Second World War to test candidates for the Administrative Class of the Civil Service on lines similar to those used by War Office Selection Boards for the selection of officers. This method of selection was known as Method II, as distinct from Method I which was the traditional method of selection by an examination comparable to a university degree examination, followed by an interview. Method II consisted of a qualifying written examination of a general character, followed by a series of personality and vocational tests in which candidates

[1] H.C. 198 of 1956–7. 4th Special Report from the Select Committee on Estimates.
[2] H.C. 223 of 1958–9. First Report from the Select Committee on Estimates. Trunk Roads.
For the Minister of Transport's criticisms of this report, see *The Times* of 22 July 1959.

were placed in the sort of situations which they might have to face as administrative Civil Servants. These tests took place at a country house run by the Civil Service Selection Board at Stoke d'Abernon.

When the Estimates Committee came to vote on the crucial question of whether or not they should recommend that the work of the Selection Board should be brought to an end, two members of the Committee voted in favour and twelve against.[1] The two members in the minority were both Conservatives, while the majority included both Labour and Conservative members. This report is also of interest as an example of the thoroughness with which a sub-committee of the Estimates Committee will go about its job. Sub-Committee D not only interviewed the First Commissioner of the Civil Service and the Head of the Personnel Department of the Foreign Office, but it also visited Stoke d'Abernon and sat in during the testing of candidates. Its report, which was generally favourable to the work of the Board, therefore, carried considerable weight. It did much to dispel fears voiced in the national Press that Method II was an unreliable method of selection and gave scope for favouritism and bias towards the products of the major public schools. The Committee's recommendation that Method II should be continued alongside Method I, but should not supplant it, was in fact adopted by the Government.

Sometimes the Estimates Committee is able to point to deficiencies in the social services. For example, in 1963 it gave prominence to the serious shortage of dentists in the school dental service. There were, at that time, less than half the number of dentists required in the service. As a result, children's teeth were being inspected much less frequently than was desirable, and very few children were receiving treatment from the school dentists. The Committee recommended that responsibility for the school dental service should be transferred from the Ministry of Education to the Ministry of Health as a means of creating greater drive in improving the service.[2] The Government did not accept this recommendation, but promised to do all it could to improve the existing service.

One limitation on the usefulness of the Committee's inquiries

[1] H.C. 203, 205 of 1947–8, p. xi.
[2] H.C. 40 of 1962–3. 1st Report from the Estimates Committee. Dental Services.

has been the lack of specialized assistance. Each sub-committee has a House of Commons Clerk to assist it. He acts as secretary of the sub-committee, but he is not specially qualified in the field of inquiry. When, in 1965, a sub-committee made an investigation of recruitment to the Civil Service they had to accept funds from an outside organization in order to get research done on their behalf. The Acton Society Trust paid the expenses of a survey, carried out by Trevor Smith of Hull University, into student attitudes to a career in the Civil Service. This survey produced some of the most interesting sections in a generally valuable report by the Committee.[1] It underlined the need for technical and scientific assistance to the sub-committee. In their Fifth Special Report earlier in the session, the Committee had asked for power to appoint outside advisers on an *ad hoc* basis, and for the finance to meet their fees and expenses.[2] This request was supported by the Select Committee on Procedure in 1965 in its Fourth Report.[3] In the session 1966—7 funds were made available to the Estimates Committee for the employment of *ad hoc* advisers and specialists.

Another difficulty which faced the Estimates Committee from time to time was that it had no power to travel overseas and take evidence outside Britain. When a sub-committee in 1962 wished to look into military expenditure overseas, they were told by the Government that there were constitutional objections to a Committee of the Commons meeting overseas, and that therefore the Government would oppose a motion for a sub-committee of the Estimates Committee to visit British overseas bases. A way round this impasse was found by the Ministry of Defence inviting members of the sub-committee and their Clerk to visit the bases. This they did, but the visit was an informal one, and although members of the sub-committee talked freely with commanders and other authorities at the bases, they were unable to take formal evidence. This they had to do when they returned to London, confirming from the Service Departments what they had heard at first-hand

---

[1] H.C. 308 of 1964–5. Sixth Report from the Estimates Committee. Recruitment to the Civil Service. See also below Chapter XV for a discussion of this report.

[2] H.C. 161 of 1964–5. Fifth Special Report of the Estimates Committee.

[3] H.C. 303 of 1964–5. p. ix at para. 16.

overseas.[1] The Select Committee on Procedure in 1965 recommended that 'the power of Select Committees to adjourn from place to place should include the power to travel abroad, with the leave of the House, when investigations require it'.[2] In the debate on Procedure on 27 October 1965, Herbert Bowden, as Leader of the House, said that the Government would support a motion, where necessary, for a sub-committee of the Estimates Committee to travel abroad and take evidence.[3] One may assume, therefore, that this limitation on the Committee's activities has been removed.

It must be emphasized that Ministers do not themselves give evidence to either the Estimates Committee or the Committee on Public Accounts. It is the senior Civil Servants who appear before these Committees and undergo cross-examination on their department's affairs. Confining the evidence to Civil Servants underlines the idea that the Committees are not questioning the policy pursued by a department, but are examining the ways in which policies are put into effect and the expenditures involved. By these means, it is felt, the notion of ministerial responsibility is preserved. The Minister answers for his policy in the full House of Commons. The Civil Servant, in giving evidence to Committees, must not be put into a position in which he seems to criticize his Minister's policy. The delicacy of the Civil Servant's role here is recognized by both Committees, and Civil Servants are, as far as possible, saved from embarrassment.

However, the idea that the Committees do not inquire into policy is a pure fiction. Almost all the reports of the Estimates Committee make recommendations about policy in the departments. The Committee can only be said to avoid discussing policy in the very broad sense that it accepts, for example, the House's decision to provide for Civil Defence, or a Hospital Service, and it then goes on to recommend how, in its view, the administration of those services can be improved.

There has been some confusion and controversy on this point over the years. Until 1960, the Committee was instructed by its terms of reference to examine the Estimates and 'to report

[1] H.C. 282 of 1962–3. 10th Report from the Estimates Committee. Military Expenditure Overseas.
[2] H.C. 303 of 1964–5 p. ix at para. 16.   [3] H.C. Deb. Vol. 718, Col. 186.

what, if any, economies consistent with the policy implied in those Estimates may be effected therein'. In 1960 the terms of reference were changed to read: 'and report how, if at all, the policy implied in those estimates may be carried out more economically'. This change, it was felt, would give more scope to the Estimates Committee. In the first five years of the 1950s, in particular, the Committee had complained that it was confined and restricted by its terms of reference; and on the other hand, the Government complained that the Committee was overstepping its powers.[1]

The Select Committee on Procedure recommended in 1965 that the terms of reference of the Estimates Committee should be further modified to enable it 'to examine how the departments of state carry out their responsibilities and to consider their Estimates of Expenditure and Reports'.[2] The Leader of the House, Herbert Bowden, was not in favour of this change when he spoke on the Debate on Procedure on 27 October 1965.[3] The terms of reference, therefore, remained unchanged for the session 1965–6. There is no reason, however, why this should seriously inhibit the Committee's activities. Even if one only considers the reports mentioned above, it is clear that many recommendations on matters of policy have been made by the Committee. It is clear, too, that these recommendations have often been very useful. It may be contended that some of the recommendations have not always been very sound and that others have merely echoed official policy in the departments. Even where this has been the case, the Committee's investigations have helped to inform M.P.s and the public about the work of Government departments.

The Impact of the Committees

How often were reports of these committees discussed in the Commons? Until 1960 very rarely, and this was a cogent criticism of procedure in the Commons. However, in July 1960 the Home Secretary announced that, in future, three parliamentary days in each session would be set aside for debates

[1] See the evidence of H. R. M. Farmer (Clerk of Committees in the Commons) to the Select Committee on Procedure. H.C. 303 of 1964–5. Fourth Report from the Select Committee on Procedure p. 25 at question 32.
[2] H.C. 303 of 1964–5 p. ix at para. 16.
[3] H.C. Deb. Vol. 718 Col. 183.

on reports of the Public Accounts Committee and the Estimates Committee. Good use has been made of these opportunities. Perhaps the most outstanding debate on a Report of the Public Accounts Committee was that of 29 April 1964 on the Ferranti contract for the development of the Bloodhound guided missile.[1] One of the most thoughtful debates on an Estimates Committee report was the debate on 24 January 1962 when the earlier reports of the Estimates Committee on Treasury Control and the Plowden Committee's report on the Treasury were considered together.[2]

These debates are far from being the only means available for giving publicity to the Committees' findings. As has been seen, their reports normally get good publicity in the Press, they are talked about by M.P.s, and they are available for the interested public to study. But the debates help to concentrate criticism on a department and they also give a valuable opportunity to chairmen and members of the Committees to explain their work.

A particularly good example of such an opportunity well taken was the debate, on 30 November 1961, in which Harold Wilson, as Chairman of the Public Accounts Committee, discussed the contemporary role of the Committee. He pointed out that the emphasis in the Committee's work had been steadily changing. 'It would be true to say that the Committee now devotes less attention to the problem of due economy merely for the sake of past events and locking the stable door after the horse has gone and is now spending more of its time drawing attention to any failure of administration, of methods and systems which has a bearing on the future.'[3] It does this without much overlapping with the work of the Estimates Committee. The exact division of labour is hard to describe. Perhaps it is best to define it by saying that the Public Accounts Committee is concerned with aspects of expenditure that have revealed defects of administration or faulty planning. The Estimates Committee is engaged in examining whole fields of administration and considering where improvements can be made.

To sum up, we may say that the activities of the Estimates

[1] H.C. Deb. Vol. 694 Cols. 408–546.
[2] H.C. Deb. Vol. 652 Cols. 208–346.
[3] H.C. Deb. Vol. 650 Col. 640.

Committee since 1945, and the renewed vigour of the Public Accounts Committee, have produced more information about what goes on in Government departments than was available before. While, then, the scope of Government has increased enormously since before the Second World War, Parliament's agencies for informing itself about the activities of Government have been greatly strengthened.

There are, however, many who complain that sources of information are still too few. Those who think this way have for some time been advocating specialist committees of the Commons. The re-organization of the Estimates Committee into specialized sub-committees, carried out in December 1965, was a partial concession to this point of view. It had been recommended by the Fourth Report of the Select Committee on Procedure in 1964–5.[1] But many voices had been raised, inside and outside the Commons, in support of specialist committees of a wider character. This is one of the proposals for reform of the Commons which we shall examine in the next chapter.

For Reference

L. A. ABRAHAM and S. C. HAWTREY, *A Parliamentary Dictionary*, 2nd ed. (Butterworth, 1964).

A. BARKER, 'A Study of Commons Supply Procedure', *Political Studies*, February 1965.

G. CAMPION, *Introduction to the Procedure of the House of Commons*, 2nd ed. (Macmillan, 1964).

D. N. CHESTER and N. BOWRING, *Questions in Parliament* (Clarendon Press, 1962).

B. CHUBB, *The Control of Public Expenditure* (Clarendon Press, 1952).

E. A. COLLINS, 'The Price of Financial Control', *Public Administration*, Autumn 1962.

A. H. HANSON and H. V. WISEMAN, *Parliament at Work* (Stevens, 1962).

N. JOHNSON; Parliament and Administration: The Estimates Committee 1945–65 (Allen and Unwin, 1966).

N. JOHNSON, 'Parliamentary Questions and the Conduct of Administration', *Public Administration*, Summer 1961.

ERSKINE MAY, *Parliamentary Practice*, 17th ed. (Butterworth, 1964).

H. MORRISON, *Government and Parliament*, 3rd ed. (Oxford University Press, 1964).

P. G. RICHARDS, *Honourable Members*, 2nd ed. (Faber 1964).

[1] H.C. 303 of 1964–5 p. ix, para. 16.

E. Taylor, *The House of Commons at Work*, 5th ed. (Penguin, 1963).
K. C. Wheare, *Government by Committee* (Clarendon Press, 1955), Chapter VIII.

H.C. 92-I of 1958–9. Report from the Select Committee on Procedure.
H.C. 188 of 1964–5. Second Report from the Select Committee on Procedure.
H.C. 303 of 1964–5. Fourth Report from the Select Committee on Procedure.
H.C. 153 of 1966–7. First Report from the Select Committee on Procedure.
H.C. 282 of 1966–7. Second Report from the Select Committee on Procedure.
Reports of the Public Accounts Committee.
Reports of the Estimates Committee.
Standing Orders of the House of Commons. Public Business.

CHAPTER VII

Reform of the House of Commons

THE many proposals for reforming the House of Commons that have been made in recent years can be grouped under four main headings. First, and most radical, have been suggestions for setting up a system of specialist committees. Second, many people have pointed to ways in which opportunities for debate in the House itself, and the general quality of debates, could be improved. Third, there have been proposals for loosening the ties of party discipline in the House. Finally, there has been much discussion of ways in which the control of the House over delegated legislation could be improved. The first three lines of reform will be discussed in this chapter while the control of delegated legislation will be examined in Chapter VIII.

PART ONE: *Proposals for Specialist Committees*

Those who have suggested various systems of specialist committees of the House of Commons have included academic authorities, a few back-benchers in the Commons and, less frequently again, former Ministers. In the first category can be instanced H. J. Laski writing in 1925 in his book *A Grammar of Politics*, and later in 1951 in his *Reflections on the Constitution*.[1] In 1959, A. H. Hanson and H. V. Wiseman submitted a memorandum to the Select Committee on Procedure advocating specialist committees.[2] Another series of proposals was made by Bernard Crick, in his Fabian pamphlet, *Reform of the Commons*, also published in 1959.[3] He repeated these proposals,

---

[1] H. J. Laski, *A Grammar of Politics*, 4th ed (Allen & Unwin, 1955).

H. J. Laski, *Reflections on the Constitution* (Manchester University Press, 1951), pp. 52–3.

[2] This memorandum was printed as an article in *Public Law*, Autumn 1959, pp. 277–92.

[3] Bernard Crick, *Reform of the Commons* (Fabian Society, 1959), esp. pp. 29–39.

with certain important variations, in a book published in 1964, *The Reform of Parliament.*[1]

In 1965, evidence in favour of specialist committees was presented, in a Memorandum to the Select Committee on Procedure, by the Study of Parliament Group.[2] This group, which had been formed in 1964, included on the academic side, besides Hanson, Wiseman, and Crick, D. N. Chester, Warden of Nuffield College, Oxford, and Professors Max Beloff, Peter Bromhead, J. A. G. Griffith, W. J. M. Mackenzie, and W. A. Robson. In addition, officers of both Houses of Parliament were members of the group and its chairman was Sir Edward Fellowes, former Clerk of the House of Commons.

Of former Ministers, Lloyd George had advocated specialist committees in his evidence to the Select Committee on Procedure in 1931.[3] So also did L. S. Amery in *Thoughts on the Constitution* published in 1947.[4]

The common element in all these suggestions is the proposal for a series of committees of the Commons which would concern themselves with the work of government departments, taken either singly or in cognate groups. For example, Crick advocated a committee on Defence and Services, another on Foreign Affairs, another on Economics and Finance, and so on. But when it comes to the powers that the innovators think their committees should enjoy, there is considerable variation. Crick in 1959 suggested committees which would debate, inquire into activities of the departments, take the Committee Stage of legislation (and possibly the Report Stage too), examine the departmental estimates, and scrutinize delegated legislation issued by the department. By 1964 Crick had changed his mind in one respect. He no longer thought that these specialist committees should take the Committee Stage (or Report Stage) of bills. Otherwise he still proposed the same range of powers. Lloyd George had advocated committees of a similar type.

Hanson and Wiseman, on the other hand, following Laski's

---

[1] Bernard Crick, *The Reform of Parliament* (Weidenfeld and Nicolson, 1964), esp. pp. 198–201.

[2] See H.C. 303 of 1964–5. Fourth Report from the Select Committee on Procedure, esp. pp. 137–8.

[3] H.C. 161 of 1931, pp. 43–50.

[4] Amery, op. cit., pp. 53–4.

ideas in his *Grammar of Politics*, argued for committees which would be mainly advisory. Their chief function would be to inquire into policy and administration in the departments; they would not consider legislation, except when consulted by Ministers about draft legislation or draft statutory instruments. They could also examine cases of complaints against departments raised by M.P.s and could assess the merits of statutory instruments currently lying before the House.

The committees which Laski suggested in 1951 were to be purely advisory. They would allow a Minister to give information and to exchange views with a group of Members, from the Government and the Opposition sides, who were specially interested in the affairs of his department. Amery, too, envisaged similarly restricted functions for specialist committees.

The Study of Parliament Group in 1965 recommended that the Estimates Committee should be divided into specialized sub-committees. This suggestion was, as we have seen, taken up by the Procedure Committee and put into effect in December 1965 by the Estimates Committee.[1] The Group suggested in addition that there should be a series of specialist committees which would initially be concerned with Scientific Development, with the Prevention and Punishment of Crime, with the Machinery of Government (National, Regional and Local), with Housing, Building, and Land Use, and with the Social Services. Eventually, specialist committees should cover the whole field of administration. Their functions would be to scrutinize and advise. As new specialist committees were set up, the Estimates Committee would devolve its relevant functions to them.

Up to this point, the Study of Parliament Group seems to have been of one mind. But there then come references to possible further functions of the specialist committees which indicate that there were differences of opinion among the Group. For example, the memorandum states: 'We note other suggestions for committees to examine proposals for legislation before bills are drafted. Our specialist committees could perform such a function if desired.'[2]

It is clear that objections can be made to some of these

[1] See above, pp. 137–8 and 147.
[2] H.C. 303 of 1964–5, p. 138.

schemes which are not appropriate to others. It is a mistake to lump together all proposals for specialist committees and to dismiss them on the grounds that they are derived from the American or French system. Such comments have been made frequently by Ministers, and notably, in recent years, by Herbert Morrison and R. A. Butler giving evidence as Leaders of the House to successive Select Committees of Procedure. Morrison even argued on these lines in 1946, when rejecting the proposal that the Public Accounts Committee and the Select Committee on Estimates should be merged into one Public Expenditure Committee.[1] R. A. Butler made a similar objection in 1958 to Jo Grimond's proposal for a Standing Committee on Colonial Affairs.[2] Herbert Bowden, Leader of the House in 1965, rejected the suggestion that the terms of reference of the Estimates Committee should be widened to enable it 'to examine how the Departments of State carry out their responsibilities'. He explained his opposition to the idea in the following terms: 'The real question is whether or not we want to develop a system of specialist committees, not exactly like, but something akin to, the American Congressional Committees and similar committees which exist in certain European countries, or whether we feel that the proper place for policy discussions, as distinct from financial administration, is on the Floor of the House.'[3]

This bogey of the American and French systems deserves to be laid. The fact is that the committees of Congress have even wider powers than the specialist committees proposed by Crick in 1959. Congressional committees investigate and have power to sub-poena witnesses. They play a decisive part in legislation and vote the departmental estimates. These powers on their own—the power to consider legislation and to approve finance—would be sufficient to enable them to intervene in the running of departments. Since all departments need finance, and most departments need legislation, it is important that they should retain the goodwill of the relevant committee or committees. But the influence of Congressional committees is greatly

---

[1] H.C. 189-I of 1946. Third Report from the Select Committee on Procedure. Question 3260 at p. 111.
[2] H.C. 92-I of 1959. Report from the Select Committee on Procedure. Question 1161 at p. 189.
[3] H.C. Deb. Vol. 718, Col. 183.

enhanced by the system of separation of the powers. The President has no control over Congress except through patronage and through persuasion. Committees can go their own way and are, in fact, the key institutions of both Houses of Congress. The position would obviously be quite different in the British system. Even if specialist committees of the Commons had power to legislate and vote finance, they would still be controlled by the government of the day through the machinery of the party whips.

Similar observations can be made about the committee systems of many European parliaments. In France in the Fourth Republic, for example, the committees of the National Assembly considered legislation and the estimates as well as inquiring into the activities of departments. But the power of these committees was increased immeasurably by the absence of coherent and stable majorities for the government.

To sum up then, American and French committees have, or had (in the case of the Fourth Republic), wider powers even than those proposed by Crick in his 1959 pamphlet. They also operate, or operated, in systems quite unlike our own in which the Executive has much less control over the Legislature. Even so, it would seem wise not to concentrate too many functions in the proposed specialist committees of the Commons. In particular, to give them power to take the committee stage of legislation, in addition to the power to scrutinize administration, would be to risk giving them too much influence over departmental policy. If, then, we rule out the idea that specialist committees should consider legislation, what are the arguments for and against specialist committees which would only scrutinize administration and report to the House?

The case for such committees has been well stated by the Study of Parliament Group. 'The main weakness in Parliament's present methods of scrutinizing administration, and indeed of debating policy matters, is the limited ability to obtain the background facts and understanding essential for any detailed criticism of administration or any informed discussion of policy. Specialist committees, working on lines similar to those of the Estimates Committee or Nationalized Industries Committee (itself a fairly recently established specialist committee) could go a long way to remedy this.'[1]

[1] H.C. 303 of 1964–5, p. 137.

The case against specialist committees of this type is twofold. First, it can be argued that such committees would weaken a Minister's control over his department. They would, it is implied, become so well-informed about policy planning in the departments that they would become rival centres of authority to the Minister. This is less likely to happen if the committees' functions are limited to scrutiny alone. It is also less likely to happen if, as a general rule, the specialist committees only hear evidence from Civil Servants and not from Ministers. This, as we have seen, has been the invariable practice of the Public Accounts Committee and the Select Committee on Estimates. It helps to ensure that, as a rule, the function of the committee is to gather information about what is being done in the departments. This does not mean that the committees do not concern themselves with policy. We have seen that their reports are most useful when they do.[1] The point was well put by the Study of Parliament Group when they stated that the proposed specialist committees 'would be mainly concerned with administration and would normally seek to avoid matters of policy which are controversial between the major political parties'.[2] In other words, specialist committees would normally consider those areas of policy which are less sensitive in the party context. This again, in general, has been the practice of the Estimates Committee.

The second objection to specialist scrutiny committees is possibly more weighty. Many opponents of specialist committees consider that they would lessen the importance of debates on the Floor of the House. Members rightly pride themselves on the fact that debates in the House can be very valuable occasions for extracting information from Ministers, and for making clear to the public the attitudes of the Government and the Opposition. If, before the debate, Members' lips are sealed by having information revealed to them in committee which they cannot make use of in the debate, then debate on the Floor of the House is likely to lose its vitality. This would be most prone to happen in the case of a Defence Committee, as was argued in the Procedure Debate in October 1965 by J. J. Mendelson.[3]

[1] See above Chapter VI, esp. pp. 144–5.
[2] H.C. 303 of 1964–5, p. 137.
[3] H.C. Deb. Vol. 718, Cols. 240–8.

It would happen to a much lesser extent with subjects which did not have a security aspect. Even here, however, Michael Foot has argued that in the specialist committees 'all the topics of debate in the House would be hashed and rehashed before they ever got to the House of Commons itself. By the time they got here, we would find the subject utterly boring or would be told by the members of the specialist committees that they knew so much more about the subject than the others that the rest of us were not supposed to speak on the matter.'[1] The only way to test this argument was to give specialist committees a trial. The question was what sort of committees should one start with?

Various committees had been suggested. For example, the Socialist Commentary group of twelve Labour M.P.s proposed, in July 1964, that there should be specialized committees on the welfare services and on colonial affairs and that 'ultimately there ought to be a Select Committee on Defence, though this may be too controversial for immediate implementation'.[2] The Liberal Party, in its manifesto for the 1964 General Election, advocated specialized committees on economic affairs, foreign policy, and defence.[3] In 1965 the Study of Parliament Group in effect recommended starting from the other end with subjects such as the prevention and punishment of crime, housing, and the social services, which sometimes, although by no means always, tend to be less a matter of acute party controversy.[4]

On 21 April 1966, the Prime Minister, Harold Wilson, told the Commons that the Government was going to discuss with the two Opposition parties the suggestion for setting up one or two parliamentary committees to concern themselves with administration in the departments. This would be an experiment in specialist committees and the Prime Minister's own feeling was that it would be best made in the field of the home departments. He mentioned specifically Home Office affairs, education, and housing and local government. He suggested that

[1] H.C. Deb. Vol. 718, Col. 208.
[2] Socialist Commentary Supplement, July 1964, p. x, para. 49.
[3] In its manifesto for the 1966 General Election, the Liberal Party repeated these proposals and also advocated a specialized committee on Science and Technology.
[4] For the full list of committees proposed by the Study of Parliament Group see above, p. 151.

the committees might hear evidence from Ministers, senior Civil Servants, and outside experts. He thought that the committees should be run on informal lines and should not be required to publish all the information they received. This idea was later criticized by many M.P.s who maintained that the chief value of the reports from the Estimates Committee, for example, lay in the publication of evidence received. The Prime Minister indicated that he had yet to be convinced of the value of specialist committees on foreign policy and defence.[1]

After discussion between the party leaders, it emerged that the Conservative Opposition was in favour of a Committee on Science and Technology. This proposal was supported by Labour and Liberal Members, many of whom also favoured a Committee on Agriculture. On 14 December 1966 the Leader of the House, Richard Crossman, announced in a Procedure Debate that these two committees would be set up on an experimental basis. They would be empowered to examine witnesses and to hear evidence in public. By the end of September 1967, both committees had made a considerable impact. The Select Committee on Agriculture had published its first report: on the preparations being made by the Ministry of Agriculture against Britain's possible entry into the European Economic Community.[2]

The Committee had encountered resistance from the Foreign Office to its proposal to visit the British delegation to the Community in Brussels. Nevertheless, the Committee had won its case and had both visited the British delegation in Brussels and had informal meetings with Dr. Mansholt, the Commissioner in charge of agriculture, and members of the E.E.C. staff. The Committee's report pointed to inadequacies in the staffing of the British delegation and, as a consequence, its failure to provide sufficient information about the working of the agricultural policy of the Community.

The Committee on Science and Technology had not, in September 1967, issued a report. It was carrying out two separate inquiries: on the nuclear reactor programme, and on the problem of oil pollution.

[1] H.C. Deb. Vol. 727, Cols 75–79.
[2] H.C. 378–xvii of 1966–7. Report of the Select Committee on Agriculture.

A Defence Committee of the Commons

The case for a Defence Committee is rather different from the case for other specialist committees. It seems certain that a Defence Committee would meet behind closed doors and that members of the committee would often not be able to pass on to the full House information which they had received—for example, certain facts divulged by the Chiefs of Staff. This would seem a sound reason for not having such a committee if it could be shown that worthwhile information on defence at present emerged from debates in the House. In general, it cannot be said that it does. This is probably inevitable because the crucial facts on defence questions cannot normally be made public. As a result, the debate between the parties often assumes an air of unreality. For example, in the years 1962–4, the Conservative Government's insistence on maintaining its 'independent deterrent', against the Labour assertion that the deterrent was not independent and that the Nassau agreement about its use must be re-negotiated, were widely contrasting positions which were eventually seen to have been equally unrealistic. It seems certain that if there had been a Defence Committee of the Commons, which included in its membership both the Defence Ministers and the leading spokesmen on defence from the Opposition, such a wide gulf would not have developed between the parties. Opposition leaders could have been told the real capabilities and limitations of the Polaris-armed submarine, while Ministers would have heard a more effective, because better informed, exposition of the Opposition argument.

It can similarly be argued that a Defence Committee of the Commons would have been of immense value in the 1930s. It would have allowed the Opposition to be given the essential facts about the military preparedness of Britain relative to that of Nazi Germany. It would have helped Opposition spokesmen, such as Hugh Dalton, to persuade the Labour Parliamentary Party of the need for re-armament, and it would have allowed the Government to see what the Opposition would, or would not, stand.

The objections to a Defence Committee could be twofold. First, it might be alleged that it could result in leaks about Britain's defence capabilities. Second, it might increase the tension between the front and back benches, particularly on the Opposition side. Opposition leaders, it could be claimed, would find themselves under fire from their back-benchers for supporting Government policy on defence without being able to reveal their reasons for so doing. It is undeniable that there might be embarrassments here, but it seems probable that the balance of advantage is on the side of a Defence Committee.

It was significant that in 1964 tentative approaches were being made towards a bi-partisan policy on defence. On 16 January 1964, Harold Wilson, as Leader of the Opposition, asked the Prime Minister to institute private talks on defence between himself and the Defence Minister on the one hand and the Opposition leaders on the other. The Prime Minister, Sir Alec Douglas-Home, turned down the suggestion. Then on 16 December 1964, Harold Wilson, now Prime Minister, renewed this suggestion.[1] This was not taken up by the then Leader of the Opposition, Sir Alec Douglas-Home, nor was it by his successor, Edward Heath. When Wilson made his offer to the Leader of the Opposition, the Liberal Leader, Jo Grimond, welcomed the idea but said that Liberal leaders and some back-benchers should also be given private information on defence by the Government.[2] The logic of Grimond's position is sound enough and surely points to the need for a fully fledged Defence Committee of the Commons.

There had once before been informal talks between Opposition leaders and the Government on defence. This was in 1949 when Sir Winston Churchill, as Leader of the Opposition, complained to the Attlee Government that Parliament was not being given the full facts on defence. Attlee then invited Churchill, and other leading Conservatives, to a series of informal discussions with members of the Government. Thereafter the practice was allowed to lapse. This can always happen with an informal arrangement; but a Defence Committee, once set up, would almost certainly become a permanent feature.

Such a Defence Committee would of course be quite different in structure from the sort of specialist committees we have previously discussed. It would include the Prime Minister and the Defence Minister, and the Leader of the Opposition and

[1] H.C. Deb. Vol. 704, Col. 441.
[2] H.C. Deb. Vol. 704, Col. 618–19.

the Shadow Defence Minister; whereas the other specialist committees would consist of back-benchers. This different structure would indeed accord with a quite different role. The function of the Defence Committee would be to provide some common ground between the leaders of the parties on defence matters; the function of the other specialist committees would be to provide information for use in debate in the Commons, and in consideration of departmental policy by the informed public.

The Select Committee on Nationalized Industries
We have seen that the Select Committee on Nationalized Industries has been referred to as a prototype of such a specialist committee.[1] This Committee was set up in 1955 largely because Members had experienced frustration in questioning Ministers about the administration of the nationalized industries. Since Ministers are not responsible for the day to day administration of these industries, questions on such topics were inadmissible. It was hoped that a Select Committee would provide the House with some information about the working of these industries.

In its first form the Committee was a disappointment. Its terms of reference were too limited. In 1956 its terms of reference were widened: it was now instructed 'to examine the Reports and Accounts of the Nationalized Industries established by Statute . . .' Since the widening of its terms of reference, it has published many informative reports and is generally thought to be a success. The Committee has thirteen members, made up in relation to party strengths in the full House. Its chairman is a back-bencher on the Government side. The chief weakness of the Committee, as with the Estimates Committee, is that it does not have a specialized staff to assist it. One of the Clerks of the Commons acts as Secretary of the Committee, but this is not enough. As far back as 1959, the Committee reported that it needed a specialized staff to help in assessing problems of accounting policy and management organization.[2] The Macmillan Government did not respond to

---

[1] For example by the Study of Parliament Group in 1965. See above, p. 153.
[2] See H.C. 276 of 1958–9. Special Report from the Select Committee on Nationalized Industries.

this suggestion but it did agree to appoint a second clerk from the House of Commons staff to assist the Committee.[1]

PART TWO: *Suggestions for Improving Opportunities for Debate in the House and for Making Debates More Effective*

While specialist committees could possibly improve the flow of information about administration in the departments, two points should be made here about the campaign for specialist committees. First, some of those who have argued for specialist committees have not taken full account of the extent to which the Commons has improved its methods of gaining information about the departments since 1945.[2] For example, Bernard Crick's statement in 1959 that 'Parliament is ceasing to be an efficient critic of the Executive' and that 'the power of Parliament to offer informed and well disseminated criticism has declined, is declining and should be increased' would seem to be a considerable over-statement to say the least.[3] Second, relatively few Members of Parliament have been in favour of specialist committees. For every Member in recent years who has favoured specialist committees, there have been many more who have urged the need for finding more time for debate in the House. Indeed, it was the frustration experienced by many back-benchers who found themselves, all too often, elbowed out of participating in major debates which led to the setting up of the Select Committee on Procedure in 1958.

Finding More Time for Debates

One line of suggestion was that a time limit should be placed on speeches and that Privy Councillors should lose their right to priority in debate. As we have seen in Chapter VI, neither of these ideas has yet been adopted.

The other main line of criticism was that insufficient time was being found in the House for major debates on policy and

---

[1] For an account of the work of the Select Committee on Nationalized Industries see A. H. Hanson, *Parliament and Public Ownership* (Cassell for Hansard Society, 1961).

See also David Coombes, *The Member of Parliament and the Administration. The Case of the Select Committee on Nationalized Industries* (Allen and Unwin, 1966).

[2] See above, Chapter VI, pp. 136–47.

[3] B. Crick, *Reform of the Commons* (Fabian Society, 1959), pp. 1 and 2.

administration and for Private Members' motions. As Anthony Wedgwood Benn put it in seconding the motion for a Select Committee on Procedure: 'Because of the volume of routine business, our great debates are too late, too short and, in many cases, never take place at all. We ought somehow "to clear the decks".'[1] The Select Committee on Procedure reported in 1959 that one of the most efficient ways of 'clearing the decks' was to make full use of standing committees. It recommended that some standing committees could be smaller, that their composition should be changed and that virtually all bills should be sent to them at committee stage. The Macmillan Government accepted these recommendations and acted upon them. Between 1959 and 1964, as has been noted in Chapter V, virtually all bills except those of constitutional importance were taken in standing committee at committee stage. After the General Election in October 1964 the Wilson Government continued to make extensive use of standing committees.

Such a use of standing committees is, then, an excellent way of reducing the time spent on legislative business on the floor of the House and thereby providing more time for debates on policy and administration.

It has also been suggested that the report stage of many bills should be taken in standing committee. There are powerful arguments against such a move, as Members not on a standing committee would then be deprived of any chance to move detailed amendments to a bill. For this reason the Procedure Committee in 1959 turned down the suggestion.

Another proposal for saving time in the whole House has much more to commend it. This is the suggestion that the Finance Bill should be taken in standing committee. The Finance Bill, which embodies the annual proposals for taxation, takes up a great deal of the time of the House, in the summer, while it is exhaustively debated at committee stage. The Procedure Committee, in 1959, recommended that the Finance Bill should be sent, in whole or in part, to standing committee at committee stage.[2] The Macmillan Government did not accept the recommendation, and it was evident from the debate on 8 February 1960 that opinion as to its advisability was

[1] H.C. Deb. Vol. 581, Col. 681. 31 January 1958.
[2] H.C. 92-I of 1958–9, pp. viii–ix.

divided on both sides of the House.[1] In 1965 the Procedure
Committee recommended that parts of the Finance Bill should
be taken in standing committee, and that a timetable for the
passage of the Bill should be drawn up by a select committee of
the House. The Leader of the House, Herbert Bowden, turned
down both suggestions.[2] Yet, in most sessions, debates on the
committee stage of the Finance Bill are thinly attended and
tend to be monopolized by Members with an expert interest
in the subject. They seem to be pre-eminently debates which
would be better taken in standing committee. The Finance Bill
in the session 1964–5 was exceptional. It contained two major
reforms, in the introduction of corporation tax and in capital
gains tax, and was highly controversial. But major measures of
nationalization or of land reform are taken in standing committee and are equally controversial. There seems to be no adequate reason for not taking the Finance Bill in entirety in
standing committee. There would still be report stage in the
whole House which would preserve the rights of all Members
to move amendments.

Morning Sittings

Another proposal made to the Procedure Committee of 1958–9
was for morning sittings of the House. The Labour Members on
the Committee favoured the suggestion that there should be
morning sittings on two days a week between 11 a.m. and 1 p.m.
It was proposed that this time should be used for discussing
current topics, and reports of Royal Commissions and select
committees, including the Estimates Committee. The majority
of the Committee turned down the idea on the grounds that
morning sittings would impose too heavy a burden on Members, and especially on Ministers who require the mornings for
administration in their departments or for service on Cabinet
Committees.[3] The Macmillan Government concurred with the
majority view here, but they did arrange from 1960 onward
for the discussion on three days per session, on the floor of

---

[1] H.C. Deb. Vol. 617, Cols. 33–184.

[2] H.C. Deb. Vol. 718, Cols. 181–2.

[3] H.C. 92-I of 1958–9. Report of the Select Committee on Procedure, pp.
xiii–xv and xxxix–xli.

the House, of reports of the Estimates Committee and the Public Accounts Committee. One of these days has been found out of Government time and two have been Supply days. As we have already seen, in Chapter VI, this time has been well used and has proved a useful innovation.

The Macmillan Government also found more time, after the Procedure Committee Report, for discussing private Members' motions. In the session 1959–60, four half-days (part of two Mondays and two Wednesdays) were set aside for private Members' motions in addition to the ten Fridays already allocated. Similar arrangements have been made in subsequent sessions.

Some Members, however, continued to press for morning sittings and were influenced both by the desire to provide more time for debate on the floor of the House and by the feeling that the traditional daily timetable was no longer appropriate. Thus the Socialist Commentary group of members proposed in July 1964 that the House should sit from 10 a.m. to 7 p.m., instead of its present normal hours—from 2.30 p.m. to 10.30 p.m. (on Mondays, Tuesdays, Wednesdays, and Thursdays). They suggested that proceedings should begin with a half-hour debate similar to the present adjournment debate. Question Time should then follow, from 10.30 a.m. to 11.30 a.m., and be followed by the ordinary business of the day. To minimize the demands on Ministers, they suggested that private Members' bills and motions should be taken in the mornings, as should the discussion of statutory instruments. Some other types of Government business would also have to go on in the mornings, but the Socialist Commentary group suggested that departments should be represented in the mornings by junior Ministers or Parliamentary Secretaries, that is apart from the rota of senior Ministers who would be answering questions at Question Time.

This radical proposal for rearrangement of the sittings of the House did not win wide support. However, in August 1966 the Procedure Committee suggested that, as an experiment, the House should sit on Wednesday and Thursday mornings, when the main business taken would be discussion of delegated legislation and non-controversial bills. The Leader of the House, Richard Crossman, told the Procedure Committee in December

1966 that the Government proposed to make such an experiment, but had decided to have morning sittings on Mondays and Wednesdays, so as not to conflict with the sittings of Standing Committees which take place on Tuesday and Thursday mornings. During the morning sittings, the House could not be counted out and divisions called in the morning would not be taken until the end of the evening's business.[1]

Opinions differed as to the success of this experiment which was undertaken from February to July 1967. The majority of Conservatives, who had initially been strongly opposed to the idea, were not converted. On the other hand, Richard Crossman told the House on 19 April 1967 that, from the Government's point of view, the experiment was proving a success.[2] Business which might otherwise have taken a lot of time late at night had been dealt with expeditiously in the mornings. He allowed, however, that it had imposed an extra strain on the Speaker and the staff of the House.

Reforms in Voting Procedure

Another idea for saving time in the House has been considered by the Procedure Committee. This was the suggestion for mechanical voting. At present the House takes from 8 to 11 minutes to divide. As on some days there are many divisions, it can happen that a lot of the time of Members is taken up in walking through the division lobbies. Electronic systems of voting are employed in the Parliaments of Belgium, Sweden, India, and Finland. The Clerk of the House of Commons was asked, in 1958, to circulate a questionnaire to the Officers of these Parliaments, and the answers received were published in an appendix to the Report of the Select Committee on Procedure.[3] In each of these Parliaments every Member has his personal desk in the Chamber from which he votes by inserting a key in the voting machine in his desk. He then can press a 'yes', 'no' or 'abstain' button and record his vote. The systems are reliable and permit very rapid divisions. The total time taken in voting, between the beginning of the division and the announcement of the result, is generally between two and five minutes.

[1] H.C. Deb. Vol. 738, Cols. 489–494.
[2] H.C. Deb. Vol. 744, Cols. 601–2.
[3] H.C. 92-I of 1958–9, pp. 218–21.

But the system cannot be exactly copied in the Commons because there are only 346 seats on the floor of the House, whereas there are 630 Members. It is, therefore, impossible for each Member to have a seat allocated to him.

It would be possible to have a variation of the scheme whereby voting machines would be installed in the division lobbies, or in a room immediately adjacent to the Chamber. This would not save much time, however, for the Palace of Westminster is so rambling that it is necessary to allow six minutes for Members who are not in the Chamber to get to the division lobbies. Therefore, even if electronic voting were installed in the lobbies, divisions would take at least six minutes as against the eight to eleven minutes at present. The Procedure Committee therefore reported against the proposal in 1959.[1] In 1966, they made a further enquiry and came to a similar conclusion.[2]

If, at some time in the future, the administrative capital of Britain should be moved out of London, as some town planners now advocate (York has been suggested, for example), an entirely new Parliament building would be necessary. Such a new building could be designed with a larger Chamber, although it would probably be better not to include a desk for every Member on the floor of the House as this would make the Chamber too large and destroy the informality of debate. More important would be the possibility of grouping Members' rooms, committee rooms, libraries, restaurants etc. all round the Chamber so that Members could quickly get to the division lobby. Then, equipping the lobby with electronic voting machines might be worthwhile.

Two other reforms in voting procedure are worth considering: one is proxy voting, and the other is voting after a period of delay. The idea of proxy voting was turned down in 1959 by the Select Committee on Procedure, who felt that: 'A Member's duty in voting is one that must remain personal to himself. It cannot be transferred.'[3] The idea was revived in 1965, but this time it was suggested that proxy votes should be allowed only for Members who were sick and for whom a medical certificate had been produced. This was to prevent sick

[1] H.C. 92-I of 1958–9, pp. xx–xxi.
[2] H.C. 283 of 1966-7, pp. iii–iv.
[3] H.C. 92-I of 1958–9, p. xxi at para. 37.

Members being brought to the House by ambulance in order to have their names added to the division lists, in a period of small majority when their votes might decide the future of the Government. The Select Committee on Procedure voted in favour of this proposal, although the five Conservative Members on the Committee voted against it.[1] In the event, the Wilson Government did not ask the House to implement the report since the Opposition Chief Whip offered to make proxy votes for sick Members unnecessary by undertaking to provide a pair, on all occasions, for sick Members on the Government side.

The proposal for voting after a period of delay has been made by Christopher Hollis.[2] His suggestion was that all the divisions on the motions and amendments in a day's business should be taken at one time. He suggested that this should be at the beginning of the next day's business. We have seen that an experiment on these lines was made in 1967 for morning sittings only. If generally adopted, it would have some advantages. For example, it would allow Members working on committees to carry on with their work undistracted.

The Welsh Grand Committee

One reform which was suggested only tentatively by the Procedure Committee in 1959 was taken up and acted upon by the Macmillan Government. This was the proposal made originally by Ness Edwards, the Member for Caerphilly, for a Welsh Grand Committee. The Procedure Committee suggested that such a committee should be set up 'If need arose for more discussion of Welsh affairs in addition to the present Welsh day on the floor of the House'.[3] The Macmillan Government decided that there was such a need, and the Welsh Grand Committee was set up for the first time in the session 1959–60. It consisted at first of all the Members who sat for constituencies in Wales and Monmouthshire, 36 in number, together with 25 Conservative Members from outside Wales to give the Conservatives a majority on the Committee, proportional to their majority in the full House. After the 1964 General Election,

[1] H.C. 361 of 1964–5. Fifth Report from the Select Committee on Procedure. Voting Arrangements for Sick Members.
[2] In a review by Christopher Hollis of Bernard Crick's *The Reform of Parliament* in the *Sunday Times*, 7 June 1964.
[3] H.C. 92-I of 1958–9, p. xxv.

the Committee was reduced in size to a total of 41, as only five Conservatives had to be added from outside Wales and Monmouthshire to make the Labour majority on the Committee proportionate to the majority in the full House.

The Committee normally meets four times each session, on a Wednesday morning, to discuss Welsh problems and the work of a department or a group of departments in Wales. Valuable debates have taken place on such subjects as industry, employment, agriculture, forestry, education, and tourism in Wales. From 1960 to 1964, the Minister for Welsh Affairs, or his Minister of State, was always present and he was accompanied by the junior Minister from the department whose affairs in Wales were under discussion. In the Wilson Government, the Minister responsible was the Secretary of State for Wales, and the first meeting of the Committee in the session 1964–5 was to consider the constitutional changes which were involved in the creation of this new office. A debate of great importance to all Welshmen was the debate on 14 December 1965, in the Grand Committee, on the recommendation of the Hughes Parry Committee for equal validity for the Welsh language, with English, inside Wales.

The Welsh Grand Committee is not entirely similar in type to the Scottish Grand Committee, because the latter can also consider estimates and legislation relating exclusively to Scotland. There are no Welsh estimates or Welsh bills, so the Welsh Committee is purely a forum for debate and an opportunity for questioning Ministers. Both committees are well liked by Scottish and Welsh Members. They are not, however, analogous to specialist committees. They are, indeed, general in scope although particular to the region (or nation, if that word is preferred) that is concerned. There is a case for regional committees for the English regions. We shall return to this suggestion in Chapter XVI.[1]

Back-Benchers Are Now More Active
We have seen that a major cause of dissatisfaction amongst Members has been the inadequacy of opportunities to take

[1] See below, p. 400.
The Prime Minister, Harold Wilson, in his speech to the Commons on 21 April 1966, said that he hoped that the House would give consideration to the appointment of regional parliamentary committees for the English regions. H.C. Deb. Vol. 727, Col. 81.

part in debate on the floor of the House. At the same time we should recognize that the average Member of the House now shows greater keenness to take an active part in the House of Commons than did his predecessor, ninety, sixty, or even thirty years ago. This increased interest and activity can be accounted for in two ways. First, many more Members are now 'Constituency Members': that is, they keep in close touch with their constituents and act as a channel of enquiry and pressure upon Ministers. Second, many more Members take a serious, rather than a dilettante, interest in policy questions in their chosen spheres of specialization.

Both these developments are desirable. As the scope of government has enlarged, so the need for more effective channels of opinion between the citizen and government departments has increased. Equally, with the growing complexity of government has come a need for more fully informed and careful scrutiny by Members. But the consequences of these developments are important too. In the nineteenth century, most private Members were content, as a rule, to leave speech-making to the front benches. In 1886, Gladstone spoke for three and a half hours when introducing the first Home Rule Bill. Lord Halifax commented, in 1957, that 'Even at the end of the nineteenth century, private members of the House of Commons were still conducting themselves a good deal on the model of a jury, before whom the respective arguments were set out by the leaders on each side, and who recorded their judgment at the end, but did not greatly wish to intervene themselves'.[1] Nowadays back-benchers are much more anxious to get a word in, while the time allocated for debates has shrunk because of the increased pressure of business. The result has been frustration and impatience which is not, as many have maintained, an indication that the House of Commons is in low water but is instead a product of the higher level of interest and ability among Members.

Members are more and more coming to regard themselves as full-time legislators and rightly so. The days of 'amateur status' are numbered. Already, the demands of committee work are such that an unfair load is being placed on Members who devote their whole time to the affairs of the House, and do

---

[1] The Earl of Halifax, *Fulness of Days* (Collins, 1957), p. 71.

not combine membership with participation in another profession such as the bar, commerce or industry. If the average
Member is to be as well informed and as active in House of
Commons business as he needs to be, and as in most cases he
wants to be, he will have to give up the idea of pursuing
another career at the same time. This does not mean, as many
supporters of amateur status have claimed, that Members will
lose touch with the occupations from which they are drawn
and become a class apart. If the majority of Members devote
all their time to their work in the House, they can still preserve
their contacts with the professions which they followed before
entering the House.

M.P.s' Salaries

If a Member must now consider his work in the House as a full-
time occupation, and if he is to do it well, then his salary must
take account of this fact. It must also take account of the very
heavy expenses which are associated with his work. If a Member is to do his job properly he must have secretarial assistance.
No secretaries are provided by the Commons, so he must employ
his own secretary or, at the very least, share a secretary with
another Member. Again, Members whose constituencies are
at any distance from London must maintain two homes, but
at present the only help they are given is free rail travel
(during parliamentary sessions) between London and their
constituency, constituency and home, and home and London.
A mileage allowance can be claimed for travel by car instead.
The Member's basic salary should therefore be sufficiently large
to attract able men to the Commons who will regard their
work there as a full-time occupation, and it should include an
extra element to cover expenses such as secretarial assistance
and the cost of living away from home for part of the week.

For a long time, these essential facts about the Member's
position were not widely appreciated in Britain. Members'
salaries were raised to £1,750 in 1957 (including an element of
£750 for expenses which was nevertheless subject to tax).
Even in 1957 this was an inadequate salary. By 1960 it had
become clearly inadequate, and yet no increase in salary was
agreed to by the Government until November 1964. By this
time, many Members were suffering real hardships. It is likely

that the quality of membership would have severely declined had it not been known, well before the 1964 Election, that salaries would be substantially raised after the election. In December 1963 the Home Government had appointed a small Committee consisting of the chairman of the National Incomes Commission, Sir Geoffrey Lawrence, H. S. Kirkaldy, and Professor W. J. M. Mackenzie to recommend a new level of salaries for Ministers and M.P.s, and also to consider the level of allowances for Members of the House of Lords. All three political parties, in effect, agreed to implement the recommendations of the Committee. In November 1964 the Lawrence Committee reported, recommending that the M.P.'s salary should be raised to £3,250 a year (£2,000 basic salary plus £1,250 taxable allowance for expenses).

The Wilson Government accepted this recommendation. It did not however accept the Committee's recommendation about Ministers' salaries. The Committee had recommended that the Prime Minister's salary should go up from £10,000 a year to £18,000, and senior Ministers' salaries from £5,000 to £12,000. The Government thought that the increase was too great and decided that the Prime Minister's new salary should be £14,000 and the salaries of senior Ministers should be £8,500. The Lawrence Committee also recommended the creation of a contributory pension scheme for Members of the Commons. The Government accepted this proposal.

The salary of £3,250 for Members is reasonable but by no means generous since, as we have seen, it must cover payment for secretarial assistance and other expenses. What still gives cause for anxiety is that the M.P.'s salary may again be allowed to fall far behind the level of comparable occupations. For this reason the best course would be to equate the Member's salary, as Bernard Crick suggested in 1959, with the salary of a senior grade in the civil service.[1] A point on the salary scale of an Assistant Secretary would be most appropriate. If this were done, the whole subject of Members' salaries need not become a matter of controversy again.

Facilities for Members
Important although the question of salaries is, this is not the

[1] Crick, op. cit., p. 38.

only aspect of the position of Members which has been in need of radical reform. Until recently, no back-bencher had a room of his own in the Palace of Westminster. Each Member had only a minute locker, not large enough to take an ordinary brief-case, and this was the sum total of private office facilities accorded to Members. When he needed to write to constituents he would either have to write in longhand in one of the writing rooms, or if lucky enough to be able to afford a secretary, he might be able to dictate to her *sotto voce* in one of the corridors of the House.[1] A start has been made to remedy this situation. Rooms for Members are being constructed inside the Palace of Westminster and a site in Bridge Street is being developed for the same purpose. In 1967 there was still a grave shortage of rooms. Many Members were sharing rooms with three or four others.

Another grievance that has been voiced by Members in recent years has been the lack of sufficient research assistance. Here again there has recently been some improvement. There are now thirteen graduate Clerks in the House of Commons Library, of whom six are primarily concerned with undertaking research for Members. This in no way compares with the 223 people employed in 1962 by the Legislative Reference Service of the American Library of Congress. The contrast is even more marked when it is considered that the Legislative Reference Service includes many highly skilled specialists in law, education, international affairs, housing, economics etc.[2]

No similar specialists have as yet been appointed to the House of Commons Library staff. It is apparent that if the staff of the Commons were strengthened in this way, Members could be much more effective in their work of criticizing the Government and keeping a check on the activities of Government departments. The specialists could also be available to assist the sub-committees of the Estimates Committee, and the Select Committee on Nationalised Industries, in their inquiries. Clearly one would not expect the House of Commons Library staff to be expanded to anything like the scale of the Legislative

[1] See especially Anthony Wedgwood Benn's account of the poverty of facilities in the House in the Procedure Debate on 31 January 1958. H.C. Deb. Vol. 581, Col. 685.

[2] Crick, op. cit., pp. 66–9 and 218–26.

Reference Service, but even the appointment of a few specialists on economic, scientific, and social services questions would be a great benefit. Another field in which Members are in great need of specialist assistance is in drafting bills and amendments. The Procedure Committee in 1959 recommended that an officer, or officers, of the House, with knowledge of legislative drafting, should be provided in order to assist private Members.[1] R. A. Butler, when leader of the House, promised to look into the matter but did not, in fact, give effect to the recommendation.

Televising Debates

One reform about which there is much difference of opinion in the Commons is the proposal for televising debates. Not long before his death, Aneurin Bevan said in 1959 in a debate in the Commons that if Parliament was to continue to exert a real influence in the nation, it must allow its proceedings to be televised. Relatively few front-benchers have since come forward with a similar view. One to do so has been Iain Macleod who, as Leader of the House in March 1963, told the House that he favoured an edited daily version on television of the day's proceedings.[2] Another Minister in the Macmillan Government, William Deedes, suggested the continuous televising of Commons debates on a special service which would be piped to subscribers such as—'schools, universities, newspaper offices, political clubs and so on'.[3] Harold Wilson in December 1963 thought that there might be a case for experimenting with a daily edited version. On the whole, he said, he was slightly against it, but he was prepared to be convinced.[4] Herbert Bowden, from 1964 to 1966 Leader of the House in the Wilson Government, had been more emphatically opposed when he was Opposition Chief Whip. He told the House in 1963 that the idea of televising proceedings 'frightened' him. 'Let me remind the House that this is a debating Chamber. Through you, Mr. Speaker, we address each other in debate. We are not speaking to the country or to the world outside. It is true that

---

[1] H.C. 92-I of 1958-9, p. xii.
[2] H.C. Deb. Vol. 673, Cols. 1791 and 1792, 15 March 1963.
[3] *Daily Mail*, 18 July 1963.
[4] Harold Wilson in a discussion with Norman Hunt, *The Listener*, 21 December 1963, p. 833.

reports of our debates appear in *Hansard*. But the very intimacy of our debates would be lost if the atmosphere were not as it is' . . . that is, if the television cameras were brought in.[1] Similar objections were advanced by Allan Segal in an appendix to Bernard Crick's *The Reform of Parliament*.[2]

These critical views tend to overlook the fact that while the continuous televising of proceedings in the House has numerous drawbacks, an edited daily version does not. A continuous television transmission would be often dull, often unintelligible to the viewer. It would invite Members to address viewers rather than the Chamber, it might produce jockeying for position, for the opportunity to speak at peak viewing times. A short evening programme lasting half an hour on the lines of 'Today in Parliament' would have none of these drawbacks. It would, in fact, be an illustrated account by a parliamentary correspondent of the highlights of the day's proceedings. The danger here would be that it would be presented in a biased way. But similar programmes, on B.B.C. and on I.T.V., reviewing the day's proceedings at the party conferences have been very successful and have been very fairly edited. There is no reason why similarly high standards of fairness should not be maintained in a televised 'Today in Parliament'.[3] Such a programme would certainly do something to increase public interest in, and understanding of, the Commons.

On 24 November 1966 the House debated the first report from a Select Committee which had been specially set up to examine the possibility of having the proceedings of the House televised.[4] The Leader of the House, Richard Crossman, proposed that proceedings should be televised on closed circuit television for five weeks, after which the House would vote again to decide whether a daily edited programme should be made. The House voted by a majority of one against making such an experiment.

The Reform of Parliamentary Privilege

There is one further field for reform which should be noted.

[1] H.C. Deb. Vol. 673, Col. 1748. 15 March 1963.
[2] Crick, op. cit., pp. 262–9.
[3] See especially here—Robin Day, *The Case for Televising Parliament* (Hansard Society, 1963).
[4] H.C. Deb. Vol. 736, Cols. 1606–1730.

There is a need, long overdue, for the reform of parliamentary privilege. Certain of the privileges of Parliament are essential. For example, it is highly desirable that Members' speeches in the Commons should be protected. That is, writs of libel cannot be served upon Members for speeches they make in the House. This is a valuable safeguard of freedom of expression in the House. What is more open to question is whether it is necessary for the House to be able, as at present, to punish for contempt 'imputations against the good name of the House'. It is, at present, immaterial whether or no the imputations complained of are justified. For example, in July 1965 a complaint of breach of privilege was made by a Conservative Member against the Chancellor of the Exchequer, James Callaghan. It was claimed that the Chancellor had said in a speech at Swansea on 3 July that certain Conservative Members were spokesmen for financial interests rather than for their constituents. The Speaker ruled that this was a *prima facie* case of breach of privilege and, after a vote in the House, the question was referred to the Committee of Privileges.

The Committee reported that there had been no contempt of the House in view of the explanation of his speech, given at the Committee's request, by the Chancellor, and in particular by his statement that he had not intended to imply 'that Honourable Members who possess interests are acting or were acting improperly in discussions on the Finance Bill'. What was most significant, however, was that the Clerk of the House, Sir Barnett Cocks, in a memorandum to the Committee, pointed out that the House did not accept justification as a defence in cases of contempt.[1] This seems to be altogether too wide a conception of privilege. As Iain Macleod has pointed out, Members could protect themselves sufficiently by using the ordinary law of defamation against scurrilous attacks made on them outside the Commons.[2]

What is needed, however, is a re-definition and restriction of the scope of privilege, not a re-organization of the Committee of Privileges. The organization of the Committee is well adapted

[1] H.C. 269 of 1964–5. Third Report from the Committee of Privileges: Complaint Concerning Speech of the Chancellor of the Exchequer.

[2] Iain Macleod, 'The Future of Parliamentary Privilege'. Article in *The Spectator*, 13 August 1965, pp. 200–1.

to its task. It consists, as a rule, of the Leader of the House, one of the Law Officers of the Crown, the Leader of the Opposition and the Liberal Leader, and eleven other Members, from both sides of the House, most of them senior back-benchers.

PART THREE: *Party Discipline in the House*

One of the most frequently voiced criticisms of the modern House of Commons concerns party discipline. L. S. Amery argued that 'the most serious political menace to our whole system of parliamentary government lies in the enormous development of the party machine', meaning the development he had witnessed within his own lifetime.[1] In 1958, Sir Robert Boothby criticized the rigidity of the party machines in the Commons and deplored the growing tendency in the country to regard Members 'as not much more than the recognized fuglemen for Abbey House and Transport House'.[2] Michael Foot has contended that in the Commons 'two well whipped forces confront one another in formal, prearranged combat. Speeches of Gladstonian power or Disraeli-ite wit are unlikely to shift a single vote. We need look no further for the pall of unreality and tedium which descends on so many parliamentary debates'.[3]

What substance is there in these criticisms? To attempt some answer it is necessary to examine the machinery of party organization in the House and the ways in which party discipline is invoked. Both the Conservative and Labour parties have a Chief Whip and about eleven assistant Whips—who are all Members of the House of Commons.[4] The Conservative Chief Whip is always appointed by the Leader of the Conservative Party. The Labour Chief Whip is appointed by the Leader of the Labour Party when Labour is the governing party, but is elected by the Parliamentary Labour Party when Labour is in opposition. When a party is in power, the Chief Whip and the eight most senior of his assistants are members of the Government and receive salaries.

The main function of the Whips is to inform Members of their

---

[1] Amery, op. cit., p. 42.
[2] H.C. Deb. Vol. 581, Col. 688.
[3] Michael Foot, *Parliament in Danger* (Pall Mall Press, 1959), p. 14.
[4] The expression 'Whip' derives from the hunting field. The whipper-in or 'Whip' is the person who manages the hounds.

party of the current business of the House, of the times when the attendance of Members is required and of the way in which they are expected to vote. They impart this information by means of a weekly notice, sent through the post to all Members, which is also known as a 'whip'. The whip gives details of business in the House in the forthcoming week. The degree of underlining indicates how important it is for a Member to attend. Double underlining means that the business is important and a division is expected; triple underlining, in a 'three-line whip', indicates that a vital vote will take place and that everyone is required to attend and vote. When the division takes place the Whips indicate to their respective packs how they are to vote by acting as tellers for the 'ayes' or the 'noes' as the case may be. Sometimes, when the division bells ring, many Members will flood in to vote as their Whips direct without any clear idea of what is at issue.

This is the machinery of party control, but how is the party attitude decided and how is party discipline enforced? These are the crucial questions which must be examined if the degree of rigidity of the party machines is to be assessed. On the Conservative side, the attitude of the party is determined by its Leader, both when it is in opposition and when it is the governing party. When the Conservatives are in power, of course, the Whips act on the instructions of the Leader of the House and of individual Ministers in charge of bills, although the Prime Minister and the Cabinet exert an overall control. When Labour is in power, the position is similar, but, when Labour is in opposition, the attitude of the party is often decided by majority vote at a meeting of the Parliamentary Labour Party.

The Leader of the Conservative Party, although in form an autocrat, keeps in close touch with trends of opinion among Conservative Members. The Whips provide one of the channels of communication, their recognized secondary function being to communicate feelings amongst the rank and file to the party leaders. As Peter Richards has said, the Whip is 'in turn, advocate, lightning conductor and interpreter'.[1] Also important are the committees of Conservative back-benchers. The Conservatives have seventeen of these committees ranging from Defence, Trade and Industry, Foreign Affairs, and Finance to

[1] P. G. Richards, *Honourable Members*, 2nd ed. (Faber, 1964), p. 148.

Health and Social Security. Each committee elects a chairman, vice-chairman, and secretary for the current session. Any Conservative can attend meetings of any of the committees. But naturally there is a hard core of specialists in each committee and the total attendance varies widely according to the interest taken in the topic under discussion.

The Chairman of a committee may be a former Minister and he may be a potential Minister. For example, Enoch Powell was Chairman of the Committee on Finance in the session 1959–60. He had been Financial Secretary to the Treasury before he resigned from the Government in January 1958. In July 1960 he was appointed Minister of Health. Not all chairmen become Ministers, of course, but all chairmen have the opportunity to exert considerable influence. Ministers do not normally attend meetings of these committees, but a Minister is quite often invited to attend when a committee wants to know his intentions or to thrash out a difference of opinion with him.

Even when a Minister does not attend a committee meeting he may receive a report of what has occurred. One of the Whips is attached to each committee, and he makes a report to the Chief Whip which may be sent on to the Minister. In some cases the secretary of the committee is the Minister's parliamentary private secretary, who also reports to his Minister. Also frequently in attendance at committee meetings are research officers from Conservative Central Office whose function is partly to keep in touch with opinion amongst Members, and partly to provide information and undertake research for the committee.

Each week during the session there is a meeting of all Conservative back-benchers known as the Conservative and Unionist Members' Committee. It is sometimes called the 1922 Committee because it first began to meet in that year. It receives reports of the party committees, it may discuss some matter of current policy, and it may consider complaints about the activities of the Whips. The Committee elects annually its Executive Committee, but the members of this Executive have no claim to sit on the front bench when the Conservatives are in opposition.

The organization on the Labour side is similar but with one

major and some minor differences. The major difference is that the Parliamentary Labour Party consists of all Labour Members, including the Leader of the Party and Members of the Cabinet or Shadow Cabinet. When Labour is in opposition, the Parliamentary Labour Party elects, early in the session, the Leader of the Party, Deputy Leader, and twelve members of the Parliamentary Committee. Together, they constitute the Committee with the addition of the Chief Whip, the leader of the Labour peers, the Chief Whip of Labour peers and one elected representative of Labour peers.

The Labour Party has a series of specialist groups similar in range to the Conservative committees. Like the Conservatives, Labour has developed specialist groups on Defence, Foreign Affairs, Commonwealth and Colonies, for example. There are differences of detail (the Conservatives have their committee on Finance while Labour has an Economic group) but the overall pattern is similar. The Labour specialist groups each elect a chairman and vice-chairman. Like the Conservative committees they have their hard-core of regular attenders but are open to any other Labour Members who are interested. Unlike the Conservatives, they do not report direct to the main organization of the party in Parliament, that is to the Parliamentary Labour Party. Instead they report to the Parliamentary Committee which then reports to the Parliamentary Labour Party. The chairmen of the Labour specialist groups, when Labour is in opposition, are usually 'Shadow Cabinet' spokesmen for the department under consideration. These 'shadow ministers' may be members of the Parliamentary Committee or they may be other Labour Members who have been invited by the Leader of the Party to join him on the front bench.

When Labour is in office the organization is different. The Leader of the Labour Party is Prime Minister. He no longer acts as Chairman of the Parliamentary Labour Party; instead a prominent back-bencher is elected. For example, Emmanuel Shinwell was Chairman from October 1964 until April 1967 when he was succeeded by Douglas Houghton.[1] The other

[1] Emmanuel Shinwell was a Minister in the minority Labour Governments of 1924 and 1929–31. In the Attlee Government he was Minister of Fuel and Power from 1945 to 1947 and Minister of Defence from 1950 to 1951. Douglas Houghton was Chancellor of the Duchy of Lancaster in the Wilson Government from October 1964 to January 1967.

officers of the Party are also back-benchers and there is no Parliamentary Committee. In its place, a Liaison Committee is brought into being, consisting of a majority of back-benchers and a minority of Ministers with the Chairman of the Parliamentary Labour Party as its Chairman. This Liaison Committee helps to keep a Labour Government in touch with back-bench opinion, but Labour Ministers have full freedom of action. They do not have to seek the approval of the appropriate specialist group or of the Parliamentary Labour Party. But of course a Labour Government tries to maintain good relations with the Parliamentary Labour Party and to retain the willing support of Labour Members.

Are the specialist committees and the main party meetings in the House primarily a device for keeping Members in check? Alternatively, are they as much a means for permitting Members to influence the leadership? Some of those who criticize the present party organization in the Commons maintain the first opinion. For example, Michael Foot has spoken of 'Whips and Scorpions'—the party committees being, in his view, the scorpions. He was particularly critical of meetings of the Parliamentary Labour Party. 'No formal agenda,' he claimed, 'exists for these meetings, often a major decision may be taken on a matter about which no prior notice is given. Resolutions on issues of supreme importance may be passed even though their terms have never been circulated in advance.' The meetings sometimes take place in an atmosphere of highly charged emotion, particularly when the leadership is being challenged, and reasoned, calm consideration of the issues at stake is impossible.[1]

There have been meetings of the Parliamentary Labour Party to which some of these criticisms could be held to apply. But there have been other meetings, too, of which it has been said that discussion has been of a high order. As a general picture of the way in which the Parliamentary Labour Party conducts its affairs, it seems likely that Foot's description is inaccurate. Certainly the impression he gives of the Labour Leader manipulating opinion in the Parliamentary Party, virtually as he thinks fit, is a misleading one. There have been many occasions when a Leader of the Labour Party has had to make concessions to a

[1] Foot, op. cit., p. 17.

point of view in the Parliamentary Party which he did not share. For example, in 1953, Clement Attlee was invited by Sir Winston Churchill, at that time Prime Minister, to take part in a discussion of party leaders on the reform of the House of Lords. Attlee put this suggestion to a meeting of the Parliamentary Labour Party which, by a narrow majority, decided that he should reject the invitation, though in 1948 Attlee had taken part as Prime Minister in a similar discussion of all party leaders on Lords reform.[1] Again, in 1954, the Parliamentary Labour Party was divided on the question of German re-armament. Attlee and a majority of the Parliamentary Party were in favour, but feelings ran high in the Labour Movement. So Attlee decided that the Parliamentary Party would not take a stand for or against German re-armament until the issue had been voted upon at the Annual Conference of the Labour Party.[2]

On the Conservative side, there have been numerous examples of back-bench rebellion. Criticism, centred in the Conservative committee on Housing and Local Government, played a big part in inducing the Minister of Housing and Local Government to provide more safeguards for the tenant in the Rent Bill of 1957. Again, the Suez policy of successive Conservative Governments was under fire from sections of Conservative Members from 1953 to 1954 and from 1956 to 1958. In 1960 the Budget was coolly received by Conservatives, both in the Conservative Finance Committee, and in the Budget debates in the House. The Budget itself was not greatly modified. But, in subsequent months, several changes in economic policy were made which pleased Conservative critics of the Budget, and in July one of the Government's chief critics, the Chairman of the Conservative Finance committee, Enoch Powell, was brought into the Government as Minister of Health.

These are only a few examples, on either side of the House, of the frequent attempts which are made by back-benchers to influence the leadership of their party. In these attempts the

[1] See Anthony Wedgwood Benn, *The Privy Council as a Second Chamber* (Fabian Society, 1957), p. 7.

[2] The Annual Conference, by a small majority, voted in favour of German re-armament.

party specialist committee is much more an aid than a hin-
drance to the back-bencher. Far from being a scorpion applied
by the leadership to the rank and file, it is more often a lever
which the back-bencher can try to apply in order to stimulate
Government action or alter its direction. Neither does the
existence of party committees mean that important debates
usually take place there rather than on the floor of the House.
Although it is true that crucial discussions often take place in the
party committees, the important speeches by which the Prime
Minister and the Leader of the Opposition attempt to influence
opinion are still made, by and large, in the House. Similarly,
critics from the back-benches do not confine their criticism to
the party meeting. Members on both sides of the House are free
to criticize their own party's policy in the House and to attempt
to convert majority opinion to their own views.

The Parliamentary Labour Party has only very rarely disciplined a Labour Member for speaking against established
Labour policy. Foot quotes the case of Aneurin Bevan from
whom the Parliamentary Labour Party withdrew the whip in
1955 on account of a speech he made in the House, and not for
failing to vote as the Party had decided.[1] But Bevan's speech
was a direct challenge to Attlee's leadership on the question of
nuclear weapons. It was, too, the culmination of an intensive
campaign against Attlee's policy waged on several fronts.
Bevan's case must be regarded as quite exceptional here.

Freedom to speak against party policy is one thing; freedom
to vote contrary to a party decision in the Parliamentary
Labour Party is quite another. The practice in the Labour
Party has at certain times been defined by Standing Orders
and at other times by a code of conduct. For example, Hugh
Gaitskell, as Leader of the Labour Party, said that the code
voted by the Parliamentary Labour Party in November 1959
made clear that Labour Members are expected to observe
majority decisions of the Parliamentary Labour Party, especially in the matter of voting, 'although the right of individual
members to abstain on grounds of deeply held conscientious
conviction is recognized'.[2] This 'conscience clause' is now

[1] Foot, op. cit., p. 18.
[2] Quoted from a statement by Hugh Gaitskell as reported in *The Times* of 25
November 1959.

G

fairly liberally interpreted. It had long been recognized that it applied to such questions as Sabbath observance, temperance, gambling, and conscription. Since 1945 it had also been reckoned to apply to differences on foreign policy if deeply and sincerely held. But it is a right only to abstain from voting, not to vote against the party decision.

What happens if a Labour Member votes against his Party? One such deviation would produce a reprimand from the Chief Whip and possibly an interview with the Leader of the Party. Repeated voting against the Party would result in the withdrawal of the whip. The Member concerned is then no longer an official Labour Member. He forfeits the right to attend meetings of the Parliamentary Labour Party and of Labour subject groups, he no longer receives the weekly notices sent out by the Whip's office.

Withdrawal of the whip may, or may not, result in expulsion from the Party. Four Labour Members (H. L. Hutchinson, J. F. Platts-Mills, L. J. Solley, and K. Zilliacus) who had the whip withdrawn during the 1945–50 parliament, were subsequently expelled from the Labour Party by a decision of the National Executive Committee, confirmed by Annual Conference. On the other hand, eight Labour Members who lost the whip during the 1951–55 parliament (Aneurin Bevan, G. Craddock, S. O. Davies, E. Fernyhough, E. Hughes, J. McGovern, S. Silverman, and V. Yates) fared better. They were not expelled from the Labour Party and had the whip restored to them before the 1955 election.

The difference in treatment resulted partly from the different gravity of the offences: the earlier rebels were held to be more persistently in revolt than the later group. Even more significant, perhaps, was the fact that the leading rebel in 1955, Aneurin Bevan, had a great deal of support in the Labour Party outside parliament and an impregnable position in his own constituency (Ebbw Vale). The leadership did not therefore want to force the issue to the point of expulsion. Normally, expulsion from the Party is equivalent to depriving a Member of his seat at the next election. The Labour Members who were expelled between 1945 and 1950, and who stood in the 1950 election as Independent Labour candidates, were all easily defeated by official Labour candidates. The threat of withdrawal of the whip, and possible subsequent expulsion from the Party, is therefore in most cases a very effective sanction.

The Conservatives have less rigorous discipline in the House than Labour. Individual Conservatives, or groups of Conservative Members, fairly often abstain or vote against the Party in order to register their disapproval of the Party line. Such action does not normally result in the whip being withdrawn. In fact, on the Conservative side, it is quite a frequent occurrence for Members to resign the Conservative whip in protest against their Party's policy. This was done by the Conservative Members, Lord Hinchingbrooke, Paul Williams, J. Biggs-Davison, L. Turner, Anthony Fell, Angus Maude, Sir Victor Raikes, and P. Maitland in May 1957. They were protesting against the Conservative Government's decision to allow British shipping to use the Suez canal. It was not until over a year later that five of the eight re-applied for the Conservative whip and were re-admitted. One of the group, Patrick Maitland, had come back earlier into the fold and two others, Sir Victor Raikes and Angus Maude, had resigned from Parliament.

Similarly, the Member for Caithness and Sutherland, Sir David Robertson, resigned the Conservative whip in February 1959 in protest against the Government's failure, in his view, to develop the Scottish Highlands. He fought the 1959 election as an Independent Conservative, and such was the strength of his position in the constituency that he was returned without official Conservative opposition. He continued to sit in the Commons as an Independent Conservative in the 1959–64 Parliament.

In these examples, the Conservative organization in Parliament appears surprisingly tolerant towards sustained opposition within its ranks. It must be remembered, however, that all these rebellions were relatively small in scale and did not threaten the Conservative majority. At times, in recent years, Conservative Whips have been very energetic behind the scenes to prevent a larger-scale rebellion developing, particularly on the Suez question. But while the Conservative organization in Parliament presents a reasonably tolerant picture, several local Conservative associations have shown marked intolerance to non-conformist Members.

Between 1956 and 1959 three Conservative Members failed

to secure readoption by their local associations. They were Nigel Nicolson at Bournemouth East, Sir Frank Medlicott in Central Norfolk, and Montgomery Hyde in North Belfast. Nicolson and Medlicott were objected to because they opposed the Eden Government's ultimatum to Egypt in October 1956 and the landings at Port Said. Medlicott, who resigned the Conservative whip, had it returned to him a year later. But, in the meantime, relations between him and his constituency association had become so strained that he announced that he did not wish to be readopted at the next general election.

Nicolson did not resign the Conservative whip and remained in good standing with the Conservative leadership in Parliament. Nevertheless the executive of the Bournemouth East and Christchurch Conservative Association voted by a large majority to adopt another candidate at the next general election. Nicolson refused to knuckle under and, after prolonged dispute, the national Chairman of the Conservative Party, Lord Hailsham, intervened. He persuaded the executive of the Bournemouth East association to agree to a ballot open to all members of the Conservative Party in the constituency. The ballot would decide if Nicolson was, or was not, to remain the Conservative candidate. The ballot, which took place in February 1959, did not reflect the executive's large majority against Nicolson. 3,671 votes were cast for him, 3,762 against.[1] Nevertheless it was a majority against him and another candidate was adopted for the 1959 general election.[2]

Nicolson had been unpopular with his local association not only for his views on Suez but also for supporting the abolition of capital punishment. This was the principal issue upon which Montgomery Hyde differed from his association in Belfast North. He was not re-adopted for the 1959 general election and so he too was excluded from Parliament. He had asked for a ballot to be held in the constituency to decide the dispute in the same way as matters were settled in Bournemouth East. But no such ballot was held.

In addition to these three Conservatives who had protracted

[1] A. Ranney, *Pathways to Parliament* (Macmillan, 1965), p. 65.

[2] For Nicolson's own account of his controversy with the Bournemouth East Conservative Association, see Nigel Nicolson, *People and Parliament* (Weidenfeld and Nicolson, 1958).

disputes with their local parties and eventually emerged the losers, one Conservative, Anthony Nutting, first resigned from the Government (he had been Minister of State for Foreign Affairs) in opposition to the Government's Suez policy, and then resigned his seat when his local association made it clear that they did not share his views. On the other hand one of his former colleagues in the Government, Sir Edward Boyle, who resigned on the same issue, was not rejected by his local association in the Handsworth division of Birmingham. When, a few months later, Macmillan became Prime Minister, Boyle re-entered the Government as Parliamentary Secretary to the Ministry of Education.[1] More recently, in January 1965, Aubrey Jones, at that time Conservative Member for Hall Green, successfully resisted an attempt to supplant him made by the finance and general purposes committee of his constituency association. When the issue reached the full executive of the association, the move to adopt another candidate was defeated.[2] Soon afterwards, he resigned his seat on accepting appointment as head of the Wilson Government's Prices and Incomes Board.

On the Labour side there was only one case during the Suez crisis of a Member resigning after disagreement with his local association. Stanley Evans resigned his seat at Wednesbury when called upon to do so by his local party. They objected to his support for military action against Egypt. He was the only Labour Member of Parliament to take this line. But Evans himself stated to the Press that the Parliamentary Labour Party had not proposed to withdraw the whip from him and considered his decision to abstain in the division on Suez to be covered by the conscience clause.[3]

The record shows more cases of intolerance in local Conservative associations towards non-conforming Conservative Members than has been shown by local Labour Parties towards deviating Labour Members. On the other hand, discipline in the Parliamentary Labour Party is generally tighter than the discipline which is imposed on Conservative Members

---

[1] Sir Edward Boyle was Economic Secretary to the Treasury when he resigned in November 1956 on the Suez issue.

[2] See *The Times*, 25 January 1965 and the *Sunday Times*, 31 January 1965.

[3] See statement in the *News Chronicle* of 21 November 1956.

in the Commons. What is really significant is that, however deplorable the cases of heresy-hunting among the Conservatives, there were only four such cases during the 1955–59 Parliament. What is more, the net effect of discipline in the House and conformist pressure from outside has not been to produce two collections of party yes-men. In fact, the variety of opinions in the House is remarkable as is the readiness of Members to express minority views.[1] Nowadays an Independent Member who has no party affiliation is rare but, in every Parliament, there are many independent-minded members sitting in the ranks of the two great parties. Such men as Gerald Nabarro, Ted Leather, and Cyril Osborne on the Conservative side or Sidney Silverman, Emrys Hughes, and Desmond Donnelly in the Parliamentary Labour Party have never been afraid to criticize their front bench or to espouse unpopular causes which they felt to be right, while staying within the party fold.

Yet even if it is true that independence, in spirit and utterance, is compatible with party loyalty, and even if the criticisms made of the party control are held to be unjustified, would it not be desirable to have more free votes in the House of Commons? It is undeniable that when there is a free vote, the debate often has an exceptionally high quality. This was true, for example, of the debate in 1958 on the report of the Committee of Privileges on the Strauss case.[2] But this was essentially a House of Commons matter on which party differences could be laid aside. Where party policy is involved a free vote is inappropriate. The interested public wants to know where a party stands on the issue which is before the House. If a party should be divided three ways between those who are in favour, those who vote against, and those who abstain, who is to say where the party stands? Clear identification of parties with policies, which the British public has come to expect, then goes out of the window. But although there is not a strong argument in favour of many more free votes in the House of Commons, and although party discipline is not at present

---

[1] An interesting analysis of the variety of opinions to be found in the 1955–59 Parliament in the two main parties is to be found in S. E. Finer, H. B. Berrington and D. J. Bartholomew, *Backbench Opinion in the House of Commons, 1955–59* (Pergamon Press, 1961).

[2] H.C. Deb. Vol. 591, Cols. 208–346.

unduly severe, there is need for constant vigilance against the growth of a spirit of intolerance either within the House itself or in the party organizations outside.

For Reference

L. S. AMERY, *Thoughtts on the Constitution* (Oxford University Press, 1947).

D. COOMBES, *The Member of Parliament and the Administration. The Case of the Select Committee on Nationalized Industries* (Allen and Unwin, 1966).

B. CRICK, *Reform of the Commons* (Fabian Society, 1959).

B. CRICK, *The Reform of Parliament* (Weidenfeld and Nicolson, 1964).

M. FOOT, *Parliament in Danger* (Pall Mall Press, 1959).

HANSARD SOCIETY, *Parliamentary Reform 1933–60* (1961).

A. H. HANSON and H. V. WISEMAN, 'The Use of Committees by the House of Commons' in *Public Law*, 1959.

A. HILL and A. WHICHELOW, *What's Wrong with Parliament* (Penguin, 1964).

H. J. LASKI, *Reflections on the Constitution* (Manchester University Press, 1951).

A. RANNEY, *Pathways to Parliament* (Macmillan, 1965).

P. G. RICHARDS, *Honourable Members*, 2nd ed. (Faber, 1964).

THE STUDY OF PARLIAMENT GROUP, *Reforming the Commons* (P.E.P., 1965).

H.C. 161 of 1931. Special Report from the Select Committee on Procedure on Public Business.

H.C. 189-I of 1946–7. Third Report from the Select Committee on Procedure.

H.C. 92-I of 1958–9. Report from the Select Committee on Procedure.

H.C. 303 of 1964–5. Fourth Report from the Select Committee on Procedure.

H.C. 153 of 1966–7. First Report from the Select Committee on Procedure.

H.C. 283 of 1966–7. Third Report from the Select Committee on Procedure.

CHAPTER VIII

The Control of Delegated Legislation

THERE has been much controversy over the last thirty years, and more, about the control—or rather, as is alleged, the lack of control—exerted by Parliament over delegated legislation. The controversy rose to its height in 1929 when no less a person than the Lord Chief Justice, Lord Hewart, roundly attacked the practice of delegating legislative and judicial powers to Ministers. The title of his book *The New Despotism* gives a good indication of the dangers which he discerned in these procedures.[1]

The Report of the Committee on Ministers' Powers, 1932
In response to the widespread concern which his book produced, the second Labour Government appointed a strong Committee on Ministers' Powers. Its first chairman was the Earl of Donoughmore. It included two senior public servants, Sir John Anderson, and Sir Warren Fisher who was at that time Permanent Secretary at the Treasury and Head of the Civil Service. The eminent historian of English law, Sir William Holdsworth, was a member, and also on the committee were several leading barristers, six Members of Parliament and one of the best known theorists of the Labour Movement, H. J. Laski. This representative and high-powered committee heard a great deal of evidence and produced, in 1932, a most useful report.[2] It is divided into three sections: Section I which is introductory and discusses the problem as a whole, Section II which deals only with delegated legislation, and Section III which is concerned with judicial or quasi-judicial decision by Ministers. Only Sections I and II will be discussed here.

The Committee had no doubt about the need for delegated

---

[1] Rt. Hon. Lord Hewart of Bury, *The New Despotism* (Benn, 1929).

[2] Cmd. 4060 of 1932. Report of the Committee on Ministers' Powers.

See also H.C. 32-57-2 of 1932. Minutes of Evidence to the Committee on Ministers' Powers.

legislation in a modern State: 'The truth is that if Parliament were not willing to delegate law-making power, Parliament would be unable to pass the kind and quantity of legislation which modern public opinion requires.'[1]

They advanced six reasons for delegating legislative powers. First, pressure upon parliamentary time is so great that it is desirable to leave some procedural and subordinate matters for regulation, so as to enable Parliament to concentrate on the essential principles in legislation. Second, matters of great technicality, where expert knowledge is required, are often best left to regulation. For example, the question of whether or not a drug should be placed on the poisons list is clearly a matter for experts. Third, there is often a need, in a complex scheme of reform, to take powers by regulation to deal with unforeseen contingencies, and many kinds of administrative difficulties, which may arise in the application of the Statute. A good example was to be found here in the National Health Insurance Regulations. If there had been no power to make such regulations, all the matters dealt with would have had to be settled by Statute with consequent delay and inconvenience to the public. Fourth and fifth, the use of regulations gives great advantages in permitting flexibility and scope for experiment. Finally, there is often need for the Government to act quickly in an emergency. This is not only the case in wartime, but in certain fields at any time. For example, the Minister of Agriculture needs to have power to check diseases in animals, at any time, by regulation.[2]

But although the Committee said that delegating some legislative powers to Ministers was inevitable and indispensable, they emphasized that there were abuses and dangers which needed to be guarded against. In the first place, they thought that the machinery of Parliamentary control was inadequate. 'There is at present no effective machinery for Parliamentary control over the many regulations of a legislative character which are made every year by Ministers in pursuance of their statutory powers, and the consequence is that much of the most important legislation is not really considered and approved by Parliament.'[3]

The Committee found much variety of statutory provision

---

[1] Cmd. 4060 of 1932, p. 59.　　[2] Ibid., pp. 51–3.　　[3] Ibid., p. 6.

for control by Parliament. The Statutes delegating legislative powers to a Minister would sometimes state that a regulation, made under the Statute, must lie before Parliament for a specified number of days during which it would be subject to annulment if either House voted a 'prayer' for its withdrawal. This is commonly known as the 'negative procedure'. Another practice was for the Statute to state that a regulation must lie before Parliament for a specified period during which it had to be approved by a resolution in each House if it was to remain in operation. This is known as the 'affirmative procedure'. A third general type was provision for a regulation to lie in draft, subject either to the affirmative or negative procedure. Finally, there were also examples of regulations being required to lie before Parliament but not subject to annulment.

It is obvious that of these provisions the affirmative procedure gives Parliament greatest control, for if the government does not find time for the regulation to be debated and voted it must lapse or fail to come into operation. The negative procedure only comes into effect if Members are sufficiently vigilant to examine the regulations which lie before the House to see if they contain undesirable features. The provision for laying a regulation without possibility of annulment gives least control of all. In theory the most important powers exercised by regulation should be subject to the affirmative procedure, those of less importance to the negative procedure, and those of only minor importance subject to laying only. But the Committee observed that in fact no coherent principle had been followed in deciding which procedure should be adopted.

Another cause for concern was that the number of regulations issued annually had grown immensely during the First World War, and the output of regulations had been considerable in many of the post-war years. The number of regulations lying before Parliament often made it very difficult for the nominal methods of control to be effective. It was very hard indeed for Members to keep informed of the content and meaning of the regulations theoretically subject to annulment or requiring an affirmative resolution.

The situation was made the more serious by the fact that some delegated legislative powers seemed undesirable or potentially dangerous in character. The Committee pointed to examples of Ministers being given power to legislate on matters of principle. For example, a succession of acts starting with the Poor Law Amendment Act of 1834 and culminating in the Poor Law Act of 1930 had given extraordinarily wide powers, first to the Poor Law Commissioners and later to the Minister of Health. The later Act stated that: 'For executing the powers given to him by this Act the Minister shall make such rules, orders and regulations as he may think fit for—(a) the management of the poor. . . .'[1]

The Committee also found numerous examples of regulations which imposed a tax. For example, the Import Duties Act of 1932 imposed a general *ad valorem* customs duty of ten per cent on all goods imported into the United Kingdom other than exempted goods. The Treasury was given power, on the recommendation of the Board of Trade, to make exemptions, or to impose supplementary duties against countries which discriminated against British goods. Orders made under the Act which increased customs duty were to be subject to the affirmative procedure, other orders to the negative procedure in Parliament. This was a very wide delegation of powers which the Committee spoke of as 'obviously one of the most important delegating enactments which Parliament has ever passed.'[2]

Another type of potentially dangerous delegated legislative power was found in what came to be known as 'the Henry VIII clause'. (It acquired this nickname because Henry VIII was associated with the attempt to make royal proclamations equal in force to statute law. His Statute of Proclamations of 1539 claimed this right and remained in force until his death in 1547.) The Committee found eight examples of Acts of Parliament passed between 1888 and 1929 which conferred upon Ministers power to modify the provisions of the Act. They also found numerous examples of Acts of Parliament which gave Ministers power to amend other Acts.[3]

Potentially dangerous as this power might seem, the Committee found that, in most cases, it applied to technical and minor matters and was intended to obviate the passage of a

---

[1] Poor Law Act, 1930, subsection 1 of section 136.
[2] Cmd. 4060 of 1932, p. 36.
[3] Op. cit., pp. 36-8 and 123-7.

series of new Acts differing only in slight detail from the Acts which they replaced. For example, the Juries Act of 1922 gave power to the Executive to adapt existing enactments by Order in Council, as necessary to give full effect to the Act. The Rating and Valuation Act of 1925 gave powers to the Minister which were wider in scope. Section 67 of this Act provided at sub-section (1): 'If any difficulty arises in connection with the application of this Act to any exceptional area . . . the Minister may by order remove the difficulty . . . and any such order may modify the provisions of this Act so far as may appear to the Minister necessary or expedient for carrying the order into effect.' But Ministers were only to exercise this power for a stated period—for less than four years from the passage of the Act. The Donoughmore Committee hesitated to condemn the use of the Henry VIII clause altogether, but it did urge that it should only be used when it was 'demonstrably essential'. The Minister should be expected to justify 'up to the hilt' the grant-ing of such powers, and where they were given by Parliament 'the clause should always contain a maximum time limit of one year after which the powers should lapse'.[1]

Finally, the Committee pointed to cases in which Parliament had delegated legislative powers to Ministers in such a way that judicial control over the use made of these powers was excluded. Judicial review of the acts of Ministers is an important aspect of the rule of law in Britain. The Common Law Courts may not rule upon the legality of a Statute in Britain, because Parliament is the sovereign law-making body. But the Courts can decide whether or not a Minister is acting within the powers (*intra vires*) delegated to him by Parliament when he makes an order or regulation. If the Minister is acting beyond his powers (*ultra vires*), they will find for the citizen and against the Minister in any judicial action brought by either party. But the Committee found that in certain Statutes, for example the Housing Act of 1925, a provision of the following kind was used: 'The Minister may confirm the order and the confirma-tion shall be conclusive evidence that the requirements of this Act have been complied with, and that the order has been duly made and is within the powers of this Act.'

This sort of provision had not been tested in the Courts when

[1] Ibid., p. 61.

the Committee made their report, but it seemed likely that it would make judicial control over Ministerial powers very difficult. The Committee commented: 'the clause is objectionable, and we doubt whether it is ever justified'.[1] If Parliament decided on any occasion that a Minister needed to be given power to make a regulation which could not be challenged in the Courts, it should state plainly in the Statute that that was its intention, and a period of challenge of at least three months from the passage of the Act should be allowed.[2]

Proposal for Scrutinizing Committees

Because there were undesirable, or highly questionable, types of delegation and because of the 'quantity and complexity' of subordinate legislation, the Donoughmore Committee recommended that both Houses of Parliament should establish scrutinizing committees. These committees should have a dual task. First, they should examine 'every Bill, containing any proposal for conferring legislative powers on Ministers, as and when it is introduced'. Second they should scrutinize 'every regulation, made in the exercise of such powers and required to be laid before Parliament, as and when it is laid'.[3] Every Bill containing a provision for delegating legislative power would be referred to the scrutinizing committee for report immediately it had received its first reading. The second reading should not take place until seven days after the report of the committee had been received. In making its report the committee would be instructed to state:

1. whether the precise limits of the power were clearly defined;
2. whether any power to legislate on a matter of principle or to impose a tax was involved;
3. whether any power to modify the provisions of the Bill itself or any existing statute was proposed;
4. whether power was being given to make regulations which would be, or might be, immune from challenge in the Courts;
5. whether the memorandum submitted by the Minister (the Donoughmore Committee suggested that every Bill delegating legislative powers should be accompanied by a

[1] Op. cit., p. 41.   [2] Ibid., p. 65.   [3] Ibid., p. 63.

Memorandum from the Minister explaining the nature of the powers proposed) gave an accurate account of the proposals in the Bill.

These were the principal heads under which it was suggested the committee should report.[1]

In reporting on a regulation lying before Parliament it was suggested that the committee should state:

1. whether any matter of principle was involved;
2. whether the regulation imposed a tax;
3. whether it was immune from challenge in the Courts;
4. whether it consisted wholly or partly of consolidation;
5. whether there was any special feature of the regulation meriting the attention of the House;
6. whether there were any circumstances connected with the making of the regulation meriting such attention.

In this way a committee in each House would be able to keep a check on delegated legislative power both at the source, in the Bill, and at the outflow, when regulations came to lie before Parliament. In carrying out these functions, the Donoughmore Committee recommended that the scrutinizing committee in each House should have a permanent staff and should have the assistance of the Counsel to the Lord Chairman of Committees in the case of the Lords committee, and the Counsel to the Speaker in the Commons.[2]

The report of the Donoughmore Committee, in so far as it related to delegated legislation, had three important consequences. In the first place, it dispelled the wildest fears about delegated legislation which had been fanned by Lord Hewart's *New Despotism*. On the other hand, and in the second place, it made clear that certain undesirable forms of delegation were currently in use. The report seems to have had a profound effect on senior Civil Servants in this respect, for since 1932 regulations which impose a tax have become very rare, and regulations which are immune from challenge in the Courts are almost unknown.[3] The 'Henry VIII clause' has not been used at all since the publication of the Report.[4] In the third place, the report had an important long-term result. It prepared the way for the establishment of a scrutinizing committee in the

---

[1] Op. cit., pp. 67–8.   [2] Ibid., pp. 68–9.   [3] See below pp. 198–9 and 208.
[4] See C. K. Allen, *Law and Orders*, 2nd ed. (Stevens, 1956) p. 102.

House of Commons, although one was not actually set up until twelve years later, in 1944.

There was already a scrutinizing committee in the House of Lords, but with restricted functions. In 1925 the House of Lords had set up a Special Orders Committee whose function it was to examine all orders which required an affirmative resolution. This committee has continued to function, but its terms of reference have never been widened.

The response to the Donoughmore Committee's suggestion for a House of Commons committee was at first not at all encouraging. W. I. Jennings, for example, writing in 1939 in the first edition of his study of Parliament, commented that the idea of a committee to examine all regulations laid before the House of Commons was impracticable. The task was too great and no Members would be found to undertake it.[1]

The House of Commons Creates Machinery for Scrutiny

The Second World War changed the situation in this as in so many other fields. In August 1939, on the eve of the war, Parliament passed the Emergency Powers (Defence) Act, 1939. This Act gave to the Government the most sweeping powers to regulate by Order in Council virtually every aspect of national life. Regulations were issued in increasing number, dealing with such subjects as detention, propaganda, press censorship, curfew, rationing, and many aspects of trade and production. The war-time peak was reached in 1942 when 1,900 statutory rules and orders of general application were issued. In the House of Commons, there was increasing disquiet as parliamentary scrutiny of more than a fraction of the orders laid had become patently impossible. In May 1943, after a debate on parliamentary control, the Government rejected the suggestion for a scrutiny committee.[2] But a year later, the Government was more co-operative. On 17 May 1944, a debate took place on the Motion of a Conservative back-bencher, Hugh Molson. The Motion asked for a Select Committee to be set up, charged with the duty of examining all 'Statutory Rules and Orders and other instruments of delegated legislation presented to

---

[1] W. I. Jennings, *Parliament* (Cambridge University Press, 1939) p. 491.

[2] The debate took place on 26 May 1943.   H.C. Deb. Vol. 389, Cols. 1593–1694.

Parliament'. Herbert Morrison, Home Secretary, replied that the Government were now willing for such a committee to be set up, but asked for the Motion to be withdrawn so that the Government could introduce their own Motion.[1]

On 21 June 1944 a sessional order, proposed by the Government, was approved which set up the Select Committee on Statutory Rules and Orders. This Committee has been reappointed in every subsequent session but has been known since 1946 as the Select Committee on Statutory Instruments. By its original terms of reference, it was instructed to consider every Statutory Rule or Order laid before the House, subject to affirmative or negative resolution, and to draw the special attention of the House to any Order etc. on any of the following grounds (here summarized):

1. that it imposed a charge on the public revenues;
2. that it was immune from challenge in the Courts;
3. that it appeared to make unusual or unexpected use of the powers conferred by the Statute under which it was made;
4. that there appeared to have been unjustifiable delay in the publication of it;
5. that its form or purport called for elucidation.

The Committee was given the assistance of the Counsel to the Speaker. It was empowered to require any Government department to submit a memorandum explaining any Rule or Order under consideration, or to send a witness to explain it. It was instructed, indeed, to give Government departments the opportunity to give such explanations before reporting any Rule or Order to the House. The Committee was to consist of eleven Members, five being the quorum.

Subsequent changes in terms of reference of the Committee have included some further grounds on which Rules and Orders may be reported to the House. In November 1945 it was given power to report an instrument on the grounds of delay in laying it before Parliament. Since 1947 it has been able to report instruments on the ground 'that there appears to have been unjustifiable delay in sending a notification to the Speaker under the proviso to subsection (1) of section four of the Statutory Instruments Act, 1946, where an instrument has

[1] H. C. Deb. Vol. 400, Cols. 202–99.

come into operation before it has been laid before Parliament.'[1] The committee has also been given power to report instruments which claim to have retrospective effect although no such power has been given in the Statute under which they have been made. One further change has been made in the organization of the Committee: its quorum has been reduced to three.

The Experience of the Statutory Instruments Committee

It will be seen that the terms of reference of the Committee are distinctly similar to the terms of reference which the Donough-more Report recommended such a committee should have in considering instruments. The Committee also has the assistance of the Counsel to the Speaker, as the Donoughmore Report suggested. The chief difference between the Donoughmore proposals and the Committee's actual powers is that the Committee is not empowered to consider Bills delegating legislative power. It can examine only the instruments as they are laid.

The Committee has been a success since its earliest days. In the first two years of its existence the Committee came across many cases of unjustifiable delay in the publication of instruments. In its first Special Report for the session 1944–45, it pointed to a particularly bad case of delay. The Ploughing Grants Regulations of 1945 had been signed on 31 January 1945, but they were not on sale to the public until 2 March, and were not laid before the House until 6 March. The Committee commented that this was a very lax interpretation of the requirement in the parent statute that instruments should be published and laid before the House 'as soon as may be'. The Committee said too that they had 'encountered a tenacious disposition on the part of the Department [the Ministry of Agriculture and Fisheries] to assert that the delay in respect of the Ploughing Grants Regulations was natural and justifiable'.[2] This was a particularly bad case, both in regard to the length of the delay and the arrogant attitude of the department concerned.

---

[1] See below p. 198. The phrase Statutory Instrument has been used since 1946 to describe all the many kinds of subordinate legislation made under authority of a Statute.

[2] H.C. 82 of 1944–5. First Special Report of the Select Committee on Statutory Rules and Orders.

In the following two sessions, the Committee reported numerous other cases of delay, but never of such a serious character. The departments clearly did a lot to speed up their procedure, and by 1948 cases of delay had become rare. This can then be counted the first main achievement of the Committee. It was an important one too, in that the twin principles of parliamentary sovereignty and the rule of law are infringed if there is a long delay between the making of an instrument and its laying and publication. While there is delay, the department concerned is administering an ordinance which Parliament cannot negative, because it has not been laid before either House, and the general public cannot know about, because the instrument has not been printed.

The second main achievement of the Committee was also linked to the question of delay. This was to persuade the Attlee Government to introduce the Statutory Instruments Bill which became the Statutory Instruments Act of 1946. This Act made important reforms, on lines recommended in the Committee's Special Reports, in the procedure of laying and publication of instruments. It provides that, normally, instruments which must be laid must reach Parliament before they come into operation. Where, exceptionally, this principle is departed from, the Speaker and the Lord Chancellor must be immediately notified by the department concerned, which must also give its reasons for failing to comply with the normal procedure. Similarly, the Act provides that no one can be convicted under an instrument which has not yet been published unless the prosecution can show that the accused had been informed of the content of the instrument. Another important reform made by the Act was the provision which requires all instruments, subject to the negative procedure, to lie before the House for forty days. This has introduced a welcome uniformity, for all instruments subject to the negative procedure are now open to challenge for forty days irrespective of the period of challenge mentioned in the parent statute.

The Committee has never had to report an instrument on the ground that it was immune from challenge in the Courts. It may be argued that the departments had already been made very chary of issuing such instruments by the strictures in the Donoughmore Report. This is true, but the fact that the

Committee is watching for the reappearance of any such instruments is an important safeguard. Examples of instruments which impose a charge on the public revenues, another type of instrument looked on askance by the Donoughmore Committee, have proved to be very rare. Between 1944 and 1959 the Committee on Statutory Instruments reported only one such instrument to the House. Again, the Committee with its watching brief, is an important deterrent to the departments. One of the most interesting of the grounds under which the Committee may report an instrument to the House is that it 'appears to make some unusual or unexpected use of the powers conferred by the Statute under which it is made'. The Committee reported 47 instruments under this heading between 1944 and 1959, the largest number under any heading.

Only rarely is an important constitutional principle involved, but that this heading is potentially most useful was demonstrated in the session 1945–46. On 16 November 1945, the Home Office issued an Order in Council which gave wide powers of arrest, without warrant, to a police constable who suspected a person of having been at a gaming house some days or weeks before. The Order was made under the authority of Defence Regulations which had been issued in 1939 under the Emergency Powers legislation of that year. The Committee reported it to the House on the grounds of 'unusual or unexpected use' because it seemed strange to them that powers of arbitrary arrest, given to the police in wartime to deal with enemy agents, should be used in peace-time to control gambling.[1] Shortly after the Committee's report was published, a prayer was moved in the House to annul the Order and the Home Secretary, Chuter Ede, acquiesced in the carrying of the prayer. In this case, therefore, the Committee was able to alert the Commons to negative an instrument which enlarged police powers of arrest in a most undesirable way, and a way which Parliament had clearly never intended.

It is rare for the Committee to be able to safeguard liberties of the subject in so direct a way. Most of its reports under this heading deal with more minor issues. For example, a report in February 1960 drew the attention of the House to the Teachers'

---

[1] See H.C. 40 of 1945–6 for Report of the Committee and Minutes of Evidence of examination of the Home Office witness, L. S. Brass.

Salaries (Scotland) (Amendment) Rules, 1959. They reported that some of these regulations seemed to make unusual or unexpected use of the powers conferred by Statute in that the regulations gave power to the Secretary of State for Scotland to modify the regulations while the parent Statute gave him no such power.[1] This is unexciting, but it is an important safe-guard that the Committee should be continually looking to see whether Ministers are assuming powers which Parliament has never authorized.

Similarly, the Committee's reports under the heading of need for elucidation have not had great news value. But the Committee has had an important effect on the departments in inducing them to issue better drafted and, where possible, self-explanatory instruments. In 1963 the Committee stated in their Special Report that they were 'impressed by the high standard of drafting and the obvious care which is taken to make the Instruments (many of which, by reason of their subject matter, are extremely complicated) intelligible'.[2] It has also waged an effective campaign for consolidation of instruments. It reported in the session 1947–8 that the situation as regards Air Navigation Regulations, which it had commented on in earlier reports, was getting out of hand. These Regulations had been first issued in 1923 and had since been amended 34 times. The original Regulations had been long out of print. The Committee reported that reissue of the Regulations in a consolidated form was a matter of urgency. In November 1949 they were able to note with satisfaction that the Regulations had been reissued in consolidated form.[3] So an aspect of the law which had become arbitrary and obscure to the interested public was clarified as a result of the Committee's agitation.

The Committee has more than fulfilled the hopes of the authors of the Donoughmore Report. Why has it been such a success, confounding pessimistic commentators of the 1930s?

[1] H.C. 18 VI of 1959–60 Second Report from the Select Committee on Statutory Instruments.

[2] H.C. 10–(i) of 1963–4 Special Report from the Select Committee on Statutory Instruments p. 2.

[3] H.C. 281 of 1949–50. Special Report from the Select Committee on Statutory Instruments, p. 3.

Perhaps the main reason lies in the skilled assistance given to the Committee by successive Counsels to the Speaker. The Committee was specially fortunate in that Sir Cecil Carr, its first adviser, was not only a constitutional authority but the leading expert on the drafting of delegated legislation. Before becoming Counsel to the Speaker he had been for many years editor of the annual volumes of Statutory Rules and Orders.[1] His specialized knowledge was invaluable to the Committee because to him fell the task of making a preliminary scrutiny of all instruments laid. He would select from among them those instruments which seemed to him to need examination by the Committee, as possibly coming under their terms of reference. The Committee then, when it met, had a short list of instruments needing its attention. As important as this invaluable preliminary sifting was the advice Carr gave to the Committee in the subsequent stages of examining the instruments and assessing departmental evidence, etc.

Since his retirement, the Committee has received the same sort of skilled aid and advice from his successors as Counsel to the Speaker, Sir Alan Ellis and Sir Robert Speed. Without their help the Committee's task would have been extremely difficult. But credit must also be given to the chairmen and members of the Committee in assessing the reasons for its success. The first chairman was Sir Charles MacAndrew, a Conservative Member, who continued to serve as chairman during the period of Labour Government from 1945 to 1950. As a good 'House of Commons' man, Sir Charles MacAndrew's interest as chairman lay solely in improving parliamentary control of delegated legislation irrespective of party considerations. This attitude has been shared by other members of the Committee, many of whom have given up much of their time and served on the Committee for long periods.

Sir Charles MacAndrew's success as chairman helped to establish a convention that the chairman should normally be a member of the Opposition. This convention has been followed since his retirement, subsequent chairmen being Godfrey Nicholson (Conservative), Eric Fletcher (Labour), and Graham Page (Conservative).

[1] He was also the author of two important books on delegated legislation and administrative law: see p. 209 below.

Suggestions for Further Reforms

Although it is generally recognized that the Committee has been a success, there has been some discussion about whether it should be empowered to do more. In 1946, Sir Gilbert Campion, then Clerk of the House of Commons, submitted a memorandum to the Select Committee on Procedure in which he proposed that the terms of reference of the Statutory Rules and Orders Committee (as it was then called) should be extended. He thought that the Committee should be empowered to report 'on the merits of a Statutory Instrument, as an exercise of the powers delegated' and that it should also be empowered 'to inquire into and report on any grievances arising out of Instruments actually in operation.'[1]

Sir Charles MacAndrew and Sir Cecil Carr in memoranda and in evidence to the Select Committee on Procedure opposed these suggestions.[2] On the question of merits, they were in agreement that if the Committee on Rules and Orders were to consider merits it would take a tremendous amount of time. They also considered that it would destroy the semi-judicial character of the Committee. Discussing the merits of instruments would often mean discussing matters of party controversy. As Sir Charles MacAndrew put it: 'the Committee, in the two years it has been working has really worked on non-party lines. Anyone coming into our Committee would not have the slightest idea to which party the various Members belonged. We are really semi-judicial I think in the way we run it, and as soon as merits arise, policy must be discussed and the Committee must be divided into the Government and Opposition'.[3] They were supported in this view by C. K. Allen.[4]

When the Select Committee on Procedure reported, it showed some sympathy for the view that merits should be examined, but concluded that the whole question of control of delegated legislation should be examined by a committee of the House.[5] Such an investigation was not begun until December 1952 when a Select Committee on Delegated Legislation was appointed with Clement Davies as chairman. It

---

[1] H.C. 189–I of 1945–6. Third Report from The Select Committee on Procedure, pp. xliv and xlv.

[2] Ibid., pp. 242–61.   [3] Ibid., question 4630 at p. 246.

[4] Ibid., pp. 261–82.   [5] Ibid., p. xii.

reported in October 1953 and, on the question of merits, recommended that the existing powers of the Statutory Instruments Committee were wide enough and that it should not be empowered 'to consider the merits or policy of a statutory instrument'.[1] The Davies Committee seems to have been influenced in coming to this conclusion by the knowledge that on both sides of the House unofficial machinery had been established for examining the merits of statutory instruments.

Between 1943 and 1951 there was, on the Conservative side of the House, a group of around 24 Members calling themselves the 'Active Back-Benchers' and led by Sir Herbert Williams. This group constituted itself into an unofficial vigilance committee to scrutinize delegated legislation and to put down a prayer against any instrument which they considered objectionable. During the period of Labour Government from 1945 to 1951, most prayers were put down by members of this group.[2] After 1951, when the Conservatives came to office, the group was less prominent but continued to function on a smaller scale. The specialized committees of Conservative Members also take an interest in the merits of statutory instruments issued by the departments within their sphere of specialization. From 1951 to 1959 it was normal practice for departments to send copies of instruments to the relevant Conservative specialist committees, especially if they were thought likely to be controversial.[3]

On the Labour side, there has been since 1951 a Subject Group of Labour Members which is solely concerned with statutory instruments. It consists of about twelve Members and had as its first two chairmen members of the Labour front bench, first Chuter Ede, a former Home Secretary, then G. R. Mitchison. The group examines, from the point of view of merit, all instruments which are subject to the affirmative or negative procedure. When Labour is in Opposition, it recommends to the Parliamentary Committee whether or not, in its opinion, an instrument should be opposed by the Parliamentary Labour Party. Sometimes the Statutory Instruments

---

[1] H.C. 310–I of 1952–3. Report from the Select Committee on Delegated Legislation p. xxvi.
[2] See J. E. Kersell, *Parliamentary Supervision of Delegated Legislation* (Stevens, 1960) p. 63.
[3] Op. cit., p. 65.

Group will refer an instrument to one of the other Subject Groups when it requires more specialized advice on the merits of the case. On the whole the Labour organization for scrutinizing instruments seems to have worked well.[1] Indeed the scrutiny of the merit of instruments undertaken, especially since 1951, by party committees is an important argument for continuing to leave out considerations of merit from the terms of reference of the Statutory Instruments Committee. The semi-judicial, constitutional role of that committee can be preserved, leaving the question of merit to party committees.[2]

There remains to consider other suggestions for reform. It has been noted that Sir Gilbert Campion advocated in 1946 that the Statutory Instruments Committee should be empowered to inquire into 'grievances arising out of Instruments actually in operation'.[3] The objection made by Sir Charles MacAndrew and Sir Cecil Carr to this suggestion was that it would prove very time-consuming and that such grievances were best examined through the existing channels: in the departments or through questions in the House.[4]

A somewhat similar proposal to Sir Gilbert Campion's was made to the Select Committee on Delegated Legislation in 1953 by Mr. E. A. Fellowes, at that time Clerk Assistant to the House of Commons. His suggestion was that persons aggrieved by the operation of a statutory instrument should be allowed to appeal to the House of Commons for redress of grievances. He thought that such petitions should be examined not by the Statutory Instruments Committee but by special committees of three Members nominated by the Committee of Selection in respect of each petition. The committees could hear witnesses and report to the House on the petition assigned to them. The Select Committee on Delegated Legislation rejected this proposal on the grounds that 'Aggrieved persons have their

---

[1] Ibid., p. 67.

[2] See also on the controversy over merits: A. H. Hanson, 'The Select Committee on Statutory Instruments 1944-9', *Public Administration*, Winter 1949, p. 278.

F. A. Stacey, 'The Select Committee on Statutory Instruments—a Reply to Mr. Hanson', *Public Administration*, Winter 1950, p. 333.

A. H. Hanson, 'A further note', *Public Administration*, Autumn 1951, p. 281.

[3] See above p. 202.

[4] H.C. 189-I of 1945-6, p. 243 Memorandum by Sir Charles MacAndrew, p. 244 Memorandum by Sir Cecil Carr. Also evidence by both witnesses especially pp. 247-9.

grievances brought to the attention of the House by Members and it is not necessary to establish another procedure for lodging and hearing of petitions'.[1]

Another suggestion was made by Sir Cecil Carr in his Memorandum to the Select Committee on Delegated Legislation. He put the following question to the Committee: 'Has the time come to try the Donoughmore-Scott Committee's recommendation of a Standing Committee to scrutinize the delegation while the enabling Act is still in the Bill stage?'[2] The Davies Committee did not think so and reported that it was unnecessary: 'Individual Members and unofficial Committees of Members are vigilant and can be relied upon to take close interest in any proposal in a Bill to delegate power to legislate'.[3]

A suggestion which Sir Cecil Carr pressed strongly on the Davies Committee was that the period during which instruments lie before the House should be extended from forty to fifty or even sixty days. He favoured this reform, which would necessitate amendment of the Statutory Instruments Act of 1946, because experience showed that it was quite often difficult for the Statutory Instruments Committee to make its report on an instrument within the forty-day period. This was because of the necessity of asking for a memorandum from the department concerned, considering the memorandum and then publishing the report.[4] The Davies Committee recommended, to meet this point, that the procedure should be changed so that the period of challenge should be 10 days from the date when the Statutory Instruments Committee reported on an instrument or the statutory 40 days, whichever was the longer.[5] This recommendation has not been accepted. There is clearly need for reform here on the lines of either the Davies Committee's or Sir Cecil Carr's recommendations.

The chief problem which the Davies Committee was set up to inquire into was concerned with debates in the House on instruments subject to the negative procedure. Between 1950 and 1952 the Conservative, and then the Labour, Opposition

---

[1] H.C. 310–I of 1952–3 Report from the Select Committee on Delegated Legislation p. xxxii. See also pp. 88–91 for Memorandum by E. A. Fellowes.

[2] Ibid., p. 9.   [4] Ibid., p. 9.

[3] Ibid., p. xxiv.   [5] Ibid., pp. xxvi–xxvii.

had used these debates as a means of obstructing and harassing the Government. They were able to do this because such debates were 'exempted business', that is they were exempt from the standing order which provides that the normal business of the day in the House is interrupted at 10 p.m. Debates on prayers to annul statutory instruments could therefore continue well into the night. By spinning out discussion in these debates, and by putting down one prayer for consideration after another, the Opposition were able effectively to embarrass the Government because of the need to keep large numbers of Government supporters present in the House in case of a division. It was generally felt that this was an abuse of the rules of the House, but that any curtailment of debate should still provide sufficient time for effectively debating instruments subject to a prayer. The Davies Committee found the answer by suggesting that debate on a prayer should be terminated at 11.30 p.m., and the question put to the House, unless the Speaker considered that there had been insufficient time for debate. In such a case the debate would be adjourned until the next ordinary sitting day of the House, when it would be resumed at the end of Government business for that day.[1] The House of Commons accepted this recommendation. On 31 March 1953, a sessional order on these lines was carried and it has been repassed in every subsequent session. This put an end to the practice of using debates on delegated legislation as a tactic for harrying the Government.

The Impact of Parliamentary Control

We have seen the importance of the work of the Statutory Instruments Committee and the effect it has had on departments. How much interest is taken in its reports in the Commons? There is some ground for saying that interest in the Commons has declined in recent years. S. A. Walkland has pointed out that between 1945 and 1951, the Committee reported 25 instruments on the ground that they made an unusual or unexpected use of powers (probably the most important of the heads under which the committee can report). Of these, 14 were debated in the Commons. Between 1951 and 1959, the Committee reported 22 instruments under unusual

[1] Op. cit., p. xxxii.

or unexpected use. In only 3 cases was a prayer moved to annul the instrument in question.[1]

The Committee itself has been concerned to see that the Commons takes more notice of its reports. In its Special Report in January 1961, the Committee recommended that when motions for affirmative resolution on an instrument appear on the Order Paper of the House, a note should be added stating whether the instrument concerned had been reported on adversely by the Statutory Instruments Committee. This recommendation was accepted and has become part of the practice of the House. In this way, the Committee's reports on instruments requiring an affirmative resolution are brought to the notice of the House. There remains the problem of instruments subject to the negative procedure. To ensure that they were debated, if reported upon adversely, the Committee recommended that they should only remain operative for 40 days after being reported on unfavourably by the Committee, unless during that time they were approved by an affirmative resolution. This reform would require legislation and has not been acted on.

It would help if the Committee's reports were more informative. When it draws the attention of the House to an instrument, the report merely states the heading under which this action is taken. No reasons are given. Sometimes, something can be gleaned from the correspondence with the department concerned, which is published, or from the minutes of evidence of cross-examination of Civil Servants. But if the committee explained its reasons for reporting an instrument adversely, it would make the reports both more informative and more interesting.[2]

Nevertheless, the role of the Committee is a very valuable one. The accompanying table (Table VII) shows that delegated legislation has continued to be used extensively since 1947. An average of around six instruments has been brought to the attention of the House in each session. Between October

[1] S. A. Walkland, ' "Unusual or Unexpected Use" and the Select Committee on Statutory Instruments', Article in *Parliamentary Affairs*, Winter 1959–60, pp. 61–9.

[2] S. A. Walkland argues that the Committee should issue reasoned reports, op. cit., p. 68.

TABLE VII

The Select Committee on Statutory Instruments 1947–66

Session	Total of instruments examined by the Committee	Number brought to special attention of the House
1947–48	1,189	10
1948–49	1,300	5
1950	682	7
1950–51	715	17
1951–52	930	8
1952–53	680	9
1953–54	595	4
1954–55	273	1
1955–56	581	6
1956–57	449	5
1957–58	416	2
1958–59	505	3
1959–60	495	9
1960–61	617	4
1961–62	594	2
1962–63	713	5
1963–64	760	7
1964–65	1,088	4
1965–66 (October to March)	203	2

(Source of statistics: Special Reports of the Select Committee on Statutory Instruments)

1957 and December 1966, 41 instruments were reported. Seventeen of these were under the heading of needing elucidation, 17 under unusual or unexpected powers, 2 under retrospective effect and 5 because of unjustifiable delay.[1] These figures show the continuing need for vigilance by the Committee.

We may conclude that the House of Commons now exercises a more effective control over delegated legislation than it did in the 1920s despite the increased use now made of delegated

[1] H.C. 5–VI of 1960–1. Special Report from the Select Committee on Statutory Instruments.

H.C. 10–(i) of 1963–4. Special Report from the Select Committee on Statutory Instruments.

H.C. 266 of 1966–7. Special Report from the Select Committee on Statutory Instruments.

legislative powers by governments. The effectiveness of its control has been enhanced by the enquiries of the Select Committee on Statutory Instruments. But this committee's work has been ably complemented by groups of individual Members and by party committees. Their interest reflects a more general awareness of the need for, and the possibility of, careful scrutiny of delegated legislation. In this respect, as in so many others, the House of Commons has, since the Second World War, improved its methods of keeping a check upon the work of government departments. The work of the Public Accounts Committee, of the Estimates Committee in its post-1945 form, of the Statutory Instruments Committee, and of the party committees on both sides of the House, has all helped to increase the information available to Members and to allow them to become more effective critics of the administration.

For Reference

C. K. ALLEN, *Law and Orders*, 2nd ed. (Stevens, 1956).

C. T. CARR, *Concerning English Administrative Law* (Columbia University Press, 1941).

C. T. CARR, *Delegated Legislation* (Cambridge University Press, 1921).

LORD HEWART, *The New Despotism* (Benn, 1929).

J. E. KERSELL, *Parliamentary Supervision of Delegated Legislation* (Stevens, 1960).

S. A. WALKLAND, '"Unusual or Unexpected Use" and the Select Committee on Statutory Instruments', in *Parliamentary Affairs*, 1959.

K. C. WHEARE, *Government by Committee* (Clarendon Press, 1955), Chapter VIII.

Cmd. 4060 of 1932. Report of the Committee on Ministers' Powers.

H.C. 310–1 of 1952–3. Report from the Select Committee on Delegated Legislation.

Reports of the Select Committee on Statutory Instruments.

CHAPTER IX

The House of Lords

THE House of Lords is certainly the strangest feature of the British system of government. In mediaeval times a house of nobility was commonly found in European countries. One by one all have disappeared, or lost any part in the legislative process. The British House of Lords is the unique surviving example of a legislative chamber largely composed of hereditary peers. There is an element of life peers in the House but, numerically, it is a small minority. In 1966 there were 119 life peers who had been nominated under the Life Peerages Act of 1958. To their number may be added the nine Lords of Appeal in Ordinary (Law Lords), who are life peers, and the 26 Lords Spiritual (the Archbishops and senior Bishops of the Church of England). There is therefore a non-hereditary element of just over 150 as against the whole body of hereditary peers entitled to sit in the Lords, who number more than 800. Nowadays, however, the real work of the House is carried on by life peers, by some of the hereditary peers of first creation, and by a very small fraction of the hereditary peers who have inherited their titles.

The House of Lords 1832–1911

It is difficult to explain why the hereditary peerage for so long played a predominant part in the British Upper House. Part of the explanation must lie in the fact that the majority of peers were usually intelligent enough to give way when faced with the most serious kind of confrontation with the Commons. Before 1832 the House of Lords was a powerful Second Chamber. Its power lay chiefly in the ability of some of the wealthiest peers to influence voting in the Commons. About 150 Members of Parliament were returned by rotten boroughs, some of which were under the control of great landlords who sat in the Lords. In Bagehot's phrase, the House of Lords was 'if not a directing

Chamber, at least a Chamber of Directors'. The Reform Act of 1832 brought a major change by abolishing the rotten boroughs. From then on, the House of Lords became a revising and delaying chamber only.

Conflict between the two Houses could be resolved in one of two ways: either the Prime Minister could induce the Monarch to create sufficient peers to produce a majority for the Government in the Lords, or the Lords could give way to the majority in the Commons. A precedent for the creation of peers was to be found in the action of a Tory Ministry in 1713. Faced with a hostile Whig majority in the Lords, the Tory Ministry persuaded Queen Anne to create twelve Tory peers in order to wipe out the Whig majority, and secure the ratification by the Lords of the Treaty of Utrecht. This precedent was invoked in 1832 when the House of Lords rejected the Reform Bill for a second time. The first defeat of the Bill had been followed by a General Election which confirmed the Whig Government's majority and popular support for the Bill. The Prime Minister, Earl Grey, then asked the King to promise to create sufficient Whig peers to secure the passage of the Bill in the Lords. William IV, somewhat reluctantly, gave this undertaking, but no creations were in fact necessary, as on hearing of the royal promise, the Tory leadership in the Lords decided to allow the Bill to pass.

The struggle over the Reform Bill and its outcome set the scene for the House of Lords in the next 70 years. In the mid-nineteenth century it was generally assumed that in cases of conflict between the Houses, the House of Lords might reject a bill in order to enforce reconsideration by the Commons but would eventually give way to pressure from the Commons, particularly if popular support for a proposed measure was confirmed in a General Election. In the 1850s the Conservative and Liberal strengths in the Lords were roughly equal and there was no serious conflict between the Houses. But in the later 1860s, with the Liberal Party under Gladstone adopting more radical policies, conservative tendencies in the Lords were intensified. When Gladstone became converted to the need for Irish Home Rule, his Home Rule Bill was defeated in the Commons in 1886 by the combined forces of the Conservatives and dissident Liberals, calling themselves 'Liberal Unionists'.

The Liberal peers split in a similar way. In 1893 when the House of Commons had approved Gladstone's second Home Rule Bill, the House of Lords heavily defeated it by 419 votes to 41. Since then there has always been an immense majority for Conservative and Unionist policies in the Lords and a potential hostility to non-Conservative governments. The conflict subsided for a ten-year period from 1895 to 1905 when the Conservatives held office in concert with the Unionists. But with the formation of a Liberal Government in 1905 and with Liberal success at the polls in 1906, relations between the Liberal majority in the Commons and the great Conservative majority in the Lords became very strained. A series of Government bills sent up from the Commons was rejected by the Lords, including the Land Valuation and Licensing Bills, while one of the most dearly prized Liberal measures, the Education Bill of 1906, was so extensively amended that the Government decided to abandon it.

The last straw, from the Liberal point of view, came when the Lords rejected the Finance Bill of 1909 on second reading. This was a drastic action because a convention had long been recognized that the Lords did not reject Money Bills. The Liberal Prime Minister, Asquith, then asked for a dissolution, and at the General Election in January 1910 the Liberals gained a small majority which was strengthened by the support of Labour and Irish Nationalist Members. The Asquith Government then introduced the Parliament Bill which proposed to limit the powers of the House of Lords. It was obvious that the House of Lords would reject this Bill, but the question of the creation of peers was confused by the death of King Edward VII in May 1910. His successor, George V, thus came to the throne at a moment of acute constitutional crisis. The number of creations necessary for a Liberal majority in the Lords would have been unprecedentedly large, and the King was being urged by many Conservatives on 'constitutional' grounds to refuse to create the necessary Liberal peers because the passage of the Parliament Bill would only be a prelude to the enactment of Irish Home Rule. Eventually, the King agreed to promise to create sufficient Liberal peers, if the Liberal Government could confirm its majority in a second General Election. This it was able to do in December 1910, but the need for a massive creation of Liberal peers was obviated by the passing of the Parliament Bill by the Lords in August 1911.

From the Parliament Act, 1911, to the 1950s

The Parliament Act of 1911 had two main provisions. First, it provided that Money Bills, if sent up to the House of Lords at least one month before the end of a session should, if not passed without amendment by the Lords within a month, become law, subject to the Royal Assent, without the consent of the Lords. Money Bills were defined by the Parliament Act, but for greater certainty the Act provided that the Speaker of the House of Commons should supply a certificate confirming that a Bill was a Money Bill. In the second place, the Act provided that other public bills should become law, subject to the Royal Assent, but without the consent of the Lords, if passed by the Commons in three successive sessions. It also provided that two years must elapse between the first reading in the first of these sessions and the third reading in the third session. The Lords were therefore limited to imposing two years' delay on the passage of non-financial legislation. But one category of bill was exempted from the provisions of the Act. A bill proposing to extend the maximum duration of Parliament beyond five years had to receive the consent of the Lords to become law.

The preamble to the Parliament Act implied that it was thought of by its authors as an interim measure. It began with these words:

'Whereas it is expedient that provision should be made for regulating the relations between the two Houses of Parliament:

And whereas it is intended to substitute for the House of Lords as it at present exists a Second Chamber constituted on a popular instead of hereditary basis, but such substitution cannot be immediately brought into operation:'

It was clearly the intention of many Liberals to go on from piecemeal to wholesale reform of the Second Chamber. The Lloyd George Government, during the First World War, summoned a Conference under the chairmanship of Lord Bryce to discuss the composition and powers of a reformed Second Chamber. Lord Bryce reported in April 1918 that the

H

majority of the Conference favoured a Second Chamber in which the largest element would be elected by Members of the House of Commons. It was proposed that 246 members of the new Upper House should be elected by M.P.s grouped in 13 geographic areas. Thus, M.P.s for Wales and Monmouthshire would elect 15 members of the Upper House, while Members for London constituencies would elect 27 (the allocation per area being based on population). Within each group, election would be by proportional representation so as to secure fair representation of the parties found in the Commons. A further 81 members of the Upper House would be chosen by a Joint Standing Committee of both Houses of Parliament. Initially, all the 81 chosen in this way would be chosen from the peers, in order to maintain some continuity with the House of Lords; in time only 30 of the seats would be reserved for peers. Members of both sections of the new Upper House, the 246 and the 81, would have a 12-year term, one third of each section retiring every fourth year.

As regards powers, the chief interest of the majority report of the Bryce Conference lay in its proposal for recourse to a Free Conference Committee of both Houses in cases of disagreement between the Houses. This Free Conference Committee would be composed of members of the two Houses in equal numbers with a maximum total membership of sixty. All Bills upon which there was disagreement would be referred to it, when its task would be to try and produce an agreed text. This would be the beginning of what might be a long process, with the Bill being considered again by the two Houses and then possibly referred to the Conference Committee once again. In the last analysis, no Bill would be able to pass without the agreement of the Commons; while a Bill which had the support of the Commons but was rejected by the Lords could only pass if it had secured a majority of not less than three, of the members voting in the Conference Committee. These complex proposals would have given the Upper House considerable power to delay, and in some cases obstruct, legislation approved by the House of Commons.

The Bryce Conference proposals were not acted upon, partly because the Conference report was by no means unanimous, and partly because the proposals were not acceptable either to the Right or to the Left in British politics. To the Right they would have meant an unwelcome and radical abandonment of the traditional House of Lords; to the Left the proposed new Second Chamber was to be too powerful in legislative matters, and could place too effective a brake on the initiative of the majority in the Commons. So the Lords continued unreformed and was not the subject of much controversy in the inter-war period. Conservative governments occasionally had difficulty with revolts by Conservative peers. The National Government's Agricultural Marketing Bill of 1933 was considerably amended in the Lords, against the Government's wishes. In this case, the Government did not re-submit the Bill to the Lords but acquiesced in the amendments. In most other cases of Government Bills which were amended in the Lords, for example the Coal Industry Bill of 1937–8, the Government eventually succeeded in getting its way in all matters of real importance.[1]

The short-lived minority Labour Government of 1929–31 had greater difficulty with the Lords. In particular, one of its major measures, the Coal Mines Bill of 1929–30, was drastically amended in the Lords. This experience helped to influence the Labour Party at its Annual Conference in 1934 to vote for the abolition of the House of Lords. But when Labour came to power for the first time with a clear majority, in 1945, abolition of the Lords was not in its immediate programme. In fact, the Labour Government found the House of Lords a very useful Second Chamber in the sphere of legislation.

Some Government bills which had been passed rather hurriedly in the House of Commons were extensively amended in the Lords on the Government's advice. By and large, therefore, the House of Lords proved to be a means of accelerating rather than delaying Labour's ambitious legislative programme. If there had been no Upper House, legislation would have to have been considered at greater length in the Commons to ensure adequate discussion. The Conservative majority in the Lords were content on their side not to press differences with the Government too far. When a Bill was amended in the Lords, against the Government's advice, the Lords did not

[1] See P. A. Bromhead, *The House of Lords and Contemporary Politics* (Routledge and Kegan Paul, 1958), pp. 148–50.

normally persist in their amendment when the Bill returned from the Commons with the amendment struck out.

However, the Labour Government feared that in the later stages of the Parliament elected in 1945, the Conservative majority in the Lords would become more assertive. In the first three sessions of the 1945 Parliament it was clear that any Bill rejected or drastically amended by the Lords could be repassed by the Commons in two subsequent sessions and could become law under the Parliament Act of 1911 without the consent of the Lords. But in the final two sessions of the Parliament, the Labour majority in the Commons would no longer be able to override the Lords in this way. The Labour Government feared that their Bill to nationalize the iron and steel industry, which they would not have ready until the session of 1948–9, would be rejected by the Lords and could not become law under the Parliament Act of 1911 within the lifetime of the current Parliament. Accordingly, they introduced in the session of 1947–8 a new Parliament Bill which proposed to amend the delaying period to two sessions, one year having to elapse between the second reading on the first occasion and the third reading on the second occasion.

This Bill in fact became law as the Parliament Act of 1949, but not before an attempt had been made to secure agreement on reform of the Lords. A conference of leaders of the three main parties took place in 1948. It reached a surprising measure of agreement on the question of the composition of the Upper House. The party leaders agreed on the principle that the Second Chamber should be complementary to, and not a rival to, the lower House and that therefore it should be a modification of the existing House of Lords and not a completely new type of chamber based on some system of election. They were also agreed on the principle that 'the revised constitution of the House of Lords should be such as to secure as far as practicable that a permanent majority is not assured for any one political party'.[1] They suggested that members of the Second Chamber should be called 'Lords of Parliament' and should be appointed on grounds of personal distinction or public service. They might be drawn either from hereditary

[1] Cmd. 7380 of 1948. Parliament Bill, 1947: Agreed Statement on Conclusion of Conference of Party Leaders.

peers or from commoners who would be created life peers.

These were the key principles upon which they were in agreement, but they were also in accord in suggesting that women should be eligible to be appointed Lords of Parliament, that members of the Upper House should be paid, and that peers who were not Lords of Parliament should be entitled to stand for election to the House of Commons. These agreed principles represented some major compromises on the part of the Labour and Conservative leaders.

Unfortunately they were not able to reach a compromise on the question of powers, and it was on this question that the conference broke down. Both sides were prepared to make some concession. The Conservative leaders said that they might have regarded as acceptable a period of delay of eighteen months from the second reading in the Commons—half-way between the two years of the Parliament Act of 1911, and the one year proposed by the new Parliament Bill. Indeed, as a further concession, they said that they would have been prepared to suggest, for consideration by their supporters, an even shorter period of twelve months from the third reading in the Commons. The Labour leaders, on their side, had been prepared to suggest to the Labour Party that the period of delay should be either one year from the second reading in the Commons or nine months from the third reading, whichever period was the longer. The gap that remained to be bridged between the Conservative and Labour proposals was only three months, but it could not be bridged. The conference of party leaders having been abandoned, the Labour Government went ahead with its Parliament Bill. It was able to secure enactment of the Bill under the provisions of the Parliament Act of 1911, despite its rejection in three successive sessions by the House of Lords.

Since the period of delay was fixed at one year by the Parliament Act of 1949, there seems to have been little disposition among Conservatives to extend the period. Indeed the Conservative Party manifesto at the 1955 General Election stated that, while a Conservative Government would attempt to bring about a reform of the Lords, such a reform would 'be concerned solely with the composition of the House'. Earlier, in 1953, Sir Winston Churchill as Conservative Prime Minister

had invited the Leader of the Opposition, Clement Attlee, to
take part in an all-party conference on the composition of the
Lords. Attlee declined this invitation after referring the question
to the Parliamentary Labour Party. It seems that the Labour
attitude was governed largely by the feeling that it was better
to leave the House of Lords as it was: in a state in which it
could do good, by improving legislation, but could not do
harm (i.e. obstruct Bills sent up by a Labour majority in the
Commons) because of its anachronistic composition. To
modernize the composition of the Lords might, in the majority
Labour view of the time, make the Upper House more assertive
and more inclined to use its power of delaying legislation. The
Conservatives eventually then produced their own plan for
piecemeal reform.

The Life Peerages Act, 1958

The principal element in the Conservative reform was the
Life Peerages Act of 1958. This is a very short statute which
simply gives the Crown power to appoint life peers, who may
be women. No limit is set on the number of life peers who
may be appointed. At the same time, payment of peers was
introduced for the first time by providing for an attendance
allowance for peers of three guineas a day. This could not be
considered a salary because the maximum allowance that any
peer could receive, even if he attended on every day in a
session, would not be much more than £300. The allowance
did something, however, to improve the position of those peers
who did not enjoy considerable private means. In 1964 it was
increased to four and a half guineas a day. Finally, some
attempt was made to restrain the intervention of 'backwoodsmen'—peers who did not normally attend the House but who
came in large numbers to defeat a Bill whose objects they
disliked. The Lords approved, in 1958, a new standing order
which laid down that every peer must say at the beginning of a
session whether he intended to take up his seat in the House.
If he applied for leave of absence, in this way, then he was
morally bound not to come and vote. About 200 peers now
declare their intention not to attend. This still leaves a very
large number of peers who have inherited their titles (about
600) who can attend and vote and influence the decision of the

Lords. Henry Burrows, a former Clerk at the Lords, considered in 1965 that the procedure had served no useful purpose.[1]

Clearly much the most important element in these reforms was the Life Peerages Act, 1958, which by 1966 had made a considerable impact on the shape of the House. In 1966, there were 119 life peers, created under the Act, of whom 16 were women. Of the total of 119, the largest section, 31, were former Labour M.P.s. Eighteen were former Conservative M.P.s and two were former Liberal M.P.s. In addition, there were sixteen life peers who had been active and prominent in their parties without having been in the Commons. Of these, ten were Labour, five Conservative and one Liberal. Another important category contained eminent educationists who numbered nineteen in all. There were nine company directors and nine former public servants. This last category included two former colonial governors, the former Permanent Under-Secretary at the Foreign Office, Lord Caccia, and three former heads of nationalized industries, Lords Beeching, Hinton and Plowden. There were four authors or journalists, three life peers with legal experience, three trade union officials and two voluntary social workers (see accompanying Table VIII).[2]

The difficulty involved in this classification of life peers is that some individuals are classified by their occupation, or former occupation, while the reason for their being created life peers has been quite separate. For example, Lord Goodman is classed here as a solicitor but the reason for his peerage is to be found largely in the fact that in 1965 he was chairman of the Arts Council. Nevertheless the table does highlight some of the most important results of the introduction of life peers.

In the first place, it has brought into the Lords a sizeable element of former Labour M.P.s and Labour party workers as well as people from the professions who have Labour sympathies. Both Macmillan and Home as Premiers asked the Labour Leader of the Opposition, first Gaitskell, then Wilson, to suggest nominations. A high proportion of peers created

---

[1] Henry Burrows, 'Two Writs for the House of Lords'. Article in the *Listener* 29 July 1965, p. 149.

[2] Included amongst the former Labour M.P.s are several trade union officials. Also counted among the former Labour M.P.s is the head of a nationalized industry, Lord Robens, chairman of the National Coal Board.

TABLE VIII

Life Peers in the Lords, 1966
(Peers created under the Life Peerages Act, 1958)

Former Labour M.P.s		31
Former Conservative M.P.s		18
Former Liberal M.P.s		2
Prominent Party workers (but not former M.P.s)	Labour	10
	Conservative	5
	Liberal	1
Eminent educationists, university professors, etc.		19
Company directors		9
Former public servants		9
Journalists, authors		4
Barristers, solicitors		3
Trade Union officials		3
Voluntary Social workers		2
Others		3
	TOTAL	119

between 1958 and 1964 were recommended in this way. When Wilson became Premier, he continued to nominate a majority of life peers with Labour sympathies. The primary function of the introduction of life peers has therefore been to strengthen Labour representation in the Lords.

Its secondary function has been to introduce into the Lords eminent people from the professions of a type which was relatively rare among those created hereditary peers. The nineteen educationists and university professors, for example, are people of first-rate ability. Lords Todd and Wynne-Jones in Chemistry, Lords Robbins and Kahn in Economics, Lord Llewellyn-Davies in Architecture, Lord Holford in Town Planning, Lady Wootton and Lord Simey in Sociology, are outstanding figures in their subjects. There are prominent heads of Colleges and Universities in Lords Bowden, Franks, Fulton, James, Annan and Florey, and a former chairman of the University Grants Committee in Lord Murray. Also interesting are those who can be grouped under the heading of authors and journalists. They include Lord Snow, Lord Chalfont, who was defence correspondent of *The Times* and was created a life peer to enable him to enter the Wilson government as Minister of Disarmament, Lord Francis-Williams, and Lord Willis who was best known as the original author of the television programme 'Dixon of Dock Green'.

The company directors included leading industrialists like Lord Kings Norton, chairman of the Metal Box Company, and Lord Cole, the chairman of Unilever. Several life peers are men of many-faceted talent. For example, Lord Kings Norton is not only a leading industrialist but also an outstanding aeronautical engineer with a distinguished earlier career as a government scientist. Others are men of noticeable outspokenness and conviction. The best example here is perhaps Dr. Donald Soper who was made a life peer in 1965. Lord Soper, a Methodist Minister and past president of the Methodist Conference, had been a soap-box orator for years at Speakers' Corner in Hyde Park and on Tower Hill. He continued to make his twice-weekly appearances on the soap-box after being made a life peer. It is apparent that the power to create life peers has been used on the whole in a very imaginative way. It has brought in many brilliant men and women from outside Parliament who would have been most unlikely to have been appointed hereditary peers. Indeed many of them would have refused a hereditary peerage, as would a large number of the former Labour M.P.s.

Until the end of 1964, hereditary peers continued to be created alongside the growing body of life peers. The new hereditary peers included a fair number of former Conservative Ministers, although a good many such people chose to be life peers—for example Lords Alport, Hill, and Runcorn. Many prominent businessmen who were ennobled between 1958 and 1964 were created hereditary peers, for example Lord Marks and Lord Thomson, the newspaper proprietor. Of distinguished public servants ennobled in this period, quite a high proportion were made hereditary peers: one may instance Lord Gladwyn (formerly Gladwyn Jebb and British Ambassador in Paris), Lord Howick of Glendale (formerly Sir Evelyn Baring and Governor of Kenya), Lord Normanbrook (formerly Norman Brook, Permanent Secretary to the Treasury) and Lord Shenfield (formerly Sir Roger Makins and Chairman of the Atomic Energy Authority).

Harold Wilson, as Premier, let it be known that he would

not recommend the creation of further hereditary peers. He did, however, repair an omission in the creation of life peers. Between 1958 and October 1964 no Liberal politician was made a life peer. Wilson partly made amends by recommending the creation of Lords Wade and Byers, both former Liberal M.P.s' and Baroness Asquith of Yarnbury (formerly Lady Violet Bonham Carter), a prominent Liberal campaigner.

The position of the hereditary peerage has been further affected by the passage of the Peerage Act of 1963. This Act was the result of a personal campaign by Anthony Wedgwood Benn. His father, the first Viscount Stansgate, had accepted a hereditary peerage in 1941 in order to strengthen the meagre Labour ranks in the Lords. He consulted his elder son who had no objection to his father taking a peerage. But the elder son was killed in the war and the younger son, Anthony, who had political ambitions, found himself condemned to be, in time, politically immured in the Lords. A vigorous and popular Labour Member of the Commons in the 1950s, he set about trying to renounce the succession. But Parliament refused to pass first his private bill, then a public bill with this object. His father died in 1960. Benn then claimed that he was not disqualified from continuing to sit in the Commons, because he had renounced the peerage and had not applied for a Writ of Summons to the Lords. The House of Commons Committee of Privileges, however, considered that his renunciation had no effect and that his status as a peer disabled him from sitting in the Commons. The Conservative majority in the Commons supported this decision of the Committee. A writ was issued for a by-election in his constituency of Bristol, South East. Benn stood again and was returned with a greatly increased majority, the campaign being fought on the issue of his right to remain a Member of the Commons if supported by the electorate in his constituency. After the by-election, the defeated Conservative candidate, Malcolm St. Clair, petitioned the Election Court on the ground that Benn was disqualified from sitting in the Commons by reason of his peerage. The Court upheld this petition and the House of Commons allowed St. Clair to take his seat as the Member for Bristol, South East.

So Benn's long campaign to renounce his peerage seemed to have failed. But Parliament proved to be not wholly unsympathetic. A Joint Select Committee of the two Houses was set up which recommended that peers should be able to resign their titles and privileges and so become eligible to sit in the Commons. The peerage in each case should not be extinguished for good, for the heir of someone who had renounced his peerage would resume the title. Existing peers, it was suggested, should be given six months to decide whether to renounce their titles; newly succeeding peers, in most cases, one year. These recommendations were accepted by the Commons and in 1963 the Peerage Act became law. Other detailed changes were made by this Act. All Scottish peers were allowed to sit in the Lords, whereas previously they had elected sixteen of their number at the beginning of each Parliament. Peeresses in their own right (i.e. peeresses with a hereditary title) were to be allowed for the first time to sit in the Lords, or to surrender their titles on the same terms as other peers.[1]

Anthony Wedgwood Benn took the earliest possible opportunity to renounce his peerage under the Act. He was returned for Bristol South East at a by-election and again in the General Election of 1964. He then entered the Wilson Government as Postmaster General. Much more surprising was the decision of the fourteenth Earl of Home to renounce his peerage in October 1963. He took this action to secure election as Leader of the Conservative Party. A little earlier, another contender for the Conservative leadership, Lord Hailsham, had also decided to renounce his peerage. The departure of the two leading Conservative peers and their translation to the Commons could not fail to weaken the position of the hereditary peerage in the Lords. In fact, since 1963, it can be said that few peers who have inherited their titles figure prominently in debates in the Lords. The major part is taken by life peers and hereditary peers of first creation. The active legislators in these categories are mostly drawn from the ranks of peers who were previously M.P.s. This is not surprising, as they are experienced and skilled in the work of Parliament and are best qualified to take part in debates on legislation. The distinguished people from outside Parliament who have been appointed life peers, in general, take less part in legislative business, although

[1] For a fuller account of the Peerage Act, 1963, and its passage see B. Crick, *The Reform of Parliament*, pp. 134-41.

on a subject within their special experience they may be prominent.

The Role of the Lords

We have seen earlier that the Lords fulfils a very important role by revising in detail legislation sent up by the Commons. It can also initiate legislation, and in any session a substantial minority of Government Bills originate in the Lords. These are usually rather technical Bills which are not a matter of acute party controversy. For example, in the session 1960–61, Government bills originating in the Lords dealt with such matters as trustee investment, weights and measures, land compensation and police pensions. The work done on such Bills as these in the Lords can make their passage in the Commons smoother and speedier. On private bills, the Lords shares an equal burden with the Commons, and in considering delegated legislation also, the Lords has equal powers with the Commons. The legislative role of the Lords is then still very important and very valuable.

Its functions in the field of financial legislation have, of course, been much diminished since the Parliament Act, 1911. The House of Lords now normally gives a good part of one day to discussing the Finance Bill on second reading, but then passes the Bill through all its other stages without discussion. The time thus saved on financial legislation can be used for general debates. These debates form a valuable adjunct to debates in the Commons. Indeed, as there is more time available in the Lords, it frequently happens that a debate takes place in the Lords on a currently important topic for which no time has been found in the Commons. The quality of these debates is, by and large, very high. As the house is made up largely of elder statesmen and people experienced in public service, business, or the professions, there is usually no lack of informed opinion. Peers have no constituents and do not have to seek re-election, so party ties are looser than they are in the Commons. Party organization is maintained on parallel lines to the organization in the Commons, but there is a greater readiness to criticize one's own party and to take an independent line. In addition, there is a considerable body of peers who do not accept a party whip.

General debates in the Lords do not normally end in a division. Debate begins by a noble Lord calling attention to a particular problem or situation and moving for papers. At the end of the debate the motion is usually 'by leave withdrawn' and there is no vote. The whole importance of the debate lies in what is said, and speeches made may be influential on the Government and more rarely on public opinion.

The House is perhaps seen at its best in a debate like the one held on 19 May 1965 on Urban Planning and Development.[1] The debate was opened by Lord Llewellyn-Davies, Professor of Architecture at London University, and the architect of many hospitals. Lord Brockway said later in the debate that this was a remarkable speech—'a speech which not merely dealt with the theory of planning but which applied that theory to immediate problems. One of the advantages of the House is that it can listen to speeches of that character. I cannot imagine that speech being delivered in another place.'[2] A later speaker in the same debate was Lord Holford, the Professor of Town Planning at University College, London, and the foremost authority in this field. Also taking part was Lord Silkin, formerly Minister of Town and Country Planning in the 1945 Labour Government. This example illustrates the way in which the House of Lords can provide a forum for debate on specialized subjects which the Commons rarely touches, debate reaching a level at times which M.P.s cannot be expected to reach. Such a debate can have an important effect on informed opinion.

A classic example of an influential speech in the Lords was the contribution by Lord Keynes to the debate, in December 1945, on the negotiation of the American loan to Britain. His biographer, R. F. Harrod, says that the speech 'made a profound impression and moved opinion'.[3] A speech in the Lords which received greater publicity was the speech by Lord Tedder in 1956 criticizing the whole Suez operation on the

---

[1] House of Lords Vol. 591 cols. 458–9.

[2] House of Lords Vol. 591 col. 514. Lord Brockway, as an egalitarian, was an unwilling recruit to the House of Lords. He only accepted the Wilson Government's summons in order to strengthen Labour representation in the Lords. He soon came to value the quality of debates in the Lords. See also his article: 'Living like a Lord' in the *Spectator*, 30 April 1965.

[3] R. F. Harrod, *The Life of John Maynard Keynes*, (Macmillan, 1951) p. 617.

grounds that it was ill-conceived and based on a 'complete and utter misjudgement of world-wide political reactions to our intervention'.[1] These speeches were not only cogent in themselves but also gained greatly in effect because they were delivered by outstanding authorities in their fields.

The standard of debate in the Lords has been steadily rising in recent years and greater interest is now taken in the work of the House. The attendance of peers in the session 1964–5 was on average considerably higher than the attendance in the previous session. The House was also more assertive than it had been for some time. Two Government bills, the War Damage Bill and the Trades Disputes Bill, were amended in a major way. But the Lords did not insist on its amendments when these bills returned from the Commons. The attitude of the Lords was, then, assertive but not intransigent. In fact the atmosphere of the House was unprecedently liberal. It approved the Murder (Abolition of the Death Penalty) Bill, with only minor amendment. The Lord Chief Justice, Lord Parker, had originally moved an amendment giving to the judges discretion to fix the term of imprisonment for people convicted of murder. The sponsors of the Bill favoured a 'life sentence' which left discretion, as to the actual term served, with the Home Secretary. Lord Parker's amendment was carried at committee stage, but he himself moved a compromise amendment at report stage. This restored discretion to the Home Secretary by requiring that judges must pass a life sentence for murder, but empowering them to recommend a minimum term of imprisonment in each case. This action stands in contrast to the Lords' previous rejection of abolition of the death penalty in 1948 and 1956.

Even more liberal was the Lords decision in 1965 to support a private member's Bill, introduced by Lord Arran, to legalize homosexual acts in private between consenting adults. In the same session, a similar private member's bill in the Commons, introduced by Leo Abse, was defeated. On this issue, then, the Lords showed itself to be in advance of the Commons.[2]

---

[1] House of Lords. Vol. 200 col. 1084. Lord Tedder was Deputy Supreme Commander in Western Europe under General Eisenhower, 1943–5, and Chief of the Air Staff, 1946–50.

[2] Leo Abse's bill was eventually passed by both Houses and became law in 1967.

It is apparent that the Lords has undergone major changes since the early 1950s. The most important change has been the Life Peerages Act of 1958 and the use to which it has been put. The introduction of life peers has brought new life to the House of Lords. Nor is it wholly accurate to claim, as Bernard Crick has done, that the House is composed, besides the hereditary peers, of 'far too many retired politicians and V.I.P.s past their prime, and far too many I.B.P.s (Impossibly Busy People)—all those life peers appointed to work in the House of Lords but who, like Lords Shawcross and Robbins, never really had time'.[1] In fact the former M.P.s, as we have seen, provide the necessary legislative experience in the Lords, and the outstanding people from the professions, Lord Robbins included, attend and speak in debates in which they have special knowledge.

Alternative Forms of Second Chamber

Though one may not accept Crick's criticism of the composition of the Lords, the present position is far from satisfactory. The great anomaly lies in the fact that the 'backwoodsmen'—the hundreds of peers of inherited title who rarely attend the House—have a right to attend and outvote measures which the experienced and qualified members of the Lords would have approved. A second anomaly lies in the majority for the Conservative Party which is to be found in the whole body of peers. In view of these continuing anomalies is there a case for a more radical reform of the upper House? To answer this question it is useful to consider the possible types of Second Chamber and the experience of other countries.

One possibility is a directly elected upper House. It could be chosen by a different electoral system. For example, the new upper House could be elected by the single transferable vote while the House of Commons continued to be elected by the relative majority system. The disadvantage of direct election is that the upper House can then rival the lower House. Even if by law the Government were made responsible only to the lower House, the upper House could also claim a popular mandate and there would be endless possibilities for friction between the two Houses. Another disadvantage of direct

[1] Bernard Crick, 'How long, O Lords'—Article in the *Observer*, 4 July 1965.

election, as compared with the present House of Lords, is that party would count for as much in the Upper House as in the Commons, and much the same sort of candidate would be returned to the two Houses.

There is only really a good argument for a directly elected upper House in a country which has a federal constitution. In a federal system there is always a desire to safeguard the individual states against encroachment by the federal government. So we find that in the American constitution each state is given the right to elect two senators and only two, irrespective of its population. New York State, with a population of more than 17 million, has two senators; and Nevada, with a population of 368,000, also has two senators. Thus the Senate, which is granted very wide powers by the constitution, can be held to place a check, in the interest of the states, upon the lower House, the House of Representatives, which is, broadly speaking, elected on the basis of population. In Australia also the Senate is directly elected, ten seats being allotted to each state irrespective of population. The Soviet Union, in theory, also has a federal constitution. The Soviet of the Union is directly elected on the basis of population, while the Soviet of Nationalities is directly elected on the basis of twenty-five deputies from each Union Republic, eleven deputies from each Autonomous Republic, five deputies from each Autonomous Province and one from each National Region. But, of course, both Houses are dominated by the Communist Party and other parties are not allowed to exist, let alone contest elections. Leaving aside the question of the Soviet Union, it seems that there is an argument for a directly elected Second Chamber in a country with a federal system, but not in a country with a unitary system like Britain.

Another possibility is appointment for life. The members of the Canadian Senate, for example, are nominated for life by the Governor-General.[1] Nomination by the Governor-General means, in fact, nomination by the Government of the day. Canadian experience has been that each Government chooses as senators supporters of the party in power. The Senate therefore is an upper House in which party counts for a good deal and in which there is a long period of domination by one

[1] Since 1965 Canadian senators must retire at 75.

political party. The number of senators is limited to 110. A long period of Conservative government results in a series of Conservative nominations to vacancies in the Senate and a Conservative ascendancy there. This is only slowly reversed by Liberal governments, who for some time are faced with a hostile majority in the upper House. Eventually Liberal nominations may produce a Liberal majority in the Senate which is an embarrassment to succeeding Conservative governments and so on.[1]

A third possibility which has been canvassed is an upper House chosen by professional and vocational organizations. Some sort of chamber of this type has been advocated by many people in this country: by Sidney and Beatrice Webb in 1920 in their book *Constitution for a Socialist Commonwealth of Great Britain*; by Sir Winston Churchill, who in his 1930 Romanes lecture argued for a House of Industry; and more recently by L. S. Amery and Christopher Hollis whose proposals resembled those made by Churchill.[2] The last three writers argued for an industrial chamber which would be in addition to the Commons and Lords. But it could equally well take the place of the Lords. There is no good example of such a chamber in practice. In Italy, under Mussolini, there was a corporative chamber but this took the place of a democratically elected Parliament and was itself not freely elected. Portugal too has a corporative chamber but is also not a democracy.

The only democratic country which has any form of vocational representation in the Upper House is the Republic of Ireland. The Irish Senate since 1937 has consisted of six members elected by graduates of Irish universities, eleven nominated by the Prime Minister and forty-three members elected from five vocational panels. The manner of nomination and election of these forty-three considerably waters down the vocational character of the chamber. One half of the candidates in the five panels (which are classified as Cultural and Educational, Agricultural, Labour, Industrial and Commerical, and Administrative) is nominated by members of the two Houses of

[1] See R. Macgregor Dawson, *The Government of Canada* (University of Toronto Press, 1949) pp. 334–41. Dawson remarked that Sir John A. Macdonald stood alone as the only Prime Minister who appointed a political opponent to the Senate.

[2] See Amery, op. cit., and Christopher Hollis, *Can Parliament Survive?* (Hollis & Carter, 1949) esp. pp. 120–9.

Parliament. The other half is nominated by vocational associations. Choice from these panels is made by an electoral college consisting of the members of both Houses of Parliament, numbering 207 in all, together with all the members of the county and county borough councils, making a total electorate of nearly 1,000. Election is by proportional representation. Both the members of Parliament and the members of local authorities are predominantly party men, and it is not surprising to find therefore that they choose good party men for the Senate rather than eminent representatives of industry or the professions. As a result, the Senate is divided on party lines and has little of the character of a vocational chamber.[1] It is in fact far from being a pure example of a vocational chamber, as it combines the idea of vocational representation with another system of electing the upper House: by members of local authorities and members of Parliament grouped in an electoral college.

It would be possible to devise a chamber entirely elected by vocational organizations. Christopher Hollis speaks of a chamber 'elected by those engaged in industry, voting in occupational rather than in geographical constituencies'.[2] But there are very great difficulties involved. How is the voting to be organized in these constituencies? Would it be left to the trade unions and to the employers' associations to organize their own elections? If this were not thought satisfactory, then there would need to be State intervention in the internal affairs of unions and employers' associations in order to regularize the elections. Many would find such intervention undesirable. Another great problem is found in the question of the amount of representation which should be accorded to each occupational group. How many members should be chosen by the mineworkers as against the shipping owners or the doctors? Whatever decision about the allocation of members was arrived at, it would inevitably be arbitrary and open to dispute.

A yet more fundamental criticism concerns the very nature of a vocational chamber. It is open to question whether people elected by vocational associations would make good legislators.

---

[1] See Basil Chubb, 'Vocational Representation and the Irish Senate', in *Political Studies*, June 1954, pp. 97–111.
[2] Hollis, op. cit., p. 120.

Candidates for election to the House of Commons are in many
cases members of a vocational association, but they do not
stand as such and they must commend themselves to their party
organizations, and to the electorate, as people of all-round
ability and interest. They are elected not as doctors, steel
workers, or stockbrokers but as representatives of constituencies
including a host of trades and professions. They are therefore
likely to have much wider horizons and a clearer conception
of the national interest than the representatives of vocational
associations would have. Equally, members of a nominated
upper House can be chosen for their eminence in their industry
or profession coupled with the impression they give of po-
tentiality as good legislators. In other words, direct election or
nomination by the Government of the day are likely to produce
better legislators than any system of election by vocational
associations which would produce representatives having, in
the main, a narrower sectional interest.

Finally, there are several examples of an upper House which
is indirectly elected, in some cases by the members of local
authorities, in some cases by the members of the lower House.
The upper House in Sweden is entirely elected by members of
local councils. In France, in the Fifth Republic, the Senate is
elected by electoral colleges in each department, each electoral
college consisting of the deputies for that department, the
members of the departmental council and some or all of the
municipal councillors, the number varying broadly in relation
to the population of each commune. This system, in theory, is a
combination of election by the lower House and election by
local authorities. But the local councillors are such a numerous
element in the electoral colleges that the system can be considered as election by local authorities. Essentially the same
method was used for electing the Senate in the Third Republic,
and the Council of the Republic in the Fourth Republic. In all
three Republics, it produced an upper House which enjoyed
a high reputation and had, on average, an able membership.
In Sweden, also, the upper House elected by local authorities
has worked well.

One of the arguments against adopting this method of
election for the British upper House is that it would introduce
party politics into local elections. This argument has much less

force now than when it was raised in the Bryce conference report in 1918. Nowadays, a great many elections to county borough councils, and many elections to county councils, are fought on party lines. But the system would clearly increase party interest in local elections. It would, however, also increase the interest of the electorate and this would be no bad thing, as at present a poll as low as 30 per cent to 40 per cent is quite common in local elections. There is no doubt, however, that an upper House elected in this way would be organized on party lines, although it would be different in composition from the Commons and would tend to give more emphasis to local issues.

Norway provides an example of an upper House elected by the lower House or, more accurately, elected from the whole Parliament. The Parliament, which is called the Storting, consists of 150 members elected by universal suffrage. Its first function after election is to elect from amongst its own members the upper House, the Lagting. This Lagting has 38 members, while the remaining 112 comprise the lower House or Odelsting. They function as separate chambers except when there is a difference of view between the two chambers on legislation. They then come together in a full meeting of the Storting in which the disagreement between the chambers must be resolved by a two-thirds majority vote. This system provides for review of legislation by an upper House which is very similar in complexion to the lower House. The disadvantage of the Lagting compared with the present House of Lords is that it consists entirely of the same sort of people as the Odelsting: party politicians who are responsible to their constituents and are subject to the same kind of party discipline.

Conclusion

If, then, we survey the working of second chambers in other countries we find no system which clearly has advantages over the present House of Lords. The idea of abolition, of single chamber government, also has its disadvantages. As we have seen, the House of Lords has useful functions. It is significant, too, that two countries which have recently abolished their upper Houses, Denmark and New Zealand, both have small populations (just over $4\frac{1}{2}$ million and $2\frac{1}{2}$ million respectively). In a country with a small population, the pressure of legislation is much less than in a country the size of Britain. It is notable too that in Denmark, where the second chamber, the Landsting, was abolished in 1953, special safeguards have been provided against hasty treatment of legislation by the Folketing. The Constitution now provides that one-third of the members of the Folketing can demand a referendum on a bill which has been passed but not yet approved by the King. If 30 per cent of the electorate take part in the referendum, the bill can be defeated by a simple majority of those voting. The legislative procedure in the Folketing has also been extended, more time now being given between the readings and more time to committee stages.[1]

The existing constitution of the Lords is nearest in type to the nominated Senate in Canada. There is an essential difference, however: in the past, those nominated to the Canadian upper House have generally been supporters of the governing party, whereas since 1958 life peers have been appointed in numbers calculated to reduce the dominance of the Conservative Party in the Lords. The House of Lords is, in effect, an upper House consisting of nominated people drawn mostly from the ranks of the three main political parties, but including some non-party figures. This statement has to be qualified, because peers who have inherited their titles may attend and vote if they wish, although they play a steadily diminishing part in the proceedings of the House. The logical next step in reform would be to exclude these peers from the House.

This could quite simply be done by a statute which provided that only life peers and hereditary peers of first creation could sit in the House of Lords. Those hereditary peers of inherited title, who it was desired to have in the House, could be made life peers. The remaining body of hereditary peers could be allowed to stand for election to the Commons and to vote in parliamentary elections. With the membership of the Lords thereby much reduced, it would be reasonable to pay members more than the present four and a half guineas a day for attendance. This would permit those who wished to devote the bulk of their time to the Lords to do so. A nucleus, at least, of such 'majority-time' members would be highly desirable.

[1] See S. Thorsen: 'The Problem of Democratic Safeguards', in the *Listener* 25 July 1957, pp. 119–21.

A further reform would be favoured by many. This would permit men and women to be appointed 'Members of the Lords' without being made life peers. 'Members of the Lords' would have exactly the same rights as life peers but would not be burdened with a title. 'Members of the Lords', like life peers, should be appointed for life, because appointment for a limited term of years (subject to reappointment) might make them less independent of the Government of the day.

There remains the question of powers. We have seen that the main function of the Lords, besides its function as a largely independent forum of debate, is to revise legislation and to ask the Commons to reconsider bills in detail. To do this it does not need to be able to delay legislation for a year. In other words, the powers of the Lords under the Parliament Act of 1949 are too great. A new Parliament Act should be passed, merely requiring that legislation amended, or defeated, by the Lords should be voted again in the Commons before receiving the Royal Assent. Such a reform would mean abandoning the idea that the Lords is, in any sense, 'a safeguard of the Constitution'. The difficulty inherent in this idea has been that ever since the latter part of the nineteenth century, this 'safeguard' has only existed during the lifetime of Liberal and Labour governments. As we have seen, the Lords has been complaisant during Conservative governments. If the power of delay were taken from the Lords, the question of the party majority in the Lords would become unimportant. This reform would further emphasize and clarify the role of the Lords in modern conditions: to give advice and reasoned criticism of the government and the Commons, but not to frustrate the intentions of the Commons.

For Reference

L. S. AMERY, *Thoughts on the Constitution* (Oxford University Press, 1947).

A. WEDGWOOD BENN, *The Privy Council as a Second Chamber* (Fabian Society, 1957).

P. A. BROMHEAD, *The House of Lords and Contemporary Politics* (Routledge and Kegan Paul, 1958).

B. CHUBB, 'Vocational Representation and the Irish Senate' in *Political Studies*, June 1954.

B. CRICK, *The Reform of Parliament* (Weidenfeld and Nicolson, 1964).

HANSARD SOCIETY, *The Future of the House of Lords* (1954).
C. HOLLIS, *Can Parliament Survive?* (Hollis and Carter, 1949).

Cmd. 7380 of 1948. Parliament Bill 1947: Agreed Statement on Conclusion of Conference of Party Leaders.
The Life Peerages Act, 1958.
The Parliament Acts of 1911 and 1949.
The Peerage Act, 1963.

CHAPTER X

The Monarch and the Prime Minister

Conventions of the Constitution

WE have seen in earlier chapters that many aspects of British government are regulated by convention. When we come to examine the inter-relationship of the Monarch, the Prime Minister, and the Cabinet, we find that almost everything is regulated by convention and very little by law. It is appropriate then, at this stage, to define more fully what we mean by conventions of the constitution. The classic analysis of the subject was made by A. V. Dicey, when he was Professor of Law at Oxford, in a series of lectures which were first published in 1885. Dicey distinguished between the law of the constitution and the conventions of the constitution which he said consist of 'maxims or practices which though they regulate the ordinary conduct of the Crown, of Ministers, and of other persons under the constitution, are not in strictness laws at all'.[1]

Why then, he asked himself, are these conventions obeyed? The answer which he arrived at was that 'the conventions of the constitution are not laws, but, in so far as they really possess binding force, derive their sanction from the fact that whoever breaks them must finally break the law and incur the penalties of a law breaker'.[2] For example, it is a convention that if a government is defeated on an important issue in the House of Commons, and if it has clearly lost the confidence of the House, the government will either resign or the Prime Minister will ask the Monarch for a dissolution of Parliament. But suppose that a government, in direct violation of this convention, decided not to resign and not to ask for a dissolution. This would not be in itself illegal. The Prime Minister and his

[1] A. V. Dicey, *Introduction to the Study of the Law of the Constitution*, 10th ed. (Macmillan, 1959) p. 24.

[2] Ibid., p. 451.

colleagues in the government would not be acting in breach of any law, but before long they would be involved in a violation of the ordinary law of the land. For example, maintenance of a standing army would be illegal without the passage of the Army (Annual) Act, and a House of Commons which was in dispute with the government would clearly refuse to renew this Act. Similarly, it would refuse to pass the Finance Bill and the Estimates, with the result that much taxation and most expenditure would become illegal.

But although it is true in this case that breach of a convention involves, before long, breaking the law of the land, it is not true in every case or even in the majority of cases. For example, it is a convention that Ministers are collectively responsible for decisions made in Cabinet. Yet, in 1932, the Ramsay MacDonald Coalition Government decided to allow Ministers to speak and vote against the Government's decision to introduce a general tariff. The Conservatives, who were the predominant element in the Coalition, were anxious to introduce tariffs. The Liberal ministers in the Cabinet, and the former Labour Chancellor of the Exchequer, Philip Snowden, were strongly opposed. The opponents of tariffs proposed to resign, but the Prime Minister persuaded them to remain in the Cabinet on the basis of this 'agreement to differ'. It was a clear breach of the convention of collective responsibility but it did not involve anyone in breaking the law. Neither did it create a new precedent. There have been no similar subsequent departures from the principle of collective responsibility. This does not mean that the 'agreement to differ' was certainly wrong in the special circumstances of 1932, but it is significant that within three months the dissenting ministers had all resigned. This leads to the conclusion that the 'agreement to differ' was not only an isolated breach of the convention of collective responsibility but that it was an unwise attempt to hold together a government that was already deeply divided.

If then conventions can be broken without involving a subsequent breach of the law, why are they not broken more frequently? The answer lies in the general understanding of democratic procedures in this country by those who have to work them. A convention, in other words, is an accepted practice which is felt to be desirable and appropriate to the notions of democracy current at any one time. This means that conventions are easily adaptable, and the fact that so much of British government is regulated by convention makes it highly flexible as a system. The British system should not, however, be contrasted fundamentally with those systems of government which are regulated by a written constitution. Even with a written constitution, there is always much which must be regulated by the ordinary law and much by convention. Wherever the constitution or the ordinary law is silent, or where it is ambiguous, convention comes in. But in Britain, convention covers a wider area than, for example, in the United States, and the written part of the British constitution, the laws relating to the powers of the upper House and to elections and so on, can be changed as easily as any other laws.

Selecting the Prime Minister

The law relating to the Monarchy deals chiefly with such matters as the succession. The relations between the Monarch and his Ministers are left almost entirely to convention. Here then there has been much scope for difference of interpretation, and some interpretations have been more influential than others. Clearly Bagehot's interpretation in *The English Constitution* has been most influential of all in the nineteenth and twentieth centuries. Indeed it influenced King George V in a very direct way. In 1894, when Queen Victoria was still on the throne, J. R. Tanner, the constitutional historian, was engaged to teach the then Duke of York the law and practice of the constitution. Tanner set the future George V to study and analyse Bagehot's *English Constitution*. Sir Harold Nicolson discovered in the archives at Windsor a notebook in the Duke of York's handwriting in which he had carefully summarized Bagehot's chapters on the Monarchy.[1] In his subsequent reign from 1910 to 1935 he closely followed Bagehot's theory of the role of the Monarchy.

Bagehot maintained that the functions of the Monarchy were in part dignified, in part efficient. In its dignified functions, which Bagehot regarded as the most important, the Monarchy acted as a focus of loyalty above party; it provided a moral example to the nation and made government intelligible to the

[1] H. Nicolson, *King George V* (Constable, 1952), pp. 61–3.

masses who could not understand the intricacies of representative government. To some extent these functions are still
performed by the Monarchy, although clearly it is no longer
true (if it ever was, even in Bagehot's day) that the average
Englishman is 'not fit for an elective government' and does not
understand that the Prime Minister is the real head of the
executive and not the Queen.

It is in the efficient functions that there is more resemblance
between Bagehot's theory and subsequent practice. He argued
that the efficient functions could be divided between those
exercised at the beginning and end of a ministry and those
exercised in its continuance. In the first category come the
right enjoyed by the Monarch to invite a party leader to form
a government and the right to agree to a dissolution. In the
second category come, during the lifetime of a government,
'the right to be consulted, the right to encourage, the right to
warn'.[1]

It may seem at first sight that the right to invite a party
leader to form a government is now purely formal. When a
party wins a clear majority at a general election, and that party
has an accepted leader, he has an undoubted right to be invited
to form a government. If, however, a general election does not
produce a majority for any one party, then the Monarch's
role in selecting the Prime Minister can become important. His
role in the first instance may be relatively simple and involve
little initiative. In such a situation, the Prime Minister who
held office before the general election may or may not decide
to wait and see if he can secure the support of the new House
of Commons. Baldwin did wait to resign until he had been
defeated in the Commons after the 1923 election, but he
resigned as soon as the results were known after the 1929
general election. The Prime Minister's resignation having been
handed in, the Monarch will normally invite the leader of the
other large party in the Commons to form a government.
This is straightforward; but suppose the new Prime Minister
loses his majority, then the role of the Monarch can become
really important. For he then becomes, as the President of the
Republic was in the Third and Fourth Republics in France,
a mediator between the parties. The political system then

[1] Bagehot, op. cit. (World's Classics edn.), p. 67.

can be considerably affected by his skill as a mediator and by his personal preference in the choice of individuals to form a government.

A modern illustration of the influence a Monarch can have in such a situation is given by the part played by George V in the crisis of 1931. Labour had been in office since 1929. They were the largest single party but, not having an overall majority, were dependent upon Liberal support in the Commons. In the summer of 1931, the Government was faced with an acute financial crisis. In view of a continuing drain on our gold reserves, it was thought necessary to ask for a large loan from a consortium of New York bankers headed by Messrs J. P. Morgan and Co. On 23 August, Messrs J. P. Morgan informed the Cabinet by telegram that no loan would be forthcoming unless the British Government made severe economies in public expenditure. Such economies had been suggested to the Government at the end of July by the Committee it had appointed under the chairmanship of Sir George May. The economies proposed involved considerable reductions in unemployment relief, and in the pay of police, teachers, Civil Servants, and members of the Fighting Services.

The Cabinet was deeply divided on the question of whether to impose such economies and the Prime Minister, Ramsay MacDonald, decided to tender the resignation of his Government. He went straight from the Cabinet meeting to Buckingham Palace to submit his resignation to the King. George V had earlier in the day personally consulted the Opposition leaders: Sir Herbert Samuel for the Liberals (deputizing for Lloyd George, who was seriously ill), and Baldwin, the Conservative leader. The King had summoned them both on hearing from MacDonald of the probable division in his Cabinet. By chance, Sir Herbert Samuel had arrived at Buckingham Palace first and had suggested to the King that the best course would be for MacDonald to continue as Prime Minister and to impose the necessary economies, as head of either a reconstituted Labour Government or a National Government in which the Conservatives and Liberals would be invited to participate. This latter solution fitted in with the King's own leaning towards a National Government, and, when Baldwin arrived, the King asked him whether he would be prepared to serve in such a Government under Ramsay MacDonald. Baldwin replied that he would be prepared to; or, if MacDonald insisted on resignation, he would be ready to form a Conservative Government if assured of Liberal support to impose economies.

When MacDonald arrived in the evening to hand in his resignation, the King impressed on him that he was the only man to lead the country through the crisis, and that the Conservatives and Liberals would be willing to support him. MacDonald then asked the King if he could confer with him, and the two other party leaders, on the following morning. The King willingly agreed and at the conference on the following day, 24 August, at Buckingham Palace, the formation of a National Government with MacDonald as Prime Minister was decided upon. Ramsay MacDonald then met his Cabinet colleagues and informed them of the decision. He was received with amazement. The majority of the Labour Cabinet Ministers refused to join him in the National Government, only James Thomas, Lord Sankey and Philip Snowden deciding to do so. The subsequent history of the National Government does not concern us here. What is important is that the King's role in the formation of the National Government was decisive. When MacDonald tendered his resignation on the evening of 23 August, George V could have accepted it and could have then invited Baldwin to form a Conservative Government. The evidence shows that Baldwin would have accepted and that his Government would probably have received Liberal support. The history of this country in the 1930s would then have taken a different course. The Labour Party would not have split, and even if the Conservative Government had dealt more successfully with the financial crisis than Labour had done, the Conservatives would hardly have won the overwhelming majorities which they achieved as the dominant partner in the National Government in the General Elections of 1931 and 1935.

King George V, then, made a momentous decision when he invited MacDonald to form a National Government in 1931. He was attacked at the time from the Labour side for acting in a partisan way, and even by some critics for behaving unconstitutionally. This last accusation cannot be supported.

As the suggestion for a National Government was made by one of the Opposition leaders, Sir Herbert Samuel, it was clearly open to the King to pass on the suggestion to the other party leaders. Whether it was wise is another matter. But the evidence shows that the King was not acting in a partisan spirit. There is no evidence that he desired to weaken the position of the Labour Party electorally, although his action did have this effect at the General Election of 1931. He genuinely thought that the country needed a National Government in the economic circumstances of the time; he admired Ramsay MacDonald and wished him to continue as Premier. It must also be remembered that when the National Government was formed it was thought of as only a temporary expedient. Ramsay MacDonald gave this assurance in a broadcast message on 25 August 1931. But it proved to be more durable and to have more fundamental effects on the strength of the parties than MacDonald seems originally to have foreseen.[1]

King George V did not exceed his powers as a mediator between the parties in 1931, even if it is thought that he used those powers unwisely. The incident shows well that important powers remain to the Monarch in the event of a break up of a Government. Such occasions have been rare in the twentieth century, but they could become more frequent if the present dominance of the political scene by two parties were replaced by a three-party situation as a result of a revival of the Liberal Party, or a split in the Conservative or Labour Parties. In a prolonged multi-party situation, the role of the Monarch as a mediator between the parties would become much more important. As long as government defeats are infrequent, however, the Monarch's power to mediate between the parties remains a reserve power which is rarely called upon.

Until 1965, the Monarch also had to exercise a choice when a Conservative Prime Minister died or resigned through ill health. In such a situation, it was not the custom of the Con-

---

[1] The best short account of the 1931 crisis is to be found in Nicolson, op. cit., pp. 453–69.

See also Graeme C. Moodie, 'The Monarch and the Selection of a Prime Minister: A Re-examination of the Crisis of 1931', in *Political Studies*, February 1957, pp. 1–20; and R. Bassett, *Nineteen Thirty One. Political Crisis* (Macmillan, 1958).

servative Party to designate a new Leader who would then accept the Monarch's commission to form a government. Instead, the choice of the new Prime Minister was left to the Monarch. Once chosen as Prime Minister, he was elected Leader of the Conservative Party. Of course the Monarch was given considerable advice by 'notables' in the Conservative Party. He did have some freedom of choice, although as time went on it was more and more circumscribed. Thus when, in 1923, the Conservative Prime Minister, Bonar Law, resigned because he was seriously ill, George V could have chosen as his successor either Lord Curzon or Stanley Baldwin. Of those who were consulted by the King, Lord Salisbury advised that Curzon should be chosen, while Lord Balfour, a former Prime Minister, favoured Baldwin. Curzon was much the more experienced man, having been Foreign Secretary since 1919, a member of the War Cabinet under Lloyd George, and, before the 1914 war, Viceroy of India. Baldwin was a younger man, much less experienced as a Minister. There seems little doubt that George V could have invited Curzon to become Prime Minister and that the Conservatives would have accepted him as Leader. In fact the King chose Baldwin, influenced it would seem by the view that it was no longer possible to have the Prime Minister in the House of Lords, and by the opinion that Curzon was not personally acceptable to many Conservative ministers.[1]

On the next occasion when a Conservative Prime Minister resigned through illness, the Monarch had less freedom of choice in naming his successor. This was in January 1957. Sir Anthony Eden had to resign through ill health. As in 1923, there were two candidates for the succession, R. A. Butler and Harold Macmillan. Both were very experienced Ministers and each had a strong following. On the face of it, therefore, Queen Elizabeth II could have chosen either. But it seems that all the advice she received pointed to Macmillan. The 'two elder statesmen', whom the Queen personally received at Buckingham Palace to ask their advice, were Lord Salisbury, leader of the Conservative peers, and Sir Winston Churchill. Both recommended Macmillan. Lord Salisbury, in conjunction with

[1] See Robert Blake, *The Unknown Prime Minister. The Life and Times of Andrew Bonar Law* (Eyre and Spottiswoode, 1955), pp. 525–7.

Lord Kilmuir, then Lord Chancellor, had earlier gathered the views of members of the Cabinet. Kilmuir has stated that an overwhelming majority of the Cabinet was in favour of Macmillan. Salisbury and Kilmuir had also received reports from the Conservative Chief Whip, Edward Heath, from Lord Poole, the Chairman of the Conservative Party Organization, and from John Morrison, the Chairman of the 1922 Committee. These reports clearly indicated that the majority of back bench opinion also favoured Macmillan.[1] The Queen's secretary, Sir Michael Adeane, had also been in touch with the Conservative Chief Whip and had received similar information.[2] Nearly all the Press, however, had expected Butler to be chosen, particularly since he had been acting head of the Government for three weeks since Sir Anthony Eden had fallen ill. The choice of Macmillan was therefore a great surprise to the general public, but it is now clear that the Queen had no real alternative but to call upon Macmillan. The speed with which she acted indicates that she had little doubt about the matter. She came up to London from Sandringham in the morning, received Salisbury and Churchill at once, and sent for Macmillan almost immediately afterwards.

In October 1963, the Queen's freedom to choose a successor to Macmillan was even more circumscribed. Macmillan himself, as outgoing Prime Minister, prepared a memorandum for the Queen advising her to choose Lord Home as his successor. This memorandum he read out to the Queen from his hospital bed. She at once sent for Lord Home, and invited him to try to form a government, which he was successful in doing. In his memorandum, Macmillan set out the results of the soundings of opinion which he had caused to be made in the Cabinet by Lord Dilhorne, amongst Conservative M.P.s by the Chief Whip, Martin Redmayne, amongst Conservative peers by the Chief Whip in the Lords, Lord St. Aldwyn, and among the Conservative constituency parties. He claimed that all the soundings showed that majority opinion was in favour of Lord Home.

This view was later contested by a senior member of the

[1] Kilmuir, *Political Adventure. The Memoirs of the Earl of Kilmuir* (Weidenfeld and Nicolson, 1964), p. 285.

[2] See Dermot Morrah, *The Work of the Queen* (Kimber, 1958), pp. 159–61.

Cabinet, Iain Macleod.[1] In Macleod's view, the majority of the Cabinet had not favoured Home as first choice. He also cast doubts on the way in which opinion was canvassed by the Chief Whip and his colleagues in the Whip's office. He remarked that 'the Chief Whip had been working hard for a week to secure the maximum support for Lord Home'. In his view, the process of gathering opinions was angled in the direction of favouring Lord Home, particularly through the canvassing of second choices and of Members' general impressions about the candidates.

Be this as it may, the Queen had no choice but to accept Macmillan's advice. There is no substance in the view, put forward by Paul Johnson in the *New Statesman* (24 January 1964), that the Queen acted unconstitutionally by not seeking further advice. It is true that the morning papers on 18 October 1963 had reported that a meeting of Conservative Cabinet Ministers had been held at Enoch Powell's house the previous evening, at which a decision was taken to oppose Home's selection.[2] The Queen therefore knew of this move when she visited Macmillan on the 18th to receive his advice. But she had asked his advice and could hardly have refused to accept his memorandum. Neither is it true that Macmillan acted unconstitutionally by giving advice on the succession. Bonar Law had declined to give advice in 1923, but he could have given his views to George V if he had chosen to do so. In fact George V, through his Secretary, had specially asked for Bonar Law's advice.[3]

Whether Macmillan was wise to give advice in so comprehensive a form that it virtually prevented the Queen from asking anyone else's opinion, is another matter. His reasons for adopting this course of action seem to be clear. The situation in relation to the succession was confused. There were no less than five possible candidates: Butler, Lord Hailsham, Maudling, Macleod, and Lord Home. The time of decision was an

---

[1] In the *Spectator*, 17 January 1964, pp. 65–7, Iain Macleod reviewed the book by Randolph Churchill: *The Fight for the Tory Leadership* (Heinemann, 1964). This book was an account of the events of October 1963, largely based on interviews with Macmillan.

[2] The Ministers who met at Enoch Powell's house on the evening of 17 October were, beside Powell himself, Iain Macleod, Reginald Maudling, Frederick Erroll, and Lord Aldington.

[3] See Blake, op. cit., pp. 516–25.

inopportune one. Macmillan's health had deteriorated just
before the Conservative Party Conference was due to begin. At
the Conference, there were demonstrations in favour of some
of the candidates. Macmillan felt that, in order to prevent the
situation getting out of hand, he should personally keep control
of all the strings in the process of giving advice to the Queen.

Whatever his reasons for acting as he did, Macmillan's
methods gave rise to considerable dissatisfaction among Conservatives. One Conservative M.P., Humphrey Berkeley, had
been campaigning for some time for election of the Conservative leader by secret ballot, in a small electoral college in which
Members of Parliament would predominate. In November 1963,
another Conservative Member, T. L. Iremonger, wrote to the
Daily Telegraph arguing for a procedure for electing the Leader
which would give greater confidence to the public that the
selection process was a fair one.[1] After the 1964 general election,
feeling gained ground among Conservatives in favour of reforming the method of selection. In February 1965, Sir Alec
Douglas-Home announced, as Leader of the Conservative
Party, that the next Leader would be chosen after secret
balloting among Conservative M.P.s. Edward Heath was the
first Conservative Leader to be chosen by this method in July
1965 (see below, Chapter XII). In this way the Conservatives
moved closer to the Labour practice in choosing their Leader.

Edward Heath was chosen by this method when the Conservatives were in opposition. It seems likely that when in
office they will use a similar method. There too they will be
adopting a similar approach to Labour's. The Parliamentary
Committee of the Parliamentary Labour Party announced on
21 January 1957, that if a Labour Prime Minister died or
resigned because of ill health, the Parliamentary Labour Party
would meet and would elect a new Leader who would then
accept the Queen's commission to form a government. We may
assume that this will now be the practice on the Conservative
side. After Sir Alec had announced the new method of selection on 25 February 1965, *The Times* Political Correspondent
commented rather deliciously: 'the procedure is not intended
in any way to limit the prerogative of the Sovereign, in the
event of the sudden death of a Conservative Prime Minister at

[1] *Daily Telegraph*, 15 November 1963.

a time of crisis, from summoning a successor. But it is to be
assumed the Sovereign would normally allow the elective process to work.'[1] Whether it is a Labour or a Conservative
Premier who has to be replaced, then, the choice will now
normally be made by the party itself. We have seen that the
Monarch's freedom of choice had already narrowed down
considerably in the forty years between 1923 and 1963. This
withering of a royal power is more accurately seen not as an
aspect of a general decline in royal influence, but as a consequence of the development of an increasingly democratic
attitude within the Conservative Party.

When a party leader has been invited to form a government,
his first task is to choose his Cabinet. What influence, if any,
does the Monarch possess over the choice of Cabinet Ministers?
The convention is that the Prime Minister, when forming a
government, discusses with the Monarch his proposed allocation of offices. The Monarch may then suggest changes, but
the Prime Minister is in no way bound to act upon these
suggestions. For example, when King George VI invited Attlee
to form a Government on 26 July 1945, he asked Attlee whom
he would make Foreign Secretary. When Attlee replied that
he intended to offer the Foreign Office to Hugh Dalton, the
King urged him to appoint Ernest Bevin instead. George VI
had come to know Bevin well, as a Minister during the war,
and greatly admired his ability and strength of character.
Attlee did in fact change his mind on the following day and
offered the Foreign Office to Bevin and the Treasury to Dalton.
Both accepted, although Dalton had earlier told Attlee that
he would prefer the Foreign Office. Attlee has since said that
the King's opinion in no way influenced his decision which was
governed, in the first place, by his own estimate of Bevin's high
abilities and, in the second place, by his desire to keep Herbert
Morrison and Bevin apart as much as possible. Morrison and
Bevin did not get on well and Attlee wanted to avoid having them both concerned with home affairs.[2] This incident

[1] *The Times*, 26 February 1965.
[2] See J. W. Wheeler-Bennett, *King George VI. His Life and Reign* (Macmillan,
1958) pp. 638–9.
   Also Francis Williams, *A Prime Minister Remembers* (Heinemann, 1961), pp. 4–6,
and Hugh Dalton, *The Fateful Years. Memoirs 1931–1945* (Frederick Muller,
1957), pp. 473–5.

illustrates well the influence which a Monarch can have on the choice of Ministers. He can make suggestions, but he cannot insist on the choice of any Minister, neither can he veto any appointment which his Prime Minister chooses to make.

The Monarch and Dissolution of Parliament

We have examined the role of the Monarch in the formation of a government. We must now consider his function in the dissolution of Parliament. The Prime Minister asks the Monarch to dissolve Parliament. For more than a hundred years the Monarch has always agreed to a request for dissolution. This does not necessarily mean that the Monarch can never refuse a dissolution.

Some controversy arose over this question after the 1950 General Election when the Labour Party secured a majority in the House of Commons of only five over all other parties. There was speculation in the correspondence column of *The Times* as to whether Attlee would ask the King for an immediate dissolution and, if so, whether the King would have any right to refuse. The King's Private Secretary, Sir Alan Lascelles, contributed to this correspondence in a letter which he signed with the pseudonym 'Senex'. In this letter he argued that the Sovereign could refuse a dissolution but would not do so 'unless he were satisfied that: (1) the existing Parliament was still vital, viable and capable of doing its job; (2) a General Election would be detrimental to the national economy; (3) he could rely on finding another Prime Minister who could carry on his Government, for a reasonable period, with a working majority in the House of Commons'.[1] He had earlier advised the King in broadly the same terms but had stated that, in his opinion, the three conditions for denial of a dissolution would not be satisfied at that particular time.[2]

Attlee did not in fact ask for a dissolution until the autumn of 1951, well over a year later. It is clear from the conditions which Sir Alan Lascelles laid down in his letter to *The Times*, that he regarded the Monarch's power to refuse a dissolution as very heavily circumscribed. One may wonder indeed if all

---

[1] *The Times*, 2 May 1950.
[2] See Wheeler-Bennett, op. cit., pp. 772–5.

the conditions he mentions would ever be realized at one and the same time. We may conclude that although the Monarch, in theory, retains the power to refuse a dissolution, it would only be refused in the most exceptional circumstances.[1]

'The Right to be Consulted, the Right to Encourage, the Right to Warn'
Having examined the functions of the Monarch at the beginning and end of a ministry, we may turn to the functions of the Monarch, in Bagehot's phrase, 'during the continuance of a ministry'. We have seen that these functions were considered by Bagehot to flow from the Monarch's 'right to be consulted, the right to encourage, the right to warn'. The official biographies of George V and George VI show that these rights were often exercised between 1910, the year of George V's accession, and 1951. The Monarch can assert these rights because, in the first place, he is kept well informed. He is sent copies of Cabinet minutes, and he can examine despatches from ambassadors. It is customary for the Prime Minister and other senior Ministers to consult him personally from time to time. In these consultations, he may attempt to influence the Prime Minister towards a particular course of action, or to dissuade him from a policy to which the government is already committed or has under consideration. Thus, in 1921 King George V strongly disapproved of the activities of the 'Black and Tans' in Ireland. This was a para-military force recruited by the Lloyd George Government from ex-servicemen. It was established in order to reinforce the Irish Constabulary in its effort to combat the lawlessness and terrorism of the Irish Republicans. In fact it resorted at times to a sort of counter-terrorism against the ordinary Irish population. George V deeply deplored these activities and made his views known both to the Cabinet and to the Chief Secretary in Ireland.

Strangely enough, an American newspaper, in July 1921, published a purported interview with Lord Northcliffe in which he was reported as saying that the King had protested to his Government about the activities of the Black and Tans. Lord Northcliffe announced that he had given no such interview, and Lloyd George, in the Commons, said that the whole

[1] For discussion of the earlier precedents relating to the dissolution of Parliament see Jennings, *Cabinet Government*, 3rd ed. (1959), pp. 412–28.

story was 'a complete fabrication'.[1] Yet it did convey George V's actual feelings on the subject. But the King made no move to make his views known to the public. Here he acted with strict constitutional propriety, for although the Monarch may attempt to influence his Ministers he should not let it be known publicly that he is in disagreement with his Government. The King, however, continued to prod his Government on to opening negotiations with the Irish nationalist leader, De Valera, and urged them to be conciliatory in their attitude when negotiations were opened. At one crucial stage, in September 1921, the King was able to persuade Lloyd George to modify the whole tone of a letter to De Valera, changing what had been a largely aggressive despatch into a conciliatory one. The amended Note was approved by the Cabinet and was eventually accepted by De Valera as a basis for the conference which led to the establishment of the Irish Free State.[2]

The reign of King George VI also provides numerous examples of occasions when the Monarch attempted to influence his Government, at times successfully, sometimes without success. For example, in September 1938, George VI suggested to the Foreign Secretary, Lord Halifax, and later to the Prime Minister, Neville Chamberlain, that he, the King, should write a personal letter to Adolf Hitler. In this letter he proposed to write as 'one ex-Serviceman to another' (the King had seen action in the Battle of Jutland as a junior naval officer, Hitler had served as a corporal on the western front), urging the German Fuehrer to spare the youth of Britain and Germany from the horror and slaughter of a second world war. Both the Foreign Secretary and the Prime Minister advised against the sending of this letter on the grounds that Hitler might publish an insulting reply which would make relations between the two countries more strained. The King then abandoned the idea.[3]

An occasion when George VI was able to influence his Government was in 1943. The Viceroy of India, Lord Linlithgow, was about to retire. The Prime Minister, Winston

---

[1] Nicolson, op. cit., p. 347.

[2] Nicolson, op. cit., p. 359.

[3] See Wheeler-Bennett, op. cit., pp. 348–52.

Churchill, backed by the Secretary of State for India, Leopold Amery, suggested to the King that Anthony Eden should be the new Viceroy. Anthony Eden had been approached and was willing to take up the appointment. The King disagreed strongly and urged, on 28 April, in a letter to Churchill, that Eden could not be spared from the Government: that he was indispensable as (in many respects) Churchill's 'second-in-Command', and as a Foreign Secretary who enjoyed 'in an exceptional degree the confidence both of the United States and of our Soviet Allies'. Churchill discussed the question with the King in June, when the King was finally able to convince him that the appointment of Eden would be unwise. Instead, Lord Wavell was offered the Viceroyalty and he accepted.[1]

Another very interesting occasion was in the summer of 1944. On 30 May, Churchill had lunch with the King at Buckingham Palace. This was one of a long series of weekly luncheons at which the King and Prime Minister discussed affairs of State while serving themselves with a buffet lunch. No servants were present and they were able to speak with complete frankness. On this occasion, the King asked Churchill where he would be on the night before the Normandy invasion which was scheduled to take place within a few days. Churchill replied he would be on board one of the warships bombarding the Normandy coast. The King said that he would like to be with him and they agreed to discuss arrangement with Admiral Ramsay in two days time.

Later in the day, the King informed Princess Elizabeth, who approved the idea, and his Private Secretary, Sir Alan Lascelles, who was appalled. He urged on the King that a bomb or torpedo might deprive the country of its Sovereign and its Prime Minister at one blow. He also argued that the commander of the ship would be placed in an intolerable predicament, in having to fight his ship with two such distinguished passengers on board. On the following morning Sir Alan Lascelles discussed the project with the King again, and succeeded in convincing him that it would be wrong for either the King or the Prime Minister to sail with the invasion fleet. But George VI had considerable difficulty in convincing his Prime Minister of

[1] See Wheeler-Bennett, op. cit., pp. 699–702.

this. After an interview with the King and two strongly worded letters from him, Churchill still seemed bent on sailing with the cruiser *Belfast*. However, when on 2 June, Sir Alan Lascelles telephoned to Churchill and informed him that the King had stated that he was prepared to go himself to the quayside to prevent Churchill going on board, the Prime Minister replied that he had decided, in deference to the King's wishes, to abandon his plan of sailing with the fleet.[1]

These few examples indicate some of the ways in which a Monarch can influence his Prime Minister. The influence that a Monarch possesses will, of course, vary according to his personality, ability and experience. The Prime Minister will always listen to the views of the Monarch and take them into account, but he will give greater attention to them if he knows that his Sovereign is well informed and has long experience. Both George V and George VI were industrious, interested in political questions, and often showed much political wisdom, as the incidents just cited illustrate. They both gained a great deal of experience through following affairs of State in several administrations, and the influence of each man clearly increased as his fund of experience grew.

It seems probable that Queen Elizabeth II has been less ready to give advice to her Ministers than her father and grandfather were. She came to the throne in 1952 when she was only 26 years old. Although she had served for a time in the Auxiliary Territorial Service during the war, she did not otherwise have much experience outside the family circle, and she had been privately educated. Younger on coming to the throne, and lacking in experience when compared with her two predecessors, she has perhaps been more diffident in pressing her views on the government of the day. On the other hand, she has a reputation for great conscientiousness and industry. Time alone can tell what her ultimate influence will be.

The royal secretariat is a great source of strength to the Monarchy. The Private Secretary, as we have seen in the 1944 affair, can sometimes give advice which is very valuable to the Monarch. Most Private Secretaries have been in the royal service continuously over a long period. Sir Alan Lascelles, for

[1] Ibid., pp. 601–6.

example, served King George VI for eight years from 1943 to 1951 and was then Private Secretary to Queen Elizabeth II from 1951 to 1953. His successor, Sir Michael Adeane, had served from 1937 as Assistant Private Secretary to King George VI, and then to Queen Elizabeth, before his appointment in 1953 as Private Secretary. He is a grandson of probably the most famous of all Private Secretaries, Lord Stamfordham, who, as Sir Arthur Bigge, served Queen Victoria from 1895 to 1900, and was later Private Secretary to George V from 1910 to 1931. The Private Secretary is, of course, important not only for his experience and advice, but also as the Monarch's main channel in relations with Ministers and with the Leader of the Opposition and other political leaders.[1]

Conclusion

To sum up, we may say that the Sovereign has a reserve power to act as a sort of political umpire in a ministerial crisis. This power is rarely invoked because of the dominance of the two main parties, but it is important, and because it exists it is essential that the neutrality and impartiality of the Monarch be maintained. The Sovereign also has the day-to-day function, exercised behind the scenes, of following affairs of State and making known his views to Ministers. To these 'efficient' functions we may now add a 'dignified' function which has taken on a new form in recent years. The Queen is Head of the Commonwealth and is now the only tangible link between the member nations of the Commonwealth. These countries are entirely independent and are in no way subordinate to the British Government, but they are united in their recognition of the Queen as Head of the Commonwealth. In many Commonwealth countries the Queen is thought of with affection not only for her personal qualities, but as a symbol of ideals which are held in common by member nations. The Commonwealth has its own institutions, notably the Conferences of Commonwealth Prime Ministers which meet from time to time. Since 1964 the Commonwealth has had its own Secretariat under a Secretary-General, who has a staff of twenty-five.

We have seen that the Prime Minister must consult the Monarch and must consider the Monarch's views, but that he

[1] See Wheeler-Bennett, op. cit., pp. 817–23.

is in no way obliged to act upon them. We have seen that he must ask the Monarch for a dissolution but that his request can hardly ever be refused. The powers which the Prime Minister possesses are then very wide. He can secure a dissolution, to all intents and purposes, whenever he likes. He can appoint as Ministers whomever he thinks fit. He can dismiss Ministers and reshape his Government whenever he chooses. The party which he leads normally enjoys a secure majority in the House of Commons, so he can rely on getting the legislation he needs enacted by Parliament. On the face of it he enjoys far wider powers than the President of the United States. There are, in normal times, no 'checks and balances' to limit his freedom of action in British affairs. The restraints placed upon him by alliances with other powers and by international agreements are, of course, another matter.

But within the framework of British policy-making, what limitations are there on the freedom of action of the Prime Minister? The limitations are, in effect, only those which derive from the state of opinion in his party and in the country. He is kept in constant touch with opinion in his party through his colleagues in the Cabinet who should, as far as possible, be broadly representative of the main trends of thought in the party, and through the Whips and party committees in the House. He keeps in touch with opinion in the country largely through debates in the Commons and through comment in the Press.

As the Prime Minister enjoys such wide powers, is it not more accurate to speak of Prime Ministerial Government than of Cabinet Government in Britain? This view has been advanced particularly by J. P. Mackintosh and by R. H. S. Crossman.[1] In their opinion, developments in the twentieth century have accentuated the dominance of the Prime Minister in the British system of government. In order to assess this view we need to consider how the Cabinet has developed since 1916 and what is its present role in conjunction with that of the Prime Minister.

---

[1] J. P. Mackintosh, *The British Cabinet* (Stevens, 1962). R. H. S. Crossman, Introduction to W. Bagehot: *The English Constitution* (Fontana, 1963).

For Reference

W. BAGEHOT, *The English Constitution* (Fontana, 1963).

R. BLAKE, *The Unknown Prime Minister* (Eyre and Spottiswoode, 1955).

A. V. DICEY, *The Law of the Constitution*, 10th ed. (Macmillan, 1959).

W. I. JENNINGS, *Cabinet Government*, 3rd ed. (Cambridge University Press, 1959).

G. C. MOODIE, 'The Monarch and the Selection of a Prime Minister: A Re-examination of the Crisis of 1931', in *Political Studies*, 1957.

D. MORRAH, *The Work of the Queen* (Kimber, 1958).

H. NICOLSON, *King George V* (Constable, 1952).

J. W. WHEELER-BENNETT, *King George VI* (Macmillan, 1958).

F. WILLIAMS, *A Prime Minister Remembers* (Heinemann, 1961).

CHAPTER XI

The Cabinet

Collective Responsibility

BEFORE considering the ways in which the Cabinet has developed since 1916, it is useful to look at the conventions that govern the working of Cabinet government in Britain. The most important is the convention of collective responsibility. What essentially does it mean? It means that all Ministers must at all times support Cabinet decisions. A Minister may, of course, oppose a decision during discussion in Cabinet, but he must not, after the decision has been made, reveal that he disagreed with the majority, or that he has any reservations about the Government's policy. If he disagrees with the Government's policy to the point of wishing to criticize it in public, then he must resign.

This interpretation of collective responsibility is not maintained in every form of the Cabinet system. In France, for example, in 1959, the Finance Minister, M. Pinay, publicly criticized some of the measures being taken by the government, of which he was a member, to combat tax evasion. It was not felt that this necessitated his resignation from the government, and he remained Minister of Finance until January 1960. One can, then, have Cabinet government without full collective responsibility. Indeed there have occasionally been departures from the convention in this country, notably in the agreement amongst Ministers, in 1932, to differ in public on the question of the introduction of tariffs, which has been discussed in Chapter X.[1]

Such departures from the convention have been very rare. In general it has been thought desirable to maintain the doctrine of collective responsibility in its fullest sense. Ministers must speak with one voice and not with conflicting voices. Thereby the unification of responsibility and clarity of

[1] See above, p. 237.

responsibility, which we have earlier seen to be features of the British system, are maintained. It is understood, however, when a Minister resigns because he disagrees with Government policy, he then may reveal the nature of his disagreement with his colleagues in order to explain the reason for his resignation.

The fact of his resignation does not give a former Minister *carte blanche* to reveal everything that went on in Cabinet while he was a member of the Government. He is bound by the same rules which apply to other former Ministers. If they wish to write their memoirs, they may consult the documents which they saw as Ministers, but they may not disclose the contents of such documents without the permission of the government of the day, and in certain cases of the Queen. Cabinet documents, memoranda, and minutes of the Cabinet and of Cabinet committees, are not opened to public inspection in the Public Record Office until they are 30 years old. Even then the Lord Chancellor, who is responsible for the Public Record Office, may withhold certain documents in the public interest, especially if they relate to persons still living. So secrecy is maintained with great stringency in the interests of preserving the practice of collective responsibility.

Individual Responsibility
Interlocking with the convention of collective responsibility, is the doctrine of individual responsibility of Ministers. Members of the Government are collectively responsible for decisions made by the Cabinet, but Ministers are individually responsible for decisions made in their departments. This does not in every case mean that a Minister must resign if a mistake is made in the department for which he is responsible. It does mean that he is accountable to Parliament for everything that is done in his department and for his personal conduct as a Minister. He must account for what has happened, he must explain, but he need not always resign. Is it possible to generalize about the circumstances in which a Minister will resign?

Serious personal misconduct will clearly result in resignation. For example, in 1936, a Tribunal of Enquiry found that a member of the Cabinet, J. H. Thomas, had disclosed part of the Budget to friends who had then insured large sums with Lloyd's against a change in the income tax rate. Thomas had no alternative but to resign. For a less serious personal mis-conduct, there can be more than one interpretation of a Minister's duty. In 1947 the Chancellor of the Exchequer, Hugh Dalton, while waiting to make his Budget speech, told a lobby correspondent in the House of Commons that he was going to increase the excise on tea. The correspondent immediately telephoned an evening paper, which came out with the news before Dalton had completed his speech. It was a case of Budget disclosure, but one would have thought in a purely technical sense. Dalton had no idea that the news could get into print so quickly and no one made any money out of his revelation. Nevertheless, Dalton admitted that he was at fault and resigned. On the other hand, Lloyd George did not see fit to resign when he emerged not entirely blameless from the Marconi Affair in 1913. He and Sir Rufus Isaacs expressed their regrets to the House for an error in judgement in buying shares in the American Marconi Company, while the British Government was currently awarding a tender to the British Marconi Company for the development of wireless telegraphy. But the two Ministers did not resign although their 'errors of judgement' had been more serious than those of Dalton, and had given rise to much more public concern.

If we examine cases when departmental policy has come under heavy criticism, we can again find conflicting precedents. In 1935, the Foreign Secretary, Sir Samuel Hoare, resigned because of widespread criticism of the proposals he had agreed to with Laval for partitioning Abyssinia in Italy's favour. In this case the Cabinet had already approved the proposals, although apparently somewhat unwillingly. When the plan was made public and there was an outcry in the Commons and in the country, the Cabinet did a quick right-about-face and the Prime Minister, Stanley Baldwin, in effect repudiated his Foreign Secretary. So what had been for a short period a matter of collective responsibility was hastily referred back to Sir Samual Hoare and treated as a question of individual re-sponsibility. The Cabinet was in fact prepared for him to remain Foreign Secretary, but only on condition that he with-drew the Abyssinian peace plan and acknowledged that it had been a mistake. This he was not prepared to do.[1]

[1] Templewood, op. cit., p. 185.

Another interesting case in which departmental policy came under heavy criticism occurred in 1949. The Minister of Food, John Strachey, was strongly attacked in the House of Commons for the failure of his Ministry's scheme to develop the economic production of groundnuts in large areas of virgin territory in East Africa. This was a scheme to which Strachey was deeply committed. He had initially described it in glowing terms as a means of increasing Britain's supply of fats and of raising the standard of living in East Africa. It might be thought that the failure of the scheme would result in his resignation. But, despite criticism, he decided not to resign and was supported in this course by the Cabinet and the Parliamentary Labour Party. Here is the key difference with Sir Samual Hoare's case. In 1935 the Cabinet was not prepared to support Sir Samual Hoare without a recantation, and the Foreign Affairs Committee of Conservative back-benchers had condemned the Hoare-Laval proposals very strongly.[1]

When we turn to the question of maladministration in a department, as distinct from unpopular or ill-conceived policies, again we find conflicting precedents. In 1954, the Minister of Agriculture, Sir Thomas Dugdale, resigned when faced with criticism of his Ministry's handling of the Crichel Down affair. This celebrated case turned on the refusal of the Commissioner of Crown Lands to sell an area of land in Dorset, known as Crichel Down, to Lieutenant-Commander Marten whose family had owned part of the property before it had been requisitioned by the Air Ministry in 1937. Commander Marten, reckoning he had been treated unfairly, took up his case with the Minister with the help of his M.P., R. F. Crouch. The Minister eventually ordered a public inquiry to be made by Sir Andrew Clark, Q.C. His report concluded that there had been considerable inefficiency and lack of fairness on the part of the Civil Servants concerned. A few weeks later, the Minister, Sir Thomas Dugdale, announced his resignation to the House of Commons. Some of the Civil Servants concerned were transferred to other duties.[2]

The case is of great interest not least because the Labour

[1] See Templewood, op. cit., p. 187.
[2] See D. N. Chester, 'The Crichel Down Case', in *Public Administration*, Winter 1954, pp. 389–401.

Opposition did not call on the Minister to resign, and pressure on him to resign came from the Government back benches. It is also of interest because of other similar occasions when Ministers have not thought it necessary to resign. For example, in 1959 the Colonial Secretary, Alan Lennox-Boyd, did not resign despite severe criticisms of the administration of a camp for political detainees in Kenya. At this camp, Hola Camp, several of the detainees, former members of the Mau-Mau organization, had been beaten to death by their guards. Their deaths had been at first falsely attributed to contaminated drinking water and it was only after an inquiry that the major maladministration at the camp had been revealed. In this case it could be argued that this was something for which the Minister could not be held directly responsible, although he did know of the decision that the Mau-Mau detainees should be 'made to work' as a means to rehabilitation—a decision which proved to have such tragic consequences at Hola. Essentially, it seems that Lennox-Boyd's responsibility in the Hola case was of the same order as Sir Thomas Dugdale's responsibility in Crichel Down. The different outcome is partly to be explained by the fact that it was the Labour Opposition which called for Lennox-Boyd's resignation, while, in general, the Conservative back-benches supported him.

Again, in 1961, it was the Labour Opposition which called for the resignation of the First Lord of the Admiralty, Lord Carrington, in view of the findings of the Romer Committee. This Committee had reported that lax security arrangements had made it easier for Soviet agents to obtain secret information from certain Admiralty employees over a period of some years. The Prime Minister, Harold Macmillan, announced in the House of Commons that the First Lord had offered his resignation, but that he had refused it. In the Prime Minister's view the weakness in security arrangements was the responsibility of Boards of Admiralty over a considerable period of years, dating from before the time when Lord Carrington had become First Lord. The Prime Minister stated that he was satisfied that the Minister was acting efficiently in tightening up security arrangements.[1]

From these conflicting precedents what can we conclude

[1] H.C. Deb. Vol. 642. Cols. 1683–1688 22 June 1961.

about the convention of individual ministerial responsibility in modern conditions? What is clear is that there are a number of factors which influence the decision as to whether or not a Minister will resign. The Minister's own sense of what is fitting, his sense of honour in other words, may be decisive. The attitude of the Prime Minister is very important: whether or not he is anxious to keep the Minister and dissuade him from resignation. Also of great importance, as we have seen, is the temper of the governing party: a Minister is much more likely to resign when he is under criticism from his own side of the House.[1]

Cabinet Organization: 1916-1939

The organization of the Cabinet has been strongly influenced by the convention of collective responsibility. As it was important that differences of opinion within the Cabinet should not be made known, it was for a long time considered impossible to have a Secretary present. Therefore, the Prime Minister himself took such notes as were taken of Cabinet proceedings. His was the only record of what had transpired in Cabinet and it was not circulated to Ministers. The only written account of proceedings was the letter sent by the Prime Minister to the Sovereign after each meeting of the Cabinet. As a result, Ministers often had conflicting ideas about the decisions that had been made in Cabinet. Just as there were no minutes, so there was no agenda circulated before the Cabinet met. Ministers often had only the haziest notion of the topics that would be raised in Cabinet. In consequence they were often ill-prepared to take part in discussion. This extraordinary lack of organization persisted until December 1916 when Lloyd George set up a Cabinet Secretariat immediately on becoming Prime Minister.

The machinery lay to hand in the Secretariat of the Committee of Imperial Defence, a Cabinet committee which was first set up in 1902 and acquired a Secretary in 1904. Lloyd George was concerned in 1916 about the Asquith Cabinet's lack of co-ordination in directing the war effort. One of his

---

[2] For an excellent discussion of this question see: S. E. Finer, 'The Individual Responsibility of Ministers', in *Public Administration*, Winter 1956 pp. 377–96. See also G. Marshall and G. C. Moodie, *Some Problems of the Constitution* (Hutchinson, 1959), pp. 78–87 and A. H. Birch, *Representative and Responsible Government* (Allen & Unwin, 1964) pp. 141–9.

motives in helping to engineer the fall of Asquith was his desire to re-organize the Cabinet and enhance its efficiency. On becoming Prime Minister, he merged the Committee of Imperial Defence with the Cabinet, and the Committee's Secretariat became the Secretariat to the Cabinet. He also drastically reduced the size of the Cabinet, appointing only five Ministers to the Cabinet, while Ministers not in the Cabinet sat on committees which were chaired by members of the Cabinet. Soon after the war ended, he restored the Cabinet to its pre-war size of around twenty members, but the Secretariat remained. It had proved its usefulness in the war and, although there were some misgivings amongst elder statesmen about its continuance in peace time, those who had had experience of the War Cabinet had no doubt of the value of the Secretariat.[1]

Since 1918 the Secretariat has grown steadily in importance and has helped to enhance the efficiency of the Cabinet, both as a decision-making body and as a means of co-ordinating the whole Government machine. The Secretariat now prepares the agendas for Cabinet meetings and circulates them to all Ministers, whether members of the Cabinet or not. This enables Ministers to seek permission to attend the Cabinet if they see that a matter down for discussion will impinge on the affairs of their own departments. Cabinet Ministers can see to it that they have the necessary briefing from their advisers in relation to business that will affect their departments. The Secretariat also circulates memoranda from departments concerned, relating to items on the Cabinet agenda. Its function in circulating the minutes of Cabinet meetings is equally important. Thereby Ministers, both inside and outside the Cabinet, are kept fully informed of decisions made in Cabinet. The Secretariat performs similar functions, in the circulation of agenda and minutes, for all Cabinet committees.

This work of the Secretariat has helped to provide an answer to the problem created by the establishment of many new government departments in the twentieth century. The Wilson Cabinet in July 1967 had twenty-one members, one

[1] See the speech by Lord Curzon in support of the Secretariat in a debate in the Lords on 19 June 1918 (H. L. Deb. Vol. xxx Col. 253) and the Report of the Haldane Committee in 1918 which recommended that the Cabinet Secretariat should be given permanent form (CD. 9230 Report of the Machinery of Government Committee, p. 6, para. 10).

less than the Cabinet headed by Campbell-Bannerman in 1907. But whereas in 1907 there were no Ministerial heads of departments outside the Cabinet, in July 1967 there were five such Ministers. They were the Minister of Overseas Development, the Minister of Health, the Minister of Social Security, the Postmaster-General and the Minister of Public Building and Works. Without a Secretariat it would have been difficult to omit these Ministers from the Cabinet which, with a membership of twenty-six, would have become unwieldy.

The existence of the Cabinet Secretariat has not been a matter of controversy since 1918. The other changes in the structure of the Cabinet made by Lloyd George in 1916 did not achieve such permanence and continued to be controversial. As we have seen, Lloyd George not only introduced a Secretariat, but also cut down the size of the Cabinet to only five Ministers, only one of whom was a departmental Minister. This small War Cabinet made extensive use of committees. After the war, in January 1919, Lloyd George reverted to the large pre-war type Cabinet.

It was not until the beginning of the Second World War in 1939 that the small Cabinet was tried again. (That is if we exclude the short-lived Coalition Cabinet formed in August 1931 by Ramsay MacDonald. This Cabinet had only ten members, but after the general election in 1931 it was enlarged to include at first nineteen and later twenty Ministers.) Similarly with committees, the Committee of Imperial Defence was re-formed in 1918 and remained an important committee of the Cabinet until the outbreak of war in 1939. Otherwise, inter-war governments did not make extensive use of standing committees of the Cabinet. There was a Home Affairs Committee of the Cabinet which was first set up in 1918. But although it was originally intended that this committee should consider all questions of internal policy, it soon became, in effect, a Legislation Committee concerned with the drafting of Government bills and with planning the legislative work of a session. Again, Ramsay MacDonald set up an Economic Advisory Council in January 1930. But this was never in a full sense a committee of the Cabinet. It consisted mainly of outside experts and functioned as an advisory body. After 1931 it continued to exist but had little importance. We may conclude then that the only standing

Cabinet committee of real importance in the inter-war years was the Committee of Imperial Defence.

This type of Cabinet, consisting of around twenty Ministers (mostly heads of departments), and making little use of Cabinet Committees, was heavily criticized by L. S. Amery in 1935. The Cabinet, he said, 'is really little more than a standing conference of departmental chiefs where departmental policies come up, from time to time, to be submitted to a cursory criticism as a result of which they may be accepted, blocked, or in some measure adjusted to the competing policies of other departments'. The system, he said, 'is quite incompatible with any coherent planning of policy as a whole, or with the effective execution of such a policy. It breaks down hopelessly in a serious crisis where clear thinking over difficult and complex situations, definite decisions (not formulae of agreement) and swift and resolute action are required'.[1] In place of this type of Cabinet, Amery argued for a Cabinet organized on the lines of the Lloyd George War Cabinet. The Cabinet should be small and should consist entirely of non-departmental Ministers who would be free to plan ahead and would co-ordinate the work of the Ministerial heads of departments.[2] Amery had had experience of the Lloyd George War Cabinet as a political assistant secretary to Lloyd George. He also saw something of the disadvantages of the traditional Cabinet during his six years as a Cabinet Minister in Conservative governments of the inter-war period.

Another critic of Cabinet organization in the thirties was the Leader of the Opposition, Clement Attlee. In his book *The Labour Party in Perspective*, published in 1937, he advanced similar criticisms of the Cabinet with its predominance of departmental Ministers concerned with the particular problems of their departments. He suggested that there should be a small group of non-departmental Ministers whose function it would be to co-ordinate the policy of groups of departments. This is distinctly similar to Amery's proposal but with the difference that Attlee does not seem to have envisaged that these co-ordinating Ministers should make up the whole Cabinet and that departmental Ministers should be excluded from the

---

[1] L. S. Amery, *The Forward View* (Bles, 1935) pp. 444–5.

[2] Amery, op. cit., pp. 445–6.

Cabinet. For example, he explicitly stated that his proposals did 'not mean the supersession of the Cabinet by a small Junta and the relegation of departmental Ministers to an inferior status'.[1]

Cabinet Organization: 1939–1951

When the Second World War broke out in September 1939, the Prime Minister, Neville Chamberlain, merged the Committee of Imperial Defence with the Cabinet and reduced the size of the Cabinet. His Cabinet had nine members and made considerable use of committees. More drastic re-organization followed in May 1940 when Winston Churchill became Prime Minister at the head of a Coalition Government including Attlee and other leading members of the Labour Party. This Cabinet had only five members, four of whom were Ministers without departments, the fifth being the Foreign Secretary. The four non-departmental Ministers were each given functions in co-ordinating the work of departments and acting as chairmen of Cabinet committees.

This Cabinet was almost a replica of the Lloyd George War Cabinet. But it did not last for long in this form. By January 1941 there were four departmental Ministers in the Cabinet: the Chancellor of the Exchequer, the Minister of Labour and National Service, and the Minister of Aircraft Production, in addition to the Foreign Secretary who had been there from the outset. The total membership of the Cabinet was now eight, one half being departmental Ministers and one half Ministers without departments. This speedy abandonment of the 'Lloyd George' idea was interesting and is to be explained by the circumstances of the time and the personalities of some of the leading Ministers. Two problems were of overriding importance in the autumn and winter of 1940: how to produce more aeroplanes and military equipment of all kinds, and how to deploy the labour force efficiently to these ends. The Ministers who were in charge in these spheres were both men of dynamic and outstanding personality: Ernest Bevin at the Ministry of Labour and Lord Beaverbrook at the Ministry of Aircraft Production. It proved impossible to keep these men out of the Cabinet and, similarly, the Chancellor of the Exchequer, Kingsley Wood, was constantly needed in Cabinet counsels.

[1] C. R. Attlee, *The Labour Party in Perspective* (Gollancz, 1937) p. 174.

The committee structure of the Churchill Cabinet was also considerably modified. By 1942 the Committee chaired by the Lord President of the Council, Sir John Anderson, had become, in Churchill's phrase, 'almost a parallel Cabinet concerned with home affairs'.[1] The War Cabinet was concerned mainly with the conduct of the war and worked largely through two committees: the Defence Committee (Operations) and the Defence Committee (Supply). Parallel was the Lord President's Committee, which dealt with home affairs, and had a series of sub-committees responsible to it. This eventual organization, which worked very well, bore little resemblance to the Lloyd George-type War Cabinet with which Churchill had begun in 1940.

After the General Election in 1945, Attlee formed a Cabinet of traditional type including twenty Ministers, most of them heads of departments. In the following year, two authorities on Cabinet organization, L. S. Amery and Sir John Anderson, fired verbal broadsides on the subject. Amery, in a lecture given at Oxford, argued for a Cabinet of six Ministers, entirely free from ordinary departmental duties, who would act as chairman of Cabinet committees.[2] In May 1946, Sir John Anderson in his Romanes Lecture at Oxford had argued against this very notion of 'supervising Ministers', as he called them. He claimed that the Cabinet could be made more efficient as a co-ordinating and decision-making body by developing the system of Cabinet committees without drastically reducing the size of the Cabinet. He suggested that there should be five main standing committees of the Cabinet, in turn dealing with Defence, Economic Relations (with a different composition for internal economic problems), External Affairs, the Social Services, and Proposals for Legislation. The chairman of each committee could be either a non-departmental Minister or a departmental Minister with a dominant interest in the matters comprised within the particular group. The Prime Minister would himself, in many cases, preside. The system should be flexible, and details of the membership of committees, and of the co-ordinating functions given to Ministers, should not be

---

[1] H.C. Deb. 24 February 1942, Col. 38.
[2] See Amery, *Thoughts on the Constitution*, Chapter III, The Machinery of Government.

made public. If they were, the individual responsibility of departmental Ministers and the collective responsibility of the Cabinet would be weakened. Anderson also argued that the Cabinet's own advisory services should be strengthened. The Economic Section of the Cabinet Secretariat, set up during the Second World War, should be enlarged and the Central Statistical Office should be given permanent form.[1]

When Attlee reorganized his Cabinet in 1947, many of the changes that he made bore a resemblance to the proposals made by Anderson in 1946. We are told by Francis Williams, who was Press adviser to Attlee in those years, that Attlee was influenced by his experience of the working of the Cabinet since 1945, and by the success of such Cabinet committees as the Fuel Committee which was set up to take charge of the organization of fuel supply in the severe winter of 1946–1947.[2] The re-organized Attlee Cabinet made extensive use of committees. There were standing Cabinet committees on Defence, Economic Policy (with a different composition for production questions), the Social Services, and Legislation. Another resemblance to the Anderson proposals was that some of these committees were chaired by non-departmental Ministers and some by departmental Ministers with a major interest in the sphere of the committee. For example, the Defence Committee was chaired by the Prime Minister or by the Minister of Defence as his deputy. The Economic Policy Committee was chaired by the Prime Minister while its executive arm was chaired by Sir Stafford Cripps who was, from November 1947, Chancellor of the Exchequer. The Social Services Committee, from 1947, and the Legislation Committee were both chaired by a non-departmental Minister, Herbert Morrison, who was Lord President of the Council.

In these ways Attlee's re-organized Cabinet bore much resemblance to the sort of Cabinet which Sir John Anderson had advocated. But Attlee also made innovations of his own. He introduced what Francis Williams has described as a pyramidal structure within the Cabinet.[3] At the apex of the pyramid stood

[1] Sir John Anderson: 'The Machinery of Government', *Public Administration*, Autumn 1946, pp. 147–56.
[2] See Francis Williams, *The Triple Challenge* (Heinemann, 1948) p. 44.
[3] Ibid., pp. 44–8.

the Prime Minister. In the second tier were three Ministers, Ernest Bevin, Sir Stafford Cripps, and Herbert Morrison, to whom were given major co-ordinating functions. Ernest Bevin, as Foreign Secretary, was given general oversight not only of foreign but also of commonwealth and colonial affairs. Sir Stafford Cripps, the Chancellor of the Exchequer, was responsible for the direction of financial and economic policy and was chairman of the executive arm of the Prime Minister's Economic Policy Committee. Herbert Morrison, as Lord President of the Council, was made responsible for the co-ordination of social services and of general domestic policy in the non-economic field. He was chairman of several committees including those on Legislation, on the Social Services, and on the Socialization of Industry.[1]

These three Ministers were, in effect, Deputy Prime Ministers within their allotted spheres. Below them in the third tier came another group of five Ministers to whom were allotted co-ordinating functions of slightly less importance. These Ministers were A. V. Alexander, the Minister of Defence, whose task was the co-ordination of Defence under Attlee's overall direction; the Home Secretary, Chuter Ede, who was chairman of the Committee for Civil Defence; and three Ministers— Viscount Addison, Lord Privy Seal; Viscount Jowitt, Lord Chancellor; and Hugh Dalton, Chancellor of the Duchy of Lancaster—to whom were given a variety of co-ordinating functions according to their interest and the nature of problems which pressed for a solution.

In the fourth tier were eight senior departmental Ministers: the Secretaries of State for the Colonies, for Commonwealth Relations, and for Scotland; the Ministers of Labour, Health, Agriculture, and Education; and the President of the Board of Trade. Finally, in the fifth tier, were twenty-one Ministers of Cabinet rank who were not members of the Cabinet. These included the three Service Ministers, the Ministers of Transport, Food, and National Insurance, and six other Ministerial heads of departments.

It will be seen that the co-ordinating functions in both the second and third tiers were given partly to departmental

---

[1] See Herbert Morrison's own account of his functions in his *Government and Parliament*, 2nd ed. (Oxford University Press, 1959) pp. 18–23.

Ministers and partly to non-departmental Ministers. In the second tier, only one out of three, Herbert Morrison, was a non-departmental Minister. In the third tier two Ministers, the Home Secretary and the Minister of Defence, were heads of Departments; two, the Lord Privy Seal and the Chancellor of the Duchy of Lancaster, were non-departmental Ministers; and the fifth, the Lord Chancellor, was in an intermediate position, having a small department to help him in his function as head of the judiciary.

The advantages that can be claimed for the Cabinet as re-organized by Attlee in 1947 are that it made easier the co-ordination of the work of related departments, it relieved some of the burden on the Prime Minister, and it transferred to committees much of the discussion which would have taken place in full Cabinet. It did this without necessitating a drastic reduction in the size of the Cabinet. Attlee's Cabinet in 1947 had seventeen members and by 1951 had twenty-one. It could, then, retain its representative character and include some of the most dynamic and influential leaders of the Labour Party in Parliament. Finally, it gave co-ordinating functions in many cases to Ministers who were best placed to understand the nature of the subjects with which they had to deal: their position as senior departmental Ministers kept them in touch with day-to-day administrative problems and they benefited from the skilled advice of the Civil Servants in their departments.

The disadvantage of the pyramid arrangement lay in the very heavy burden which was placed on the shoulders of the senior departmental Ministers in the second tier, and particularly on the Foreign Secretary and the Chancellor of the Exchequer. This burden was to some extent relieved by the appointment of an additional Minister in both of these departments. Bevin had already secured, in October 1946, the appointment of a Minister of State, Hector McNeil, to act as his chief substitute in the Defence Committee of the Cabinet, in conference work, and at the United Nations. Attlee eased the position of the Chancellor of the Exchequer by appointing an additional Parliamentary Secretary, with the title of Economic Secretary to the Treasury, to assist the Chancellor, particularly in the formation of economic policy.

This device of appointing an additional Minister, or Ministers, to assist an over-extended Ministerial head of department
has been increasingly employed in recent years. Attlee
appointed a Minister of State for Colonial Affairs to assist the
Colonial Secretary in January 1948. By February 1964 the
number of Ministers of State had risen to nine and in July
1967 there were seventeen Ministers of State in the Wilson
Government. They were then distributed as follows: four at the
Foreign Office, three at the Board of Trade, three at the Department of Education and Science, two at the Commonwealth
Office, and one each at the Ministry of Housing and Local Government, the Ministry of Technology, the Home Office and the
Scottish and Welsh Offices. The salary of a Minister of State is
higher than that of a Parliamentary Secretary but is less than
that of a Minister. This reflects his intermediate position in the
government hierarchy.

Cabinet Organization: 1951–1967

The re-organized Attlee Cabinet in this, as in many other ways,
set the pattern for subsequent governments. But in the first
two years of Conservative administration from 1951 to 1953,
there was a limited experiment with different theories of
Cabinet organization, more akin to those of Amery. In the
first place Churchill's Cabinet, as initially formed in 1951, was
smaller than Attlee's had been, having sixteen as against the
Attlee Cabinet's twenty-one members. In the second place, the
proportion of non-departmental Ministers was higher, there
being in Churchill's Cabinet five non-departmental Ministers
out of a total of sixteen, while in the Attlee Cabinet there were
five out of a total of twenty-one. Finally, and most interesting,
two of the non-departmental Ministers were given specific
co-ordinating functions which were publicly announced. Lord
Woolton, as Lord President of the Council, was given the task
of co-ordinating the Ministries of Food and Agriculture. Lord
Leathers was made Secretary of State for Co-ordination of
Transport, Fuel and Power. The Minister of Transport and the
Minister of Fuel and Power were excluded from the Cabinet,
as were the Ministers of Food and Agriculture.

This arrangement came under immediate criticism from the
Opposition and particularly from Attlee and Morrison. Their

ground for criticism was principally that Ministerial responsibility was confused. Who, they asked, was responsible for agricultural policy, for example—the Minister of Agriculture or Lord Woolton, the co-ordinating Minister? The answers given by the Prime Minister did not really clarify the issue.[1] The House of Commons was left with the feeling that either the co-ordinating Ministers gave directives, on occasion, to the Ministers within their co-ordinating field, in which case those Ministers were not in a full sense responsible for policy in their departments, or else the co-ordinating Ministers only sought to harmonize the views of the 'co-ordinated' departments, in which case their role was a distinctly minor one.

The position was further obscured by the fact that both co-ordinating Ministers were in the Lords, as was the Minister of Defence appointed in March 1952, Lord Alexander of Tunis. The arrangement was rather mockingly dubbed the system of 'Overlords', and this name has since come to be loosely used to describe the role of a non-departmental Minister who is publicly given the function of co-ordinating a group of departments. The arrangement was quietly brought to an end in 1953. Lord Leathers resigned from his post as Secretary for the Co-ordination of Transport and Fuel and Power and no successor was appointed. Lord Woolton gave up the task of co-ordinating Food and Agriculture and became Minister of Materials, as well as Chancellor of the Duchy of Lancaster.

So, Churchill's 'limited Amery experiment' was brought to an end. Recent evidence has shown that Churchill originally intended to make a broader trial of Amery's ideas. When he was constructing his Cabinet in October 1951 he invited Sir John Anderson to Chartwell and offered him the post of Chancellor of the Duchy of Lancaster in the new Government. With this post was to have gone responsibility for co-ordinating the Treasury, the Board of Trade, and the Ministry of Supply. Sir John Anderson would have been made a peer and would have become the economic 'overlord' in the Government. But Sir John declined this invitation in no uncertain terms.

J. W. Wheeler-Bennett, his biographer, records that he told Churchill that, in his opinion, the position of economic

---

[1] On 6 November 1951, H.C. Deb. Vol. 493 Cols. 74-5 and on 6 May 1952 H.C. Deb., Vol. 500, Cols. 188-196.

overlord 'could have no place in the peacetime organization of government. There were Government Departments which were responsible to Ministers, and there were Ministers who answered for their departments to the House of Commons. This was the established order of things. It was inconceivable to him to have another Minister, floating, as it were, above these Departments and Ministers with no fixed responsibility for either. To Sir John, the proposed arrangement would prove intolerable, nor did he think it could possibly work, and he said as much to the Prime Minister.'[1] The offer, however, shows conclusively that Churchill was thinking along Amery's lines for re-organization of the Cabinet. If Sir John Anderson had accepted Churchill's offer there would have been, from October 1951, a more thoroughgoing experiment with Amery's ideas than there had been before in peacetime. As it was, the strictly limited experiment was quietly dropped in 1953 in face of criticism.

Between 1953 and 1967, Cabinets, both Conservative and Labour, have been constructed broadly on the lines of the Attlee Cabinet in its re-organized form after 1947. Cabinets have remained large, varying in size from twenty to twenty-three members. Co-ordinating functions have been given in some cases to departmental, in some cases to non-departmental Ministers. For example, in 1962, R. A. Butler, when Home Secretary, was chairman of the Cabinet committee concerned with negotiations over Britain's request to join the European Common Market.[2] Again, in the summer of 1965 the Wilson Cabinet gave to a committee of Ministers under the chairmanship of Herbert Bowden, Lord President of the Council, the task of working out Government policy on the control of immigration. The allotment of such co-ordinating functions has not normally been announced at the time, but it is clear that every Cabinet since 1953 has been using co-ordinating Ministers in this kind of way. Similarly, extensive use has been made of Cabinet committees since 1953 although their character and composition has not been made public. In following this practice, governments have been keeping to the recommendation

---

[1] J. W. Wheeler-Bennett: *John Anderson, Viscount Waverley*, (Macmillan, 1962) p. 352.

[2] See: 'Lord Butler on Cabinet Government: A Conversation with Norman Hunt' in the *Listener*, 16 September 1965, p. 410.

made by Sir John Anderson in 1946 that the arrangement of co-ordinating functions in the Cabinet and the composition of Cabinet committees should not be made public. This, as we saw above, was advisable, in his opinion, in order not to undermine the principles of individual responsibility of Ministers and the collective responsibility of the Cabinet.

Sometimes, government statements have announced that a committee covering a particular field was envisaged. For example, in July 1963, the Government white paper on the Central Organization for Defence announced that a Cabinet Committee on Defence and Overseas Policy would be set up. Its chairman would be the Prime Minister and other members would include the First Secretary of State, the Foreign Secretary, the Chancellor of the Exchequer, the Home Secretary, the Secretary of State for Commonwealth Relations and the Colonies, and the Secretary of State for Defence. Other Ministers and the Chiefs of Staff would be asked to attend where necessary.[1] This committee was continued, basically unchanged, under the Wilson government.

The problem of co-ordinating Ministries and of keeping down the size of the Cabinet has also partly been met by the merging of ministries. In 1953 the Ministry of Pensions was combined with the Ministry of National Insurance.[2] In 1955 the Ministry of Food was merged with the Ministry of Agriculture and Fisheries. A cynic might say that new ministries tend to proliferate as fast as old ones are merged with each other. But even a new ministry may not have an independent existence for long. A Minister for Science, for example, came into being in October 1959 and acquired a small staff. By 1965, this had been merged in the Department for Education and Science.

Departments which are grouped together are a likely target for later merger. In 1947 the three Service departments were placed in a unique relationship with the newly created Ministry of Defence. The Minister of Defence, from 1947 to 1964, was a co-ordinating Minister with a small staff of his

[1] Cmnd. 2097. Central Organization for Defence p. 2 at para. 16.

[2] In 1966 the Ministry of Pensions and National Insurance was re-named the Ministry of Social Security and, at the same time, the National Assistance Board was merged with the new Ministry.

own. He was in the Cabinet, from which the three Service Ministers—the First Lord of the Admiralty, the Secretary of State for War, and the Secretary of State for Air—were excluded. He was Deputy Chairman of the Defence Committee of the Cabinet (the Prime Minister being the full Chairman), and the three Service Ministers sat on this committee. In 1958 his powers of control over the Service ministries were increased and his staff was strengthened by the addition of the Chief of Defence Staff.[1]

This was to prove only an interim stage, however. In 1964 the Service ministries were merged with the Ministry of Defence. The successors to the Service Ministers were then called Deputy Secretaries of State for Defence, and Ministers of Defence for the Army, for the Royal Navy, and for the Royal Air Force. In January 1967 the integration of the three Services was taken a stage further. Two Ministers, outside the Cabinet, were appointed to assist the Minister of Defence. These were the Minister of Defence (Administration) and the Minister of Defence (Equipment). In place of the Deputy Secretaries of State for Defence, three Parliamentary Under-Secretaries were appointed: one for the Army, one for the Navy, and one for the Royal Air Force.

There have been other suggestions for grouping or merging ministries. Lord Butler has suggested a Minister for External Affairs who would take charge of Foreign Affairs, Commonwealth Affairs, and Colonial Affairs. He has also expressed his preference for a single Minister in charge of economic affairs, and a Minister for the Social Services under whom would be brought together the many aspects of the social services which are at present scattered among various departments.[2] In this way, the Cabinet would be reduced in size, but it would be unlike the 'Amery' Cabinet since it would consist largely of senior departmental Ministers each of whom, in the manner of the Minister of Defence from 1964 to 1967, would preside over a group of related sub-departments.

We have seen that Sir John Anderson recommended in his Romanes Lecture in 1946 that the advisory services of the

---

[1] See the white papers on 'Central Organization for Defence'—Cmnd. 6923 of 1946 and Cmnd. 476 of 1958.
[2] Butler, loc. cit., p. 411.

Cabinet should be strengthened. This recommendation was followed by the Attlee Government. The Central Statistical Office, which had been set up to advise the Cabinet in 1941, was given permanent form. Again, the Economic Section of the Cabinet Secretariat, which was also a war-time creation, was retained within the Cabinet framework until 1953. In that year the Economic Section was transferred to the Treasury. This then represented another example of the strengthening of departmental organization which was a notable trend in the period.

Harold Wilson, as Leader of the Opposition in 1964, criticized the way in which, in his view, the advisory services of the Cabinet were weakened by Conservative administrations between 1953 and 1964. He favoured strengthening the Cabinet Secretariat and restoring it to what he conceived had been its position in the Attlee Government. He wanted to see skilled advisers brought in who would assist the Prime Minister, and other Cabinet Ministers, in sizing up some of the more complex issues—in economic affairs and defence, for example.[1] On forming his Government in October 1964, Wilson was able to put these ideas into practice, at least in part. Dr. Thomas Balogh was brought in from the university world to advise the Cabinet on economic affairs, while Sir Solly Zuckerman became Scientific Officer to the Cabinet. He continued to act also as Chief Scientific Officer to the Secretary of State for Defence.

The Experience Summarized

How can we sum up the development of the Cabinet since 1916? It is most instructive to divide the period into two phases: from 1916 to 1939 and from 1939 to 1967. In the first phase, the main achievement was the establishment of the Cabinet Secretariat. Between 1916 and 1918 there was a radical experiment with a small 'policy' Cabinet, but this idea did not catch on in peacetime. Between 1918 and 1939, apart from the institution of Secretariat, the Cabinet pattern was little changed from that known before 1916.

The 1939 war brought several experiments, first with a small 'policy' Cabinet, then with a parallel Cabinet structure, the

[1] See a conversation between Harold Wilson and Norman Hunt in *Whitehall and Beyond* (BBC Publications 1964) pp. 18–23.

War Cabinet being in effect paralleled by a Home Cabinet which was for much of the war chaired by Sir John Anderson. Extensive use was made of committees, and advisory services to assist the Cabinet were brought into being. The Attlee Government, drawing upon war-time experience and the ideas of Anderson, created from 1947 a new type of Cabinet. This was a large Cabinet, but one which made extensive use of committees and in which certain key Ministers, some of whom were departmental Ministers, had important co-ordinating roles. This type of Cabinet has, by and large, been retained ever since. There was a brief and limited experiment with the Amery idea but it ended in 1953. Subsequent developments have, on the whole, strengthened the trends already visible after 1947. The major ministries have tended to acquire more influence and their Ministers have often received the main co-ordinating roles.

It is evident then that the modern Cabinet bears little resemblance to the Cabinet which Amery criticized in the 1930s. His statement that the Cabinet was 'little more than a standing conference of departmental chiefs' which was quite incapable of coherent planning of policy as a whole, or of effectively executing such a policy, may have been true of the Cabinet in 1935, but it is certainly not true of the Cabinet in 1967. The Cabinet now includes a series of high-powered ministerial committees, in many of which senior officials also play a part, and which are all articulated with the Cabinet meeting itself which is normally the final arena for decision-making. Within this structure, the main co-ordinating roles are played by senior departmental Ministers. Amery's belief that non-departmental Ministers would be better fitted for policy planning has not been borne out by experience. Lord Butler, who was the main co-ordinating Minister in the Churchill, Eden, and Macmillan governments, said in 1965 that in his view he was much more effective in Cabinet when he had a department to support him. From 1955 to 1957, he had been Lord Privy Seal, but in January 1957 he became Home Secretary. He considered that he was then able to make his case more effectively in Cabinet with the whole force of his department's advice behind him.[1]

[1] Butler, loc. cit., p. 410.

Indeed, just as we may seriously question Amery's view that non-departmental Ministers are better for policy planning, so we may also question his view that a small Cabinet is better than a large one. The great advantage of a large one is that it can be representative. Representative, that is, not only of the main departments, but also of the different countries in Great Britain, since nowadays the Secretaries of State for Scotland and for Wales are always included; and, most important of all, representative of the main trends within the majority party. This comprehensiveness helps to ensure that the main sections of the administrative machine are kept in reasonable harmony, and that the Cabinet reflects the state of opinion in the majority party in the Commons. If, by using committees, this large Cabinet of 20 or 23 Ministers can be also an efficient co-ordinator and policy planner, then it would seem to be in every way superior to a small policy Cabinet.[1]

Cabinet Government or Government by Prime Minister?

We have seen that R. H. S. Crossman and J. P. Mackintosh have claimed that Prime Ministerial government has supplanted Cabinet government in Britain. We are now in a position to examine this view. The argument is developed in two main ways. First, it is claimed that decision-making now rests either with the Prime Minister or with the departmental Ministers backed by powerful Civil Servants. The Cabinet has shrunk in importance and now, in Crossman's phrase, 'joins the other dignified elements in the Constitution'.[2] Second, several occasions are quoted when the Prime Minister has in recent times acted on his own initiative or in concert with a small group of Ministers. Crossman cites Attlee's decision to manufacture the atom bomb in Britain. This decision was taken without any prior discussion in the Cabinet and was not revealed by Attlee 'to any but a handful of trusted friends'.[3] Similarly he claimed

---

[1] R. V. Clements has argued recently that the Cabinet needs to be made larger rather than smaller. In his view, in the present Cabinet, 'a mature committee system sustains a flourishing plural executive'. Why not then, he says, include in the Cabinet all ministerial heads of departments? See R. V. Clements, 'The Cabinet', in *Political Studies*, Vol. xiii, p. 232.

[2] R. H. S. Crossman in his Introduction to W. Bagehot, *The English Constitution* (Fontana, 1963) p. 54.

[3] Ibid., p. 55.

that in 1956 'Lord Avon took the decisions and prepared the plans for the Anglo-French attack at Port Said without Cabinet consultation, and with the assistance of only a handful of his colleagues and permanent advisers'.[1] Anthony Nutting, who was Minister of State for Foreign Affairs at the time and resigned over the Government's Suez policy, has subsequently modified this picture. He has referred to two Cabinet meetings, on October 24 and 25, at which the proposed Anglo-French action was discussed and approved by the Cabinet.[2] The ultimatum to Egypt was not delivered until October 30. Nevertheless, it is true that Anthony Eden (Lord Avon) took a leading part in formulating the Suez policy and kept most of his colleagues in the dark until a late stage. Finally, J. P. Mackintosh has pointed to the 'massacre of Ministers' carried out by Macmillan in July 1962. On this occasion the Prime Minister dismissed, at one blow, the Chancellor of the Exchequer (Selwyn Lloyd), the Lord Chancellor (Viscount Kilmuir), and three other senior Ministers.

Looking first at the argument that the Cabinet has now shrunk in importance in the decision-making process, one may reasonably reply that this is to confuse the Cabinet with the Cabinet meeting. Surely the Cabinet, as an institution, includes the network of Cabinet committees which are responsible to it? Moreover, looking at the examples given of high-handed action by Prime Ministers, one may reasonably ask how far these instances are really typical. The difficulty in attempting to answer this question is that, as Cabinet proceedings are shrouded in secrecy, it is impossible to make a fair assessment until records can be consulted thirty years after the event. But some evidence is available. For example, Edward Heath has described how the decision to apply for entry to the Common Market in 1962 was only reached after a series of Cabinet meetings which had been preceded by meetings of Cabinet committees preparing the ground for the Cabinet.[3] Lord Butler has supported this picture by affirming that the decision was taken by the Cabinet after a strong recommendation from

[1] Ibid., p. 55.

[2] Anthony Nutting: *No End of a Lesson*, (Constable, 1967) p. 104.

[3] In a conversation with J. P. Mackintosh in the 'Power in Britain' broadcast on ITV, 21 February 1965.

the Cabinet Committee and the Prime Minister. But, he said, the Cabinet could have rejected this recommendation.[1] With regard to Suez and Macmillan's 'massacre of Ministers', Butler implied that these actions produced countervailing forces.[2] In other words, high-handed action by a Premier prompted resistance elsewhere in the political system, either in the Cabinet, or in the Commons, or both. After all, Eden resigned less than three months after the ultimatum to Egypt, and Macmillan only just a year after he had dismissed a third of his Cabinet. Both, it is true, were sick men at the time of resignation, but Prime Ministers do not always resign when they are ill. For example, Attlee did not resign in April 1950 when he went into hospital to be treated for a duodenal ulcer.

A recent Premier who clearly did not attempt to hold all the reins of power in his own hands was Sir Alec Douglas-Home. In an interview with Nora Beloff published in the *Observer* on 13 September 1964 he said that the most important quality needed by a Prime Minister was to know how to delegate his authority. A good Prime Minister, he said, once he has selected his Ministers, should interfere with their departmental business as little as possible.

It is impossible to generalize about the way in which Prime Ministers have conceived their role. Some, like Palmerston or Lloyd George, have been high-handed. Some, like Baldwin, have been rarely assertive and have let Ministers go their own way. The high-handed Premiers have often in the past stimulated 'countervailing forces'. For example, Lloyd George was ousted by disgruntled Conservatives meeting at the Carlton Club. Many Prime Ministers fall between the two poles of the dictatorial and the '*laisser faire*' Premier. For example, Lord Butler has recorded that Churchill was dictatorial but also 'constitutional' in the sense that he consulted people and expected things to be discussed in Cabinet.

One may conclude that the emergence of 'Government by Prime Minister' is probably a myth. Let a Dutch student of the British Cabinet have the last word here. In the view of Hans Daalder, the tradition of collective responsibility and the complexity of modern government make Prime Ministerial

[1] Butler, loc. cit., p. 410.
[2] Ibid., p. 409.

Government unlikely. 'Even the sheer burden of office prevents any Prime Minister from intervening at all closely except in the most urgent matters. If he can make his will prevail in any matter he chooses, he can only do so by leaving most things alone'.[1]

[1] Hans Daalder, *Cabinet Reform in Britain*, 1914–1963 (Stanford University Press, 1964) p. 248.

FOR REFERENCE

L. S. AMERY, *Thoughts on the Constitution*, 2nd ed. (Oxford University Press, 1953), Chapter III.

SIR JOHN ANDERSON, 'The Machinery of Government', Romanes Lecture printed in *Public Administration*, 1946.

W. BAGEHOT, *The English Constitution* (Fontana, 1963).

BBC PUBLICATIONS, *Whitehall and Beyond* (1964).

A. H. BIRCH, *Representative and Responsible Government* (Allen and Unwin, 1964).

G. CAMPION, *British Government since 1918* (Allen & Unwin, 1950), Chapter 2 by D. N. Chester.

D. N. CHESTER and F. M. G. WILLSON, *The Organization of British Central Government* (Allen and Unwin, 1957), Chapter IX.

R. V. CLEMENTS, 'The Cabinet', in *Political Studies*, 1965.

H. DAALDER, *Cabinet Reform in Britain*, *1914–1963* (Stanford University Press, 1964).

S. E. FINER, 'The Individual Responsibility of Ministers' in *Public Administration*, 1956.

J. P. MACKINTOSH, *The British Cabinet* (Stevens, 1962).

G. MARSHALL and G. C. MOODIE, *Some Problems of the Constitution* (Hutchinson, 1959).

H. MORRISON, *Government and Parliament*, 2nd ed. (Oxford University Press, 1959).

F. WILLIAMS, *A Prime Minister Remembers* (Heinemann, 1961).

F. WILLIAMS, *The Triple Challenge* (Heinemann, 1948).

CD. 9230. Report of the Machinery of Government Committee, 1918.

Cmd. 6923. Central Organization for Defence, 1946.

Cmd. 476. Central Organization for Defence, 1958.

Cmd. 2097. Central Organization for Defence, 1963.

CHAPTER XII

The Political Parties

ALMOST everywhere in a study of British politics one comes to considerations of party. We have seen that much of the strength which the Prime Minister enjoys in relation to his Cabinet, and to Parliament, flows from the support which he enjoys from his party, particularly if that party has a clear majority in the House of Commons. Conversely, if he loses support in his party, or if the party breaks up, then his days as Prime Minister are probably numbered. Again, the chief opposition party provides an invaluable check upon the government. It is the 'conscience of the nation'. It is, or should be, an alternative government and, therefore, constitutes an invaluable safeguard of democratic procedures. Yet, although parties are so important, there is not complete agreement about the ways in which they function in Britain, or indeed about what their roles should be in the democratic process. The fact is that the two largest parties, the Conservative and Labour parties, have many-sided functions and there is dispute, inside and outside these parties, about the relative emphasis which should be given to each of their main functions.

The first function of a party, if it is the governing party, is to sustain the government and, if it is the opposition party, to provide a coherent alternative to the government. This function is performed at the parliamentary level and is the oldest of the functions of British parties. The second main function of the party is to organize support in the constituencies and in the nation as a whole. This function is performed partly by developing and maintaining a network of party associations and agents in the constituencies, partly by making known the policy and principles of the party. The third function is to act as a channel of communication between party members in the constituencies and the leader of the party.

Viewed historically, political parties in Britain began with only the first function. Before 1832, there was little need to organize support in the constituencies. This was a matter for the local magnates, whether as owners of pocket boroughs or as leaders of the local community. With the extension of the franchise in 1832 and the elimination of pocket boroughs, constituency organization 'to get out the vote' first became important. So we find registration societies, from the 1830s, appearing in many parts of the country and developing even more rapidly after the Reform Act of 1867.[1] In November of that year the Conservatives established a National Union of Conservative and Constitutional Associations.[2] Ten years later, in 1877, the Liberals set up their National Liberal Federation. So we see the beginnings of the modern type of mass party organization.

With further extensions of the franchise, in 1884, 1918, and 1928, the need for a wide and active party membership became all the greater. This created new problems for the parties. In an increasingly democratic country, it was inevitable that the members of the party would want to play a part in the policy-making process in the party. But this desire can, and often does, conflict with the first and second functions of a party: to sustain the Leader in parliament and to present a coherent picture, or 'image' in the modern phrase, of what the party stands for. There is, therefore, an underlying tension in the three main parties. It is camouflaged in the Conservative Party by the party's constitution, it is underlined and made overt in the Labour Party by that party's constitutional arrangements. Neither of the main parties has the complete answer to this problem; neither has the same answer.[3]

The Conservative Party: How the Leader is Chosen
Until 1965, the Conservative Party eschewed intra-party democracy, both in the very wide powers it gave to its Leader

[1] See I. Bulmer-Thomas, *The Party System in Great Britain* (Phoenix House, 1953) pp. 18-19.

[2] This organization has had a continuous existence ever since. In 1924 it received its modern name: The National Union of Conservative and Unionist Associations.

[3] R. T. McKenzie in his book *British Political Parties*, 2nd ed. (Mercury Books, 1964), has given a very able account of the distribution of power within the Conservative and Labour parties. My analysis differs from McKenzie's in some ways, see especially below pp. 295-9.

in controlling the Party machine, and in the method by which the Leader was chosen. In theory, he was elected by a large body consisting of Conservative Members of Parliament, Conservative peers, prospective parliamentary candidates, and the members of the Executive Committee of the National Union of Conservative and Unionist Associations. In fact, this body merely acclaimed the choice of Leader which had already been decided by negotiation, behind the scenes, between the most powerful elements in the Party. This method, it was considered, prevented open faction fighting and gave the appearance of a Party united behind its new Leader. Thus, when in 1911, the Conservatives were in opposition and it was necessary to find a new Leader, there were two strongly supported candidates, Austen Chamberlain and Walter Long. In order to prevent a contest between these two a compromise candidate was found. This was Bonar Law who was known to have ability but was not strongly liked or disliked by anyone. When the meeting to elect the Leader took place, Bonar Law's nomination was moved by Walter Long and seconded by Austen Chamberlain. He was elected unanimously.

When the Conservatives were in office and a vacancy for the leadership arose, they were again able to avoid an open contest. When a Conservative Prime Minister resigned through ill health or advancing years, they left the choice of his successor to the Monarch. In some cases, the choice of successor was obvious. In 1937, Neville Chamberlain had long been unofficially recognized as 'heir apparent' to Stanley Baldwin. Similarly, when Sir Winston Churchill resigned in 1955, it was generally accepted that the Queen would invite Anthony Eden to form a government. On several occasions, as we have seen in Chapter X, there were rival contestants for the succession. In 1923 George V, and in 1957 and 1963 Queen Elizabeth II, had to make a choice. That choice was influenced by opinion among the leading Party notables, and in 1957 and 1963 the Queen merely followed the advice, in the first case, of the two senior members of the Party and, in the second case, of the outgoing Prime Minister, Macmillan.[1] The whole procedure might seem to fit well with the Conservative desire to avoid an open contest for the leadership.

[1] See above pp. 243—6.

There were, however, contrary currents moving within the Party. The method of choice in 1957 gave rise to some misgivings but these were nothing to the passions aroused by the choice of Lord Home in 1963. There was criticism, especially by Iain Macleod, of the way in which informal soundings of opinion were taken, both in the Cabinet, and among Conservative M.P.s.[1] Feeling gained ground that a secret ballot among Conservative M.P.s would be a better method of selection because no one could dispute its reliability. In February 1965, Sir Alec Douglas-Home, as Leader of the Conservative Party, announced that the next Leader would be chosen after secret balloting among Conservative M.P.s.

His statement envisaged the possibility of three ballots. At the first ballot, there would not be a decision unless one candidate secured, not only an absolute majority, but also 15 per cent. more of the votes cast than any other candidate. If this requirement was not fulfilled there would be a second ballot, not more than four days later. At the second ballot, a candidate who secured an absolute majority would be declared elected. If no candidate received an absolute majority, a third ballot would be held. At this final ballot, all except the three strongest at the second ballot would be eliminated and Conservative M.P.s would use the alternative vote system to choose the Leader. This choice would then be submitted for ratification to the traditional meeting of the Conservative M.P.s, Conservative peers, prospective candidates, and members of the Executive Committee of the National Union.

This method of selection differs in two principal ways from the Labour method of selecting their Leader. First, in the Labour Party there are only two instead of three ballots. If, at the first ballot, no candidate receives an absolute majority, at the second ballot all except the first two names are eliminated and a straight vote takes place. Second, in the Labour Party there is no large ratifying body although Labour peers join with Labour M.P.s in the Parliamentary Labour Party to choose the Leader.

The new method of choosing the Conservative Leader was soon tried out. In July 1965, Sir Alec Douglas-Home resigned as Party Leader. At the first ballot of Conservative M.P.s, on

[1] See above pp. 244-6.

27 July, Edward Heath received 150 votes, Reginald Maudling 133 and Enoch Powell 15. This gave Heath an absolute majority, but less than the required 15 per cent lead over the second candidate. However, Maudling conceded Heath the election. He withdrew from the contest and no further ballot was necessary. The choice of Heath as Leader was then ratified by the meeting of Conservative M.P.s, peers, prospective candidates, and members of the Executive of the National Union. The new method of election was generally accepted to be a success. Iain Macleod wrote in *The Spectator*: 'The Tories' cautious flutter with formalized democracy in choosing their leader has worked with smoothness and despatch'. It represented, he said, a revolution within the Tory party.[1]

The Relationship Between the Leader and His Party

The Conservative Party has, therefore, adopted a democratic method of choosing its Leader basically similar to the method long used by the Labour Party. But, once he is elected, the relationship between the Conservative Leader and the Conservative Party organization remains essentially autocratic. He appoints the Conservative Chief Whip in the Commons, whether the Party is in office or in opposition. He selects the members of the Shadow Cabinet with as much freedom, in opposition, as he enjoys when, as Prime Minister, he is choosing members of his government. He has complete control over the Party machine outside Parliament, because he appoints all the chief officers of the Party who are then responsible only to him. These are the Chairman of the Party, the Deputy Chairman, the Vice-Chairman, and the Honorary Treasurers. They control the Central Office of the Party which is housed in Smith Square, in Westminster, conveniently near to the Houses of Parliament.

The Central Office has a series of well staffed departments, devoted to Constituency Organization and Finance, Publicity and Propaganda, Speakers, Industrial Problems, Local Government, the Young Conservative Organization, the Young Britons Organization, and the Associations of Conservative teachers and university students. Two other important organizations are associated with Central Office. These

[1] *Spectator*, 30 July 1965, p. 139.

are the Conservative Political Centre, which is responsible for political education in the Party, and the Conservative Research Department. Another vitally important part of the central organization is the Advisory Committee on Policy. This committee has a key role in planning the future policy of the Party, and is closely supported by the Research Department whose Director is also Secretary to the committee. Significantly, the Chairman and Deputy Chairman of this policy committee are appointed by the Leader of the Party, as is the Chairman of the Research Department.

The Central Office works closely with, but is not in any way responsible to, the representative body of the Party, the Central Council of the National Union of Conservative and Unionist Associations, and its Executive Committee. The Central Council is a large body consisting of representatives of all the constituency associations and of provincial area councils of the Party. In addition, all Conservative M.P.s, peers, and prospective parliamentary candidates are entitled to sit on the Council. It meets at least once a year to consider a report from the Executive Committee, and to debate motions submitted by area councils and constituency associations. 'The decisions arrived at are conveyed to the Leader of the Party'.[1] The Executive Committee consists of the Leader of the Party and the principal officers, together with at least six representatives from each area council. It meets once a month.

The Annual Party Conference is organized by the National Union. It can be attended by members of the Central Council, by two representatives of each constituency association and by the certificated agents of the Party. The number attending is usually well over 4,000. The relationship between the Conference and the Leader is typical of the underlying spirit of Conservative organization. Decisions of the Conference, like decisions of the Central Council, 'are conveyed to the Leader of the Party'. He is in no way bound to act upon them. Indeed, until 1965, he did not even attend the Conference sessions, but addressed a mass rally of Party members when the Conference proper was over. At the 1965 Conference the Leader of the Conservative Party, for the first time, sat on the platform

---

[1] *The Party Organization*, Conservative and Unionist Central Office, Organization Series No. 1 (January 1961), p. 8.

throughout the Conference and replied to the debate on the Conservative policy document *Putting Britain Right Ahead*. He also gave the customary speech when the Conference ended.

For Edward Heath, as Party Leader, to sit through all the Conference debates was another indication of the increasingly democratic temper of the Conservative Party. The new passion for democracy did not, however, in 1965, bring with it a change in the traditional method of taking votes at the Conference. The normal practice has been for resolutions to be carried or rejected by a show of hands. The vote is taken simultaneously in the main hall and in the overflow hall to which the speeches are relayed by closed circuit television. It is very rare for a count to be demanded. Consequently, there is often a stronger impression of overwhelming support for the platform than would appear if a count were taken. This is how Conservatives would have it. The tradition is that differences are not pressed by a minority, when it seems to be clear where the majority stand.

Even when the Party is narrowly divided, a vote will sometimes not be claimed. This was the case at the end of a dramatic debate on Rhodesia at the 1965 Conference. Lord Salisbury had moved an amendment to the official motion on Rhodesia. Salisbury's amendment deplored the use, or threat of use, of any kind of sanctions against Rhodesia. It was passionately debated by the Conference for nearly two hours. It was apparent that there was widespread support for the amendment although, possibly, not majority support. The extent of support was not accurately ascertained, however, since Sir Alec Douglas-Home, when replying to the debate, asked the Conference not to force a vote on the amendment, and the Conference agreed not to.

There are signs here, too, of an increasingly democratic temper in the Annual Conference. At the 1967 Conference, at Brighton, delegates called for a ballot after the Chairman had declared that the resolution on comprehensive schools had been carried by a small majority on a show of hands. The ballot was held and the resolution carried by 1,302 votes to 816. This was, however, the only ballot at the Conference.

The organization of the Conservative Party then gives great authority to the Leader, and the rank and file do not, normally, openly challenge his authority. But when there is widespread dissatisfaction with the Leader, his power can melt away. Whenever there is a heavy ground-swell of opinion against the Leader, it is likely that he will resign. Thus Balfour decided to resign in 1911 when he became convinced that there was much unrest in the Party at the stand he had taken on the passage of the Parliament Bill. Austen Chamberlain's leadership was rejected in 1922 when a meeting of Conservative Members of Parliament at the Carlton Club voted against his policy of maintaining the coalition with the Lloyd George Liberals. This led to the resignation of the Lloyd George Government and to Chamberlain's replacement as Leader of the Conservative Party by Bonar Law, one of the chief advocates of ending the coalition. Baldwin had to fight a major battle to maintain his position as Leader in 1930 and 1931. The opposition to him was spearheaded by the two Conservative press Lords, Lords Beaverbrook and Rothermere. Baldwin had to display unusual vigour to throw off their challenge. Clearly, then, although the constitution of the Conservative Party gives their Leader immense power, it is a power based upon consent. If he is widely thought to have abused the trust placed in him, then his position becomes untenable.

The Labour Party: The Constitution of The Party
On the face of it, the constitution of the Labour Party presents a complete contrast. While the Conservative Party is largely authoritarian, the Labour Party is democratic. While the Leader is the central figure in the Conservative Party and the Conference and other representative organs are purely advisory, in the Labour Party the sovereign authority, according to the constitution, is the Annual Conference. Clause VI, Section 1 of the Labour Party Constitution states: 'The work of the Party shall be under the direction and control of the Party Conference which shall itself be subject to the Constitution and Standing Orders of the Party'. The Constitution and Standing Orders can be changed by the Conference. No special majority is required, although it is provided that there must be a card vote. Normally, amendments to the Constitution are only considered every third year, although the National Executive may advise consideration of amendments in other years.

The Annual Conference, therefore, is a sovereign body, subject to a written constitution, which it can itself change with little formal difficulty although there may be a formidable emotional barrier against changing some of the time-hallowed features of the constitution. Miss Sara Barker, the National Agent of the Labour Party, has very well defined the role which it is thought the Conference should play. 'The Annual Conference of the Labour Party', she says, 'is the fountain of authority. It declares policy and elects a National Executive Committee, which is responsible to the whole Movement for carrying out all phases of activity.'[1]

Just as the Labour Annual Conference is different from the Conservative Annual Conference in being the sovereign authority in the Party, so the composition of the Labour Conference is very different. The Conservative Party is a union of constituency associations beside which ancillary bodies such as the associations of Conservative trade unionists and of Conservative clubs play a very small part. The Labour Party, however, is an alliance of constituency parties, trade unions, and socialist societies. In this alliance, the trade unions are numerically most important, the constituency parties are next most important and the socialist societies are relatively tiny. This position is reflected in the composition of the Conference. The parties, trade unions, and societies are entitled to send one delegate for every 5,000 members, or part thereof, on whom affiliation fees to the Labour Party have been paid. In 1965 there were 816,765 individual members of constituency parties, 5,601,982 affiliated trade unionists and 21,146 members of Socialist Societies.[2] Whenever a card vote is demanded, the trade unions heavily outnumber the rest. In a card vote, each delegation votes for all its affiliated members. The delegates of the Transport and General Workers Union, for example, deploy well over a million votes.

The composition of the National Executive Committee also reflects the triple nature of the Party. Twelve members of the Committee are nominated and elected by the trade unions,

[1] Sara Barker, *How the Labour Party Works* (revised ed. 1955, published by the Labour Party, price 6d.) p. 11.
[2] The Royal Arsenal Co-operative Society is included among the Socialist Societies, which also include the Fabian Society, the Socialist Medical Association, and the Jewish Socialist Labour Party. Many other Co-operative Societies support the Co-operative Party which is closely associated with, but not linked to, the Labour Party.

seven are nominated and elected by the constituency parties, and one by the socialist societies. In addition, five women members are elected by the whole Conference. The Treasurer of the Party is also a member and is elected by the whole Conference, and the Leader and Deputy Leader of the Parliamentary Labour Party are *ex officio* members. These provisions ensure that the trade unions do not dominate the whole process of election to the National Executive. The influence of the constituency parties and the socialist societies has been safeguarded, since 1937, by allowing them to nominate and elect their own members. But it should be noted that it is a minority influence. The majority of members of the National Executive, 18 out of 27, are elected either by the trade unions alone, or by the whole Conference in which the trade union vote predominates.

The Leader of The Party and The Annual Conference

How does the Leader of the Parliamentary Labour Party fit into this system in which, according to the constitution, the Annual Conference is the sovereign authority? The answer to this question is not altogether clear and is, from time to time, a matter of debate within the Party.

His relationship to his supporters within parliament is clear enough. He is elected by the Parliamentary Labour Party which consists of all Labour M.P.s and Labour peers. When a vacancy has arisen (through death or resignation, for example), the election has always been contested. Indeed when Labour is in opposition, the Leader is subject to annual re-election, and he is sometimes opposed. The re-election of Hugh Gaitskell, for example, was opposed in 1960 and 1961. Nevertheless, the tenure of office of Leaders is normally considerable and this reflects their generally strong position in the Parliamentary Party.

But when we look at the Leader's position outside parliament his authority, constitutionally speaking, is much less than that of the Leader of the Conservative Party. Whereas the Conservative Leader appoints the principal officers of the Party, who then direct the activities of Central Office, the national organization of the Labour Party is responsible to the National Executive Committee which is elected by Annual

Conference. The chief full-time officials of the Labour Party are the General Secretary and the National Agent. In addition there are Overseas, Research, Press and Publicity, and Finance Departments. All are housed at Transport House, in Smith Square, only a stone's throw from Conservative Central Office.

The Party machine, then, is under the control of a committee which is almost entirely elected by the Annual Conference. The Party Leader and his Deputy sit on the committee, and enjoy great prestige there, but must accept majority decisions of the committee that concern the running of the Party. But what of matters of policy? Where is policy decided?

The Constitution states at Clause V: 'The Party Conference shall decide from time to time what specific proposals of legislative, financial or administrative reform shall be included in the Party Programme. No proposal shall be included in the Party Programme unless it has been adopted by the Party Conference by a majority of not less than two-thirds of the votes recorded on a card vote.' It also states at Clause VIII (Section 2c) that the National Executive Committee has a duty 'to confer with the Parliamentary Labour Party at the opening of each Parliamentary Session, and at any time when it or the Parliamentary Labour Party may desire a Conference on any matters relating to the work and progress of the Party'. The Constitution, therefore, seems to imply that specific proposals made by Conference are binding on the Leader of the Parliamentary Labour Party if they have secured a two-thirds majority on a card vote. However, it is still a matter for his discretion as to when such proposals shall become part of the legislative programme of the Government, if Labour is in office, or be made a cardinal point of Labour opposition.

The Constitution also provides at Clause V (Section 2) that 'The National Executive Committee and the Parliamentary Committee of the Parliamentary Labour Party shall decide which items from the Party Programme shall be included in the Manifesto which shall be issued by the National Executive Committee prior to every General Election. The joint meeting of the two Committees shall also define the attitude of the Party to the principal issues raised by the Election which are not covered by the Manifesto'. At election time, therefore, discretion is given to a joint meeting of the Parliamentary Party

Committee and of the National Executive to interpret the will of the Conference.

In between general elections the Leader has considerable freedom to initiate policy on matters on which the Conference has not pronounced. The experience of the Attlee and Wilson governments shows that, when Labour is in office, the Leader has as much freedom of action as a Conservative Prime Minister. When Labour is in opposition, the Leader of the Labour Party can, and frequently does, initiate policy by speeches in the House or by television broadcasts. The main lines of such speeches may not have been submitted for approval to either the Parliamentary Committee or the National Executive. But a wise Labour Leader will try to keep in harmony with majority opinion in these bodies.

What often happens is that the Leader of the Party, when in opposition, makes a speech taking up a position on an important matter of policy. The National Executive, when next it meets, has to decide how far it supports the Leader's initiative. Thus Hugh Gaitskell in his television broadcast on 19 October 1962, replying to a broadcast by the Prime Minister, Harold Macmillan, said that the terms provisionally negotiated for Britain's entry into the Common Market were not good enough. If no better terms could be obtained, then the question of entry should be submitted to the country at a general election. When the National Executive met, a week later, it came out in general support of Gaitskell's position. A policy document was issued by the Executive, embodying and developing Gaitskell's views, and this document was soon afterwards approved by Annual Conference.

A good deal of forward planning of policy is, of course, made by the National Executive Committee or by a sub-committee, aided by the Party research officers, and sometimes also by outside experts, which then reports to the full Committee. In the years between the 1955 and 1959 general elections, a whole series of policy statements was approved by the National Executive: on public enterprise, industry and society, colonial policy, superannuation, etc. These were then submitted to the Annual Conference, approved and later incorporated in the Labour manifesto for the 1959 general election.

The position of the Leader of the Labour Party is then clear as regards resolutions of the Conference which have been passed by a two-thirds majority. These are binding on him, but he has some discretion about timing. It is fairly clear on questions upon which the Conference has not pronounced. Here he can initiate policy but should try to get approval for his policy in the Parliamentary Party and the National Executive. What, however, of resolutions of the Conference which do not receive a two-thirds majority? Are they binding on him at all? Here the Constitution is silent. One is left to infer what the attitude of the Leader should be from the sections of the Constitution which have been quoted above.

In 1960 it was a matter of bitter dispute in the Party. At the Conference at Scarborough, two motions on defence policy which were strenuously opposed by the Leader of the Party, Gaitskell, were carried by small majorities. One, moved by the Transport and General Workers' Union, called for the rejection of any defence policy based upon the threat of the use of nuclear weapons. This motion was carried by a majority of 43,000 in a card vote of more than six and a half million. A second motion put forward by the Amalgamated Engineering Union called for 'the unilateral renunciation of the testing, manufacture, stock piling and basing of all nuclear weapons in Great Britain'. This motion was carried by a majority of 407,000 with more than six million votes cast. At the same time, the National Executive Committee's defence policy, which advocated the abolition of an independent British nuclear deterrent but retention of bases and maintenance of other obligations to N.A.T.O., was rejected by Conference. There was a majority of 297,000 against the National Executive in a total vote of well over six million.

In face of these decisions Gaitskell announced that he would not modify his policy. In a television interview, on 7 October, he forecast, rightly as it proved, that the majority of the Parliamentary Labour Party would support his policy on defence and stated that it was vital that the decisions of the 1960 Conference should be reversed at the next year's Conference. This position was strongly attacked by many of Gaitskell's left-wing critics, including Mrs. Barbara Castle.[1]

---

[1] See especially Barbara Castle, 'Labour's Wind of Change', *New Statesman*, 15 October 1960, pp. 553–4.

They asserted that Gaitskell should either accept the Conference decision and change his policy, or resign his position as Leader. These assertions are not in any way supported either by the text, or the conventions, of the Constitution of the Labour Party. The one precedent which Gaitskell's critics could quote was not, in fact, any help to their argument. In 1935, when Lansbury was Leader of the Parliamentary Labour Party and found that his pacifist position was overwhelmingly rejected by the Annual Conference, he decided to resign the leadership. But the vote in the 1935 Conference, in support of collective security and the use of force against Italian aggression, had been of the order of over two million in favour and only just over one hundred thousand against. Lansbury was then in a hopeless minority as well as having the National Executive against him. The votes against Gaitskell in 1960, by contrast, fell far short of a two-thirds majority and he felt confident of being able to get the decision reversed at the next year's Conference.

It was interesting to see how the National Executive met the situation. When Parliament resumed, in the autumn of 1960, the Parliamentary Labour Party affirmed its support for Gaitskell and his defence policy. The National Executive then decided that there should, in accordance with the Constitution, be a meeting between itself and the Parliamentary Party Committee. This meeting took place on 8 December 1960, when it was decided that, as some of the main support for unilateral nuclear disarmament had come from the trade unions, it would be right to widen consultations to include the General Council of the Trades Union Congress. A meeting of the General Council, the Parliamentary Party Committee, and the National Executive was, therefore, held on 24 January 1961, and at this meeting a statement on foreign policy and defence was approved by all three bodies. This statement, entitled 'A Policy for Peace', while calling *inter alia* for the abandonment of testing of nuclear weapons and for greater emphasis in N.A.T.O. on the development of conventional forces, gave general support to Gaitskell's position. It stated that Britain should not attempt to remain an independent nuclear power but should continue to support N.A.T.O. and to agree to the presence of American forces, including a nuclear strike force, in this country.

There followed several months of strenuous activity in the Labour Party. An organization, the Campaign for Democratic Socialism, was formed to try and increase support for Gaitskell, both in the constituency parties and the trade unions, and to counter the pressure of the Campaign for Nuclear Disarmament. During the summer of 1961, three of the largest unions which in 1960 had supported unilateral nuclear disarmament, the Amalgamated Engineering Union, the National Union of Railwaymen, and the Shop and Distributive Workers, decided to give full or qualified support to the 'Policy for Peace' document. At the Annual Conference in October 1961, the document was carried by four and a half million votes to one and three-quarter million. This represented a considerable victory for Gaitskell.[1]

From the history of this affair one important conclusion can be reached. A resolution of the Labour Annual Conference passed by an ordinary, and not a two-thirds, majority is not binding on the Leader of the Labour Party who can continue in defiance of the Conference decision, provided he retains the support of the majority of the Parliamentary Labour Party. But it can be decidedly awkward for him. An attempt will always be made to remove any such disharmony between the different wings of the Labour Movement. As we have seen, it was made, and successfully, in 1961. What would have happened if the Annual Conference had voted in 1961 once again for unilateral nuclear disarmament? In such a case it is likely that Gaitskell would either have bowed to the Conference decision or resigned his position as Leader.

It is apparent that the picture which emerges of the relationship between the Labour Leader and his party differs considerably from that drawn by R. T. McKenzie in his book *British Political Parties*. McKenzie argues in this study of the Conservative and Labour parties that 'in reality the distribution of power within the two parties is overwhelmingly similar'.[2] He claims that the Conservative Party is not so autocratic, nor the Labour Party so democratic as their respective constitutions would imply. With the first proposition

[1] For an excellent account of the organization of the Campaign for Democratic Socialism see Lord Windlesham: *Communication and Political Power* (Cape, 1966) pp. 91–150.
[2] McKenzie, op. cit. p. 582.

one would not dissent. The Conservative Party, as we have seen, is not altogether as autocratic as the constitution seems to indicate. It is also tending to become more democratic. But McKenzie's picture of the Labour Party, drawn in the early 1950s, is not accurate for the period between 1954 and 1962. He was strongly influenced by the climate in the Labour Party that existed between 1945 and 1950. In those years the Labour Party was in office with a clear majority. The Labour Prime Minister, Attlee, enjoyed great prestige and his position was never seriously challenged in the Annual Conference. In these years, the great majority of the trade union vote gave solid support to the Leader of the party, outweighing any restless tendencies in the constituency parties. So it seemed that the Labour party constitution, while in theory democratic, gave great authority to the Leader, for he received the steady support of the great unions who predominated in conference.

The situation was transformed in the 1950s by a change of leadership and temper in some of the great unions. The largest trade union of all, the Transport and General Workers' Union, with over one million affiliated members, had been led for many years by Arthur Deakin who, as General Secretary, gave consistent support to Attlee as Leader of the party. When Deakin died in 1955 his place was taken by Frank Cousins, a man of very different political outlook. Where Deakin leaned to the right of centre of the Party, Cousins was a man of the left. His influence was thrown in favour of unilateral nuclear disarmament in 1960 and the Transport Union played the decisive part in the defeat of the Executive's and Gaitskell's policy at the Annual Conference in that year. Three other big unions, the Amalgamated Engineering Union, the National Union of Railwaymen, and the Shop and Distributive workers also took up the leftist position in 1960, aligning themselves with the Transport workers on this issue. In 1961 these three unions were persuaded, as we have seen, to rally to support the Executive and so Gaitskell's position was saved. But the point is that the Leader of the party could no longer rely, as Attlee had done, on the steady support of the unions against the constituency parties.

This tendency for the big unions to go different ways had already appeared in 1954 when the A.E.U., the N.U.R., and

U.S.D.A.W. voted against the National Executive's decision to support the re-armament of Western Germany, the Executive's resolution being carried by only 248,000 votes in a total vote of well over six million. From the mid-1950s onwards, it is clear that the Leader of the Labour Party needed to pay more attention to different trends of opinion in the Party and to devote more energy to winning support both of the unions and the constituency parties. Although, in 1962, Gaitskell won the overwhelming support of both elements for his stand on the Common Market question, this was no undiscriminating support. It was based on a series of subtle compromises between some of the main schools of thought in the Party. Before the debate took place, therefore, a majority had been virtually assured for the Leader's position, but Gaitskell made certain of the outcome by delivering an eighty-minute speech to the Conference of outstanding persuasiveness and power.

Gaitskell was as successful in 1962 in uniting the bulk of the party behind his policy toward the Common Market as he had been maladroit in 1959 and 1960. There would have been conflict anyway on the question of unilateral disarmament, but Gaitskell had made his position weaker, when the conflict came, by indicating in a post-election Conference in November 1959 that he thought that Clause Four of the Labour Party Constitution should be amended. This Clause states that one of the objectives of the Labour Party is: "To secure for the workers by hand or by brain the full fruits of their industry and the most equitable distribution thereof that may be possible, upon the basis of the common ownership of the means of production, distribution and exchange, and the best obtainable system of popular administration and control of each industry or service'. Since 1959 it has been printed on every member's Party card, and it has been part of the Constitution of the Labour Party since 1918. It was a cardinal error, therefore, to suggest that it should be discarded. Gaitskell's moves on Clause Four undoubtedly intensified opposition on the, apparently unrelated, defence question. It also seems that he had not attempted to win over his leading opponents prior to the 1960 Conference. For example, he had not made any approach to Frank Cousins whose influence over the Transport and General Workers' Union was crucial. However, in 1961 he recouped his position, as we have seen, and in 1962 consolidated it on the Common Market question.

When he died in January 1963 he bequeathed to his successor a broadly united Party. This was a priceless advantage to the incoming Leader, Harold Wilson. But it should not obscure Wilson's own achievement in the ensuing twenty months, before the general election of 1964. During this period, Wilson kept the Party united by avoiding too deep a commitment to the right or the left, and, when he formed a government, in October 1964, by including in it representatives of all the main tendencies in the Party.

What may we conclude then of the relationship between the Labour Leader and his party from experience since 1945? First, a Labour Leader is in a much stronger position when his party is in office than when it is in opposition. The Labour Government's policy may be challenged at the Annual Conference, as it was for example in 1965 on Vietnam, on immigration, and on the prices and incomes policy; but the leadership is likely to be able to resist a challenge fairly easily because of the personal ascendancy of the Prime Minister and the access to information, and the expertise, which Ministers have acquired. When Labour is in office too there is great loyalty to the leadership, a desire 'not to rock the boat', to weaken the chances of the government which is, for most members of the Labour Party, at least preferable to a Conservative government. At the 1967 Conference, a resolution which called on the Government to dissociate itself from American policy in Vietnam was carried, by a small majority, against the National Executive. More significant, however, was the fact that at both the 1966 and 1967 Conferences the crucial resolutions opposing the Government's economic policies were defeated.

Second, when Labour is in opposition, the Leader is likely to have a harder task keeping his party together. He must then exercise all the arts of political management if he is to succeed. If he is wise, he will avoid committing himself to either wing of the Party. He will steer a middle course, giving, in subtle ways, encouragement to both sides. The Leader of the Conservative Party can have a similar problem when his party is in opposition. This was apparent in 1965 when the Conservative Party was divided at least three ways on the question of British action in the face of the Unilateral Declaration of Independence in Rhodesia. The right wing sympathized with the Declaration and opposed any action against the Smith regime. The left wing favoured economic sanctions and the use of force if necessary. Heath as Leader of the party produced a compromise formula in November 1965: support for sanctions 'but not punitive sanctions'. Nevertheless, the Conservative Leader, when in opposition, is called upon relatively rarely to perform this sort of balancing act. His party followers tend to be less assertive than Labour Party members and, as we have seen, the Conservative Party constitution places him in control of the Party machine, and only requires him 'to receive' the views of the Annual Conference, not to act upon them.

The Liberal Party

The Liberal Party stands between the Conservative and Labour parties in the matter of organization. Its Constitution is considerably more democratic than that of the Conservative Party but is not as democratic as the Labour Party Constitution. Thus the Liberal Party is like the Labour Party in that its annual conference, known as the Liberal Assembly, has great authority. The President, Vice-President, and Treasurers of the Party Organization are all elected annually by the Assembly while their broad equivalents in the Conservative Party, the chief party officers, are appointed by the party Leader. The Liberal Assembly elects thirty members of the Liberal Council which also includes representatives of the constituency associations, six Liberal M.P.s, six Liberal peers, and the members of the Liberal Party Committee. This committee consists of the Leader, the principal officers of the Party inside and outside Parliament, and some additional members who can be appointed by the Leader. The whole Liberal Council elects the Executive Committee which has control of the Party headquarters. The full-time officers of the Party are therefore, as in the Labour Party, ultimately responsible to the annual conference. But there is a difference in that in the Liberal Party there are two intermediary bodies, the Liberal Council and the Liberal Party Committee, interposed between the Party officers and the annual conference to which they are, in the last resort, responsible.

The Liberal Assembly resembles the Conservative Conference in that the Leader of the Party customarily gives an address on the last day of the Assembly. This address is usually received with enthusiasm and is not debated. Another respect in which the Conservative and Liberal conferences are alike is in their composition. Both are conferences of constituency organizations and parliamentarians. Neither has anything resembling the great trade union element found in the Labour Party. Finally, although the Constitution of the Liberal Party states that 'it shall be the duty of the Assembly and the Council, working in free co-operation with the Scottish Liberal Party, to define the general objectives of the party',[1] it does not say, as the Constitution of the Labour Party does, that the Annual Conference shall play a part in deciding the Party programme. The Liberal Party Constitution merely states that one of the functions of the Liberal Assembly is 'To consider resolutions on public policy'.[2] The Liberal Assembly then is more than a vast advisory committee-cum-rally, which is how one might describe the Conservative Conference. It has some control, however tenuous, over the Party officers and officials. On the other hand it is not the 'fountain of authority' which the Labour Conference is felt to be within the Labour Movement.

Conference Management

One way in which all three parties are bound to resemble each other is in their desire to present a favourable image to the public. Thus all three parties make considerable efforts to stage-manage their conferences, especially now that the conference proceedings are televised. In the business of stage-management, perhaps the most important device lies in the selection and amalgamation of resolutions. On any controversial subject there is always a wide range of resolutions sent in by the affiliated bodies, chiefly constituency parties in the case of the Conservative and Liberal parties; constituency parties, trade unions, and socialist societies, in the case of the Labour Party. There has to be some selection of resolutions and amendments, and the committee entrusted with the task may

---

[1] *The Constitution of the Liberal Party*. Revised, September 1960 (pub. by the Liberal Party Organization, price 6d) p. 3.

[2] Ibid., p. 5.

be able to do a good deal to influence the subsequent course of the debate by its skill in the choice or composition of resolutions.

In the Conservative Party, the control which the organizing committee exerts goes further, in that the committee not only selects resolutions but determines the list of speakers. At the Labour Conference, the Chairman is given a much freer rein in the selection of speakers and there is more scope for spontaneous contribution from the floor. But, even there, the debate is influenced to some extent by the choice of speakers for the National Executive, who are of course permitted much longer speeches than speakers from the floor are allowed. For example, at the 1965 Labour Conference, speeches by Ministers in the debate on Vietnam lasted for a total of 101 minutes, while only seventy-three minutes were provided for contributions from the floor.[1]

Thus the desire to create a favourable image for the party can conflict with the desire to permit expression of the views of Party members. U. W. Kitzinger has suggested that 'the more public party conferences become', through being televised, 'the more stage-management will they need from the leadership to keep the conference in hand, the less will the platform tolerate speakers against them who make their case tellingly or in such a way as to hurt the party'.[2] Yet, despite the fact that party conferences have now been televised for many years, the debate on Rhodesia at the 1965 Conservative Party Conference was a livelier affair than had been seen at Conservative Conferences for many a year. It seems likely that whenever there are major differences in the Labour or Conservative Parties, they will be effectively aired at annual conferences. It would be more damaging to the party image to hush them up. Nor is controversy within a party necessarily hurtful to the party image. The watching public is accustomed to following discussion on current affairs in BBC and ITV programmes, and conference debates which include lively controversy are not likely to be damaging to the party which permits them.

[1] U. W. Kitzinger, 'Parties and Conferences', (a Third Programme talk published in the *Listener*, 18 November 1965, p. 785.)

[2] Ibid., p. 785.

For Reference

S. H. BEER, *Modern British Politics* (Faber, 1965).

I. BULMER-THOMAS, *The Party System in Great Britain* (Phoenix House, 1953).

M. HARRISON, *Trade Unions and the Labour Party since 1945* (Allen and Unwin, 1960).

J. D. HOFFMAN, *The Conservative Party in Opposition* (MacGibbon and Kee, 1964).

U. W. KITZINGER, 'Parties and Conferences', in *The Listener*, 18 November 1965.

R. T. McKENZIE, *British Political Parties*, 2nd ed. (Mercury Books, 1964).

R. T. McKENZIE, 'Policy Decision in Opposition: A Rejoinder', in *Political Studies*, 1957.

S. ROSE, 'The Labour Party and German Rearmament: A view from Transport House', in *Political Studies*, 1966.

S. ROSE, 'Policy Decision in Opposition', in *Political Studies*, 1956.

LORD WINDLESHAM, *Communication and Political Power* (Cape, 1966).

Conservative and Unionist Central Office, *The Party Organization*.

The Labour Party, *The Constitution and Standing Orders of the Labour Party*.

The Liberal Party Organization, *The Constitution of the Liberal Party*.

Reports of the Annual Conference of the Conservative and Unionist Party.

Reports of the Annual Conference of the Labour Party.

Reports of the Liberal Assembly.

CHAPTER XIII

Public Opinion Polls

ONE important channel of communication between the citizen and the government runs through the House of Commons, the Member of Parliament speaking for his more vocal constituents. Another important channel is provided by the political parties, particularly through their annual conferences. Vying in importance with either of these channels, in contemporary Britain, is a third: the influence and opinion brought to bear by a vast range of organized pressure groups. Also, an important indication of opinion is provided nowadays by the public opinion polls. How reliable are opinion polls and pressure groups as registers of opinion? What is their role in the political process? An attempt to answer these questions will be made in this and the following chapter.

Public opinion polls have been important in Britain since 1945. The first poll appeared in this country in 1938 and was an offshoot of the organization founded in the United States by Dr. George Gallup. This poll, which is now known as Social Surveys (Gallup Poll) Ltd., was published in the *News Chronicle* from 1945 to October 1960 when that paper was absorbed by the *Daily Mail*. For a few months after the merger, it appeared in the *Daily Mail* but in 1961 the *Daily Mail* revived its own National Opinion Poll. Findings of the Gallup Poll then began to appear in the *Daily Telegraph* and later also in the *Sunday Telegraph*. Another poll has appeared from time to time in the *Daily Express*. Research Services Ltd, under the direction of Mark Abrams, has also produced polls which were published, before the 1964 and 1966 elections, in the *Observer*.

Methods of Polling Opinion

Two principal methods are used by the opinion polls: the random sample and the quota sample. The simple random sample, which has been often used to forecast by-election results in individual constituencies, works as follows. First of all the size of the sample is determined: this in practice tends to be a compromise between a size that will give the maximum precision and the size that it is possible to handle in terms of the time and money available. Thus, in studying voting behaviour in a constituency of 60,000 it might be decided that, in the circumstances, a sample of 600, that is 1 per cent of the electorate, would be sufficiently precise and would also be a suitable size for collection and analysis. To select such a sample randomly, every one hundredth name on the register of electors is marked and these people are visited by the investigators. This method probably gives as representative a sample as is possible of the electorate. There is, of course, some margin of error, but that part of it that arises from the sample can be calculated, and it is possible to predict within this margin from the sample findings how the whole body of electors is likely to vote. Other non-statistical errors may enter and will be discussed later. The method of random sampling is also one which has been used by several university teams in studying electoral behaviour in Bristol, Greenwich, and certain Lancashire constituencies. It is also a standard method of investigation in sociological research.[1]

There is also a variation of the random sample known as the stratified random sample. If, for example, a national survey is wanted, it may be desirable first to stratify the country by regions. The method is explained by C. A. Moser as follows: 'The first step is then to allocate to each region its appropriate number of interviews. If South-West England has 10 per cent. of the population of England and Wales, 200 out of the sample of 2,000 individuals would be selected from this region. Up to this point *no sampling has taken place*. Stratification is merely a way of dividing the population into a number of sub-populations.'[2] It is possible also to stratify by urban or rural area, town

---

[1] For studies of a Bristol constituency see: R. S. Milne and H. C. Mackenzie, *Straight Fight* (Hansard Society, 1954), and *Marginal Seat* (Hansard Society, 1958).

See also M. Benney and others, *How People Vote* (Routledge and Kegan Paul, 1956) for a study of the 1950 election in Greenwich and A. H. Birch and P. Campbell, 'Voting Behaviour in a Lancashire Constituency', in *British Journal of Sociology*, September 1950.

For an example of simple random sampling in a sociological study of an English market town, see Margaret Stacey, *Tradition and Change. A Study of Banbury* (Clarendon Press, 1960).

[2] C. A. Moser, *Survey Methods in Social Investigation* (Heinemann, 1958), p. 94.

size, sex, and age-group. Once the strata have been established, interviews can be selected on a random basis.

A national opinion survey based on a quota sample begins in a similar way. Strata are established by region, town size etc. and the number of interviews to be made within each area is decided upon. But then, whereas selection of the interviews is made on a random basis in random sampling, in a quota sample each interviewer is given an assignment of interviews which provides how many men and how many women, how many in each age-group, and how many in each social class he is to interview. These quotas conform to the proportions of the population known to fall within each sex, age and social class grouping. The difficulty with quota sampling lies in its dependence upon the skill and sense of responsibility of the interviewer. It is, however, much cheaper than a random sample and can be organized far more quickly. Until November 1963 both Gallup and National Opinion Polls used quota sampling for their national surveys.

The Success of the Polls
How successful have the polls been in forecasting the results of British general elections since the Second World War? As far as the Gallup Poll is concerned, it has been remarkably successful. It has correctly predicted which party would win at every general election since 1945. In 1964 the *Daily Telegraph*, in its report on polling day, was cautious in interpreting the findings of the Gallup surveys: one of them, on the basis of a quota sample, gave Labour a 3½ per cent lead over the Conservatives, and the other, from a random sample, predicted a lead for Labour of 1½ per cent. The fact remains, however, that the Gallup surveys did predict a Labour lead, although the *Telegraph* rightly warned that the margin was likely to be small. National Opinion Polls have a similarly good record, but over fewer elections, since they have only been in existence since 1958. They correctly forecast that the Conservatives would win the 1959 election, and in the 1964 election predicted a Labour lead of 3·1 per cent over the Conservatives. The success of these two polls should not, however, blind one to the fact that polling techniques are liable to a margin of error of around 3 per cent, and so cannot be regarded as infallible. Nevertheless,

the opinion polls in Britain have been so successful since 1945 that they now arouse a great deal of interest and command considerable respect.[1]

The one notorious failure which opinion polls have experienced was in the 1948 American Presidential election. The polls forecast an easy victory for Dewey, but Harry Truman defied the auguries and in a storming campaign won a majority. Two factors help to explain their failure on this occasion. One was that the last poll was taken more than two weeks before the actual polling day. It seems certain that there was a heavy swing towards Truman in this intervening period. The polls have since tried to avoid this sort of mistake by holding their last poll as near as possible to polling day. Another factor which makes for less accuracy in polling in the United States than in Britain is the regularly lower percentage poll in American elections. In the United States it is normal for about 60 per cent of registered electors to vote in Presidential elections. In Britain the percentage poll in general elections since 1945 has varied from 73 per cent to 84 per cent. Consequently the sample in a British opinion poll is nearer to a cross-section of the actual electorate who will vote than the sample in an American opinion poll can be.

The Influence of the Polls

The success of opinion polls in Britain is now very widely recognized. The Press, in commenting on election campaigns, generally takes for granted the accuracy of the poll forecasts. The *Daily Mirror*, for example, on polling day in 1959 (8 October) keyed two of its main headlines to findings of the opinion polls. The polls had agreed in discerning a higher proportion of 'don't knows' than in previous elections. The *Daily Mirror* therefore, reckoning that the way in which the 'don't knows' divided could sway the election, and assuming that many of its readers were Labour waverers, proclaimed in its main headline: 'Only a Dope Will Be A Don't Know Today'. A headline on another page spelled out the following slogan: 'To Hell With the Telly Until We've All Voted'. This was

---

[1] At the 1966 General Election, all four opinion polls correctly forecast a Labour victory. On this occasion, the prediction of Research Services Ltd. was nearest to the actual result.

keyed to another finding of the polls. The *News Chronicle* had published, on 12 January 1959, a table produced by the Gallup Poll showing that considerably more Labour voters than Conservative voters would be inclined to stay away from the poll if there was a popular evening programme on television. As an earlier inquiry had shown that Labour voters tended to vote later in the day than Conservative voters, the conclusion emerged that Labour was likely to suffer much more heavily from the counter-attraction of T.V. than the Conservatives on polling day. This was the background to the *Mirror* headline.

The party leaders are also keenly aware of the significance of the opinion polls. The indications of the state of opinion provided by the polls give a fairly clear idea of the standing enjoyed by the Government and the Opposition at any one time. The *Daily Telegraph* has normally published the Gallup Poll weekly, while the National Opinion Poll appears in the *Daily Mail* about once a fortnight. The pulse of the body politic is therefore constantly being taken. The questions asked vary, depending on the issues that are prominent at any one time. But one question is standard: 'If there were a general election tomorrow how would you vote?' The answers to this question are particularly valuable to the Prime Minister. They show him the effect that his Government's policies are having on opinion in the country and, most important of all, give him some idea of when it would be tactically wise to hold a general election. The Prime Minister has then, in the opinion polls, a new technical aid which was not available to his predecessors before the Second World War. Indeed, although it was available before 1951 its potentialities were not then realized. The Attlee Government, from 1945 to 1951, made little or no attempt to 'play the polls' in the sense of timing elections to coincide with a period of government popularity as indicated by the polls.

Since 1951 this has become an accepted technique of political leadership. It is difficult to say precisely when it emerged. What is clear is that between 1951 and 1959 a pattern of relationship began to appear between the standing of the government and the circumstances of the country, particularly the economic circumstances, at any one time. Whenever economic conditions or prospects seemed grim, when the government had

introduced austerity measures—a credit squeeze or 'pay pause'
—the government's stock, in opinion poll terms, fell. By contrast, when there was a feeling of affluence, when credit restrictions were eased and the level of consumer purchases
was high, support for the government increased.

Was it by accident or design that the unpleasant economic
measures, and the consequent troughs in government popularity, came at periods well removed from a general election?
By the time the Prime Minister had asked for a dissolution,
conditions had improved and the government was riding the
crest of the wave again. Thus, in July 1952 the Gallup Poll
gave the Labour Opposition a 10 per cent lead over the Conservatives, and in August 1954 a 6 per cent lead. But by the
spring of 1955 conditions had improved, an optimistic Budget
was introduced in April in which the Chancellor of the Exchequer announced a cut of 6d. in the standard rate of income
tax, and at the General Election in May the Conservatives
won with a lead of 3·3 per cent. over Labour. Again, in November 1957 the Gallup Poll gave Labour a lead of 12·5 per cent
over the Conservatives. This poll was taken soon after the bank
rate had been raised to 7 per cent. There was a general feeling
of gloom about the economy at that time, heightened by the
aftermath of the Suez adventure which by the autumn of 1957
had been generally recognized as a failure for the Government.
As late as May 1958, Gallup still gave Labour a lead of 11 per
cent. Yet by October 1959 the Conservatives could campaign
with the slogan: 'Life is Better Under the Conservatives.
Don't Let Labour Ruin It.' They won the 1959 election
resoundingly with a lead of 5·6 per cent over Labour.

The situation changed after the 1959 general election. For
over a year the Conservative Government continued to enjoy
a healthy lead in the opinion polls over Labour. But in the
summer of 1961 the Government hit one of its mid-term economic troughs. This time it was to have more serious consequences than before. The Chancellor of the Exchequer, Selwyn
Lloyd, introduced his 'pay pause' which was to prove very
unpopular. He also put a brake on the economy, which by
February 1963 had caused the number of unemployed to rise
to 3·9 per cent of the labour force, the highest figure since 1947.
In the same period, the Government had been conducting

prolonged negotiations with the Common Market countries. When their attempt to 'get into Europe' failed, in January 1963, through President de Gaulle's veto, this was another blow to the Government's prestige. In March 1963 the Gallup Poll gave Labour a 16·5 per cent lead over the Conservatives with no less than 50 per cent of the sample declaring their intention of voting Labour. This gap was to widen even further after the debate in June 1963 on Profumo's resignation from the Government. Yet by September 1964, the Conservatives had won back popularity to such an extent that they momentarily took the lead in the Gallup Poll. In the general election in October 1964, they were only narrowly defeated by Labour, who secured only 0·7 per cent more votes.

Did the 1964 experience then re-affirm the ability of the Prime Minister to 'play the polls'? Up to a point it did. Certainly if Sir Alec Douglas-Home had gone to the country in the spring of 1964, the polls indicated that he would have been heavily defeated. By hanging on until October he allowed time for conditions to improve. In fact there was some apparent improvement in the domestic economy and consumer purchases were rising. But at the same time, externally, the trade gap was widening and there was a drain on Britain's gold and dollar reserves. The situation at non-election times would almost certainly have called for austerity measures. The Labour Party was therefore able to argue that the appearance of affluence was a facade and that, in fact, the external economic position was serious. Two other factors were important. In the first place, Conservative popularity had sunk much lower in 1963 than it had done in the previous troughs of 1952 and 1957: the Government had much further to pull back and too little time to do it since, under the Parliament Act, October 1964 was the last possible month in which the election could be held. In the second place, the Labour opposition was campaigning more effectively than it had done for years.

When Labour gained power in October 1964, the Labour Prime Minister, Harold Wilson, was able to time the next election with an eye to the opinion polls much as Harold Macmillan had done in 1959. In August 1965 the Gallup Poll gave the Conservatives a lead of 7·5 per cent over Labour (*Daily Telegraph*, 6 August 1965). By the end of the year,

L

Labour had won back the lead. This lead was substantially increased during January and February 1966 and towards the end of February the Gallup Poll gave Labour a lead of 9 per cent and the National Opinion Poll gave it a lead of 14 per cent over the Conservatives. This provided Wilson with a great opportunity for a dissolution, and the general election on 31 March 1966 gave Labour a 6 per cent lead over the Conservatives in terms of votes and an overall majority of 97 in terms of seats in the Commons.

Clearly the introduction of opinion polling has strengthened the position of the Prime Minister in British politics and made it harder to turn out the government. The point is reinforced if one looks at examples of dissolutions in the pre-opinion poll era. Would Stanley Baldwin, for example, have asked for a dissolution in 1923, only just over a year after the previous general election, if there had been opinion polls to inform him how his party stood in the country? The polls presumably would also have indicated that the majority opinion in the country was not then in favour of the introduction of tariffs. As it was, his decision to seek a mandate for the abandonment of free trade brought a major electoral setback to his party and let in the first Labour government.

Some commentators feel that opinion polls have weighted the scales too heavily in favour of the Prime Minister in Britain. They do not suggest that the polls should be made illegal—this would be intolerable in a democratic society—but they ask whether the Prime Minister should not lose the right to ask for a dissolution. The British Parliament, they suggest, could have a fixed term, like the American House of Representatives, although a four-year rather than a two-year term would seem more in keeping with British practice.[1]

It is not only the Prime Minister, however, who can learn from opinion polls. Opposition leaders also can make use of them. The opinion polls had some important lessons for Labour in opposition between 1951 and 1964. Above all, they showed that Labour lost support through disunity, particularly in 1960 and 1961. It was still, seemingly, lack of confidence in Labour's ability to form an alternative government which prompted

---

[1] See R. L. Leonard, 'Public Opinion Polls' in *Aspect*, March 1963, p. 66, and Norman Hunt, 'Interested Parties' in the *Listener* of 20 July 1961, p. 85.

the Liberal revival in 1962, when the Liberals won the Orpington by-election and gained the support of more than 25 per cent of the Gallup sample. When, however, the Labour Party settled its differences at the 1962 Conference, Labour began to forge ahead in popularity. This Harold Wilson was able to maintain and increase after being elected Leader in January 1963.

The parties have also benefited from polling techniques by commissioning their own private opinion polls. The Conservatives used such polls to prepare the way for their 1959 campaign and Labour followed suit between 1962 and 1964. The National Executive Committee of the Labour Party commissioned a survey of 'target voters' by Dr. Mark Abrams. These were the uncommitted voters in the marginal constituencies. The theory behind the survey was that these were the voters who would decide the general election. It was therefore important to know which sort of appeal from Labour would be most successful in winning their support. The survey indicated that these uncommitted electors were most interested in issues that affected themselves—housing, consumer protection, town planning and roads, education, and the care of old people. They placed a premium on managerial efficiency and sought an end to the government's 'stop-go' policy.[1] The Labour Party acted on this information and placed the emphasis in its campaign in 1963 and 1964 on just this kind of issue. The polls also showed that Harold Wilson had considerable personal popularity and for this reason a great deal of Labour's publicity was directed to putting across his personal image. This led to the Conservative accusation that Labour was a 'one-man band', but the tactic seems to have been none the less successful.

The polls have also at times helped to determine the attitude of a political party to its leader. The continued poor showing of Sir Alec Douglas-Home in the opinion polls in 1965 played some part in inducing his resignation as Leader of the Conservative Party in July of that year. Both the Gallup Poll and the National Opinion Poll found repeatedly that he was rated much lower than Harold Wilson in all the qualities expected of a political leader. The National Opinion Poll reported that 11 per cent of all voters in the sample said that they would be

[1] Butler and King, op. cit., p. 69.

more likely to vote Conservative if Sir Alec resigned his position as leader. These findings lent weight to the views of those
in the Conservative 1922 Committee who claimed that Sir
Alec was a liability as a leader. If, however, the polls played a
part in persuading him to resign, they do not seem to have
influenced the choice of his successor. On the morning of 27
July 1965, the *Daily Mail* gave great prominence to a National
Opinion Poll which indicated that 44 per cent of the voters
who had been polled favoured Maudling as leader, against
only 28 per cent who were for Heath. The *Daily Express* poll,
published the same day, produced a similar majority for
Maudling. Yet, later that day, Conservative M.P.s voted by
an absolute majority for Heath as their new leader.

Random Versus Quota Sampling

In discussing earlier the influence of polls on the political
system in Britain, reference was made to the effect of the Gallup
Polls. At this point it is necessary to note that from 1963 onwards the two main opinion polls have sometimes diverged in
their findings. Sometimes, indeed, the Gallup Poll has put
Labour in the lead while the National Opinion Poll has
divined a lead for the Conservatives. This was the case for
example in the first half of September 1964. This sort of diver-
gence inevitably prompted the question whether one poll was
more trustworthy than the other. The reliability of the *Daily
Express* poll cannot be discussed as its methods of investigation
and sampling have not been revealed. As far as Gallup and the
National Opinion Polls are concerned, their methods are
known and since November 1963 they have differed. Until then,
both polls used quota sampling methods. In that month,
National Opinion Polls decided to go over to random sampling.
The Gallup Poll continued to use a quota sample, although for
a period before the 1964 general election it ran its own random
sample, in parallel—largely, it would seem, as a means of testing out the quota sample. At this time the Gallup Poll claimed
that its quota survey comprised more than 2,000 interviews
distributed over 200 constituencies, while its random survey
consisted of 1,750 interviews in 340 constituencies.[1] The National Opinion Poll had stated a month earlier that their random

[1] *Sunday Telegraph*, 11 October 1964.

sample comprised 2,353 interviews in 100 constituencies.[1]

Which is the better method, the quota sample or the random sample, for opinion polling on a national scale? Many would say that the random sample is likely to be more accurate, but it is more expensive and it is difficult to organize quickly. National Opinion Polls implicitly recognized this when they held their poll in July 1965 on the candidates for the Conservative leadership. The poll had to be taken quickly if it was to be in the *Daily Mail* on the day of the Conservative M.P.s' ballot. It was taken on 25 and 26 July and published on the 27th. National Opinion Polls announced that in order to make this possible they had used the quota sampling method.

Dr. Henry Durant of the Gallup Poll has claimed that the random sample is less reliable in that it tends to miss many of the more 'active' people: shift-workers, long-distance lorry drivers and young people who are either at work or out in the evenings. This is because the National Opinion Poll interviews take place in the home. The opposing criticism has been made of Gallup, by National Opinion Polls, that the Gallup quota under-selects older and 'less active' people who tend to be home-bound.

The rights and wrongs of this controversy are difficult to establish. The comparison between Gallup's own quota and random samples gave no conclusive evidence. Sometimes their results agreed, sometimes they were at variance but in no consistent direction. On occasion the random sample favoured Labour, and the quota sample Conservative; on other occasions the position was reversed.[2] The most reasonable conclusion would seem to be that there is a margin of error in each method of sampling. The statistical error in a random sample can be calculated. There remain other non-calculable and non-statistical errors involved in polling, whether the respondents are selected by an entirely random method or by a method which involves some deliberate human judgements. Again, where the margin of difference between the parties is small, prediction becomes more difficult whatever method is used, for the difference may be less than the margin of error involved in sampling itself. Neither method then is infallible.

[1] *Daily Mail*, 11 September 1964.
[2] See Richard Rose, 'Bias from Sampling in Opinion Polls', article in *The Times*, 28 September 1964, p. 11.

Nevertheless opinion polls are unlikely to misinterpret a general trend, if they are published at frequent intervals, since a freak result stands out and can be ignored.

Attitude Polls

Attitude polls, in contrast to polls on voting intention, are much less reliable. Most people, when asked how they are going to vote, can give a clear answer which indicates their definite intention in voting or abstaining. But when people are asked, for example, whether or not they are in favour of Britain entering the European Common Market, the pattern of answers cannot be regarded as a clear guide to governmental policy. This is for three reasons. First, many people who are interviewed may lack adequate information. Those who answer 'don't know' will include several different categories: those who are apathetic, those who honestly admit lack of information, and some people who are well informed but consider that a clear-cut answer to the question is not possible. Second, sampling opinion normally gives no scope for the 'weighing' of opinion. The opinion of those who are better informed counts for no more than that of those who are ill informed. Third, the answer to the question may vary according to the way in which the question is phrased. For example, in March 1957, a poll was held in areas then affected by shipyard strikes. One of the questions asked was worded as follows:

'Were the unions right or wrong to call an official strike when all wage increases were turned down?'

The question could equally well have been phrased as follows:

'Were the unions right or wrong to call an official strike and to refuse to submit the dispute to arbitration?'

Neither of these formulations of the question (the first actual, the second hypothetical) contains an untruth. Wage increases *had* been turned down by the employers and the unions *had* refused to submit the dispute to arbitration. But each of the two questions emphasises a different aspect of the strike: the actual question an aspect favourable to the unions, the hypothetical question an aspect favourable to the employers. It can be confidently asserted that, if the second question had been asked, a different pattern of answers would have appeared because some people would have been influenced by an emphasis in the question on the employers' side to the dispute.

The Gallup Poll and the National Opinion Poll have a good record in keeping their questions as neutral as possible. But this example illustrates the danger which lies in opinion polling if it should come under irresponsible direction. One must also always look very sceptically at an opinion poll which is specially commissioned by an organization anxious to make propaganda in a particular direction. Fortunately, the Gallup Poll and the National Opinion Poll are independent organizations. It is important for a poll to be proved accurate, for on this depends its popularity among newspaper readers and the continued support of the business firms that pay for market research inquiries. Both the Gallup Poll and the National Opinion Poll are active in the field of market research. An important duty of course falls upon the newspapers who print the findings of the polls. It is incumbent upon an editor not to suppress a poll which is unfavourable to the party that his newspaper supports, and not to twist the findings of the poll by misrepresenting its general tenor. The *News Chronicle*, the *Daily Mail*, the *Daily Telegraph*, the *Sunday Telegraph* and the *Observer* have all maintained high standards in this respect.

British opinion polls have not then suffered, by and large, either from the biased formulation of questions or from distorted interpretation in the Press. There remain, however, the two fundamental weaknesses of attitude polling that have already been mentioned: that many of those questioned have inadequate information, and that the findings of a poll do not give greater weight to those who have fuller information.[1] For these reasons it is important that Members of Parliament, Ministers, and Civil Servants should not consider themselves bound by opinion polls. It would appear that the majority of Members of the Commons argued in this way when they voted in 1948, 1956, and 1965 for the abolition of capital punishment. Opinion polls taken in November 1947 showed that 65 per cent of the sample favoured the retention of the death penalty, and in December 1955, 61 per cent still supported capital

---

[1] For a very full and interesting discussion of the shortcomings of polls as a measure of public opinion see D. E. G. Plowman, 'Public Opinion and the Polls', *British Journal of Sociology*, Vol. xiii, pp. 331–50.

punishment. But the majority of Members took their stand on principle, or on the ground that most electors could not know that in countries where the death penalty had been abolished the average rate of murders committed annually had not increased.[1]

There seems to be no danger that legislators in Britain are becoming too subservient to public opinion polls. Provided that their deficiencies, particularly in attitude polling, are recognized they have a valuable part to play. They give an indication of the state of opinion even if it is partly ill-informed opinion; they indicate how opinion is changing, and they provide a challenge for politicians, bent on reform, to make their views better known and understood. But if a Member of Parliament decides to give greater weight to the views of individuals whom he knows to be well informed, or whom he knows to be closely affected by an issue, than to the findings of an opinion poll, he is probably on sure ground.

Just as politicians should not be over-sensitive to the polls, so there is no cause for them to be afraid of opinion polling. It was surprising that the Speaker's Conference on Electoral Law should have proposed, in 1967, that the results of public opinion polls should not be published, or broadcast, during a period of seventy-two hours before the close of a parliamentary election.[2] This very illiberal proposal was poorly received by *The Times* and other newspapers on the day of publication of the Conference report (17 May 1967). As a spokesman of the National Opinion Poll accurately commented in the *Guardian*, there is no evidence that the polls have either a bandwagon effect in favour of the party shown to be in the lead, or a boomerang effect in favour of the party placed second.[3]

---

[1] See J. B. Christoph, *Capital Punishment and British Politics* (Allen & Unwin, 1962) esp. pp. 43, 54, and 109 for analyses of opinion polls on the capital punishment issue.

[2] Cmnd. 3275. Conference on Electoral Law, p. 4.

[3] Martin Cox, of the National Opinion Poll, reported in the *Guardian*, 17 May 1967.

For Reference

M. ABRAMS and R. ROSE, *Must Labour Lose?* (Penguin, 1960).

H. BLUMER, 'Public Opinion and Public Opinion Polling' in the *American Sociological Review*, Vol. 13.

D. E. BUTLER and A. KING, *The British General Election of 1964* (Macmillan, 1965).

D. E. BUTLER and A. KING, *The British General Election of 1966* (Macmillan, 1966).

D. E. BUTLER and R. ROSE, *The British General Election of 1959* (Macmillan, 1960).

H. J. EYSENCK, *The Psychology of Politics* (Routledge and Kegan Paul, 1954), Chapters 2 and 3.

THE GALLUP POLL, *The Gallup Election Handbook* (1966).

R. L. LEONARD, 'Public Opinion Polls' in *Aspect*, 1963.

R. S. MILNE and H. C. MACKENZIE, *Marginal Seat* (Hansard Society, 1958).

C. A. MOSER, *Survey Methods in Social Investigation* (Heinemann, 1958).

D. E. G. PLOWMAN, 'Public Opinion and the Polls' in the *British Journal of Sociology*, Vol. xiii.

R. ROSE, 'Political Decision Making and the Polls' in *Parliamentary Affairs*, 1962.

R. ROSE, *Politics in England* (Faber, 1965).

CHAPTER XIV

Pressure Groups

PRESSURE groups are not new. They are as old as politics. Whenever a body of individuals group themselves together to achieve an end which demands some kind of pressure on government or legislature, they may be termed a pressure group. How then do we distinguish pressure groups from political parties? The difference lies, first, in the fact that a pressure group does not present a programme extending over a wide range of political issues and, second, in that pressure groups do not normally contest elections but seek to influence the general public and those who are elected, the Members of Parliament and the Government.

In several recently published studies in Britain there has been a tendency to avoid the term 'pressure group'. S. E. Finer speaks of 'The Lobby', Allen Potter of 'Organized Groups in British Politics', and J. W. Grove distinguishes 'sectional groups' from 'pressure groups properly so called' because they come into existence to promote a particular programme.[1] This delicacy of approach is unnecessary and perhaps misleading. It is prompted partly by the feeling that many sectional groups are only incidentally pressure groups; also by the idea that the term pressure group has 'emotive overtones'.[2] But if a sectional group does sometimes apply pressure to the centres of political power it is surely in that aspect a pressure group? Thus the Automobile Association is not primarily a pressure group, but its officers recognize that the application of pressure on government and parliament is one of the most important of its activities. The Annual Report for 1962 by the Committee of the

---

[1] S. E. Finer, *Anonymous Empire. A Study of the Lobby in Great Britain*, 2nd ed. (Pall Mall, 1966).

Allen Potter, *Organized Groups in British Politics* (Faber, 1961).

J. W. Grove, *Government and Industry in Britain* (Longmans, 1962) esp. pp. 125–7. But compare: J. D. Stewart, *British Pressure Groups* (Clarendon Press, 1958).

[2] Grove, op. cit., p. 126.

Automobile Association was quite frank about this. It stated (at p. 17) that: 'None of the Association's activities on behalf of Members is more important than the application of pressure in the corridors of power—the lobbies of the Houses of Parliament and the committee rooms of Government Ministries. The Standing Joint Committee, in which the Association joins forces with the Royal Automobile Club and the Royal Scottish Automobile Club, is the action group which carried out this task.' Nor should it be thought, with reference to Grove's 'emotive overtones', that pressure group activities are undesirable. They are an essential part of a democratic society. Certain forms of pressure group activity are undesirable and society may need to provide some safeguards against abuses. But pressure groups are essential channels through which the government is informed of the views of sections of the public. Therefore the term 'pressure group' will be used throughout this chapter.

Two Main Types of Pressure Group
We may distinguish two main types of pressure group. First, and numerically most important, are the 'interest' groups. They can be subdivided for convenience of classification into producer groups and consumer groups. The producer groups include well over two thousand employers' associations.[1] Such associations may link small employers such as ironmongers or large employers like the shipbuilders who are organized in the Shipbuilding Employers' Federation. Most of the employers' associations are themselves grouped in one great peak association which was established in 1965, the Confederation of British Industry. This Confederation combines the former major peak associations: the Federation of British Industries, the British Employers' Confederation, and the National Association of British Manufacturers. The Confederation is a large organization offering many services to its members including business education, statistics, exporting advice, etc. It was quickly faced with a minor rival, for in April 1965 the Society of Independent Manufacturers was formed. This Society began partly as a protest against the decision of the Confederation to admit the nationalized industries as associate

[1] Grove, op. cit., p. 128.

members. A few of its members are medium-sized firms, but the majority are small manufacturers.

Also classifiable as producers' associations are the trade unions. Like the employers' associations they vary greatly in size from tiny unions with only a few hundred members to the largest union of all, the Transport and General Workers' Union which in 1966 had 1,443,738 members. Most of the unions are also linked in a peak association, the Trades Union Congress. In farming, the largest association of employers and the self-employed is the National Farmers' Union, while farm workers are predominantly organized in the National Union of Agricultural Workers. Broadly in the same category of producers are the organizations of those who provide professional services, such as the British Medical Association, and the British Dental Association.

While producers are by and large very well organized, the second main sub-division of interest groups, the consumers, are much less well organized. There are some powerful bodies, such as the Automobile Association and the Royal Automobile Club, which may be considered associations of road users. Most other consumer bodies, such as the Consumers' Association (representing the interests of household consumers especially) and associations of patients in the health service, are, as yet, in an early stage of organization.

The second type of pressure group may be termed the 'ideas' group. An 'ideas' group may be distinguished from an 'interest' group in that its members do not stand to benefit materially from the end which they seek to achieve. Thus members of the National Campaign for the Abolition of Capital Punishment were prompted by idealistic motives. So are members of the Africa Bureau (in London) and the Africa Councils (in provincial centres) whose aim it has been to oppose racial discrimination and to press for self-determination in British African territories. Many other associations such as the Howard League for Penal Reform, the League for the Abolition of Cruel Sports, and the Movement for Colonial Freedom can be placed in the same category.[1] They are not as powerful as the interest groups, have little funds and few if any permanent

---

[1] S. E. Finer calls such organizations 'cause groups', op. cit., p. 3. In general, his 'cause groups' seem to be identical with my 'ideas' groups.

staff, but they have some considerable achievements to their credit.

A third possible type is the *ad hoc* committee which comes into existence to promote a particular object and then dissolves. An example was the Equal Pay Campaign Committee whose object it was to press for equal rates of pay for men and women in the public services. It dissolved itself in 1956 when it had succeeded in persuading the government of the day to under-take to introduce equal pay by stages.[1] Another example was the Popular Television Association which was set up to cam-paign for the introduction of commercial television in Britain. The Association achieved its object with the passage of the Television Act of 1954.[2]

It is difficult to differentiate the *ad hoc* group from the other two groups. For example, if the National Campaign for the Abolition of Capital Punishment had achieved its object in 1957, one might call it an *ad hoc* group. Because it secured only a partial success in that year it continued to campaign for abolition. Again, the Popular Television Association lapsed in 1954 but was revived in 1961 under the title of the National Broadcasting Development Committee. In its second manifesta-tion its main objects were to secure a second channel for com-mercial television, and the introduction of commercial sound broadcasting. Both, however, may be termed *ad hoc* campaigns as there was no continuing organization between 1954 and 1961.

An essentially *ad hoc* group which has had a continuing ex-istence has been the organization 'Britain in Europe' which was set up to campaign for British entry into the Common Market. Its chairman was Lord Gladwyn, the former British Ambassa-dor in Paris. Its membership included leading members of all political parties and other distinguished people. In the spring of 1961, 150 of them signed a declaration calling upon the Macmillan Government to apply for membership of the Com-mon Market. Three months later, in July 1961, Macmillan announced that his Government had decided to make this

[1] See Allen Potter, 'The Equal Pay Campaign Committee: A Case-Study of a Pressure Group' in *Political Studies*, February 1957, pp. 49–64.

[2] See H. H. Wilson, *Pressure Group: Commercial Television* (Secker and Warburg, 1960).

application. President de Gaulle's subsequent veto on the application left scope for the organization to renew its campaign at a later stage.

Undoubtedly there are difficulties in the two-fold classification that has been suggested: interest groups and ideas groups. There is some overlapping and some groups are difficult to place. For example, where do the Association of Municipal Corporations and the County Councils Association fit in? These are associations of local authorities. Can they be termed producer groups? In a sense they can as they are producers of services in education, health, sewage disposal, etc.

Having examined the main types of organized pressure groups it is well to recognize that there are interests in British society which are not organized but can still exert great pressure on the government. The best example is the 'City'. The City has no formal constitution. It is a heterogeneous collection of finance houses, stockbrokers, insurance companies, and so on. They are all located in, or associated with, the City of London and have a common interest in finance. We may describe them perhaps as an 'established interest' but not as an organized interest group. Yet, the influence of the City can be very great. Lord Butler has said: 'I think the Governor of the Bank of England is the greatest friend of the Chancellor of the Exchequer because he brings him the news of the City ... the Governor sees the Chancellor at least once a week and tells him, of course, the position of sterling and the position of the pound in overseas markets, so the Governor is a man without whom the Chancellor of the Exchequer cannot easily get on'.[1] The Governor is head of a nationalized institution (the Bank of England was nationalized in 1946) and is appointed by the Queen on the advice of the Chancellor of the Exchequer. His importance, however, lies here in the fact that he is the intermediary between the Government and this amorphous but very powerful interest, the City.

How Pressure is Exerted

Pressure groups in central government exert pressure in three main directions: on government departments, on parliament

[1] Lord Butler on Cabinet government. A conversation with Norman Hunt printed in the *Listener*, 16 September 1965, p. 409.

and on the general public. The different types of pressure group give differing emphasis to these three channels.

The interest groups, and particularly the producers' groups, are above all concerned with maintaining close relations with government departments. They often may achieve all they require through contacts with Civil Servants in the departments concerned with their activities. Many of them are in a strong position here. Organizations such as the National Farmers' Union have very experienced officers and a highly skilled permanent staff. They are admirably placed to give advice to the Ministry of Agriculture, Fisheries and Food on the devising and application of agricultural policies. With advice goes influence which is exerted, not only through the bewildering variety of advisory committees which assist government departments, but often also through informal contacts between officers of associations and Civil Servants. But while interest groups prefer to achieve their objects by direct negotiation with government departments, they may not be altogether successful. If not, they may resort to the second main channel of pressure: on parliament. Every trade association and almost every large firm will be prepared, if it seems necessary, to approach sympathetic Members of Parliament and ask them to move amendments or put down questions on their behalf. Many large firms also have a full-time staff whose function it is to keep a constant check on bills or statutory instruments that are before the House. They are sometimes to be seen in the seats reserved for the public in standing committees and in the corridors of the House. This sort of watching brief over activities in Parliament is also carried on by bodies like the Association of Municipal Corporations and the County Councils Associations.

Many firms or trade associations have their own spokesmen in the Commons. Andrew Roth in an analysis of the business associations of M.P.s established that, in 1963, 360 M.P.s, or well over half the total membership of the House, had a substantial present or past business connexion. He also stated that a check of the 100 biggest businesses in Britain showed that one in three had, or had had, some connexion with an M.P.[1] Many

---

[1] See Andrew Roth, *The Business Background of Members of Parliament* (Parliamentary Profile Services Ltd., 1963), pp. xvi and xxvi.

trade unions, as we have seen earlier, also have representatives
in the House. In the House of Commons elected in 1966, twenty
five unions had members whom they had sponsored. Out of a
total of 132 sponsored Members, the mineworkers and the transport workers had twenty-seven each, the engineers had seventeen and the general and municipal workers with ten were also
well represented. Trade unions, like trade associations, prefer
if they can to influence government departments directly and
tend, like the trade associations, to use Parliament as a channel
of second resort.

The third channel—pressure on the public—is relatively unimportant for interest groups. Generally speaking it is only
firms who are threatened with nationalization who campaign
openly for public sympathy. They may then resort to extensive
advertising and poster campaigns. But on the whole this is an
exceptional activity for business firms or trade associations.
'Prestige' advertisements in newspapers, paid for by individual
firms, are of course common enough nowadays, but their intention is to project a generally favourable image to the public,
to investors and to potential customers rather than, in most
cases, to promote any particular campaign.

While interest groups give more attention to pressure on
government departments and less attention to Parliament and
public opinion, ideas groups tend to give less emphasis to contacts with government departments and more attention to
Parliament and the general public. This different emphasis is
a matter of necessity rather than choice. Most interest groups
have something to 'sell' government departments: the expert
advice of their officers and their ability to ease the way for
departmental policies. In return they can expect a ready and
sympathetic consideration for their views. An ideas group cannot normally be useful in the same way to Civil Servants. They
may indeed get a polite, or even sympathetic, hearing but
there is not likely to be the continuing consultation that
proceeds between a department and a major interest group
such as the National Farmers' Union or the British Medical
Association.

Perhaps an exception here is the Howard League for Penal
Reform which has gained a special relationship with the Home
Office by virtue of its moderate attitude and the store of

information which its permanent staff has amassed on penal questions all over the world.[1] It is also active in giving information to friendly M.P.s, but its mode of operation is very different from that of the National Campaign for the Abolition of Capital Punishment, for example, whose whole emphasis lay on influencing M.P.s and the general public.

Standing perhaps midway between these organizations is a body like the Africa Bureau which exists primarily to influence parliamentary and public opinion but also greatly values its contacts with government departments. During the later 1950s it was sometimes useful to Ministers, particularly when it provided a channel of informal contact between Ministers and African leaders at junctures when the British Government was not prepared to open formal negotiations. Members of the Executive Committee of the Bureau were also at times asked for their opinion by the responsible Ministers including the Colonial Secretary, the Commonwealth Secretary, the Minister for Central African Affairs and, on occasion, the Foreign Secretary.

The clearest case of a group that has operated entirely at the parliamentary and public level is the Campaign for Nuclear Disarmament. Its pressure had been applied, until 1963, predominantly in two directions: on the Labour Party and on the general public. The annual Aldermaston marches, meetings in Trafalgar Square, and so forth, should be seen as a means of influencing public opinion.[2] The activities of the more extreme organization, the Committee of 100, differed in that they were an attempt to coerce the government through a campaign of non-violent resistance. There is a close parallel here with the suffragette movement in the years immediately preceding the 1914 war. The use of direct action by bodies like the Committee of 100, and by the suffragette movement, differentiates them so markedly from other pressure groups that it prompts the question as to whether they can be classified as pressure groups at all. They retain, however, certain attributes in common with the more usual pressure groups. In particular, their aim has been not to take over the government but to induce it

---

[1] See Christoph, op. cit., pp. 28–9.
[2] For a study of the Campaign for Nuclear Disarmament see Christopher Driver, *The Disarmers, a Study in Protest* (Hodder & Stoughton, 1964).

to adopt certain policies within a relatively restricted field.

We have seen that interest groups will sometimes appeal to public opinion through poster and advertising campaigns, although this is not their normal method of applying pressure. Similarly, some interest groups have resorted to public demonstration if other tactics have failed. For example some groups of Civil Servants and nurses have taken part in protest marches to advertise their grievances over pay awards. The National Union of Teachers organized a mass lobby of M.P.s in 1963 which, although primarily directed toward parliament, was of such a scale as to make it something of a public demonstration. An official of the union was reported in *The Times* of 28 March 1963 as saying that, in his belief, 7,000 teachers had taken part in lobbying on the previous day. *The Times* reported that teachers queued for up to two hours outside Parliament, in steady rain, waiting for their turn to see their M.P.s. Even more spectacular demonstrations by members of interest groups took place during the winter of 1964–5. Aircraft workers, threatened with redundancy by the impending cancellation of the TSR2, marched in force from Hyde Park to Westminster and lobbied their M.P.s. Farmers, disgruntled by the terms of the farm price review, held agricultural parades and gave away live chickens, not forgetting in the process the Minister of Agriculture, who received his from a farmer during a Panorama discussion on BBC television.

Such activities have been exceptional for interest groups. Employers' groups in particular enjoy, by and large, a continuing and generally harmonious relationship with government departments. The question is: is this continuing relationship in the public interest? There is a danger that a government department may be 'captured' by an interest group. J. W. Grove discusses this point but concludes that the opposite danger, capture of a sectional group by a department, is more real in Britain.[1] In other words, the teeth of a group may be drawn, or at least its 'bite' reduced, by constant association with government officials. One may question whether this is in fact the greater danger. Undoubtedly, the leading officers of an interest group are often led to adopt a more 'responsible' attitude through contact with Ministers and Civil Servants.

[1] Grove, op. cit., p. 61.

But if they are 'captured' by the official side, they are likely to be subjected to severe protests by their members.

British and American Pressure Groups Compared

The pressure group that probably established the closest relationship with a government department in the post-1945 period was the National Farmers' Union. Peter Self and Herbert J. Storing suggested that the relationship between the Union and successive governments from 1945 to 1961 was probably 'unique in its range and its intensity'.[1] But even though they claimed that in this period the Ministry allowed the National Farmers' Union 'to set the pace—or to hold it back', they do not agree that the department was 'captured' by the Union. They say of this period: 'It would be misleading to suggest that the Ministry simply succumbed to Union pressure, or developed anything like the dependent relationship upon a specialized clientele which characterizes, for example, some American government agencies'.

This brings one to another interesting and instructive question: whether it is true that pressure groups are relatively less powerful in Britain than in the United States. Here, observers from overseas can differ considerably. Maurice Duverger, for example, has argued that: 'In countries like Britain, where only two parties dominate, and two well disciplined parties, a certain equilibrium can develop between the political organizations which express national interests, and the pressure groups which voice sectional interests. On the other hand, if the parties lack cohesion (as in the U.S.A.) or are very numerous (as in France where several also are lacking in discipline) they offer little resistance. Then Parliament is essentially the field of battle in which the pressure groups struggle for power.'[2]

On the other hand, Samuel Beer has argued in a very able article that: 'If we had some way of measuring political power, we could quite possibly demonstrate that at the present time pressure groups are more powerful in Britain than in the

[1] Peter Self and Herbert J. Storing, *The State and the Farmer* (Allen & Unwin, 1962), p. 230.
[2] M. Duverger, *La VIe République et le régime présidentiel* (Librairie Arthème Fayard, 1961), p. 21 (my translation).

United States'.[1] He based his argument on three principal grounds. He pointed out first that interest groups are much more concentrated in Britain than in the United States. For example, around 90 per cent. of British farmers are members of the National Farmers' Union while in the United States there were, in 1956, three farmers' groups whose total membership included only about 30 per cent. of all American farmers. Second, he contended that, so to speak, the prizes are higher in Britain than in the United States. As Britain is a unitary state, and British governments since 1945 have been committed to the welfare state and to a controlled economy, pressure groups can win more valuable concessions from government departments than are usually possible in the United States. Third, he argued that, although British interest groups are unspectacular and work to a large extent behind the scenes, the continuing relationship which they enjoy with government departments gives them very great influence in the shaping of departmental policies, influence beyond that normally possessed by their American counterparts.

With much of this argument one must agree, conceding the force especially of his first and second points. The third point is much more debatable. Granted that the continuing relationship does exist, it remains true that a British ministry normally subjects the claim of a pressure group to the test: 'Is it in the public interest?' Also the question of what is the public interest, in any particular case, is determined by the Minister and his advisers, or by the whole Cabinet. When indeed we find a department conceding virtually the whole of the case put up by a pressure group, it is normally because the department considers the case to be well argued and the policy advanced to be in the public interest. Thus British governments have paid vast sums since 1945 in support of the farming community, not primarily because this was demanded by the National Farmers' Union, but because it was thought to be in the national interest that approaching 50 per cent. of Britain's food supplies

[1] Samuel H. Beer, 'Pressure Groups and Parties in Britain', *American Political Science Review*, March 1956, pp. 1–23.

See also Samuel H. Beer, 'Group Representation in Britain and the United States' in *Annals of the American Academy of Political and Social Science*, September 1958, pp. 130–41.

should be produced at home, for reasons of defence and of improving the balance of payments.

The concept of the national interest is also strengthened and unified, as Duverger argues, by the predominance of two well-organized political parties in Britain. Each party has its conception of the national interest which is embodied in its programme. The individual M.P. therefore is protected to some extent from group pressures by the over-riding compulsion of party discipline. By contrast, an American Congressman is often subject to severe pressures in his congressional district. An interest group will sometimes cease contributing to a Congressman's election campaign fund and switch support to his opponent, in either the main or the primary election, if his opponent is more amenable. This can be a particularly serious threat to a legislator, since in the United States the national parties give little financial support to individual Congressmen in fighting elections, and the existence of the locality rule may mean political death for the Congressman if he is defeated in his own district. The extent to which, in Britain, party discipline will prevail over constituency pressure was illustrated at the time of the cancellation of the TSR2 aircraft by the Wilson Government in 1965. Several Labour M.P.s, who had in their constituencies aircraft factories that were involved, were pressed hard to oppose the cancellation. They spoke against it and some, for example Maurice Edelman, took part in deputations to ministers, but none voted against the Government on this issue.

A comparison of the strength of American and British pressure groups is nevertheless made difficult by the fact that they operate within different political systems and use different techniques. Because of the separation of powers the main focus for interest group pressure in the United States is Congress, while in Britain it is government departments. It is clear that American pressure groups are much more powerful in relation to Congress than British pressure groups are in relation to Parliament. When we come to consider the relationship between pressure groups and departments, however, the contrast is not so clear cut. Certainly some American departments are more closely influenced by pressure groups through the agency of powerful Congressional committees, but over the whole range of government activity British pressure groups are certainly very influential. The success or failure of pressure groups depends also to a large extent on the climate of opinion in a country. American interest groups have been very successful in the past, for example in promoting high tariff legislation. L. H. Chamberlain attributed the passage of four of the major tariff measures since 1890 to interest group pressure. These were the McKinley Act of 1890, the Dingley Act of 1897, the Fordney-McCumber Act of 1922, and the Hawley-Smoot Act of 1930.[1] But although pressure groups were the initiators, and played a part in creating a climate of opinion, these tariff laws would not have been passed had there not been a general consensus in favour of protection.

It is also undeniable that, in the American context, pressure groups have greater power to obstruct the Executive than in Britain. Many examples could be cited here. Perhaps the most striking recent example has been the ability of the American Medical Association to resist for eight years the federal provision of medical care for the elderly. First introduced in 1957 by Representative Forand, and later backed by President Kennedy, a Medicare-Social Security Bill was not finally approved by Congress until 1965. It was signed by President Johnson on 30 July 1965. During the intervening period, the American Medical Association had expended vast sums in publicity directed against Medicare proposals.

The Role of the Government Department

British interest groups are not well placed to obstruct the government, but most of them do have a continuous influence over departmental policy. Not even the strongest of them, however, control government departments. This is, as we have seen, the conclusion of Self and Storing about relations between the National Farmers' Union and the Ministry of Agriculture, Fisheries, and Food. On the other hand, these authors clearly felt that the relationship between the interest group and the Ministry in this case had become undesirably close. In particular, they considered that it had induced, up until 1958, an unfortunate rigidity in Government policy in the matter of agricultural price support. 'The Government,' they say, 'was

[1] L. H. Chamberlain, *The President, Congress and Legislation* (New York, 1946). See also his article with the same title in the *Political Science Quarterly*, Vol. lxi, pp. 42–60.

slow to explore more flexible and more selective methods of support for which the Agriculture Act provided, because of the Union's strong opposition to any departure from the conventions which it had managed to get established.'[1] By the time that, in 1963, the cost to the government of agricultural support had risen to approaching £364 million a year, it had become clear that other and less costly methods of aid to the farming community had to be devised. It could be claimed that other methods should have been found sooner and that they might have been found sooner if the ministry had not depended so heavily on advice from one source: the National Farmers' Union.

This illustrates one of the chief dangers of pressure group influence in contemporary Britain: that a government department may be prepared to accept too uncritically the advice tendered by a powerful interest group. In this way the public interest may be over-ridden, or rather over-clouded, by a group interest. Similarly, a powerful organized group may drown the voice of numerically larger but unorganized interests in society. This is particularly the case in relation to producer groups. The producers, both employers and trade unionists, are in general well organized; consumers are often not organized at all. It was realization of this fact, coupled with dissatisfaction engendered by the bewildering claims and counter-claims of advertisers, which led to the founding in 1957 of the Consumers' Association. This association was initially modelled on the American Consumers' Union and has as its main aim the giving of independent advice on the relative qualities of products and services available to the consumer. Since 1957 it has published a magazine, *Which?*, giving the results of systematic tests made on goods varying from zip-fasteners to motor cars. In 1967 this magazine, which is sent to members, had a circulation of well over 400,000. In 1966 there were ninety-three local consumers' groups which were joined in a Federation of Independent Local Consumer Groups having links with the Consumers' Association.

The success of the Consumers' Association has stimulated the development of other organizations of consumers. In the field of education, the Confederation for the Advancement of State Education is an organization mainly of parents who have

[1] Self and Storing, op. cit., p. 232.

children in State schools. In September 1967 there were over one hundred local associations for the advancement of State education affiliated to the central body. In relation to the Health Service there have been similar developments. London-based organizations include the Association for the Improvement of the Maternity Services, the Patients' Association and the National Association for the Welfare of Children in Hospital.[1] Parallel organizations have appeared in the provinces, including the Association for the Welfare of Children in Hospital (in South Wales) and branches of the Patients' Association. All these are essentially consumers' organizations. They are beginning to provide an invaluable counter-balance to the well-organized producers' associations of doctors, teachers, education authorities, etc. They are still very thin on the ground but it is an important beginning.

The continued imbalance between producers' and consumers' groups prompts a number of very interesting questions for both government departments and parliament. When a government department sees that consumers are not organized, should it try to create a consumers' organization? The answer is probably in the negative, because such organizations should always be voluntary bodies. However, government departments and local authorities should do all they can to encourage the development of such organizations. In the past, some government departments, hospital boards, hospital management committees, and local education authorities have been receptive to ideas put forward by consumer groups and have welcomed their activities; but others have not been so encouraging.

A similar principle should be followed where there are rival groups in any field. It may be inconvenient for a government department to negotiate with more than one group, but it should surely do so on democratic grounds. This is not always done. Eckstein has pointed out, for example, that the Medical Practitioners' Union and the Socialist Medical Association were at one time virtually excluded from negotiations with the Ministry of Health.[2] Undoubtedly they are minority organizations, and their views are generally less representative than those

---

[1] Until 1965, the Mother Care for Children in Hospital.

[2] Harry Eckstein, *Pressure Group Politics: The case of the British Medical Association* (Allen & Unwin, 1960), p. 159.

of the British Medical Association, but they should not be excluded from the process of consultation. This leads one to a related question: should the government be concerned with the degree to which a group is, or is not, democratic in its internal structure? It might be claimed that there is no guarantee whatever that the views of the officers of the British Medical Association are representative of majority opinion in the general body of doctors. Should Parliament therefore lay down certain standards to which pressure groups must conform? Should statute require, for example, that officers must be elected each year at an annual general meeting, or annual delegate meeting, the delegates themselves being democratically accredited in branch meetings? This suggestion has some attractions but also some grave disadvantages. The chief objection to the proposal is that it would involve government interference in the internal affairs of voluntary associations.

If, however, oversight was given to an authority independent of the government there could be less objection to the idea. There already exist the Registrar of Friendly Societies and the Charity Commissioners. Part of their function is to safeguard the interests of members of associations registered with them and of the wider public. The Conservative Party, in their manifesto at the 1966 general election, suggested the creation of a Registrar of Trade Unions and Employers' Associations. He would be concerned with such questions as the rules governing the admission of members, election and responsibility of officials, finance, and disciplinary powers. Such a Registrar would regulate a large sector of producers' groups. It would be reasonable to establish also a separate Registrar who would be concerned with professional associations, consumers' groups, ideas groups, etc.

Pressure Groups and Parliament

What of pressure groups and Parliament? Is the present situation satisfactory? One major criticism has been made in recent years. It is argued that not only are many M.P.s connected with business firms, but these relationships are not always made clear when important issues are at stake. On occasion, M.P.s have combined in a campaign in Westminster and Whitehall which has had far-reaching results.

The most spectacular example in recent years was the campaign for the introduction of commercial television. This campaign was led by a small group of Conservative M.P.s some of whom had, through connexion with an advertising agency or electronics firms, a direct financial interest in the outcome. They succeeded in inducing an initially uninterested Conservative majority in the Commons, and a hostile Cabinet, to agree to the creation of the Independent Television Authority which was to provide channels for commercial television broadcasting companies. In this campaign, they were powerfully assisted by certain officials in the Conservative Party Central Office.[1] Anxiety about what can be achieved in this way has led Norman Hunt to suggest that M.P.s, like Ministers, should be required by law to give up directorships when they take their seats in Parliament. They could then, in his words, 'act as brokers, as it were, of pressure group demands', considering impartially the claims of interest groups and interpreting the public interest.[2]

A related question is the desirability of allowing M.P.s to hold positions in, or to be consultants for, public relations firms. Are they not then also in danger of losing the independence and impartiality towards interests which an M.P. should show? There was some anxiety on this question particularly in the 1959–64 Parliament.[3] The anxiety was increased by the fact that at that time Members' salaries were very inadequate. The attraction for a Member of a public relations consultancy was therefore very strong. With the major increase in salary which followed the 1964 general election, Members could be financially independent. There remains the criticism that Members are not required to reveal any connexion with a public relations firm, although it is customary for a Member to declare an interest when he speaks on a subject connected with his business affairs. There is also the question of overseas visits provided for Members by public relations firms. There are very few opportunities for Members to make study tours abroad at public expense. Consequently, the attraction of a free tour is

---

[1] See Wilson, op. cit.

[2] Norman Hunt, 'Interested Parties' in the *Listener*, 20 July 1961, p. 84.

[3] See Ian Waller, 'Pressure Politics: M.P. and P.R.O.' in *Encounter*, August 1962, pp. 3–15.

considerable. Such an offer was made to numerous M.P.s by the public relations firm 'Voice and Vision' in 1961. This firm offered a conducted tour of the Central African Federation at its expense. The forty M.P.s who went on these tours (19 Conservative, 20 Labour, and 1 Liberal) were, it seems, taken on a carefully selected itinerary designed to support the case for the maintenance of the Federation. This campaign did not, however, succeed.

There is a danger perhaps in looking too hard at campaigns, like that for commercial television, which have succeeded, and of passing over too readily the many campaigns which have failed. There is some ground for arguing that the campaign for commercial television was an exceptional case and that normally M.P.s and governments are much tougher in resisting the demands and blandishments of pressure groups. One of the most remarkable failures in a pressure group campaign was that of the groups who sought to defeat the Resale Prices Bill in 1964. They were headed by a well-organized Resale Price Maintenance Co-ordinating Committee whose steering committee consisted of officers of the Stationers' Association, the Proprietary Articles Trade Association, the Electrical Wholesalers' Federation, the British Motor Trade Association, and the National Chamber of Trade. All these interests, together with such bodies as the Pharmaceutical Society and the Wine and Spirit Association, worked hard to influence M.P.s against the Bill, particularly on the Conservative side of the House. The Bill was modified in detail but in important respects it went through unchanged. This is another example of what can be done by an energetic minister, Edward Heath, when backed by the Cabinet, even in the face of a phalanx of pressure groups to which his party might be expected to be particularly sensitive.

In Britain, then, the general picture is not one of governmental and Parliamentary subservience to pressure groups. The groups have access to Ministers, but they cannot command. What does give cause for anxiety, however, is the fact that much pressure group and public relations activity goes on behind the scenes. There is need for more publicity. Greater publicity could be ensured by legislation requiring that all pressure groups must register, making a public statement of their name,

objects, sources of funds, and officers' names. An impartial
authority of the type already suggested, a Registrar, or Regis-
trars, would examine the accounts, the constitutions, and the
annual reports of all registered groups.

The United States has had federal legislation since 1946
which aims to secure the registration of lobbyists in Congress,
but the 1946 Federal Regulation of Lobbying Act has only been
a limited success, partly because there has been no effective
law enforcement agency to ensure that lobbyists do register.[1]
Regulation is also confined to paid lobbyists who are attempting to influence legislation in Congress. American experience
does not therefore provide a clear model for any system of
registration in Britain. But neither does it show that registration of pressure groups is impracticable.

There is another step which could be taken in addition to
providing for registration of pressure groups. M.P.s could be
required to state publicly all their sources of income in addition
to their salaries as Members. If this were thought to be too
great an intrusion into their private lives, it should be thought
of as a necessary consequence of their becoming Members and
as a less draconian alternative to Hunt's suggestion that they
should be required to give up all directorships. Reforms such
as these would reduce some of the abuses that can attend pressure group activity in Britain. At the same time they would not
inhibit pressure groups from playing their valuable, and indeed
essential, part in the democratic process.

FOR REFERENCE

S. H. BEER, *Modern British Politics* (Faber, 1965).

S. H. BEER, 'Pressure Groups and Parties in Britain' in the *American Political
Science Review*, 1956.

J. B. CHRISTOPH, *Capital Punishment and British Politics* (Allen and Unwin,
1962).

C. DRIVER, *The Disarmers, a Study in Protest* (Hodder and Stoughton, 1964).

H. ECKSTEIN, *Pressure Group Politics: The Case of the British Medical Association*
(Allen and Unwin, 1960).

S. E. FINER, *Anonymous Empire*, 2nd ed. (Pall Mall Press, 1966).

J. W. GROVE, *Government and Industry in Britain* (Longmans, 1962).

[1] See Belle Zeller, 'The Regulation of Pressure Groups and Lobbyists', in the
Annals of the American Academy of Political Social Science, September 1958, pp. 94–103.

The Political Quarterly, 1958, Special Issue on 'Pressure Groups in Britain'.

A. POTTER, *Organized Groups in British Politics* (Faber, 1961).

P. SELF and H. J. STORING, *The State and the Farmer* (Allen and Unwin, 1962).

J. D. STEWART, *British Pressure Groups* (Clarendon Press, 1958).

I. WALLER, 'Pressure Politics. M.P. and P.R.O.' in *Encounter*, 1962).

H. H. WILSON, *Pressure Group: the Campaign for Commercial Television* (Secker and Warburg, 1960).

CHAPTER XV

The Machinery of Administration

WE have seen that some interest groups have a very nearly continuous influence over governments. But easily the strongest continuing influence is provided by the machinery of administration itself: by the permanent officials of the Civil Service. The work that these officials do and their relationship with Ministers is, therefore, of special interest to the student of government.

The Character of the British Civil Service

The British Civil Service has certain outstanding characteristics. It is a career service in the sense that no permanent appointments within the service are made through political patronage. It is recruited in its three main grades—Administrative, Executive, and Clerical—by open and competitive examinations. Even the most senior officials, the Permanent Secretaries of the great departments of State, are members of this career service which they entered, in most cases, through competitive examination to the Administrative grade.

The fact that it is a career service of this type, recruited in this way, has many important consequences which we shall examine; but it is worthwhile first to notice the stages by which the British Civil Service came to acquire its present character. Until 1870, nearly all appointments were made on the basis of patronage under the control of the Ministers heading the respective departments. A cogent report prepared by Sir Stafford Northcote and Sir Charles Trevelyan in 1853 had argued the case for selection by open competitive examination under the aegis of an impartial Civil Service Commission. In 1855 the Government did set up such a Commission, but it was only given power to hold qualifying examinations, the actual process of selection remaining in the hands of the separate departments.

The India Office, however, adopted the system of open competitive examination in 1858, and its success there helped to prepare the ground for Gladstone's Order in Council of 1870. This historic decision provided for open competition for all departments except the Home Office and the Foreign Office. There were to be two types of competition: an examination at the level of a University degree examination which was to recruit entrants to Class I, within which were to be brought all higher posts in the Civil Service, and an examination intended to pick out some of the best products of the grammar schools and from which Class II of the Civil Service was to be filled. The Civil Service Commissioners were made the examining authority for both sorts of examination.

In this way the pattern of the modern Civil Service in Britain was created. It has since been modified in detail. The Home Office and the Foreign Office were brought within the open competitive system. In 1920 the two main grades of the Civil Service, Classes I and II, were replaced by three grades. The old Class I was re-named the Administrative Class, while the old Class II was sub-divided into the Executive and Clerical Classes. Another important change has been the addition of an interview to the written examinations for selection to the Administrative and Executive grades. The interview became part of the selection process for the Administrative Class after the First World War, and for the Executive Class after the Second World War. Another important innovation was made in 1945 with the introduction of what is now known as Method II for recruiting entrants to the Administrative Class. The older system of a degree-type examination followed by interview is known as Method I, while Method II consists of a written examination of a more general character, plus vocational and personality tests and an interview. The results of this last innovation will be discussed later on.[1]

What in general have been the effects of selection by open competitive examination since 1870? What sort of Civil Service has it produced? There is no doubt that it has produced a Government Service staffed, particularly in the Administrative and Executive grades, by men and women of very high intellectual calibre. It has also produced a Civil Service which

[1] See below pp. 348–51.

stands outside the party political contest, providing, in the orthodox view, an efficient and loyal administrative machine for whichever political party is victorious at the polls. This generally favourable view is the one held by many students of British Government. But unorthodox and critical views are also heard. Examples of two such views are provided by Ramsay Muir and Brian Chapman.[1]

Muir may be taken as representative of the view that the supposedly loyal Civil Service in Britain is, in fact, a controlling bureaucracy masked, as he claims, 'by the doctrine of ministerial responsibility'. Chapman's strictures are somewhat different. His criticism of the Civil Service, as at present organized, is that it is a closed corporation kept apart from, one might almost say cloistered from, the world outside Whitehall. As a consequence, in his view, the quality of advice given to Ministers has suffered and this goes far to explain the many mistaken policies that, again in his view, were followed by British governments in the decade before 1963.

Muir's View Examined
Let us examine what we may term 'the Muir view' first. Muir allows that 'It would, of course, be a grave blunder to suggest that Ministers are always and in all respects, merely the puppets of the bureaucracy, merely the cover behind which their power is wielded' . . . 'But it remains true that, over the field of central administration taken as a whole, the continuous and persistent influence of the Civil Service is the dominating fact; and, therefore, that the element of bureaucracy is of vital importance, though its strength is masked by the doctrine of ministerial responsibility.'[2] Outstanding individuals, such as Joseph Chamberlain, Haldane, or Lloyd George, can as Ministers make an impact on their departments. But they are exceptional; in general, Muir argues, the influence of the Civil Service predominates in policy making.

It is undeniable that a vast number of decisions on matters of policy were in Ramsay Muir's day and are today, made by Civil Servants. Many of these decisions will be taken by

---

[1] See Ramsay Muir, *How Britain is Governed* (Constable, 1930) and Brian Chapman, *British Government Observed* (Allen & Unwin, 1963).

[2] Muir, op. cit., pp. 57 and 58.

Civil Servants of the rank of Assistant Secretary or Principal who will often have charge of a division or branch within a great department but with whom the Minister will have very little personal contact. He can only know at all well the senior Civil Servants in his department, particularly the Permanent Secretary, with whom he will normally have daily contact, and his own Private Secretary from whom he will get constant help. He will also know the Deputy Secretary or Secretaries and will come into contact with some of the Under-Secretaries. But from this level downwards, through the Assistant Secretaries and Principals, there cannot be continuous personal contact between Minister and official. Yet officials in all these grades must take, from time to time, important decisions on matters of policy.

How far is it true then to say that the Minister decides policy; or indeed, in the normal course of events, is it ever true? The answer is that in an important sense it is true. This is because it is a widely understood principle in the Civil Service that where a Minister's policy is known, Civil Servants will act in accordance with it. Where his policy is not known they will try 'to interpret the mind of the Minister', deducing from what is known of his policy what his attitude would be in the specific case to be decided. This does not mean that Civil Servants, in giving advice, are 'yes-men' to their Ministers; but neither, except on rare occasions, are they obstructionists. Lord Strang, a former Permanent Under-Secretary at the Foreign Office, has put the position very well: 'A civil servant, saving personal honour and conscience, must do as he is bid. He may, indeed should, put forward his views and he is entitled, up to a point, to press his advice, but he must be ready to reconsider and in the end he must comply. The orders which he receives are the responsibility of the Minister. The civil servant must fulfil them to the best of his capacity.'[1]

There have, of course, been occasions when Civil Servants have attempted to obstruct Ministers. One delicious incident has been described by Mary Agnes Hamilton in her biography of Arthur Henderson and has been corroborated by Hugh Dalton in the first volume of his memoirs.[2]

[1] Lord Strang, *Home and Abroad* (Deutsch, 1956), p. 126.
[2] Mary Agnes Hamilton, *Arthur Henderson* (Heinemann, 1938), pp. 289–90. Hugh Dalton, *Call Back Yesterday: Memoirs 1887–1931* (Muller, 1953), pp. 222–3.

M

When Arthur Henderson became Foreign Secretary in 1929, in the second Labour Government, he was determined to make a number of radical changes in the conduct of foreign policy. In particular, he was anxious to give more emphasis to support for the League of Nations. With this in mind, he announced to the senior officials of the Foreign Office that he intended to bring in Lord Robert Cecil, who had at one time been a Conservative Minister and had for a long time devoted himself to support for the League, to advise on League of Nations Affairs.

The officials were strongly opposed to this importation of an 'outsider', neither a member of the Government nor a Civil Servant, into the Foreign Office. Arthur Henderson was told that there was no room available for Cecil in the building. Whereupon, Henderson took his Civil Servants on a personal tour of the building until he found a room that was not in use. It was, in fact, a conference room where he directed that Lord Cecil was to have a desk in one corner and his Private Secretary, Will Arnold-Forster, in another corner. In this matter, as in a number of others, Arthur Henderson asserted his authority in his early days as Foreign Secretary. He also, for example, had copies of the Labour Manifesto at the general election sent to all the senior officials, with instructions that answers to parliamentary questions and drafts for speeches were to be formulated in the light of the Labour programme on foreign affairs. Dalton, who was Henderson's Parliamentary Under-Secretary at the time, has described the rapid effect this decision had on the content and tone of drafts submitted by the senior officials. Indeed, before long, Henderson had won the complete loyalty of his staff. He proved to be an outstandingly effective Foreign Secretary.

There is evidence that senior Civil Servants are nowadays generally more aware of their responsibilities when faced with a change of government. James Callaghan has described his first visit to the Treasury on being made Chancellor of the Exchequer after the Labour victory at the polls in October 1964. He was agreeably surprised to find that the Civil Servants had studied the Labour manifesto at the general election and Harold Wilson's speech at Swansea, in January 1964, on Labour's economic policy. They had prepared a memorandum which was waiting for him, discussing the ways in which the incoming government's policies could be implemented and the difficulties involved.[1]

What happens when there is a fundamental incompatibility between a senior official and his Minister? This rarely happens but an example is found in the career of Sir Robert, later Lord, Vansittart who was Permanent Under-Secretary at the Foreign Office for a time while Neville Chamberlain was Prime Minister. Vansittart was totally opposed to Chamberlain's policy of appeasement of Nazi Germany. The situation became intolerable, for although the Prime Minister was not himself Foreign Secretary, he had taken over complete direction of foreign policy. A solution was found to the apparent impasse by creating a new post of Diplomatic Adviser to His Majesty's Government to which Vansittart was appointed. A new Permanent Under-Secretary was brought in and Chamberlain did not, of course, ask Vansittart for advice.

There have been other occasions when Civil Servants have been hustled out more quietly, and also occasions when the official rather than the ministerial view has prevailed. But it would be quite wrong to present a picture of constant friction between Ministers and Civil Servants, or of general inability on the part of Ministers to control their Civil Servants. In general, the relationship between them is very good. It is a partnership in which both sides benefit from the diverse qualities and experience of the other. The great advantage of having permanent officials at the highest levels is that they make available to new Ministers an unrivalled fund of experience. The American practice whereby the equivalents of our Permanent Secretaries, Deputy Secretaries and Under-Secretaries, are political appointments has corresponding disadvantages. But the British career system should not be allowed to become too rigid, nor should it work to reduce the chances of men of forceful personality reaching the highest positions.

There is not much evidence that it has this last effect. Many British Permanent Secretaries have been men of considerable dynamism as well as great intelligence, but they have also been loyal servants to their Ministers. Sir Robert Morant, for

---

[1] James Callaghan in a discussion with Norman Hunt in the ITV series 'Power in Britain', 28 February 1965.

example, was a man of very forceful character who was the real author of the Balfour Education Act of 1902. But he was also picked out by a dynamic Liberal Chancellor of the Exchequer, Lloyd George, as the man to establish the new system of National Insurance in 1911.

A more recent example of a powerful and original Civil Servant who was also teamed at one time with a strong Minister, was Sir Godfrey Ince. As Permanent Secretary to the Ministry of Labour, Ince played the major part in determining the methods by which a vast and rapid demobilization was carried out after the Second World War. To him also must go most of the credit for the procedures, generally very efficient, which dealt with the manpower shortage in industry in the years after 1945. But while, from 1945 to 1950, he could be thought of as an initiating Civil Servant working with a Minister who was not a forceful personality, he had previously worked with great success with one of the strongest Ministers of modern times, Ernest Bevin.

It is interesting to note Earl Attlee's tribute to the loyalty of senior Civil Servants during the lifetime of the Labour Government between 1945 and 1950. He commented: 'There were certainly some people in the Labour Party who doubted whether the civil servants would give fair play to a socialist government, but all doubts disappeared with experience'.[1]

Chapman's View Examined

We have seen that Brian Chapman's criticism of the higher Civil Service is different from that of Muir. His criticism is not that senior officials are not susceptible of political control, but that they are too narrow in outlook: 'The British Civil Service at the higher levels is a closed corporation of a kind unknown in most European countries'.[2] It is a closed corporation in the sense that it is not sufficiently open to outside influences.

The remedies Chapman proposes are threefold. First, each Minister should have the equivalent of the French '*cabinet du ministre*', a group of advisers on policy who would include some persons brought in by the Minister from outside the Civil

---

[1] Earl Attlee, 'Civil Servants, Ministers, Parliament and the Public', Chapter 2 in W. A. Robson, ed., *The Civil Service in Britain and France* (Hogarth Press, 1956), p. 16.

[2] Chapman, op. cit., p. 23.

Service and some Civil Servants. Second, he argues in favour of advertising all posts in the Civil Service above the rank of Assistant Secretary. Third, he wants to see the French system of training Civil Servants adopted in this country.

Let us take each of these ideas in turn. There is a good deal to be said in favour of adopting the French system of the *cabinet du ministre*.[1] It would be a means of introducing new influences and new ideas into a Ministry; it would also give valuable stimulus to younger Civil Servants recruited to the Minister's policy-making staff. It would not involve a radical re-organization of existing machinery. The private offices of Ministers already perform these functions to some extent. It has long been the practice to appoint some of the ablest younger Civil Servants as private secretaries to the Minister and his junior Ministers. Together with the junior Ministers (the Minister or Ministers of State and the Parliamentary Secretaries) they can form a policy-making team as well as having duties in the preparation of parliamentary business, answers to parliamentary questions, etc. By bringing in some outside advisers the private office could be strengthened and made more like the *cabinet du ministre*. It would not be an entirely new departure. Henderson's appointment of Lord Robert Cecil and Arnold-Forster to advise him on League of Nations affairs was essentially the same idea.

The methods and terms of appointment would, of course, have to be considered carefully. Most such advisers should probably have a short-term engagement or consultancy with no undertaking that they will become established Civil Servants, though it should be possible for them to be transferred to the established staff where it seemed desirable. There is a precedent here in the many able men who were brought into the higher Civil Service during the Second World War from business or the universities. Many of them left Government service after the war, but some of those who stayed on and became established have since attained great distinction in the Service. An outstanding example is Sir Laurence Helsby who was appointed Joint Permanent Secretary of the Treasury and Head of the Civil Service in 1963. Until the Second World

[1] For a discussion of the *cabinet du ministre*, see A. Dutheillet de Lamothe, 'Ministerial Cabinets in France' in *Public Administration*, Winter 1965, pp. 365–81.

War he was a university lecturer in economics, and he entered Government service, in the Treasury, in 1941.

It should be a matter for each Minister to decide whether or not to set up a form of *cabinet du ministre*. Some Ministers would not want or need it; in some departments it would be less desirable than in others. In many cases, the best places to bring outsiders into a department would be at other levels—at the equivalent of Under-Secretary or Assistant Secretary or at Principal level within a branch, rather than in the Minister's private office. It is very doubtful, however, whether it would be desirable to do as Chapman suggests and to advertise all posts in the Civil Service above the rank of Assistant Secretary. This would strike at the whole character of the Civil Service as a career service. It would weaken the *esprit de corps* of the Service and, by reducing its attractiveness as a career, would tend to lower the average quality of men and women entering the Administrative Class.

Some moves have been made, however, since 1963, to bring into the Administrative Class people with experience in industry, local government, or the professions. In June 1964, the Douglas-Home Government announced that the Civil Service Commission were to be permitted to appoint up to six Principals a year by open competition from candidates between 30 and 35 who had had a responsible post in industry or commerce, the universities, or professions. The Commissioners were also asked to recruit by advertisement, from outside the Service, up to three Assistant Secretaries each year between the ages of 40 and 45. In their report published in 1965 they announced that the first six Principals had been recruited by open competition. Three were from business or commerce, one was from local government, and one was a grammar school headmaster.[1] In their report for 1966 the Commissioners announced that they had recruited, as Principals, 10 people from outside government service between the ages of 30 and 36. They had also recruited another 41 Principals from people aged 36 to 52. Many of this latter group had been members of the Armed Forces or of the Overseas Civil Service.[2]

[1] Report of Her Majesty's Civil Service Commissioners for the period 1 January to 31 December 1964, p. 2.
[2] Civil Service Commission: Annual Report, 1966, for the period 1 January to 31 December, p. 9.

At a higher level, the Wilson Government in the autumn of 1964 brought in several expert advisers from the university world, and from industry, to assist in policy-making in particular at the economic ministries. Nicholas Kaldor came from academic life to the Treasury, to assist in formulating policy on taxation. H. F. R. Catherwood gave up his post as Managing Director of the British Aluminium Company to become chief industrial adviser at the Department of Economic Affairs. Sir Donald MacDougall, the economist, came over from the National Economic Development Council to be director-general of the Department. John Jukes came from the Atomic Energy Authority to be his deputy. John Grieve Smith came from the Iron and Steel Board to assist them. In addition, six businessmen came in to assist Catherwood. In these various ways then, the Civil Service is ceasing to be so much of a 'closed corporation'.

Even in 1963 when Chapman wrote *British Government Observed*, however, the British Civil Service was not as much of a closed corporation as he implied. For one thing he did not take account of the development of the Scientific Civil Service since 1945. In many departments, nowadays, the number of scientific or professional Civil Servants in senior positions equals or exceeds the number of senior administrative Civil Servants. These professional and scientific Civil Servants are all selected by interview, often after public advertisement. Many of them have had considerable outside experience before entering Government service. It seems probable, however, that the Civil Service has not been making the best use of able people recruited from outside in this way. Until recently it was very unusual for Civil Servants to pass from the Scientific to the Administrative class. In 1964, the Civil Service Commission held an internal competition which resulted in eleven Scientific Officers being recommended for transfer to the Administrative Class as Principals.[1] But transfer at a higher level seems to be, as yet, extremely rare. The Institution of Professional Civil Servants stated in 1965, in evidence to the Estimates Committee, that it knew of no case of a scientific or professional Civil Servant being appointed to the post of Assistant

[1] Civil Service Commissioners' Report for 1964, p. 2.

Secretary or Under-Secretary.[1] Yet the need for senior administrators with a scientific background is, in many departments, only too clear.

In another respect the Higher Civil Service is much less narrow in background than it was before the Second World War. Before 1939 there was relatively little promotion from the Executive to the Administrative grades, the latter forming a sort of exclusive caste. During and after the war, a large number of posts in the Administrative grade had to be filled from the Executive grade. Those promoted proved, by and large, to be of excellent calibre. By 1953 more than one half of the then 703 Assistant Secretaries had come up from the Executive grade.[2] Since 1945 the number of promotions from the Executive Class has been normally exceeded by the numbers of Assistant Principals appointed by Methods I and II. In 1964 for example, there were 48 appointments to the grade of Assistant Principal, but in the same year there were also 31 internal promotions to the Administrative Class, not counting the eleven promotions from the Scientific Civil Service already mentioned.[3]

Another important development which has influenced the character of the Administrative Class has been the introduction of Method II as an alternative to selection by Method I. Method I is the traditional method of selection. It begins each year (normally the final year of a candidate's university degree course) with a qualifying examination taken in January or April. This consists of an essay, an English paper and a general paper. Those who achieve the qualifying standard in this examination are invited to an Interview Board which sits between May and July. This Board, sitting under the Chairmanship of a Civil Service Commissioner, assesses a candidate's personal qualities in conjunction with the reports provided by referees. There follows, in July, a written examination in optional subjects which are set, to quote the Civil Service Commission, 'with the aim, so far as practicable, of enabling any candidate to take the examination without offering subjects outside his

---

[1] H.C. 308 of 1964–5. Sixth Report from the Estimates Committee. Recruitment to the Civil Service, p. 248.

[2] See F. Dunnill, *The Civil Service. Some Human Aspects* (Allen and Unwin, 1956), p. 13.

[3] Report of the Commissioners for 1964, pp. 2 and 11.

university course'.[1] When these optional papers have been marked, the marks are added to those gained in the interview for each candidate, and a list of candidates in order of the totals gained is compiled. Those at the top of the list are declared successful, the exact number being determined by the number of vacancies to be filled and the Commissioners' estimate of the ability of the top group of candidates.

Method II begins with the same written examination in compulsory subjects—essay, English, and general paper—which is taken by the Method I candidates. Those who achieve the necessary standard in this examination are invited to the Civil Service Selection Board which sits between February and May. Candidates are tested at this Board in groups of five, undergoing, over a period of two days, a series of tests, exercises, and interviews. Two of the exercises, in the words of the Civil Service Commission, 'bear some analogy to the work which a successful candidate will have to do in the public service. Both are based on a lengthy dossier describing a situation which, although imaginary, has a substantial basis in fact. In the first exercise the candidates study the dossier and write an answer to a question of policy arising from it. The second is an oral exercise in which the candidates form a committee to study a number of problems related to the central theme of the dossier. Each candidate is allotted a problem and takes the chair to expound his problem and to guide his committee to a solution; when not in the chair he is a member of the committee. These exercises provide some evidence of intellectual quality, practical ability, and judgment; in addition the committee exercise should display each candidate's personality, and, in particular, his effectiveness in dealing with his fellows in discussions and arguments.'[2]

---

[1] Cmnd. 232 'Recruitment to the Administrative Class of the Home Civil Service and the Senior Branch of the Foreign Service. Statement of Government Policy and Report by the Civil Service Commission' (July 1957), p. 21. It should be noted that the Civil Service Commissioners are not able to achieve their aim in relation to many degree courses at the civic universities. The Method I examination subjects were derived initially from Oxford and Cambridge degree courses. Although they have been adapted, they cannot take account of all the many variations in university courses up and down the country. Consequently many candidates from civic universities find themselves at a disadvantage in the Method I examination, having to take subjects outside their university course.

[2] Cmnd. 232, p. 22.

Other exercises and tests include group discussions on current affairs and written intelligence and cognitive tests. Each candidate is also interviewed by the Group Chairman, by a Psychologist, and by a third member of the Directing Staff who acts as Observer. At the end of the whole process, these three assessors give their opinion of each candidate and they agree on a mark for his performance based on all the evidence. The top two-thirds to three-quarters of those assessed by the Civil Service Selection Board then go forward for interview by the Final Selection Board which sits from March to May. This Final Selection Board, under the chairmanship of the First Civil Service Commissioner, considers the reports of the C.S.S.B. Directing Staff, the marks obtained in the written examination, and its own assessment of a candidate's personal qualities in the interview. From all these sources a total mark is awarded and the order of merit in the whole Method II examination is determined. The names of those successful in the Method II examination are announced in May, but they are still provisional in that appointment of these successful candidates is dependent on their securing at least second-class honours in their degree examination.

Since Method I and Method II have continued side by side since the Second World War, it is possible to make some comparison of their effectiveness. The Select Committee on Estimates recommended in their Report in 1948 that the careers of Civil Servants selected by the two methods should be followed up. This was done by the Civil Service Commission and a report giving their findings appeared in 1957. A further statement was provided by the Commission in its memorandum to the Estimates Committee in 1965.[1] The Commission analysed departmental assessments of 132 Administrative Civil Servants who had entered since 1945 by Method II, and 231 who had entered by Method I. They found that 59·1 per cent of those who had entered by Method II were reported as doing work that was very good indeed or distinctly above average. Of those selected by Method I, only 35·1 per cent were rated in these highest categories. At the other end of the scale, 6·8 per cent of those selected by Method II were considered unsatisfactory or rather below standard, while 14·3 per cent of those selected by

[1] H.C. 308 of 1964–5, pp. 27–8.

Method I were so rated. It would seem that the group selected by Method II has a markedly better record.

One must not, however, overlook the fact that many undergraduates prefer Method II because the results are known in May, while they would have to wait until August for the results of Method I. But even taking this factor into account, it would seem that the Method II examination has proved its worth. It is perhaps even reasonable to infer that by placing emphasis largely on potential administrative ability rather than predominantly on scholarship it is selecting a higher proportion of men and women who are really fitted for their career. At the same time Method II does not fail to attract to the Civil Service some of the ablest products of the universities. In 1962, of those successful by Method I, and appointed to departments, 2 out of 10 (20 per cent) secured Firsts in their degree examinations. Of those successful by Method II, and appointed to departments in the same year, 14 out of 33 (over 42 per cent) secured Firsts. Since 1961, Method II has also become the main avenue for selection to the Administrative Class. In 1966, of those successful and appointed to departments in the Home Civil Service, more than five-sixths (66 out of 78) were selected by Method II.

Disquieting Features

There are, however, two disquieting features about recruitment to the Administrative Class. First, for several years now the Commission has been unable to fill all the vacancies. For example, in 1964 there were 88 vacancies but only 48 appointments were made.[1] Therefore, in the view of the Commission, insufficient men and women of the necessary calibre are coming forward. Second, out of those appointed, a very high proportion were educated at Oxford or Cambridge University. Indeed, if the periods 1948–56 and 1957–63 are compared, it appears that the proportion of successful candidates from Oxford and Cambridge went up from 70 per cent to 85 per cent. Again, comparing the same periods, the proportion from boarding schools went up from 31 per cent to 37 per cent, while those from local authority schools went down from 42 per cent to 30 per cent.[2]

[1] H.C. 308 of 1964–5, p. vi.   [2] Ibid.

These figures were a source of some concern to the Estimates Committee. In their investigation in 1965 they heard evidence from numerous authorities on these points. The most interesting evidence was provided by Trevor Smith and Daniel Lawrence of the University of Hull.[1] They carried out a survey of third-year undergraduates at that university. The survey was made at the request of the Estimates Committee and was financed by the Acton Society Trust. A 20 per cent sample of Hull University students in their third year, from all Faculties, Arts, Science, and Social Science, was asked questions which it was hoped would throw some light on students' preferences for one profession rather than another. The most interesting conclusions which emerged were as follows. First, a large proportion of the students surveyed considered that a high degree of personal freedom in carrying out one's job was the most important attribute they would look for in choosing their career. They did not think that they would find this freedom in the Administrative Class of the Civil Service. As Trevor Smith commented, this is really a mistaken assumption and it reflects a generally inaccurate idea on the part of most students of what is involved in the career of an administrative Civil Servant.

A large section of those surveyed, for example, said they thought the Civil Service was unattractive because of 'red tape'. Many clearly did not think that the Administrative Class gave scope for personal initiative, which in fact it certainly does. Smith and Lawrence linked their findings on this question with an analysis of the social background of the students they surveyed. They found that the parents of only 49 per cent of the students in their sample were in the Registrar General's classification of social class I or II. Only 7 per cent had at least one parent who was a graduate and only 16 per cent had been to a boarding or direct grant school. By contrast Oxford and Cambridge have a much higher proportion of students from upper-middle and middle class homes, and from homes where one or both parents are graduates, and they have a much higher proportion of students who have attended a boarding or direct grant school. Smith's argument is that in these milieux more encouragement is given to young men and women to try for the Administrative Class of the Civil Service. There is a self-

[1] H.C. 308 of 1964–5, especially pp. 199–219.

perpetuating factor, in that as Administrative Civil Servants have, in the past, been drawn predominantly from the higher social classes, from graduates of Oxford and Cambridge, and from boarding schools or 'independent' grammar schools, the role of the Administrative Class is better understood in these sectors of the population.

The second interesting finding that emerged from their survey was that a large proportion of students at Hull want to enter a profession in which their degree knowledge will be fully used. The Administrative Civil Service scores poorly here because of the system of recruiting for the Home Civil Service in general, rather than for specific departments. The authors suggested, for example, that graduates in social administration would be more likely to try for the Administrative Class if they knew they would be going for positions in one of the social service ministries instead of taking 'pot luck' in the whole Home Civil Service.[1]

Finally, the survey showed that a high proportion of students do not want to spend the whole of their working lives in London. This applies to students from Southern England only slightly less than to those from the North. The 'Great Wen' is perhaps at last beginning to repel rather than to attract the intellect of the nation. To the extent then that departments are successful in moving out of London, the Civil Service Commission's task in recruiting may be made easier.

The survey covered only students at Hull and there is a clear need for similar surveys to be made at other civic universities. It is likely that the results would not be very different since the social composition of students at other civic universities is generally similar to that at Hull. But the survey needs to be made. The Estimates Committee recognized this and also recommended that the whole question of recruitment to the Civil Service should be thoroughly investigated. They proposed that 'A Committee of officials, aided by members from outside the Civil Service, on the lines of the Plowden Committee, should be appointed to initiate research upon, to examine and to report upon the structure, recruitment and management of the Civil Service'.[2] The Wilson Government accepted this recommendation and in February 1966 announced the appointment

[1] H.C. 308 of 1964–5, p. 233.   [2] H.C. 308 of 1964–5, p. xxxv.

of a strong committee with these terms of reference under the chairmanship of Lord Fulton, the Vice-Chancellor of the University of Sussex. The committee initially comprised four senior Civil Servants, two M.P.s (Sir Edward Boyle and Mrs. Shirley Williams), two academics (Norman Hunt and Lord Simey), two business men, and the general secretary of the National and Local Government Officers' Association.

The Estimates Committee was concerned to know why more students from the civic universities do not compete for the Administrative Class. This is an important question. Equally important is the question why more of those who compete do not succeed. The success rate for civic universities is regularly much lower than for Oxford and Cambridge. In the years 1957–63, taking the Method II competition alone, there were 1,749 candidates from Oxford and Cambridge. Of these, 260 were successful. In the same period there were 841 candidates from other universities, and of these only 33 were successful. The picture in relation to Method I is similar. 135 out of 523 Oxford or Cambridge entrants were successful in this period, while only 34 out of 406 from other universities succeeded.[1]

How are we to explain the greater success, on average, of Oxbridge students? One can rule out the idea that the academic standard is higher at Oxford and Cambridge. The fact is that in some fields the two older universities have outstanding teachers and scholars and well-thought-out courses, while in others they fall well behind many of the good departments at other universities both in arts and sciences. But while the academic standard is not higher at Oxford and Cambridge, as far as the formal side of university education goes, the undergraduate at the ancient universities enjoys numerous advantages on the informal side. The collegiate system, the life of the common-room, the varied and vigorous university societies provide, for those who want it, a more stimulating intellectual atmosphere than is generally found at civic universities. It is these things which help the Oxford and Cambridge man, or woman, to acquire a lively interest in things outside his degree curriculum and to show just that adaptability and many-sidedness which is likely to help him shine in the Method II examination.

[1] H.C. 308 of 1964–5, p. 29.

The answer for the civic universities is not to provide a slavish imitation of the Oxford and Cambridge system, but to help to enhance the quality of life on the campus in all ways that are appropriate. Much is already being done, by giving greater emphasis to tutorials and seminars, to increase the opportunities for contact between students and staff. The building of halls of residence is also valuable. Equally important is the encouragement of student societies. Here it should be remembered that many civic universities are much more remote from London than Oxford or Cambridge are and find it harder to attract good visiting speakers. Universities should then make generous grants to student societies, and particularly to party and non-party political societies, to enable them to pay the expenses of visiting speakers. University staffs could also, generally speaking, do much more than they do at present to encourage their abler students to compete in the Administrative Class examinations.

It is to be noted that, since the Estimates Committee Report in 1965, candidates from civic universities have improved their success rating. In 1965, of the successful candidates in examinations for the Administrative Class, 24 per cent were from civic universities, 78 per cent from Oxford and Cambridge. In 1966, of those successful, 35 per cent were from civic universities, 65 per cent were from Oxford and Cambridge. But in 1966 more than 50 per cent of the candidates were from the civic universities.[1]

Another way to widen the field of recruitment to the Administrative Class would be to attract more women entrants. Government service is in general a good employer of women. Equal pay for men and women was introduced in 1961 for the Home Civil Service and the Foreign Service. Women have already reached some of the highest ranks in the Civil Service. Two women have achieved the rank of Permanent Secretary: Dame Evelyn Sharp was Permanent Secretary at the Ministry of Housing and Local Government, as was Dame Mary Smieton at the Ministry of Education. The Civil Service is also reasonably enlightened in the employment of married women. For example, married women are encouraged to continue their careers by the provision of generous maternity leaves. But married women who leave the Service are not reinstated if they

[1] Civil Service Commission Annual Report, 1966, p. 8.

have been away for more than seven years (or for a shorter period, if their previous service was less than seven years). The Estimates Committee recommended in 1965 that this rule should be changed so as to bring back more married women into the Service.[1] The Civil Service clearly could also do much more to publicize the relatively good conditions which it provides for women.

Training Administrative Civil Servants

We have seen that Chapman has proposed that Britain should adopt something like the French system of training Administrative Civil Servants. In France in October 1945, the decision was made to set up a National School of Administration (*École Nationale d'Administration*). This school organizes 29-month courses which every entrant to the administrative class must follow. In the first year some students are sent to work in the office of a provincial Prefect where their task is to find out as much as possible about administration in the field and about conditions in the provinces. Other students spend their first year working in an embassy. In the second year they all attend lectures and seminars which are given by university teachers or by senior Civil Servants or senior officials of nationalized industries. Some of the courses given are specialized, others are more general, dealing, for example, with aspects of industrial economics or administrative law.

At the end of this first academic period, which lasts ten months, students are sent for two months to acquire experience in the administration of an industrial or commercial company or of a bank. They then study, for five months, in seminars, a variety of social questions and topical administrative problems. This is a very well devised system which gives the student administrator an admirable combination of experience and theoretical training. What is more, the practical experience gained is not only of the working of the machinery of government both at central and local level, but also of the administration of business or industry.[2]

[1] H.C. 308 of 1964–5, p. xxxi.
[2] For an account of the *École Nationale d'Administration*, as organized in 1958, see Brian Chapman, *The Profession of Government* (Allen & Unwin, 1959), pp. 114–24.
See also F. Ridley and J. Blondel, *Public Administration in France* (Routledge and Kegan Paul, 1964), pp. 31–43, and H. Parris, 'Twenty Years of *L'École Nationale d'Administration*' in *Public Administration*, Winter 1965, pp. 395–411.

The British system of training compares very unfavourably with that of the *École Nationale d'Administration*. The long-established practice in Britain has been for the newly appointed Assistant Principal, who has just entered the Civil Service through the Method I or II examination, to be put in the care of a Principal who is in charge of one branch of the affairs of a department. The Assistant Principal works with him, learning, 'on the job', how business can be handled and policy formulated and applied. He will be moved around a little, working with more than one Principal during his spell as an Assistant Principal, and possibly having a period in the Minister's private office. But it remains true that the training he receives is very narrow. It is confined to only small sections of the whole machinery of central government. It does not provide experience in local government, industry, the nationalized industries, or the trade unions. Until recently it did not include any provision for the systematic academic study either of the problems of government as a whole or of the specialisms with which an Assistant Principal's own Ministry is concerned.

The deficiencies of the British system of training are slowly being recognized and since the Second World War a start has been made to improve matters. The Treasury began by organizing a three-week course on the structure of government for Assistant Principals in their first year. Speaking to a conference on 'The Study and Teaching of Public Administration' in 1961, Sir Maurice Dean, then Permanent Under-Secretary for Air, recognized that this was not enough. He suggested that Assistant Principals should go to a university for one term 'perhaps after two years in a department, to study public administration in an academic setting'.[1]

This idea was in part acted upon in 1963. A Centre for Administrative Studies was set up in London and began to receive its first students in October of that year. In 1965 the Centre was providing two sets of courses. All Assistant Principals in the Home Civil Service were attending a three-week course at the Centre after six months' service in a Government department. The subject of this course was the Structure of Government and it comprised the structure and problems of local govern-

[1] Sir Maurice Dean, 'The Public Servant and the Study of Public Administration' in *Public Administration*, Spring 1962, pp. 17–28.

ment, parliamentary procedure, financial control, the preparation and progress of legislation, and a few sessions dealing with aspects of administrative law. The second set of courses lasted for twenty weeks and was attended by all Assistant Principals in their third year of service. About 60 per cent of the time in this course was given to economics, about 15 per cent to statistics and the remaining 15 per cent to the relations of government and industry, both in the nationalized and the private sectors. The permanent staff of the Centre at that time consisted of three Administrative Civil Servants, but numerous lectures and seminars in the courses were given by visiting lecturers from the universities.[1]

These courses are valuable innovations, but they do not radically change the traditional system of training. This is still largely based on apprenticeship, on 'learning on the job'. The inadequacy of the system is the more apparent when one considers the academic background of those Assistant Principals who have entered the Civil Service from the universities. A high percentage of those successful in the Method I and Method II examinations have studied Classics or History. Relatively few have studied Economics or Politics. This contrasts sharply with the French practice by which nearly all entrants to the National School of Administration have studied at institutes of political science.

There may be advantages in retaining the British practice of recruiting Administrative Civil Servants from the ablest graduates whatever their field of study. But once recruited surely they should be helped at once to acquire some knowledge of government and the social sciences and some grasp of the specialisms with which their department is dealing? A three-week course in government and twenty weeks on economics and statistics is not going to go very far to do this. What is needed is at least a two-year course of training which should be provided, as soon as practicable, for all entrants to the Administrative Class. Such a course should include both theory and practice.

On the theory side, it should comprise the study of adminis-

[1] See C. D. E. Keeling, 'Treasury Centre for Administrative Studies', in *Public Administration*, Summer 1965, pp. 191–8. (This is an account of the work of the Centre by its first Director).

trative, economic, and social questions together with studies in the specialized fields with which the relevant departments have to deal. For example, trainee administrators in the Ministry of Health should study aspects of social medicine. Those entering the Ministry of Education should follow courses in educational theory and method.

On the practical side, experience should be provided in different divisions of the Ministry concerned (and in some cases of other Ministries), in a local authority, in a nationalized industry, in private industry, and in a trade union. Assistant Principals in departments which have regional offices or out-stations, such as labour exchanges or the local offices of the Ministry of Pensions and National Insurance, should work for a period there too. Those in the Ministry of Health should spend some time with hospital boards and in the hospitals themselves. Assistant Principals in the Ministry of Defence should spend some time at the Staff College and in training establishments of the armed services.

It would be highly desirable to have all the studies, both practical and theoretical, under the general supervision of the Centre for Administrative Studies. Assistant Principals would be required to furnish to the Centre reports on all the various phases of their course, both practical and theoretical. The Centre would, on its side, keep a record of the progress and standard of trainees.

It is highly probable that the introduction of a two-year training course of this type would improve recruitment to the Administrative Civil Service. For one thing an entrant would have to choose a department or group of departments. The survey made by Smith and Lawrence indicates that most students would prefer to do this. For another, good students have had their appetite whetted for further study when they come to the end of their first degree course. They would, therefore, be attracted by a training course which would provide opportunities for further study coupled with interesting experience in different kinds of organization, inside and outside government service. The idea of training on the job under the guidance of a few Principals, of varying ability and enthusiasm, is far less attractive.

Another advantage of a two-year training course is that it

would increase the number who could be taken in each year to the Administrative Class. We have seen that, under the existing system, the Commissioners have frequently not filled all the vacancies. With a training course, it would be possible for them to be less cautious and take in more people, since some of the candidates who seemed diffident, and not altogether impressive, at the Method II examination, or in the interview, would prove their ability during the course.

There is little doubt that a two-year training course would prove its worth. The time has passed when a first degree course in Classics, or English, followed by training on the job, is enough to equip the average Administrative Civil Servant for the work he will have to do. The scope of Government service is now too large, and the problems with which it has to deal too specialized, for policy questions to be sifted by highly intelligent, but haphazardly trained, general administrators.

The Treasury

Standing at the centre of the machinery of administration is the Treasury. This department has always had a key role in government, but its functions have increased very markedly since 1939. Before 1939 it had three main tasks: preparation of the budget, control of departmental estimates, and control of staffing in the departments. To these functions were added, during and after the Second World War, the conduct of negotiations in overseas finance, and the planning of economic policy as a whole. In 1954 the Treasury was organized in five 'sides'—Economic Affairs, Supply, Home Finance, Overseas Finance, and Establishments—with the heads of all the 'sides' responsible through a single Permanent Secretary to the Chancellor of the Exchequer. Its organization, at that time, was the subject of an extended study by an American scholar, Samuel H. Beer, who came away with the impression that the Treasury was working well, combining effectively its new functions in the sphere of planning and overseas finance with its traditional functions in the control of supply, the budget, and establishments.[1]

Stresses and strains were, however, soon to appear. The first change, made in 1956, was not primarily a result of overloading in the Treasury. In the autumn of that year, the single Perma-

[1] Samuel H. Beer, *Treasury Control* (Clarendon Press, 1956).

nent Secretary of the Treasury was replaced by two Joint Permanent Secretaries. One of them, Sir Roger Makins, was put in charge of Home Finance, Overseas Finance, Supply, and Economic Affairs. The other, Sir Norman Brook, was made Head of the Civil Service and put in charge of Establishments, but continued also to be Secretary of the Cabinet. The principal object of this strange re-organization was to keep Sir Norman Brook as Secretary of the Cabinet, where the Government found his services invaluable, while not denying him the position of Head of the Civil Service which is accorded to the Permanent Secretary of the Treasury.[1] A subsidiary object was to share out the burden of running the Treasury between the two Joint Permanent Secretaries. Here, lopping off Establishments was not very successful, since control of Establishments remained intermingled with control of Supply which was still the responsibility of the other Joint Permanent Secretary.

A more rational and thorough re-organization followed in 1962. This had been preceded in 1958 by a report of the Estimates Committee, on Treasury Control, which led to the setting up in 1959 of a small committee composed partly of Treasury officials and partly of outsiders.[2] This committee, under the Chairmanship of Lord Plowden, reported in 1961.[3] The 1962 re-organization implemented many of the Plowden recommendations although the changes made at the highest level had not been suggested by the committee. The association of the Secretary of the Cabinet with the Treasury was now ended. The new Secretary to the Cabinet, Sir Burke Trend, was given no other function besides looking after the Cabinet Office. One of the two Joint Permanent Secretaries of the Treasury, Sir Lawrence Helsby, was made responsible for the Management side of the Treasury. The other, William Armstrong, was given responsibility for the Financial and Economic sides.

Within each Joint Permanent Secretary's sphere of control, very considerable organizational changes were made. The

[1] See D. N. Chester, 'The Treasury, 1956' in *Public Administration*, Spring 1957, pp. 15–23 and D. N. Chester and F. M. G. Willson, *The Organization of British Central Government* (Allen and Unwin, 1957), pp. 338–40.

[2] H.C. 254-I of 1957–8. Sixth Report from the Select Committee on Estimates. Treasury Control of Expenditure.

[3] Cmnd. 1432. Control of Public Expenditure. Report of the Plowden Committee.

Management side was sub-divided into a Pay and Conditions of Service group and a Management group. This differed from the old Establishments organization in that pay and conditions of service questions were no longer shared with the Supply side of the Treasury, the old mixed joint Supply and Establishment divisions having been abolished. The Joint Permanent Secretary (Management) was made, therefore, fully master in his own house, which the Joint Permanent Secretary (Establishments) had not been between 1956 and 1962. Another significant change was the creation of a distinct Management group, under his control, the emergence of this group indicating, as the Plowden Committee recommended, an increased emphasis on management techniques.

On the Financial and Economic sides the changes were also far-reaching. The old Home Finance and Overseas Finance sides were combined into one Financial and Monetary group under a Second Secretary. The old Supply side was transformed and emerged as the Public Expenditure and Resources group, also under a Second Secretary. It was transformed not only by taking away all Establishments functions, but also through the acceptance of the Plowden Committee's recommendations that 'decisions involving substantial future expenditure should always be taken in the light of surveys of public expenditure as a whole, over a period of years, and in relation to the prospective resources'.[1] Responsibility for making such surveys was given to a special division called the Public Expenditure Surveys division. Alongside this division within the Public Expenditure Group were five divisions dealing with the major blocks of expenditure: on defence; on the social services; on agriculture, towns, and transport; on public enterprises; on arts and science. Finally, the National Economy Group, under a Third Secretary who reported directly to the Joint Permanent Secretary, was concerned with the balance of the national economy as a whole, dealing with short-term economic trends, long-term reviews of resources, problems of economic growth, and incomes policy.

This re-organization, carried through in 1962, certainly created a more rational pattern in the Treasury than had existed before. But the criticism was heard that it was still trying

[1] Cmnd. 1432, p. 5, para. 7.

to combine too many functions. Harold Wilson, when Leader of the Opposition, said in 1964 that in his view economic planning should be the function of a separate department distinct from the Treasury. He favoured this course for three main reasons. First, the Treasury was overloaded. Some Chancellors of the Exchequer had been made physically ill by the impossible burden. Second, the Treasury tended to become obsessed with balance of payments difficulties. This was a proper Treasury concern but it too often resulted in the whole Treasury being pervaded 'with the idea that we must hold down production'. Third, because of its widespread responsibilities, the Treasury 'had not been doing its traditional job of economizing and cutting out waste'.[1]

The Department of Economic Affairs

On forming a government in October 1964, Wilson was able to act on these ideas. A new Ministry, the Department of Economic Affairs, was set up under George Brown. The Department was organized into four groups: Economic Planning, Industrial Policy, Economic Co-ordination, and Regional Policy. Economic Planning was headed by Sir Donald Mac-Dougall who came from the National Economic Development Council where he had been economic director. The head of the Industrial Policy Division was H. F. R. Catherwood, himself an industrialist. The function of this Division was to work closely with industry in trying to promote efficiency and economic growth. The Economic Co-ordination group was put in charge of a senior official from the Treasury, D. A. V. Allen. It was concerned with the application of the prices and incomes policy, with the relationship of public expenditure programmes to the use of resources and economic growth and efficiency, and with the implementation of the growth plan. The Regional Policy Group was put under the direction of a senior Civil Servant who had been transferred from the Home Office, A. W. Peterson. This group was responsible for regional policy and planning—both economic and physical. It was also responsible for co-ordinating the work of the economic planning boards set up in the regions.

[1] Harold Wilson in a conversation with Norman Hunt printed in *Whitehall and Beyond* (BBC Publications, 1964), pp. 16–17.

The creation of the Department of Economic Affairs meant that the Treasury lost some of its responsibility for economic planning, although it continued to be concerned with economic policy in relation to financial policy. Close liaison was maintained between the Treasury and the Department of Economic Affairs on those subjects which required joint action or planning. This liaison was not only at ministerial level. The senior officials concerned at the two Ministries, Sir William Armstrong (Treasury) and Sir Eric Roll (Economic Affairs), set up a joint committee. But the Department of Economic Affairs was recognized to be the main co-ordinating ministry in economic questions. This was exemplified by the fact that George Brown became Chairman of the National Economic Development Council. This was a position which had been held in the previous Conservative government by the Chancellor of the Exchequer.

The N.E.D.C. (Neddy) continued to be a high-powered advisory body to the Government. It also was the main arena in which Ministers could meet leading industrialists, trade unionists, and heads of nationalized industries. The Wilson Government added a new member, the head of the newly created National Board for Prices and Incomes, Aubrey Jones. The N.E.D.C. continued to have the help of its permanent staff in the National Economic Development Office, headed by Sir Robert Shone.[1] This Office, in its turn, had representatives on all the Economic Development Committees (Little Neddies) set up for industries or groups of industries.

The pattern of organization in the Department of Economic Affairs, established in the winter of 1964–5, continued without any major modification until August, 1967. In August 1966, Michael Stewart took George Brown's place at the head of the Department, but the internal organization remained much the same. In August 1967, the Prime Minister, Harold Wilson, announced that he was himself taking over responsibility for the Department, but that its day-to-day administration would be carried on under the oversight of Peter Shore as Secretary of State for Economic Affairs. Shore became a member of the Cabinet. At the same time, some of the functions which the

---

[1] In April 1966 Sir Robert Shone resigned and was replaced by H. F. R. Catherwood from the Department of Economic Affairs.

Department had acquired, notably in the field of co-ordination of overseas economic policy, were transferred to the Board of Trade.

It was known that ever since October 1964 the Prime Minister had been the final co-ordinator of economic policy. The changes made in August 1967 indicated that he was taking more direct control of this sector of government. Significantly, he also became Chairman of N.E.D.C., a step which had been advocated since September 1966 by the Confederation of British Industry.

To sum up, it would be inaccurate to see the Department of Economic Affairs as merely hiving off from the Treasury the function of economic planning. It is certainly the chief ministry for economic co-ordination and planning. But it has also developed new fields and new forms of government organization. The creation of regional economic planning boards, for example, has brought together the chief government officials in each region and facilitated more effective regional planning than was possible before. The parallel creation of economic planning councils in the regions has brought in industrialists, trade unionists, local councillors, and university and other experts to advise on the formulation and implementation of regional plans. This is a new level of governmental organization, standing mid-way between the central government and the local authority, but without necessarily detracting from the functions of the latter.[1] It could be a most fruitful development, making possible both a degree of devolution from Whitehall and the emergence, in time, of effective centres of regional government.

For Reference

Sir D. Allen, 'The Department of Economic Affairs' in *The Political Quarterly*, 1967.

BBC Publications, *Whitehall and Beyond* (1964).

S. H. Beer, *Treasury Control* (Clarendon Press, 1956).

Lord Bridges, *The Treasury* (Allen & Unwin, 1964).

S. Brittan, *The Treasury under the Tories, 1951–64* (Penguin, 1964).

[1] See Frank Stacey, 'Regionalism and the Economic Planning Councils' in *The Municipal Review*, November 1965, pp. 662–4.

For a differing view see Brian C. Smith, *Regionalism—3. The New Regional Machinery* (Acton Society Trust, 1965).

B. CHAPMAN, *British Government Observed* (Allen and Unwin, 1963).

B. CHAPMAN, *The Profession of Government* (Allen and Unwin, 1959).

D. N. CHESTER and F. M. G. WILLSON, *The Organization of British Central Government* (Allen and Unwin, 1957).

C. H. DODD, 'Recruitment to the Administrative Class 1960–64' in *Public Administration*, 1967.

F. DUNNILL, *The Civil Service. Some Human Aspects* (Allen and Unwin, 1956).

C. D. E. KEELING, 'Treasury Centre for Administrative Studies' in *Public Administration*, 1965.

W. J. M. MACKENZIE and J. W. GROVE, *Central Administration in Britain* (Longmans, 1957).

R. MUIR, *How Britain is Governed* (Constable, 1930).

H. PARRIS, 'Twenty Years of L'École Nationale d'Administration' in *Public Administration*, 1965.

J. F. PICKERING, 'Recruitment to the Administrative Class 1960–64: Part 2' in *Public Administration*, 1967.

F. RIDLEY and J. BLONDEL, *Public Administration in France* (Routledge and Kegan Paul, 1964).

W. A. ROBSON (ed.), *The Civil Service in Britain and France* (Hogarth Press, 1956).

P. SELF, 'The Education of Administrators' in *The Political Quarterly*, 1967.

C. H. SISSON, *The Spirit of British Administration*, 2nd ed. (Faber, 1966).

Annual Reports of H.M. Civil Service Commissioners.

Cmnd. 232, Recruitment to the Administrative Class of the Home Civil Service and the Senior Branch of the Foreign Service. Statement of Government Policy and Report by the Civil Service Commission. 1957.

Cmnd. 1432, Control of Public Expenditure. Report of the Plowden Committee.

H.C. 308 of 1964–5, Sixth Report from the Estimates Committee. Recruitment to the Civil Service.

CHAPTER XVI

Administrative Tribunals

A SYSTEM of administration should not only be efficient: it should also be fair. To ensure that departments do give fair treatment to the citizen it is essential that there should be provision for fair-minded adjudication of disputes between the citizen and the State. In so far as such adjudication is found in Britain, it is provided partly by the ordinary courts of law and partly by administrative tribunals.

The common law courts act as a check upon abuse of power by the executive, but only in strictly limited ways. They can rule, for example, upon the question of whether or not the Minister (meaning usually, of course, the Civil Servant acting in his name) is acting within the powers conferred upon him by statute or regulation. If he is not, if he is acting '*ultra vires*', then the Minister's action is unlawful and the court will find for the citizen and against the Minister. Similarly, the courts can require, in many cases, a central department or a local authority to carry out a duty or a function which is clearly laid down by statute. The order which a court makes to require an authority to perform its lawful functions is known as an order of 'mandamus', having been developed from an ancient prerogative writ of this name.

But by far the greatest number of disputes between central departments and the citizen are decided by administrative tribunals. Thus, someone who is dissatisfied by the decision of a local office of the Ministry of Social Security about his entitlement to a grant in the National Insurance Scheme, may appeal to the Local National Insurance Tribunal. There are 202 such tribunals in Great Britain, one for every National Insurance Area. In 1965 they considered 30,581 appeals. If the Local Tribunal finds against the citizen, he may, in certain cases, appeal to the National Insurance Commissioner. The Commissioner, or one of his eight deputy Commissioners, heard 1,676 appeals in 1965.

Someone who is dissatisfied with the amount of Supplementary Benefit accorded him, may appeal to his local Supplementary Benefits Tribunal. There are 152 such tribunals in Britain, and in 1965 they decided 9,582 cases.[1] Anyone who has a complaint against a doctor, dentist, chemist, or optician in the National Health Service can make his complaint to his local Executive Council. There are 159 Executive Councils in Britain and in 1965 they dealt with 1,134 complaints. In the field of Income Tax, the eight Special Commissioners who hear appeals under Section 8 of the Income Tax Act, 1952, dealt with 2,567 appeals in 1965. These are only examples and by no means an exhaustive list of administrative tribunals in this country.[2] But they illustrate the wide range of tribunals now in existence and the extensive use which is made of them by the public.

Dicey's Opposition to Administrative Tribunals

These tribunals have not, however, developed in any really systematic fashion. They are an accretion rather than a well thought out system. Indeed, until recently, any systematic overhaul of the role and organization of administrative tribunals was hampered by the tendency among influential lawyers to view the very existence of administrative tribunals with distaste. This attitude stems from the teaching of A. V. Dicey in his lectures on the Law of the Constitution first given at Oxford in the 1880s.[3] Dicey maintained that administrative tribunals were incompatible with the rule of law. He argued that in Britain 'there can be with us nothing really corresponding to the 'administrative law' (*droit administratif*) or the 'administrative tribunals' (*tribunaux administratifs*) of France. The notion that lies at the bottom of the 'administrative law' known to foreign countries is that affairs or disputes in which the government or its servants are concerned are beyond the sphere of the civil courts and must be dealt with by special and more or less official bodies. This idea is utterly unknown to the law of England, and, indeed, is fundamentally inconsistent with our

---

[1] In 1965 they were still known as National Assistance Tribunals.

[2] Appendix C of the Annual Report of the Council on Tribunals for 1965 gives a full list of the Tribunals which have been placed under its supervision and gives, in most cases, the number of appeals dealt with by each type of tribunal during the year.

[3] A. V. Dicey, *The Law of the Constitution*, 10th ed. (Macmillan, 1959), especially Part II, the Rule of Law.

traditions and customs.'[1] This sort of reasoning was, by and large, reproduced by Lord Hewart in his book, *The New Despotism*, published in 1929.[2]

The Dicey view was based upon two fundamental misconceptions, first about the nature of administrative justice in France and other continental countries, and second about the ability of the ordinary courts of law in Britain to cope with the whole range of disputes between the citizen and the State. W. A. Robson in his study *Justice and Administrative Law*, first published in 1928, had early on exposed these misconceptions.[3] But it was not until 1954 with the publication of C. J. Hamson's *Executive Discretion and Judicial Control* that the inaccuracy of Dicey's description of the French *Conseil d'État* was fully appreciated.[4] Dicey had maintained that an administrative court, like the *Conseil d'État*, was bound to be less favourable to the citizen and to give less effective redress against State officials than was given in Britain by the common law courts. In fact, Hamson was able to show that the *Conseil d'État* had a long tradition of fairness toward the individual appellant, and that it gave, in many cases, much more effective redress to the individual than is given in Britain by the common law courts. In particular, Hamson pointed out that the *Conseil d'État*, as an adjudicating body within the executive and consisting in part of lawyers and in part of administrators, is able to command the production of documents by Ministries, and to rule upon the exercise of ministerial discretion, in a way which is not attempted by the British common law courts.

The Advantage of Administrative Tribunals

The inadequacy of the common law courts to take on all the cases considered by administrative tribunals became increasingly obvious after 1945. Extensive use had been made of

---

[1] Ibid., p. 203.

[2] Rt. Hon. Lord Hewart of Bury, *The New Despotism* (Benn, 1929).

[3] W. A. Robson, *Justice and Administrative Law*, 3rd edition (Stevens, 1951).

[4] C. J. Hamson, *Executive Discretion and Judicial Control. An Aspect of the French* CONSEIL D'ÉTAT' (Stevens, 1954). In his introduction to the 8th edition of *The Law of the Constitution*, published in 1915, Dicey did acknowledge the existence of administrative tribunals in Britain and implied that in certain circumstances they might be more appropriate than the ordinary law courts. He did not, however, modify the main text of his book.

administrative tribunals in the inter-war years, and, indeed, from well before the First World War. But the passage of the National Insurance and National Insurance (Industrial Injuries) Acts of 1946, the National Assistance Act of 1948, the National Health Service Act of 1946, and the Town and Country Planning Act of 1947, to name only some of the Acts of this period giving powers of adjudication to Ministers, brought a large increase in the number of cases dealt with by administrative tribunals. Nor was it only a question of the volume of business. Administrative tribunals had proved to have certain advantages over the common law courts. These advantages can be summed up under three headings: cheapness to the appellant, the informality and intelligibility of proceedings, and the possession of specialized knowledge by members of the tribunals.

Appeal to many tribunals, in fact, costs the appellant nothing. Indeed, if someone appeals to a Local National Insurance Tribunal, not only is there no charge, but he is allowed to claim for travelling expenses and for a subsistence allowance, or for compensation for loss of earnings through attendance at the tribunal. If he is able to appeal further to the National Insurance Commissioner, this again need cost him nothing. Similarly, someone who lodges a complaint with a National Health Service Executive Council, against a doctor, dentist, chemist, or optician, has to pay no fee for the hearing of the complaint by the appropriate Service Committee of the Executive Council. If he then appeals to the Minister against the decision of the Executive Council, he may have to pay costs if the Minister's decision goes against him. (In practice, the Minister very rarely awards costs at this stage.)

The simplicity and informality of proceedings is also an attraction to the appellant. Although, since the Franks Report, most tribunals permit him to be legally represented, the atmosphere is not like that of a court of law. The procedure is kept as simple as possible, the chairman aiming to combine fairness with intelligibility and informality.

Finally, it is an advantage that members of tribunals have special knowledge appropriate to the cases which come before them. For example, a Local National Insurance Tribunal consists of a Chairman, who usually has legal knowledge, and one representative of employers and one representative of employees in the locality. Similarly, a Medical Service Committee of an Executive Council consists of the Chairman who is a layman, three other laymen, who may have been appointed either by the local authority or by the Minister, and three general practitioners who are appointed by the local medical committee.[1] To give yet another example, the Ministry's Inspectors, who conduct public hearings of appeals under the Town and Country Planning Acts, are usually architects or have other relevant specialized training. This sort of composition of tribunals helps to ensure that they have, in general, a sound grasp of the issues which are likely to arise and can rapidly and effectively assess the technical arguments put forward by the parties. Where provision is also made for representation of sections of the public, as with the insurance tribunals and the medical service committees, the object is to ensure that some members of the tribunals will be sympathetic to the circumstances of an appellant.

Criticisms and Anxieties

Enough has been said to indicate that many tribunals have over the years proved their effectiveness and popularity. This could not be said, however, of the whole range of administrative tribunals. In the 1950s there was increasing public disquiet about certain types of ministerial tribunal and inquiry.

An example of this was provided by local inquiries into planning appeals. To appreciate the significance of the criticism these inquiries provoked, it is necessary to say something of the nature of planning appeals. Under the Town and Country Planning Acts, the County and County Borough Councils are given authority to give, or withhold, planning permission for any type of proposed new building or development of land. Someone who is refused planning permission by the local authority may appeal to the Minister of Housing and Local Government who sends one of his Inspectors to hear the appeal. The inquiry is held in the locality concerned, and the parties may be represented by counsel.

The actual conduct of the inquiries was not much criticized; indeed it had, and has, many praiseworthy features, particularly

---

[1] The local medical committee is the general practitioners' own representative committee.

the practice of the Inspector visiting the site of any proposed development to make a first-hand inspection. What was much criticized, however, was the fact that when the Inspector had completed his inquiry the text of his report to the Minister was not disclosed. It remained entirely confidential, so that when the Minister announced his decision in the case it was impossible to tell how fair-minded the Inspector had been in conducting the inquiry and whether or not the Minister had concurred with his conclusions. Similar criticisms were voiced in relation to other forms of inquiry concerned with the acquisition of land by public authorities and with inquiries into the development plans of local authorities.

Some forms of tribunal also came under attack. For example, there was criticism of the Rent Tribunals set up under the Furnished Houses (Rent Control) Act of 1946 to fix the rents of furnished flats or houses under a certain rateable value. No provision was made in the Act for appeal from a decision of a Rent Tribunal, apart from the very limited appeal which lies from any tribunal to the High Court on the basis of *ultra vires*, or failure to observe natural justice in hearing a case. Some cases which reached the High Court showed up defects in the procedure of certain Rent Tribunals.[1]

There was also a more general disquiet about the lack of system in the organization of administrative tribunals, and a feeling that there might be defects in other tribunals of the kind that had been revealed in the Rent Tribunals. The time was ripe for an official inquiry, but, strangely enough, the immediate cause of the establishment of an inquiry into administrative tribunals was an affair itself unconnected with tribunals. This was the celebrated Crichel Down affair which concerned the refusal of the Ministry of Agriculture to return to its previous owner land that had been requisitioned before the Second World War.[2] This was an exercise of ministerial discretion with which no tribunal was concerned. But the interest in the affair helped to bring to a head public anxieties over ministerial inquiries into the development or acquisition

[1] See the *Paddington Rent Tribunal Case* (1949), *R.* v. *Brighton Rent Tribunal* (1950) and *R.* v. *Kingston-upon-Hull Rent Tribunal* (1949) quoted by C. K. Allen in *Administrative Jurisdiction* (Stevens, 1956), pp. 75–7.

[2] See above, Chapter XI, p. 259.

of land, and increased the concern in some sections of the public about administrative jurisdiction in general.

The Franks Committee Report

The Lord Chancellor set up a powerful committee in November 1955, presided over by Sir Oliver, later Lord, Franks. Franks, originally a university teacher, had been an Administrative Civil Servant during the Second World War and, after the war, had been Provost of Queen's College, Oxford, British Ambassador in Washington, and Chairman of Lloyds Bank. The committee included many very able people, including Dame Florence Hancock, a leading trade unionist; Lord Justice Parker, later to become Lord Chief Justice; a former Labour Minister of Town and Country Planning, Lord Silkin; and the Professor of Government and Administration at Oxford University, Kenneth Wheare. The committee also included three M.P.s—Roderic Bowen and Douglas Johnston, who were also Queen's Counsel, and Major John Morrison. This committee, after extensive hearings, produced a report which is a landmark in the development of administrative tribunals in this country. Its full title is the Report of the Committee on Adminstrative Tribunals and Enquiries of 1957 (Cmnd. 218), but it is commonly known as the Franks Report. The terms of reference of the Committee were:

'To consider and make recommendations on:

(a) The constitution and working of tribunals other than the ordinary courts, constituted under any Act of Parliament by a Minister of the Crown or for the purposes of a Minister's functions.

(b) The working of such administrative procedures as include the holding of an enquiry or hearing by or on behalf of a Minister on an appeal or as the result of objections or representations, and in particular the procedure for the compulsory purchase of land.'[1]

[1] A committee had been set up 26 years before with, in part, similar terms of reference. This was the Committee on Ministers' Powers which was appointed in 1929 and submitted its report (Cmd. 4060) in 1932. This Committee was instructed to inquire into powers exercised by Ministers of the Crown 'by way of (a) delegated legislation and (b) judicial or quasi-judicial decision'. Its report under (b) made no great impact because the need for regularizing and systematizing the position of administrative tribunals had not, as yet, been fully realized. See also above Chapter VIII, pp. 188–95.

The Franks Committee was particularly concerned about the great variety in administrative tribunals as regards both their procedure and their constitution. 'It is no doubt right that bodies established to adjudicate on particular classes of case should be specially designed to fulfil their particular functions and should, therefore, vary widely in character. But the wide variations in procedure and constitution which now exist are much more the result of *ad hoc* decisions, political circumstance and historical accident than of the application of general and consistent principles'.[1] Accordingly the Committee recommended that two standing Councils on Tribunals, one for England and Wales and one for Scotland, should be set up whose function would be to keep under review the constitution and working of existing tribunals. They should also advise on the constitution, organization and procedure of any proposed new types of tribunals.

The Government accepted this recommendation with only minor modification. The Tribunals and Inquiries Act of 1958 set up only one Council on Tribunals, with a Scottish Committee. This adaptation of the Franks suggestion has much to recommend it. Many types of tribunal are identical in constitution and procedure throughout Great Britain; a minority are differently constituted in Scotland. It is also desirable that there should be unity of approach which the device of one Council with a Scottish Committee helps to ensure.

The principal function of the Council on Tribunals is to keep under review the constitution and working of tribunals listed in the First Schedule to the Act of 1958. It is also its function to give advice on new rules of procedure for tribunals and inquiries, and the appropriate rule-making authority, whether the Lord Chancellor, the Secretary of State for Scotland or a departmental Minister, must consult it for this purpose. In carrying out its main function, of supervising the constitution and working of tribunals, the Council can act on its own initiative, or after reference by a member of the public, or by the Lord Chancellor or another Minister.

The principles by which it judges existing, or proposed, tribunals are by and large those laid down in the Franks Report. The Franks Committee recommended that as far as possible all

[1] Cmnd. 218, p. 30 at para. 128.

tribunals should be characterized by 'openness, fairness and impartiality'.[1] Thus, wherever possible, tribunal hearings should be open to the public, although it was recognized that in some cases, for example Medical Service Committee hearings of complaints against doctors, it is desirable to keep hearings private as the professional reputation of the doctor concerned might otherwise be unjustly impaired. Similarly tribunals, such as the National Assistance Tribunals, which were concerned with intimate personal or financial circumstances, could reasonably sit in private.

As regards fairness, the Franks Committee had numerous principles to suggest. They recommended, for example, that the right to legal representation should be conceded in all types of tribunal with only rare exception. They suggested that all tribunals should be required to give reasoned decisions and that appellate tribunals should publish selected decisions and circulate them to lower tribunals. They urged that there should be provision for appeal on fact, law, and merits from all tribunals of first instance to an appellate tribunal, except where the tribunal of first instance is exceptionally strong and well qualified. Examples of such exceptionally well qualified tribunals were the Pensions Appeal Tribunals.

They considered that there should be opportunity to appeal on a point of law to the courts from all tribunals except from the National Insurance Commissioner, the Industrial Injuries Commissioner, and from National Assistance Appeal Tribunals. Their reason for exempting the first two of these is that the Commissioners in these cases are very well qualified people. The National Insurance Acts provide that the Commissioners and their deputies must be barristers or advocates of not less than ten years' standing (and their salaries are in fact higher than those of County Court judges). The Franks Committee's argument in exempting the National Assistance Tribunals is different, being based partly on the view that national assistance questions need to be decided as quickly as possible.[2] But they emphasized that there should be appeal to the courts from all tribunals, without exception, by way of certiorari. This is the procedure whereby the courts can quash the decision of a

[1] Cmnd. 218 esp. p. 5 at para. 23.
[2] Cmnd. 218, p. 42 at para. 182.

tribunal on the grounds that it has acted *ultra vires* or has failed to observe the principles of natural justice—for example, by refusing to hear one party to the case.

As regards inquiries, perhaps the Committee's most important recommendation was that Inspectors' reports to the Minister should be published. They also recommended that in land acquisition or development inquiries, the local authority should be required to make a full statement of their case before the inquiry so that objectors would have the opportunity of knowing the arguments which they would have to contest. Under the heading of impartiality, the Committee was concerned that members of tribunals should, as far as possible, be independent of the Ministry with whose affairs they were concerned. They therefore recommended that chairmen of tribunals should be appointed by the Lord Chancellor and that members of tribunals should be appointed by the Council on Tribunals.[1] They also recommended that all chairmen of tribunals exercising appellate functions should have legal qualifications and that chairmen of tribunals of first instance should ordinarily have legal qualifications.[2]

Implementation of the Report

These are some of the principal recommendations of the Franks Committee selected from a comprehensive and detailed Report. How far have these recommendations been implemented? The Government accepted the Committee's recommendation that the Lord Chancellor should appoint chairmen of tribunals. They did not accept its suggestion that the Council on Tribunals should appoint members of tribunals. As regards inquiries, Departmental Circulars have put into effect many of the most important recommendations of the Franks Committee. For example, local authorities have been told to give a full statement of their case for development, or compulsory purchase, before an inquiry. Inspectors' reports of such inquiries are now published and their reports of planning appeal inquiries are disclosed to the parties concerned, that is to the appellant and to the local authority.

On the question of provision for appeals from tribunals, the

---

[1] Cmnd. 218, pp. 11–12 at paras. 48–54.
[2] Cmnd. 218, p. 12 at para. 55; p. 13 at para. 58.

Tribunals and Inquiries Act of 1958 implements two important recommendations of the Franks Committee. Section 10 seeks to ensure that no tribunal shall be exempt from proceedings by way of prerogative writs. Section 8 provides, as the Franks Committee suggested, that appeal can lie from all tribunals, except from the National Insurance and Industrial Injuries Commissioners and the National Assistance Appeal Tribunal, to the courts on points of law. The Government have not, however, implemented the Franks Committee's suggestion that there should be a right of appeal on merits from Rent Tribunals to a County Court judge sitting with a valuer as assessor. The Council on Tribunals has approved of this omission on the grounds that the Committee's suggestion would mean appeal from an expert to a less expert tribunal and that it would involve undesirable delay.[1]

The Council on Tribunals

The Council on Tribunals has proved an effective body and its Annual Reports have attracted considerable interest. Its chairman until 1967 was Lord Tenby who, as Major Gwilym Lloyd-George, was Home Secretary from 1954 to 1957. After his death in 1967 he was succeeded by Lady Burton of Coventry. Of the other fourteen members in 1967, two were university teachers including Professor H. W. R. Wade, one of the foremost academic authorities on administrative law. Three were leading barristers or solicitors. Three were businessmen. One was a landowner. There was one prominent trade unionist, Lord Collison, of the Agricultural Workers Union. One member, Sir William Murrie, was formerly Permanent Secretary of the Scottish Home Department. All the members of the Council give their services free except for the Chairman who receives a salary. The Council has a small full-time staff, headed by a Secretary, with offices just off Whitehall. The Scottish Committee includes three members of the full Council and four additional members. It has a separate Secretary and offices in Edinburgh.

In general, the Council on Tribunals has received full co-operation from Departments in carrying out its function of

[2] Annual Report of the Council on Tribunals for 1962, pp. 11–12 at para. 50.

supervising tribunals. But it has encountered some difficulties where rules of procedure require hearings in private. Members of the Council regularly visit tribunal hearings to see for themselves whether proceedings are conducted in a fair-minded way. In the case of the Service Committees of the National Health Service Executive Councils, hearings are in private. Until 1965, this meant that members of the Council on Tribunals were only able to attend if the parties to the dispute did not object. In 1965 the Minister of Health issued new regulations which removed this limitation.[1] The position remained unsatisfactory, however, in respect of proceedings before National Insurance Local Tribunals. Regulations provided that when the tribunal were considering their decision, or when questions of procedure were being discussed, only members of the tribunal and the Clerk to the tribunal might be present. This led to the Council's observer being excluded at this stage. The Council recommended in 1964 that the regulations be amended to permit their observer to be present, but it was not until 1966 that the Ministry accepted this recommendation.[2]

Notwithstanding these, on the whole, minor difficulties, the Council on Tribunals has made a considerable impact. It scored a major success on the question of consideration by the Minister of new evidence, or expert opinion, after his Inspector's report on a planning inquiry has been submitted to him. Its attention was drawn to this question by reference from one of the objectors in the well publicized Chalkpit Case. This case, which dragged on from 1958 to 1961, arose from the refusal of Saffron Walden Rural District Council to allow the owners of certain land in Essex to develop it by digging chalk. The owners accordingly appealed to the Minister of Housing and Local Government and a planning inquiry was held in December 1958. At the inquiry, neighbouring landowners objected to the proposal on the ground that the chalk dust would damage their crops and livestock. The Inspector recommended that planning permission should not be given.

In September 1959, however, the Minister announced that

[1] The National Health Service (Service Committees and Tribunal) Amendment Regulations 1965 (S.I. 1965 No. 1366).
See the Annual Report of The Council on Tribunals for 1964, p. 7.

[2] Annual Report of the Council on Tribunals for 1965, p. 2 at para. 6.

Committee recommendations clearly avoided committing this country to a system of administrative law which stood parallel to the system of civil law. In fact, their recommendation that there should, with few exceptions, always be provision for appeal on points of law from administrative tribunals to the ordinary courts helped to ensure that common law principles would be applied in the sphere of administrative jurisdiction. We have seen that the Government accepted this recommendation and that it was embodied in the Tribunals and Inquiries Act, 1958.

An Ombudsman for Britain? The Whyatt Report

It is, then, possibly an objection to the *Conseil d'État* type of machinery that it would, or might, involve creating an entirely separate system of administrative law.[1] This objection does not, however, apply to the Ombudsman. The case for an Ombudsman was well stated in this country in a report, published in 1961, by 'Justice', the British Section of the International Commission of Jurists. This report, entitled *The Citizen and the Administration: The Redress of Grievances*, was prepared by a Committee under the direction of Sir John Whyatt, formerly Chief Justice of Singapore.[2] The Whyatt Report was invaluable not only for its discussion of the case for an Ombudsman but also for its survey of the gaps in the existing provision of administrative tribunals. For example, it pointed out that in the Health Service, while there is a well devised machinery, in the Service Committees of Executive Councils, for considering complaints against general practitioners, there is no system of tribunals for hearing complaints against hospital doctors or administrators.[3]

The Whyatt Committee made the valuable suggestion that the Council on Tribunals should be given the function of pointing to the gaps in the system of tribunals and recommending the creation of new tribunals. The Committee also suggested

[1] For other objections to the adoption of the *Conseil d'État* system in Britain, see below, pp. 399–400.

[2] *The Citizen and the Administration: The Redress of Grievances*, A Report by 'Justice'. (Stevens, 1961).

Another early statement was by T. E. Utley, *Occasion for Ombudsman* (Johnson, 1961).

[3] *The Citizen and the Administration*, p. 19.

that a General Tribunal should be established to hear miscellaneous appeals from discretionary decisions which are not covered by the existing specialized tribunals. This tribunal should, in its opinion, hear appeals against types of discretionary decision which would not be sufficiently frequent to justify establishing a special new tribunal. It instanced, for example, appeals against discretionary decisions refusing permits for vivisection.[1] The General Tribunal would be different from Robson's proposed general administrative appeal tribunal, in that the General Tribunal would hear appeals on discretionary matters not covered by existing tribunals and it would not hear appeals from other tribunals.

The creation of more tribunals to fill present gaps and of a General Tribunal would narrow down the field which would be the responsibility of the Ombudsman. The Whyatt Committee considered that he would be left with complaints about maladministration as distinct from complaints about discretionary decisions by officials. They maintained that complaints against discretionary decisions should, in fact, be a matter for tribunals, while complaints of maladministration should be a matter for the Ombudsman. This distinction, however, is difficult to sustain, as the Committee themselves implied when they said that the Ombudsman may sometimes investigate a decision by an official that is 'so harsh and unreasonable as to offend a sense of justice'.[2] But, in general, they considered that the Ombudsman should be concerned with the abuse of authority over people in confinement (in prisons or mental hospitals, for example), with the abuse of other forms of administrative authority, and with complaints about loss or damage to citizens caused by the inefficiency, negligence or error of officials. However, the distinction which they made between complaints against discretionary decisions and complaints against maladministration was not altogether a wise one. It is not, generally speaking, made in other countries that have an Ombudsman.

It is necessary to describe here the origin of the office of Ombudsman and the different forms that it has taken in Sweden, Denmark, and New Zealand.

[1] op. cit., pp. 31–3.
[2] op. cit., p. 35, at para. 73.

The Swedish Ombudsman

The modern form of Ombudsman in Sweden dates from 1809. The Swedish word '*Ombudsman*' means simply a spokesman or representative, and his function may be thought of as acting as 'people's representative' against harsh and unfair public officials. Until 1915 there was only one Ombudsman who investigated complaints against both civil and military administration. In that year a second Ombudsman was appointed to deal with all military matters, and a civil and a military Ombudsman have since continued to exist side by side. The jurisdiction of the civil Ombudsman is very wide. He can investigate complaints against public officials in both central and local government. Until 1957, the administration of cities was exempt, but in that year, municipal officials were brought under his jurisdiction. He has power to prosecute officials for negligence or maladministration. Normally, of course, he does not resort to prosecution. If he finds a complaint to be justified he recommends to the department concerned that a decision be changed and advises the complainant to make a new approach to the department.

The Ombudsman is appointed by the Parliament (*Riksdag*), and is always a person with a distinguished background, usually a judge. As well as investigating complaints sent to him, he initiates inquiries of his own by going on tours of inspection. In these tours he is concerned particularly with the prisons and mental hospitals, for persons under confinement are thought of, rightly, as needing special protection against the abuse of authority. Similarly, the military Ombudsman visits army camps to look for cases of abuse. Those in confinement or under military authority have a guaranteed right to communicate with the Ombudsman. No prison governor may open a letter sent by a prisoner to the civil Ombudsman, nor may a commanding officer interfere with a letter addressed to the military Ombudsman. The civil Ombudsman has powers over the judiciary. He can call to account magistrates who have abused their powers and can point out that a court has incorrectly applied the law. Both the civil and military Ombudsman have access to official documents.

The Danish Ombudsman

The Ombudsman in Finland has similar powers, but in Denmark, the office differs in a number of ways. It was not established there until 1954. It is modelled on the Swedish pattern but with important differences, which follow from the different constitutional structure of Denmark. In Sweden, the idea of ministerial responsibility for the actions of civil servants had not developed as it had in Denmark. Consequently, it was for long thought that an Ombudsman would not be appropriate for Denmark and, when the idea was accepted, the law establishing the office placed more emphasis on his responsibility to parliament than is given in the Swedish case.

The Danish Ombudsman is responsible to a special committee of parliament. If a Minister appears to him to have committed a civil or criminal offence, he does not prosecute the Minister, but refers the case to the special committee. He also informs this committee of any weakness he discovers in the administration of the law. He has power to direct that officials be prosecuted, but in practice this power is rarely used. Normally it has been sufficient for the Ombudsman to issue a report criticizing the authority concerned, for the departure from fair standards to be corrected.[1] The Danish, unlike the Swedish, Ombudsman has no powers over the judiciary. He can investigate complaints against local government officers on matters 'for which recourse may be had to a central government authority'.

The Parliamentary Commissioner (Ombudsman) in New Zealand
The office of the Ombudsman in Denmark aroused great interest in Britain because it was felt rightly that British constitutional conventions are nearer to those of Denmark than to those of Sweden. For the same reason the Danish pattern seemed more attractive to New Zealand, and in 1962 the New Zealand Parliament established the office of Parliamentary Commissioner, or Ombudsman. The first is his official title according to the Parliamentary Commissioner (Ombudsman) Act, 1962. But the secondary title, Ombudsman, is more frequently used.

The Ombudsman is responsible to Parliament and his

---

[1] For a fuller account of the Ombudsman in Sweden and Denmark, see D. C. Rowat, ed., *The Ombudsman. Citizen's Defender* (Allen and Unwin, 1965), Chapters 1 and 3. See also B. Chapman, *The Profession of Government* (Allen and Unwin, 1959), pp. 245–59, and 'Justice', op. cit., pp. 45–60.

powers are similar to those of the Danish Ombudsman with the following differences. First, he is empowered only to consider complaints against central government departments and national organizations such as the New Zealand Army and the Air Board. He cannot consider complaints against local authorities. Second, his jurisdiction within his allotted sphere is simply and effectively defined by saying that he is not authorized to investigate matters which are susceptible of appeal on merits to a law court or an administrative tribunal.[1] All other matters, in practice, are his concern, including the exercise of discretionary authority where, in his opinion, it has not been exercised in a fair or humane way.

In his report dated 31 March 1963, Sir Guy Powles, the New Zealand Ombudsman wrote: . . . 'Our laws contain provisions empowering Departments or organisations to exercise discretion in individual cases, but I have found that sometimes the Department or organisation follows a firm rule of practice. I am concerned to see that this discretion is genuinely exercised on the merits, as Parliament must have intended when it passed the law in question, although in a large Department delegation is necessary and this creates problems. I have recommended reconsideration in several instances, and this has always been done.'[2]

The Ombudsman instanced, in this report, several cases in which he had recommended that discretionary authority should be differently exercised. These included matters of import licensing, immigration, and social security benefit.[3]

It is apparent that the New Zealand Ombudsman regards it as within his province to consider the use of discretionary authority, and not only in cases where its manner of exercise involves such a high degree of unfairness that it can be called maladministration. The wide authority given to the New Zealand Ombudsman to consider the exercise of discretionary powers stems from the provision in the Act which states that he may report on any administrative decision which is in his opinion 'unreasonable'.[4]

---

[1] New Zealand Statutes 1962 No. 10. *The Parliamentary Commissioner* (*Ombudsman*) *Act*, Section 11, Subsec. 5.

[2] *Report of the Ombudsman for the six months ended 31 March 1963* (R. E. Owen, Government Printer, Wellington, New Zealand), pp. 5 and 6.

[3] op. cit., pp. 8 and 11.

[4] *The Parliamentary Commissioner* (*Ombudsman*) *Act*, 1962, Section 19.

A third difference between the powers of the New Zealand and the Danish Ombudsman lies in the fact that the former cannot initiate a prosecution. The sanction behind his recommendation to a department is that if the department does not give effect to the recommendation, he may report this to the Prime Minister or to Parliament. Despite these differences, the office of Ombudsman in New Zealand is closely modelled on its Scandinavian predecessors. There are numerous similarities of detail, for example, in the provision that any prisoner, or person confined in a mental hospital, may write to the Ombudsman without having his letter opened or delayed by the prison or hospital authorities.[1] This provision is copied directly from Swedish law.

There seemed to be a sound argument for modelling a British Ombudsman on the New Zealand pattern. The New Zealand Ombudsman had been fitted into a parliamentary system of the British type. His terms of reference would be appropriate to British conditions, as would the relationship to Parliament and the administration which has been devised for him. Experience with the Ombudsman in New Zealand had not produced any evidence in support of two of the principal objections to an Ombudsman which had been advanced in discussion in Britain.

First there was the contention that the Ombudsman's investigating role would rival that of M.P.s in their work of interrogating and controlling the administration. In fact, it could be a useful adjunct and support to the work of M.P.s who could not, on their own, deal effectively with the whole body of complaints against the administration.

Second, there was the contention that the Ombudsman's inquiries would unduly harass officials.[2] There was little evidence that this was happening in the Scandinavian countries or in New Zealand. In New Zealand and Denmark experience had shown that the number of complaints every year which were found by the Ombudsman to have been unjustified greatly outnumbered those found to be justified. The New Zealand Ombudsman, for example, reported in March 1963,

---

[1] *The Parliamentary Commissioner (Ombudsman) Act*, 1962, Section 13.
[2] See a statement of this point of view in an article by Brian Chapman, 'The Ombudsman', *Public Administration*, Vol. 38 (1960), pp. 303–10.

that of 117 complaints which he had investigated in the previous six months, he had only found twenty-six that were justified. This, as he pointed out, was a much higher proportion
than those annually found to be justified by the Danish Ombudsman. In 1961, for instance, the Danish Ombudsman found
sixty-four complaints to be justified out of 414 investigated.[1]
In the year ended 31 March 1964, the New Zealand Ombudsman investigated 389 complaints of which he found eighty-one
to be justified.[2] In the majority of cases, therefore, the administration got a clean bill of health after the Ombudsman's
investigation.

The New Zealand Ombudsman reported in May 1964 that
his work had been made easier 'by the willing co-operation
received from Ministers of the Crown, permanent heads of
Government Departments and their officers'. He pointed out
that 'In so far as thorough and independent investigation of
malpractice establishes that those allegations are unfounded,
the Office [of Ombudsman] acts as a valuable shield to the
administration, while at the same time, members of the public
can be assured that any such allegations, if reasonably supported by evidence or inference, will be carefully investigated'.[3]
He was also able to report that in fifty-two of the eighty-one
cases in which he found that the complaint was justified, the
Department concerned 'itself rectified the matter before it was
necessary to complete a full investigation'. In no case, in the
preceding year, had he found it necessary to report to the
House of Representatives that a recommendation had not been
complied with.[4] This seemed to provide strong evidence that
an Ombudsman could be effective and still retain good relations with the administration.[5]

A British Parliamentary Commissioner

The Whyatt Committee reported, in 1961, before the Parliamentary Commissioner Act had been passed in New Zealand.
They were not, therefore, able to draw upon New Zealand

---

[1] *Report of the Ombudsman* (New Zealand) 31 March 1963, p. 5.
[2] *Report of the Ombudsman for the year ended 31 March 1964* (New Zealand Government Printer, 1964), p. 4.
[3] Ibid., p. 5. [4] Ibid., p. 4.
[5] See also J. F. Northey, 'New Zealand's Parliamentary Commissioner' in
Rowat (e.d) op. cit. pp. 127–43.

experience. The Whyatt Committee suggested that the Parliamentary Commissioner should have a position similar to that of the Comptroller and Auditor-General and should be responsible to Parliament. They suggested, however, largely it would seem in order to lessen the fears of some of those who were opposed to an Ombudsman, that his powers should be somewhat hedged about, at any rate at first. They proposed, for example, that the Commissioner should, for an initial period, receive complaints only from Members of Parliament and peers. They proposed that the Commissioner should not have power to compel the production of all documents by the departments, including the internal minutes, but only the correspondence in the case concerned. They also suggested that a Minister should be entitled to veto a proposed investigation. They did not consider that the Commissioner should be empowered to investigate complaints against local authorities.[1]

The Macmillan Government considered these proposals for a year and then decided to turn them down. In November 1962 the Government stated, in a written answer, that it did not intend to set up a Parliamentary Commissioner since it 'would seriously interfere with the prompt and efficient despatch of business', it would not be reconcilable with the principle of Ministerial responsibility and there was, in the Government's view, already adequate provision for the redress of complaints about maladministration through the citizen's right of access to his M.P.[2]

There the matter rested, at least as far as the Conservative Administration was concerned. However, the Labour Opposition took up the idea and in July 1964, Harold Wilson, as Labour Leader, announced that, if a Labour Government was returned at the forthcoming general election, it would set up a Parliamentary Commissioner, broadly on the lines proposed in the Whyatt Report. The proposal was put into the Labour Manifesto and, after Labour's success at the polls in October 1964, the work of planning the necessary legislation began.

In October 1965 the Government produced a White Paper, 'The Parliamentary Commissioner for Administration' (Cmnd 2767), outlining its proposals. The Parliamentary Commissioner

---

[1] 'Justice', op. cit., esp. pp. 79–81.
[2] H.C. Deb. Vol. 666, Col. 1125.

Bill embodying these proposals received its Second Reading in the Commons on 18 October 1966 and became law in March 1967. Sir Edmund Compton, the former Comptroller and Auditor-General, had been appointed to the office of Parliamentary Commissioner in September 1966, before the bill became law, and in April 1967 he began to investigate complaints.

The powers of the Parliamentary Commissioner and his relationship to the House of Commons follow fairly closely on the lines recommended in the Whyatt Report. There are, however, certain important differences. In some ways, his position is much stronger than the position which the Whyatt Committee envisaged for him. For example, the Act gives him access, when investigating a complaint, to all relevant departmental files and does not limit him to the correspondence in the case, as the Whyatt Committee cautiously suggested. The Act does allow a Minister to direct that the Commissioner shall not publish items in the departmental files, but it does not allow the Minister to refuse to open the files to the Commissioner. Again, whereas the Whyatt Committee had proposed that a Minister should be able to veto a proposed investigation by the Commissioner, the 1967 Act gives no such power of veto to a Minister.

We have seen that the Whyatt Committee proposed that, during an initial (possibly five-year) period, complaints should only be submitted to the Commissioner through M.P.s or peers. The Act is more restrictive than this. It provides that complaints can only be submitted through M.P.s and there is no mention of the restriction remaining in force for only a limited period. Peers are not given a look in. The Act does, however, provide that members of the public may ask any M.P. to forward their complaints to the Parliamentary Commissioner. They are not limited to the M.P. who represents their own constituency. At second reading, and during committee stage of the Bill, some M.P.s indicated that they thought this procedure might cause difficulties. Some asked, with reason, why the public should not have direct access to the Parliamentary Commissioner, as well as having access to him through an M.P.

The Parliamentary Commissioner will report to a committee of the House of Commons. In general, his position is similar to

o

that of the Comptroller and Auditor-General. Indeed, during the passage of the bill his status was brought closer to that of the Comptroller. The bill as originally introduced provided that he could only be removed from office 'by Her Majesty in consequence of an Address from the House of Commons'. At Report Stage, an amendment, moved by the Conservatives and supported by the Minister, modified this provision to require an Address from both Houses of Parliament before a Commissioner could be removed. He thus received a security of tenure as complete as that enjoyed by the Comptroller and Auditor-General.

During the passage of the Bill, there was much criticism of the spheres from which the Parliamentary Commissioner is excluded. He may not investigate complaints against local authorities or against nationalized industries. He cannot look at complaints about personnel matters in the armed forces or in the Civil Service. He may not investigate complaints against the police, whether the Metropolitan Police or the local police forces. He cannot consider complaints which arise from the contractual and commercial transactions of government departments. He cannot consider complaints from within the national hospital service.

The Government found itself under attack for every one of these exclusions. Some points, however, can be made in its favour. First, the list of central departments against which the Commissioner can receive complaints is very extensive. In a country with a population of more than 52 million, he is going to have a big task merely dealing with the matters which have been allotted to him. It is significant that Britain is the first large modern state to appoint an Ombudsman. His predecessors are to be found in countries with a relatively small population, from New Zealand with a population of $2\frac{1}{2}$ million to Sweden with a population of $7\frac{1}{2}$ million.

Second, the Minister in charge of the Bill, Richard Crossman, made it clear that he would like to see similar machinery developed for some of the excluded sectors. For example, he spoke of the desirability of having, in time, a Parliamentary Commissioner for the armed forces. Similarly, he hoped that local authorities would develop their own machinery of Ombudsmen. Some M.P.s said, rightly, that this would not be a satisfactory alternative. It is important that a complaint against a local authority should be made to an officer who is quite independent of the authority itself. The case for regional Ombudsmen, who would receive complaints both against local authorities and against many of the central departments, is a very strong one.

Finally, the Commons inserted, at Report Stage and at the Minister's instance, a provision which allows the Queen by Order in Council to remove any of the excluded matters from Schedule 3 of the Act. This means that a government can quite simply bring one of the excluded sectors, for example the hospitals, within the Parliamentary Commissioner's sphere of investigation. The introduction of a statutory instrument, subject only to annulment in either House, will be sufficient to widen the scope of the Act.[1]

The Act follows the Whyatt Report in distinguishing between complaints about maladministration, which are subject to investigation by the Commissioner, and complaints about discretionary decisions not involving maladministration, which he cannot investigate. We have seen that this distinction is not made by the New Zealand Parliamentary Commissioner (Ombudsman) Act which allows the Ombudsman to report on any unreasonable exercise of discretionary power by a government department.

It is regrettable that similar powers were not given to the British Parliamentary Commissioner. His restriction to maladministration can only really be defended on the grounds that it was necessary to limit the number of cases he would have to investigate. But the result of preventing overloading, in this way, is likely to be that very large numbers of complainants will suffer frustration and disappointment when they find that their complaints cannot be taken up, on the grounds that they do not involve 'maladministration'. Much will depend, however, on the way in which the Commissioner interprets the phrase 'injustice in consequence of maladministration' (Clause 5 Subsection (1)(a)). Since these words are not capable of an exact definition, they do leave the Commissioner with considerable scope for widening, or narrowing, his jurisdiction as he thinks fit.

[1] See Parliamentary Commissioner Act, 1967. Clause 5. Subsection (4).

It is important to recall, in this context, that the Whyatt Committee, while recommending that the Commissioner should be confined to questions of maladministration, also proposed that the machinery of administrative tribunals should be enlarged so as to deal effectively with all complaints against discretionary decisions not involving maladministration. Crossman, when introducing the Parliamentary Commissioner Bill at Second Reading, told the Commons that the Government was tackling this second part of the Whyatt Committee's recommendations through its Tribunals and Inquiries Bill.[1] In fact this bill, which became law in December 1966, is a very minor measure which has the effect of bringing certain statutory inquiries, which previously had been outside the scrutiny of the Councils on Tribunals, within its purview. The Act does not give the Council on Tribunals power to recommend the creation of new statutory tribunals, nor does it set up a General Tribunal as the Whyatt Committee also recommended.

The fact that the Wilson Government has not acted upon the Whyatt Committee's recommendations for the widening and strengthening of the machinery of administrative tribunals, leads one to ask how satisfactory is the existing machinery, even when supplemented, as it now is, by the work of the Parliamentary Commissioner. To give a full answer to this question one would need to employ a team of investigators looking at all aspects of the tribunal system. The author has attempted, however, to take one sector within the system, the Health Service, and to look at that in some depth.

A Case Study: Tribunals in the Health Service[2]
There are three branches to the Health Service in Britain: the practitioner services (medical, dental, pharmaceutical and ophthalmic) which are administered by Executive Councils, the hospital service, and the local authority services. The local authority services were not examined as not falling within the ambit of central government. Of the other two services, the practitioner services were taken first since they have a well

[1] H.C. Deb. Vol. 734, Col. 45.
[2] For the fuller study on which this section is based see Frank Stacey, 'The Machinery for Complaints in the National Health Service', *Public Administration*, Spring 1965, pp. 59–70.

developed machinery of statutory tribunals for examining complaints.[1]

On the face of it, the machinery of tribunals in the practitioner services seems to be very fair. Complaints are investigated by the Medical Service Committee, the Dental Service Committee or the Pharmaceutical Service Committee, according to whether the complaint is against a general practitioner, dentist or chemist. There is also an Ophthalmic Investigation Committee which hears complaints against opticians.

Each Service Committee consists of a Chairman (who is always a layman), three members of the profession concerned (appointed by the local medical, dental or pharmaceutical committee), and three laymen. The laymen are drawn either from five laymen who are appointed to each Executive Council by the Minister of Health, or from eight who are appointed by the local authority. Apparently, therefore, in each Service Committee the laymen are in the majority. This would seem to be a safeguard for the complainant. But, in fact, the representatives of a local authority on an Executive Council are, in some cases, doctors. Thus it can and occasionally does happen that some of the 'laymen' on a Medical Service Committee are themselves doctors and there is a professional and not a lay majority on the Committee. The regulations should be amended to ensure that the lay members are laymen in a full sense.

After the Service Committee hearing, the Executive Council considers its report and decides whether to dismiss the complaint, whether to recommend to the Minister that the practitioner concerned be penalized (by withholding part of his salary, for example), or whether, in the most serious cases, representation to the National Health Service Tribunal should be made that the practitioner concerned should be excluded from the health service list. Either the complainant or the practitioner may appeal to the Minister against a decision of the Executive Council except where proceedings are to be taken before the Tribunal. The Minister decides whether or not there is to be an oral hearing of appeal, although a practitioner may

[1] For the regulations governing these tribunals, see especially S.I. 1077 of 1956. The National Health Service (Service Committees and Tribunal) Regulations, 1956.

insist on an oral hearing if the Executive Council has recommended that part of his salary be withheld.

The appeal committee consists of a chairman who always has legal knowledge and is usually one of the Minister's legal advisers, and two other members. If the practitioner is a doctor, one of these is always selected from a panel of doctors and the other is normally one of the Minister's medical advisers. The same principle for composing the appeal committee is followed in the case of dentists, opticians and chemists. The parties at the appeal committee can be represented by counsel, whereas they cannot be so represented before the Service Committee.

This whole machinery seems to be well devised and, by general agreement, proceedings before the Service Committees and on appeal are in general fair and conducted with humanity. There are, however, two drawbacks. The first is that the ordinary person very often finds it very difficult to present his complaint against the practitioner. Without expert assistance he may not be able to do justice to his case at the Service Committee hearing, or he may even be unable to present it sufficiently well to secure a hearing. If the chairman of a Service Committee rules that there is no prima facie case, the complaint can be disposed of without a hearing. A Clerk to an Executive Council is instructed to advise a complainant about the way in which he can make his complaint and the rules governing Service Committee procedure. But he is not expected to give him any further advice.

The Franks Committee recommended that expert assistance should be provided for complainants. They suggested that 'complainants should be entitled to apply for the services of a departmental or Executive Council official to assist them in presenting their cases before Service Committees'.[1] This recommendation has still not been acted upon. The Council on Tribunals noted in its report for 1961 that, in some areas, the Citizens' Advice Bureaux have given help in tribunal hearings to appellants who do not belong to any organization which might assist or represent them.[2] But to imagine that the Bureaux might provide a general service of this kind would be quite

---

[1] Cmnd. 218, Report of the Committee on Administrative Tribunals and Enquiries, p. 45, para. 200.

[2] *Report of the Council on Tribunals for the year ended 31 December 1961*, p. 6, para. 24.

unrealistic. For one thing, Bureaux in many areas would not be keen to take on this role, regarding themselves as primarily information centres rather than as agencies whose function it is to intervene in disputes on behalf of patients against doctors, etc. For another, the Bureaux are, in general, quite inadequately financed to permit such work, being dependent upon very modest grants from local authorities and private donations.

There is a strong case, therefore, for having an official in each Executive Council, one of whose functions it would be to act as a Patient's Adviser. He would assist a complainant in preparing his case and in replying to the subsequent submission of the practitioner. As the Franks Committee commented: 'The Minister, in addition to being in a broad sense the employer of the practitioners in the National Health Service, has a general responsibility in regard to the proper treatment of National Health Service patients. He should not, therefore, be indifferent to the proper establishment of the facts of complaints and should be anxious to see that complainants do not go unassisted.'[1]

The second drawback to the existing system for making complaints lies in the machinery for appeal to the Minister. The regulations state that the Minister may award costs on appeal, and Executive Councils are instructed to inform the parties of this fact. The effect of this provision is to discourage many complainants from appealing to the Minister, if the Executive Council dismisses their complaint. It is a thoroughly undesirable provision, especially in view of the fact that the Minister anyway has the power to refuse an oral hearing to a complainant on appeal. The scales are first weighted against the patient by this power to refuse him an oral hearing, whereas the practitioner must, in most circumstances, be allowed one. They are further weighted by the power to award costs, which hits at the patient far more than at the practitioner, who is backed by the funds of his professional defence union. It is true, as we have seen, that the Minister does not often award costs, but that does not make the practice of threatening costs any the less discreditable. Provision for appeal from tribunals of first instance is a most valuable way of ensuring that tribunals use fair-minded

---

[1] Cmnd. 218, Report of the Committee on Administrative Tribunals and Enquiries, para. 199.

procedures and follow generally uniform methods of interpreting the law. The regulations should be amended to exclude all mention of costs so that the right of appeal to the Minister can be effectively enjoyed.

The machinery for complaints in the practitioner service, therefore, has its defects, but they could be quite easily rectified in the ways that have been described. Otherwise the system is well devised and fair. When we come to consider the hospital service, however, we find a complete absence of formal machinery for complaints. This was, as we have seen, commented on by the Whyatt Committee.[1] What then is the procedure when a complaint is made against a hospital doctor?

If the complaint is not of the most serious character (i.e., not one that, if justified, would involve the dismissal of the doctor), it is normally first taken up by the Chairman or Secretary of the Hospital Management Committee. He will call for reports from the doctors and nurses concerned and may interview them. He will then interview the complainant and tell him whether or not, or how far, he feels the complaint to be justified. If the complainant then appeals to the Hospital Board for the region, a similar procedure will be followed, reports then being considered by a group of Board members. If he then appeals further to the Minister, the Minister will ask the Board to furnish him with a report and documents in the case. These will then be studied by the Minister and a reply sent to the complainant.

This machinery compares unfavourably with the machinery of the Service Committees, Executive Councils, and ministerial appeal committee in the practitioner service. In the informal hospital system there was until March 1966 no provision for confrontation between the complainant and the doctor, and it was not easy to check the truth of one's account against the other's.[2] Even now there is no really impartial or balanced

[1] 'Justice', op. cit., p. 38.

[2] In a circular issued in March 1966, the Minister of Health advised Hospital Management Committees and Boards of Governors to allow the complainant, accompanied by a friend, to be present during the investigation of complaints. The complainant should be allowed to state his case at the investigation and the same privilege should be accorded to the person complained against. See Ministry of Health circular H.M. (66) 15 dated 7 March 1966. The circular, it will be noted, only gives advice to the hospital authorities and it is not generally made available to complainants.

tribunal to assess the facts. The procedure on appeal also compares unfavourably. The committee which hears appeals from Executive Council findings is a well qualified and balanced committee. Its proceedings are thorough and permit a re-examination *de novo* of the case with a rehearing and cross-examination of the parties concerned. An appeal from a Hospital Board is, by contrast, normally considered by one or more officials who go over the papers which have been sent on to them. It is likely that if they find that the doctor's and nurse's accounts substantiate each other, for example, they will conclude that there is no reason to question the findings at management committee and regional level. This is bound to be a less searching and thorough review than that provided for by the ministerial appeal committee in the practitioner service.

When a serious complaint is made against a doctor in the hospital service, one that may involve his dismissal, the normal procedure now is for the case to be first investigated by the Chairman of the Hospital Management Committee concerned, with the help of the Hospital Board's Senior Medical Officer and its Legal Adviser. If they find that there is a prima facie case, the Board will appoint an investigating panel. The chairman of this panel always has legal knowledge and the panel will include a doctor, normally in the same specialism as the doctor complained against. The panel examines the respondent and witnesses, who may be cross-examined. The respondent may be legally represented. He can appeal to the Minister against the findings of the investigating panel. If he does appeal, the Minister can appoint a further committee to consider the case, but he is unlikely to do so. The likeliest course is for senior officials to examine the records of the investigating panel and all evidence submitted, and to recommend to the Minister whether the panel's findings be upheld or rejected.

Again, the machinery compares unfavourably with the machinery for considering the most serious complaints in the practitioner service. In particular, the provision in the practitioner service for a hearing by the National Health Service Tribunal, on representation by an Executive Council, has much to commend it. The chairman of this Tribunal is appointed by the Lord Chancellor, and of its two other members, one is appointed by the Minister, after consultation with the Association of Executive Councils, and one is a practitioner appointed by the Minister from panels of doctors, dentists, etc. according to the subject of the case. The Tribunal, being statutory, comes under the supervision of the Council on Tribunals. Perhaps the greatest defect of the complaints machinery in the hospital service is that it is all non-statutory and, therefore, none of it comes under the supervision of the Council on Tribunals.

When, therefore, we survey the machinery for complaints in the Health Service, we find that one part of it, the practitioner service, is basically sound but has several defects of detail. When we look at the hospital service, we find that the defects are much more serious. There is a strong case for establishing a statutory system of administrative tribunals for the hospital service.

If the Council on Tribunals had power to recommend the creation of new tribunals it might well propose a statutory system of tribunals for the hospitals. Alternatively, the hospitals could be brought within the sphere of investigation by the Parliamentary Commissioner. At committee stage of the Parliamentary Commissioner Bill, in November 1966, an amendment was carried, against the Minister, which brought the hospitals within the scope of the bill. At Report Stage, a Government amendment was carried which took them out again, although each one of the eleven M.P.s who spoke on the amendment, except the Minister himself, opposed this move. There would seem to be an unanswerable case for either creating a system of statutory tribunals in the hospital service or allowing the Parliamentary Commissioner to investigate complaints from within the hospitals.

Although one may regret the fact that the Parliamentary Commissioner is being limited to maladministration and that nothing is being done to widen the scope of administrative tribunals, there are certain grounds for hope in the new system. First, the Parliamentary Commissioner has been made a member of the Council on Tribunals. Second, the 1967 Act does not exclude him from considering complaints which could go to a tribunal (See Clause 5 Subsection (2)). He will, therefore, be brought into contact with the work of tribunals; and so it may be possible for him on occasion to indicate, either formally or informally, where there are gaps in the system and where existing tribunals are not functioning satisfactorily.

Summary

To sum up, we may say that, since 1945, great strides have been made in improving the machinery through which a citizen can seek redress against a government department. Individual tribunals have been improved, a degree of oversight of them has been ensured through the work of the Council on Tribunals, and a Parliamentary Commissioner has been set up to fill some of the gaps which remain. The system is still far from perfect or complete but it has been improved out of all recognition, even when compared with the situation only thirty years ago.

It must be recognized, however, that some students of the subject are not happy about recent developments. In particular, they have favoured, instead of an Ombudsman, the adoption of machinery modelled on that of the *Conseil d'État*. Perhaps the best-known exponent of this point of view has been Professor J. D. B. Mitchell of the University of Edinburgh.[1] One of his contentions has been that, while an Ombudsman works well in a country with a small population, he is unlikely to be successful in a densely populated country like Britain. The *Conseil d'État*, however, is a proven success in France which has a population similar to that of Britain. He also considers that what is needed above all, in Britain, is 'a court of administrative equity', which will include members drawn from the Civil Service and which will be able to require higher standards of practice from the public authorities.

The most fully developed scheme for machinery modelled on that of the *Conseil d'État* was put forward by the Inns of Court Conservative and Unionist Society in January 1966.[2] They suggested that an investigating and a judicial division should be grafted on to the Privy Council. The investigating division would establish the facts. If it was not satisfied by a government department's reply, after the investigation, it would refer the case to the judicial division which would include judges and

[1] See J. D. B. Mitchell, 'The Ombudsman Fallacy' in *Public Law*, 1962, pp. 24–33 and the same author, 'The Irrelevance of the Ombudsman Proposals' in Rowat (ed.) op. cit. pp. 273–81.

[2] See Inns of Court Conservative and Unionist Society, 'Let Right be Done'. (Conservative Political Centre, 1966).

senior Civil Servants as well as representatives of industry, the trade unions and the professions. The judicial division would have power to require redress, or the payment of compensation, to the aggrieved person.

There are four main arguments against these proposals. First, they would fit less well into the machinery for Parliamentary scrutiny of the administration than the Parliamentary Commissioner does. Second, it is likely that the apparatus of the investigating and judicial divisions would be cumbersome and slow-moving. It would be inappropriate for many of the cases with which an Ombudsman can deal quickly by use of informal procedures. Third, the British public is not likely to have much confidence in a judicial division of which senior Civil Servants would be members—'They would be judges in their own cause.' Finally, the scheme contains a proposal that if a complainant lost his case before the judicial division he would have to pay costs. This would largely destroy the value of the system to the ordinary person. To be fair to the scheme, this is not an essential part of it. There is no payment of costs before the *Conseil d'État*. The only charge to the complainant, in France, is the few francs which it costs him to make his original petition.

Perhaps the strongest argument, however, against the *Conseil d'État*-type machinery is that we now have a Parliamentary Commissioner. If he proves a success within his limited sphere of investigation, we can go on to appoint regional Ombudsmen with power to investigate complaints against local authorities and against those activities of central departments which are not within the original Parliamentary Commissioner's sphere. Each of the regional Ombudsmen should report to a committee of the Commons consisting of the M.P.s for each English region. In the case of Scotland or Wales, the Ombudsman would report to the Scottish or Welsh Grand Committee.

For Reference

C. K. Allen, *Administrative Jurisdiction* (Stevens, 1956).
L. J. Blom-Cooper, 'An Ombudsman in Britain?' in *Public Law*, 1960.
B. Chapman, *The Profession of Government* (Allen & Unwin, 1959).
S. A. de Smith, 'Anglo-Saxon Ombudsman?' in *Political Quarterly*, 1962.
J. F. Garner, 'The Council on Tribunals' in *Public Law*, 1965.
W. Gellhorn, *Ombudsmen and Others* (Oxford University Press, 1967).

J. A. G. GRIFFITH and H. STREET, *Principles of Administrative Law*, 2nd ed. (Pitman, 1957).

C. J. HAMSON, *Executive Discretion and Judicial Control. An Aspect of the French* CONSEIL D'ÉTAT (Stevens, 1954).

A. MACDONALD, 'A Public Watchdog' in *Social Service Quarterly*, 1966.

G. MARSHALL, 'The New Zealand Parliamentary Commissioner (Ombudsman) Act, 1962' in *Public Law*, 1963.

G. MARSHALL, 'Tribunals and Inquiries: Developments since the Franks Report' in *Public Administration*, 1958.

J. D. B. MITCHELL, 'The Ombudsman Fallacy' in *Public Law*, 1962.

J. D. B. MITCHELL, 'Administrative Law and Parliamentary Control' in *The Political Quarterly*, 1967.

W. A. ROBSON, *Justice and Administrative Law*, 3rd ed. (Stevens, 1951).

D. C. ROWAT (ed.), *The Ombudsman. Citizens' Defender* (Allen & Unwin, 1965).

M. H. SMITH, 'Thoughts on a British Conseil d'État' in *Public Administration*, 1967.

F. STACEY, 'The Machinery for Complaints in the National Health Service' in *Public Administration*, 1965.

T. E. UTLEY, *Occasion for Ombudsman* (Johnson, 1961).

H. W. R. WADE, *Administrative Law* (Clarendon Press, 1961).

WHYATT COMMITTEE, *The Citizen and the Administration: The Redress of Grievances*. A Report by 'Justice'. (Stevens, 1961).

Annual Reports of the Council on Tribunals.

Cmnd. 218. Report of the Committee on Administrative Tribunals and Enquiries, 1957 (The Franks Report).

Cmnd. 2767. The Parliamentary Commissioner for Administration.

Parliamentary Commissioner Act, 1967.

CHAPTER XVII

Conclusion

How can we sum up the changes which have occurred in the British political system since the Second World War? Many of them have been made in response to some immediate problem or event. There has been no grand design in which each particular change may be said to play its part. But is it possible to identify any clear trend in the development of the system?

Can we say that the trend has been to make the political system more egalitarian, in principle, and in practice? Can we say that Members of Parliament have now more opportunities for criticizing and checking the activities of the Executive; or has the trend been in the other direction, are the powers of Parliament dwindling? Or have there been trends in entirely different directions?

The changes in the law of elections have been in an egalitarian direction. For example, the abolition of the business and university votes in 1948 ended plural voting and established the principle of 'one man, one vote'. The new system of re-drawing constituency boundaries, first put into effect in 1948, had as one of its aims the attainment of 'equal electoral districts', one of the planks in the programme of the nineteenth-century Chartists. We have seen that this aim has been very imperfectly achieved.[1] But the new system, with its provision for periodic reviews by impartial boundary commissions, is on the whole a fair one and could be modified to bring about greater equality in the size of constituencies.

The tighter restriction placed, in 1948, upon the amounts which candidates may spend during the election campaign was intended to provide greater equality in the contest between the wealthier and the less wealthy political parties. In practice these restrictions have been partly off-set by the continued

[1] See above pp. 22—5.

freedom of political parties, and of quasi-political organizations like Aims of Industry, to spend whatever they like *between* elections. The Conservative Party has clearly been the chief gainer in this situation, and the only move to equalize the position between the two main parties has been the provision in the Companies Act of 1967 which requires the disclosure to shareholders of amounts donated by companies to political funds.

Two other important changes have been made in an egalitarian direction. The decision made by the Conservatives in 1949 to limit severely the amount which candidates, and M.P.s, may contribute to their local Conservative associations, and towards the cost of the election campaign, has, in principle, placed less wealthy Conservatives on an equal footing with the well-to-do. In practice, it has not brought about, as yet, a spectacular change in the composition of Conservative membership in the Commons. Another major change was the adoption by the Conservatives, in 1965, of election by secret ballot among M.P.s as the method of choosing their Leader. Taken together with the decision that the Conservative Leader should be present during the Annual Conference, it signifies an increasingly democratic temper within the Conservative Party.

When we turn to Parliament and ask whether the powers of Parliament have dwindled or increased, the answer cannot be a clear-cut one. We can say that, since 1945, the House of Commons has become more efficient as a legislative chamber. By taking nearly all important legislation in standing committee, at committee stage, it has greatly increased its output of legislation. The increased output has not meant, by and large, that bills have not been adequately discussed. Many people now feel that legislation could be dealt with more rapidly yet, and could still be thoroughly discussed, if a procedure for an agreed time-table on every bill were introduced.

When we turn to the question of the ability of Members of Parliament to criticize administration, we find contrary views. We have seen that Bernard Crick maintains that the power of Parliament in this field 'has declined' and 'is declining'.[1] On the other hand one can point to the greater information about the activities of government departments provided by the

[1] See above p. 160.

Estimates Committee since 1945. One can point to the newly created Select Committee on Nationalized Industries, and to the Select Committee on Statutory Instruments, and the improvements it has brought in the scrutiny of delegated legislation. One must agree with Crick, however, that the facilities provided for M.P.s are very inadequate and that there should be much more provision for research assistance to Members. We have seen that there is a strong case, too, for the limited experiment with specialist committees which is now proceeding.

There are different views also about the changes which have taken place in the House of Lords. What has been the effect of reducing the period during which the Lords may delay legislation from two years to one? Has it reduced in importance one of the means of checking the Executive, or does it recognize the essentially advisory role of the Lords, as has been argued in these pages?[1] Has the Life Peerages Act, 1958, brought a new vitality to the Lords or has it merely given a new kind of title to more and more 'Impossibly Busy People'?

Again, there are different views about trends in the Cabinet. J. P. Mackintosh and R. H. S. Crossman have maintained that Government by Prime Minister has replaced Cabinet Government. It has been argued above that the weight of evidence is against this view.[2]

Some of the most interesting developments since 1945 have been outside Westminster and Whitehall. Pressure groups, for example, have become better organized, but at the same time better understood. This has led to consideration of the safeguards which can be provided against the less desirable activities of pressure groups. It has also led to the appearance of a variety of consumer groups which are attempting to counterbalance some of the very powerful producer groups. As yet, the consumer groups are scarcely more than minnows in this pond, but they are in their early stages of development.

The changes in the field of administrative tribunals have also been of great interest. Tribunals have proliferated since 1945 but, since the Franks Report, they have been systematized and regularized as never before. The Council on Tribunals now provides a check, although not a fully adequate one, that

---

[1] See above p. 234.
[2] See above Chapter XI and especially pp. 277–80.

tribunals under its jurisdiction are working fairly. A Parliamentary Commissioner has been set up with a limited sphere of investigation. It is to be hoped that he will, in time, be supplemented by regional Ombudsmen, so as to provide machinery for complaints against all government departments, both central and local.

This leads to one last speculation. Government in Britain has become more powerful and more complex. Parliament has improved its methods of scrutinizing and checking up on the government, but needs to be encouraged to do more by developing its committee system and setting up its own research agencies. The methods by which people can secure redress of their grievances against government departments have been improved, in some instances, and could be improved even further by the institution of regional Ombudsmen. But how far have developments in Britain, since 1945, encouraged greater participation by the citizen in government? The answer is, probably, hardly at all. Can anything be done to improve participation? The answer could lie, in part, in new forms of local government. It could lie in the further development of consumer groups. Or the answer may principally be that, as a rule, very few people want to participate in government. What a democratic system should provide is the opportunity to participate and the opportunity to influence decisions of the government. These opportunities are provided by the British political system, with reasonable success.

Index